Bernstein's
REVERSE
DICTIONARY

Books by Theodore M. Bernstein

HEADLINES AND DEADLINES (*with Robert E. Garst*)
WATCH YOUR LANGUAGE
MORE LANGUAGE THAT NEEDS WATCHING
THE CAREFUL WRITER
MISS THISTLEBOTTOM'S HOBGOBLINS
DOS, DON'TS AND MAYBES OF ENGLISH USAGE

Bernstein's
REVERSE
DICTIONARY

Theodore M. Bernstein

with the collaboration of

Jane Wagner

Times
BOOKS

Manufactured in the United States of America. Published simultaneously in Canada by
Fitzhenry & Whiteside, Ltd., Toronto.

Designed by Tere LoPrete

Library of Congress Cataloging in Publication Data

Bernstein, Theodore Menline, 1904-
　Bernstein's reverse dictionary.

　Includes index.
　1. English language—Synonyms and antonyms.
2. English language—Dictionaries. I. Wagner, Jane.
II. Title.　　III. Title: Reverse dictionary.
PE1591.B45　　　1975　　　　423'.1　　　75-19178

83　84　85　86　87　18　17　16　15　14

. . . and this one is for Ethel

Yes, A New Dictionary

A conventional dictionary lists words alphabetically and gives you their meanings. This unconventional dictionary lists an array of meanings alphabetically and gives you the words. That is why it is called a Reverse Dictionary.

The words it discovers for you are those you have momentarily forgotten or those you never knew or those of whose meanings you were not quite certain. If I tell you how the concept originated, it may make the idea more quickly understandable.

One evening a couple of us, in the course of conversation, got onto the subject of Chinese cuisine. My friend said he was especially fond of won ton soup. That led me to remark that the words "won ton" made perhaps even more sense if they were read backward. Whereupon my friend cried out, "Yes, just like that famous sentence, 'Madam, I'm Adam.' What *do* you call that kind of sentence?" I replied, "I know the word you want, but I'm damned if I can think of it at this moment. But anyway, 'won ton' is not what that word refers to, because then 'won ton' would have to read exactly the same backward as forward. And it doesn't."

On and off, between drinks, the two of us struggled for the rest of the evening to recall that word, elusive and yet familiar to both of us.

The next morning I telephoned him in triumph. "You know what we needed?" I said. "A reverse dictionary."

"A what?" said he.

"A reverse dictionary. When we couldn't think of that word last night we would have gone to the reverse dictionary and looked under the *b*'s for 'backward,' and it would have said something like, 'backward—a sentence that reads backward the same as forward: PALINDROME.' Or we could have looked under the *r*'s for 'reverse' and it would have said, 'reverse—a sentence that reads the same in reverse as forward: PALINDROME.' Or if neither of those definitions had occurred to us, we could have tried under the *r*'s for 'right to left—a sentence that reads from right to left just as it does from left to right: PALINDROME.' Get it?"

He got it, all right, and that is how this project began.

It has entailed labor, to be sure, but it was lovable labor. I found it lovable and so did Jane Wagner, who toiled mightily and perceptively as my collaborator. Our labor involved two principal tasks. One was selecting the words to be included in this lexicon; the other was framing the definitions in ways that would make the words readily findable.

In selecting the entries, we had to hit a happy medium between commonplace, everyday words that everyone except a thirteen-month-old infant knows (and would never have to grope for) and words that are so remote from general use that only a specialist in a particular field would have occasion to employ them. Thus you won't find *and* or *the* or *boy* or *box* in this dictionary, nor will you find many words like *bradykinin* or *intratelluric* or *thysanuran*. But you will find *brouhaha* and *cholesterol* and *alliteration* and *danseur*.

Framing the definitions was somewhat more difficult. Let me first set forth two items of terminology that we used and that will be used in this introduction. The word to be defined—that is, the word the user of this dictionary is groping for—we call the *target word*. The first word or words of each definition—that is, the word or phrase that is a synonym for the target word, or at least bears a sense relation to it—we call the *clue word*. It is the clue words that are alphabetized in this vocabulary and it is the clue words that lead into definitions of the target words.

Naturally in most instances these clue words cannot be the first words that ordinarily appear in dictionary definitions, since dictionary definitions often begin with such things as "of or pertaining to" or "the act of" or "any of various substances." Phrases like those would not be helpful here; the first word of each entry must be meaningful. In addition, it must be a word that most likely would occur to the groper for a target word. Let's say the groper was groping for "Adonis"; most probably he would turn to the *h*'s and look for "handsome" or he would turn to the *m*'s and look for "man." Either way he would be rewarded: Under the *h*'s he would find "handsome man: ADONIS" and under the *m*'s he would find "man of great beauty: ADONIS." And he would be at grope's end.

Although we have tried to adhere to dictionary definitions—particularly, although not exclusively, to the concise ones in Funk and Wagnalls Standard College Dictionary—we have sometimes had to modify them so as to begin with meaningful clue words. Moreover, although our definitions give the sense of the target word accurately, their wording on a few occasions does not conform to the part of speech of the target word. For instance, one entry for the noun "agnosticism" is not a noun but rather a phrase: "God's existence questioned." Using that definition provides a helpful clue word—"God's"—and no damage is done to the word's meaning. This book is not, after all, a conventional dictionary.

Still, for a person momentarily lacking any kind of conventional dictionary whatever, this lexicon could help fill the gap. The target words appear alphabetically at the back of the book as an index, accompanied by page numbers that tell where their definitions or synonyms may be found. In other words, this reverse dictionary if used *in reverse* could be a conventional dictionary, though a very abridged one. That puts it one up on a normal dictionary, which can be used in only one direction. Of course, the definitions in this one are not so detailed nor so comprehensive as those in a conventional dictionary, and they are not intended to be. Yet they do give more than a hint of what each target word means.

This reverse dictionary is not a thesaurus either, yet within the limitation of the number of words it contains it can serve a similar purpose. The normal thesaurus throws masses of synonyms and closely or distantly related words at you, often leaving you to find your own way out of the jungle it has created. This lexicon gives you, by means of the clue words, synonyms or closely related expressions ranging from one to five or six for each target word. For the target word ACAUDAL, all that anyone needs for a synonym or a definition is "tailless." For the target word AMBIENCE, however, more is required, and in this vocabulary you will find five entries, as follows:

—atmosphere of a place or situation
—environmental distinctiveness
—feel of a place or situation
—milieu
—surroundings

Thus when using this dictionary for its principal purpose, if you could not recall the word AMBIENCE you could look under any one of those five entries and there the target word would be awaiting you. On the other hand, if you were looking for another way of saying "ambience," you could look in the index and be referred to all of those five entries. In doing that you would be using this work as a thesaurus.

Parenthetically, listing those five entries referring to AMBIENCE brings to mind one of the fascinating difficulties we encountered in devising this dictionary. We found we had to be seers—mind readers for thousands of people. We constantly kept asking ourselves the question, "If Jane Doe Smith couldn't recall Word A, what kindred word or expression to look under would pop into her mind?" We tried to think of as many relevant look-up words as we could and thus the clue words kept multiplying.

That process gave the book a lagniappe that hadn't occurred to us at first: the more entries the wider the opportunity for service to word fiends—vocabulary builders, crossword-puzzle workers and double-crostic solvers. After all, the pattern of this book is not unlike that of a crossword puzzle dictionary, though neither could replace the other. But if the crossword puzzle demanded a six-letter word for a "handsome man," you would find "Adonis" waiting for you in these pages.

If you wanted to get still more fun out of this basically serious book, you could use it to generate new word games in your living room. For instance, after the first round of cocktails, the host, leafing through these pages, could ask Guest A, "What's a word for an ancient adding machine?" If the guest came up with "abacus," the host could reward him with a second cocktail. Then the host could turn to Guest B and say, "Give me any one of a half a dozen definitions of 'abecedarian,' " and if Guest B scratched his head in vain, the host could say, "What you need is another cocktail," and give it to him. And so it could go.

Fundamentally, however, this book is designed with a serious purpose. It is intended to help all users of English, and particularly serious writers, to find words that temporarily are eluding them or words that they did not know even existed. It has as a chief purpose keeping them from settling for a second-best word by making easily available the precise word they require and should have. And needless to say, precision in language is a continuing imperative.

*   *   *

Now for three minor details that should be called to the attention of users of this dictionary:

1. The various kinds of phobias are not entered separately. They appear in a listing under the clue word "phobias."

2. Likewise, the various kinds of manias are not entered separately. They appear in a listing under the clue word "manias." This listing, as well as that of phobias, is derived in the main from Funk and Wagnalls Standard College Dictionary.

3. Terms for groups, males, females and the young of animals, birds, fish and other creatures are not entered separately, but appear in a chart headed "Creature Terms" under the letter C.

T.M.B.

New York, New York, September, 1975

Bernstein's
REVERSE
DICTIONARY

A

abandon, yield, give up: RELINQUISH

abandon an undertaking: SCUTTLE

abandoned, deserted, wretched, cheerless: FORLORN

abandoning of one's faith, party or principles: APOSTASY

abate, calm, quiet: SUBSIDE

abbreviation or sign representing a word such as the dollar sign: LOGOGRAM

abdominal pain resulting from muscular spasms: COLIC

abhorrence, disgust or dislike in the extreme: LOATHING

abide, continue unchanged: SUBSIST

ability, skill: PROWESS

ability to do something adroitly: KNACK

abnormal: ANOMALOUS

abnormal: TERATOID

abnormal, diverging from the natural order: PRETERNATURAL

abnormal or irregular arrangement of parts, as parts of the body: HETEROTAXIS

abominable, revolting, detestable: EXECRABLE

abominable snowman: YETI

about, approximately: CIRCA

about face: VOLTE-FACE

about to happen without delay: IMMINENT

about to occur: IMPEND

above all others in importance: PARAMOUNT

above comparison, preeminently: PAR EXCELLENCE

above the taste of the masses: CAVIAR TO THE GENERAL

abridge or make concise: CONDENSE

abridgement that is brief but comprehensive: COMPENDIUM

abrogate, repeal, revoke: RESCIND

abrupt, sharp emphasis: STACCATO

abrupt passage from one condition to another: TRANSILIENT

abruptly cause: PRECIPITATE

absence of government: ANARCHY

absence of life: ABIOSIS

absent-minded: DISTRAIT

absolute, complete: UNMITIGATED

absolute, full, complete: PLENARY

absolute, positive, final, decisive: PEREMPTORY

absolute, unreserved: IMPLICIT

absolute, without any qualifications: CATEGORICAL

absolute government by an individual: AUTOCRACY

absolute power, supreme command: IMPERIUM

absolute rule: AUTARCHY

absolve: VINDICATE

absorb, occupy completely, monopolize: ENGROSS

absorbed in one's thoughts: BROWN STUDY

absorbed in completely: RAPT

abstainer from alcoholic drinks: TEETOTALLER

abstaining from sexual intercourse, in accordance with religious vows: CELIBATE

abstract, concise summary: PRÉCIS

abstract, speculative philosophy: METAPHYSICS

abstract quality or essence of anything: DISTILLATION

abstruse, hidden: RECONDITE

abstruse, secret, unknown except by a few specially instructed individuals: ESOTERIC

absurd appearance given to something or someone: STULTIFIED

absurd, ridiculous: LUDICROUS

absurd, senseless: IRRATIONAL

absurdity of an argument or proposition demonstrated: REDUCTIO AD ABSURDUM

abundant, lavish, generous: PROFUSE

abundant, numerous: GALORE

abundant, plentiful: RIFE

abuse, handle roughly, manhandle: MAUL

abuse, vilify: REVILE

abuse by words: INVECTIVE

abuse or satirize in humorous prose or verse: LAMPOON

abusive, coarse in language: SCURRILOUS

abusive and defamatory words: OBLOQUY

abusive and loud: THERSITICAL

abusive denunciation, harangue: DIATRIBE

abusive, disgracing: OPPROBRIOUS

abusive language: VITUPERATION

accent, way of speaking a language: INTONATION

accent mark consisting of two dots over a letter (ü): DIERESIS OR UMLAUT

accent mark, hooklike, placed under a "c" (ç): CEDILLA

accent mark in form of an inverted "v" (ˆ): CIRCUMFLEX ACCENT

accent mark in Spanish and Portuguese (˜): TILDE

accent mark that runs from northeast to southwest (´): ACUTE ACCENT

accent mark that runs from northwest to southeast (`): GRAVE ACCENT

accented forcibly in music: SFORZANDO

accept as self-evident truth: POSTULATE

accept or conclude from evidence: INFER

accepted, popular, everyday speech: VULGATE

accepted practice: PRAXIS

accessory: APPURTENANCE

accidental, fortunate by chance rather than design: FORTUITOUS

accidental, random: HAPHAZARD

accidental occurrence: HAPPENSTANCE

accidentally acquired: ADVENTITIOUS

accompany factor or circumstance: CONCOMITANT

accomplice in crime: PARTICEPS CRIMINIS

accomplish, bring about: EFFECT

accomplished fact, done beyond recall: FAIT ACCOMPLI

accomplishment or realization of things worked for: FRUITION

accord, harmonious relationship: RAPPORT

accordion-like small instrument: CONCERTINA

accurate, certain: UNERRING

accurate, exact, precise: NICE

accurate reproduction: FIDELITY

accurate reproduction of a quotation indicated by this word meaning thus or so: SIC

accusation of wrongdoing made against a public official: IMPEACHMENT

accusation or the charging of a wrongdoing or fault: IMPUTATION

accusation or denunciation that is violent: INVECTIVE

accuse, charge with a crime: INDICT

accuse falsely: CALUMNIATE

accuse in return: RECRIMINATE

accuse of wrongdoing or imply guilt: INCRIMINATE

accustom oneself or someone to something: CONDITION

accustom to something difficult: INURE

accustomed or used to, habituated: WONT

acme, highest point: PINNACLE

acquainted or familiar with a subject: CONVERSANT

acquired object or entity: ACQUEST

acquit, justify: VINDICATE

acquit or free from accusation or blame: EXONERATE

acrid: PUNGENT

acrobats' canvas sheet stretched on a frame: TRAMPOLINE

across: ATHWART

acrostic form in which the final letters of successive lines form a word: TELESTICH

acrostic form in which the middle letters of successive lines form a word: MESOSTICH

act as a judge: ADJUDICATE

act as an official: OFFICIATE

acting hastily: BRASH

activate, lead, inspire, as a group: SPARKPLUG

active, lively: VIVACIOUS

actor or actress: THESPIAN

actor who feeds comedian lines: STRAIGHT MAN

actual, real: SUBSTANTIVE

acute, keen, sharp, biting: INCISIVE

acute, keen as in pleasure or pain: EXQUISITE

ad lib: EXTEMPORANEOUS

adage: APHORISM

add at the end: SUBJOIN

add or inject certain elements: INCORPO-
RATE

added syllable or group of syllables at the
end of a word: SUFFIX

adding machine of ancients: ABACUS

addition, increase, something added or
gained: INCREMENT

addition of a sound to the beginning of a
word: PROTHESIS

addition to a will: CODICIL

additions, insertions, interruptions in a
discourse, process or series: IN-
TERPOLATIONS

addressing a person or thing in a digression: APOSTROPHE

address to graduating class: BACCA-
LAUREATE

adept at many things: VERSATILE

adhesive, sticky: VISCID

adjective linked to a noun to which it normally would not apply: TRANSFERRED
EPITHET

adjunct: APPURTENANCE

adjust, temper, soften or regulate: MODU-
LATE

adjusted to a situation: RECONCILED

adjustment: ORIENTATION

adjustment to meet the demands of the environment: REALITY PRINCIPLE

adjustment to society's cultural norms:
ACCULTURATION, ENCULTURATION

administration or manner of governing:
GOVERNANCE

admirable or consummate: EXQUISITE

admittance: ACCESS

admonish or advise strongly, urge by earnest appeal: EXHORT

adorn magnificently, extol, celebrate: EM-
BLAZON

adroit, skillful: DEXTEROUS

adroit or ingenious creation of performance: TOUR DE FORCE

adultery, in law: CRIMINAL CONVERSATION

advance announcement of the coming of
someone or something: HARBINGER

advanced beyond what is usual for one's
age: PRECOCIOUS

advantage spot for observation: COIGN OF
VANTAGE

advantageous: EXPEDIENCY

adverb that is misplaced so it could modify either of two words: SQUINTING
MODIFIER

adverse, unfortunate: UNTOWARD

adversely influence or affect something:
MILITATE

advertisement or notice, usually distributed by hand: HANDBILL

advertising space measurement: AGATE
LINE

advertising that is sensational: BALLYHOO

advise of a fault: ADMONISH

advise or recommend strongly, urge by
earnest appeal: EXHORT

adviser or critic who is frank and severe:
DUTCH UNCLE

advisers, usually secret and unofficial:
CAMARILLA

advocacy or support, as of a cause: ES-
POUSAL

advocate or originator of a cause: PROPO-
NENT

aesthetic qualities associated with ancient
Greece and Rome: CLASSICISM

affectation of style or peculiarity of manner: MANNERISM

affected, artificial: FACTITIOUS

affected display of modesty: PRUDERY

affected in writing, behavior, etc.: PRE-
CIOUS

affectedly prim, elegant or dainty: MINC-
ING

affecter of attitudes to impress others: PO-
SEUR

affecting superiority, ostentatious: PRE-
TENTIOUS

affection that is foolish or excessive:
DOTAGE

affirmative expressed by negating its opposite: LITOTES

affront, insult: INDIGNITY

after-dinner: POSTPRANDIAL

after the fact: EX POST FACTO

after-the-event perception: HINDSIGHT

after death: POSTHUMOUS

aftereffect, reverberation: REPERCUSSION

aftermath: WAKE

aftermath of hay or grass in its second
growth: ROWEN

against, as in having influence or effect
against something: MILITATE

against change or progress, conservative:
REACTIONARY

age of a girl before which intercourse is
rape: AGE OF CONSENT

age or length of life beyond the ordinary:
LONGEVITY

aged, infirm, doting: SENILE

agent, deputy, substitute: VICAR
agent in financing: FACTOR
agent or adviser who is powerful but unofficial: EMINENCE GRISE
agent planted in organization to incite punishable actions: AGENT PROVOCATEUR
agent that remains unchanged while changing other components: CATALYST
agent who handles orders to buy and sell securities: BROKER
agency that sells articles to a number of periodicals: SYNDICATE
aggressive: BUMPTIOUS
aggressive, lively: FEISTY
aging and the aged, as a scientific study: GERONTOLOGY
aging, growing old: SENESCENT
agitated, worried, tense, bewildered: DISTRAUGHT
agitating violently: TURBULENT
agonizing, painful: EXCRUCIATING
agree: ACCEDE
agree: JIBE
agree exactly: COINCIDE
agreeable in manner or style, apt, well-chosen: FELICITOUS
agreeable to persuasion or change: AMENABLE
agreeableness: COMPLAISANCE
agreeing or conforming: CONGRUENT
agreement: CONCURRENCE
agreement: CONSONANCE
agreement, compact, pledge: COVENANT
agreement, treaty, contract: PACT
agreement guaranteed solely by the pledged word of the parties involved: GENTLEMAN'S AGREEMENT
agreement made by disputants pending final accord: MODUS VIVENDI
agreement of all concerned: UNANIMITY
agreement or opinion that is general: CONSENSUS
agreement that is mutual: ENTENTE
agricultural interest: AGRARIAN
aid, succor: SUBVENTION
aid or support as an auxiliary: ANCILLARY
aim, goal, purpose: INTENT
aimed straight at a target and close enough so the projectile does not fall appreciably: POINT-BLANK
aimless wandering: MEANDERING
air attack with machine-gun fire from low-flying planes: STRAFE

air column swirling around a vertical axis: WHIRLWIND
aircraft carrier: FLATTOP
aircraft enclosure, especially one housing an engine: NACELLE
aircraft on a single military mission: SORTIE
aircraft workshop or shelter: HANGAR
air-cushion vehicle: HOVERCRAFT
airhole: SPIRACLE
airplane landing that is perfect: THREE-POINT LANDING
airplane pilots' nervous disorder: AERONEUROSIS
airplane's prospective passenger who fails to claim reservation: NO-SHOW
airtight: HERMETIC
airy, light, spiritual: ETHEREAL
alarm, bell signal: TOCSIN
alarm, upset, disturb: PERTURB
Albuquerque resident: ALBUQUERQUEAN
alcoholic appetizer: APERITIF
alcoholic derelict: WINO
alcoholic liquor, given to: BIBULOUS
alcoholic liquor added in small quantity to a beverage: LACE
alcoholic strong liquor: SCHNAPPS
alcoholism, craving for alcohol: DIPSOMANIA
ale or beer and ginger ale mixed: SHANDYGAFF
alert, watchful: VIGILANT
alienated, estranged: DISAFFECTED
alignment with a margin: FLUSH
alikeness of a trait, characteristic or viewpoint: COMMON DENOMINATOR
all at one time: HOLUS-BOLUS
all life held as sacred: AHIMSA
all kinds of things accepted, as by the mind: OMNIVOROUS
all performers take part, in music: TUTTI
alleviate, extenuate: PALLIATE
alley lined with dwellings that were formerly stables: MEWS
alliance: COALITION
alliance of two or more business concerns for a venture: CONSORTIUM
all-important thing: BE-ALL AND END-ALL
allowable, permissible: TOLERABLE
allowance, salary, pension: STIPEND
allowing unusual freedom, lenient: PERMISSIVE
almighty: OMNIPOTENT
almost, nearly: WELL-NIGH
alms or charity: ELEEMOSYNARY

alone: ISOLATED

alphabetic characters of one language used to represent the letters of another: TRANSLITERATION

alphabet in small letters used in printing: LOWER CASE

alphabet matters: ABECEDARIAN

altar boy: ACOLYTE

altar boy who carries the censer: THURIFER

alter a female animal by removal of ovaries: SPAY

alter or deter the plans of someone by persuasion: DISSUADE

alteration, destruction, mutilation, especially of a legal document: SPOLIATION

alternate, change places: INTERCHANGE

altitude, instrument for measuring: ALTIMETER

altogether, entirely: IN TOTO

always prepared: SEMPER PARATUS

amaze, astound: FLABBERGAST

amazement, fear or panic that is sudden and paralyzing: CONSTERNATION

amazing, hard to believe: INCREDIBLE

amazing, wonderful: PRODIGIOUS

ambiguity, usual unintentional and because of grammatical looseness: AMPHIBOLOGY

ambiguous, insincere: LEFT-HANDED

ambiguous or oracular: DELPHIC

ambiguous talk: DOUBLE TALK

ambiguous, uncertain in origin or character, double meaning, dubious: EQUIVOCAL

ambush: WAYLAY

amends, restoration to proper condition: REPARATION

American Indian male who is married: SANNUP

among other things: INTER ALIA

amount: QUANTUM

amount by which a stock or bond may sell above its dollar value: PREMIUM

amount of stock an individual has sold even though he didn't own it and hasn't yet paid for it: SHORT POSITION

amount that must be paid by customer even though he uses his broker's credit for purchase: MARGIN

amulet or charm: TALISMAN

ammunition belt over shoulder: BANDOLIER

ammunition wagon: CAISSON

amuse, distract, entertain: DIVERT

amuse, entertain: REGALE

amuse or occupy oneself, frisk about, frolic: DISPORT

amusement: DIVERTISSEMENT

amusement, pastime: DIVERSION

anagram, or word puzzle: LOGOGRIPH

analysis of something that has happened; an after-death examination: POST-MORTEM

analysis or interpretation of a word, passage or work: EXEGESIS

analyze, break up or separate into parts: RESOLVE

ancestor dating furthest back, forefather: PRIMOGENITOR

ancestral line: PEDIGREE

ancestry, pedigree: LINEAGE

anchor for small boats: KILLICK

ancient, outmoded, old-fashioned, out of step with the times: ANTEDILUVIAN

ancient, venerable, gray- or white-haired: HOARY

ancient writing: PALEOGRAPHY

"and" symbol (&): AMPERSAND

and the following: ET SEQ.

angel of the highest rank: SERAPH

angle iron or metal bracket used to strengthen a corner or angle of a structure: GUSSET

anger, embitter: RANKLE

anger, enrage: INCENSE

anger or offense shown: BRIDLE

anger roused by injustice or baseness: INDIGNATION

angry, enraged: IRATE

angry, resentful: IN HIGH DUDGEON

angry and frowning stare: GLOWER

angry argument: ALTERCATION

angry behavior: BELLICOSITY

angry dispute, quarrel: WRANGLE

angry or irritated state: SNIT

angry or sullen look, scowl: LOWER

anguish, distress, pain, suffering: TRAVAIL

animal and plant functions and processes, as a science: PHYSIOLOGY

animal and plant structures, as a study apart from function: MORPHOLOGY

animal bereft of its horns: POLLARD

animal doctor: VETERINARIAN

animal or plant selected as representative of a new species: HOLOTYPE

animal or plant surviving from an earlier period or type: RELICT

animal preservation after death by stuffing and mounting skins: TAXIDERMY animal worship: ZOOLATRY

animals living in a given area: FAUNA

animals that are warm-blooded and whose offspring are fed with milk from female mammary glands: MAMMALS

animate or pervade: INFORM

ankle bones, as a group: TARSUS

annihilation or destruction of an entire people or national group: GENOCIDE

annotate a text between the lines: INTERLINE

announce officially, put into effect: PROMULGATE

annoy, weary, vex: IRK

annoy or harass with taunts or questions: HECKLE

annoy or taunt by reminding of a fault: TWIT

annoying, irritating: VEXATIOUS

annoying, provoking, prodding person: GADFLY

annually recurring, said of certain Mediterranean summer winds: ETESIAN

annul: INVALIDATE

annul, as a law or a right: ABROGATE

annul, suspend: SUPERSEDE

answer sharply: RETORT

antagonist or opposing thing that threatens retribution or defeat: NEMESIS

antagonistic, hostile: INIMICAL

antagonistic, hostile, resisting: REPUGNANT

antic, caper: DIDO

antic, caper: GAMBADO

anticipatory: PREVENIENT

anti-government in any form: ANARCHIC

antiquated: ANTEDILUVIAN

anxiety: DISQUIETUDE

anxiety, agitation, nervous excitement: DITHER

anxiety about one's health, often over imagined symptoms: HYPOCHONDRIA

anxiety or concern: SOLICITUDE

anxiety or state of suspense: ON TENTERHOOKS

apartment consisting of single room with kitchenette and bathroom: EFFICIENCY APARTMENT

apartment house in which occupants own shares of stock in the building: CO-OPERATIVE

apartment house in which units are owned separately by individuals: CONDOMINIUM

apathetic: PHLEGMATIC

apathetic, lackadaisical, indifferent: LISTLESS

apathetic, unconcerned: INDIFFERENT

apathy, sluggishness, dullness: LETHARGY

apathy, stupor: TORPOR

ape-like: SIMIAN

apex, top: VERTEX

apologetic: DEPRECATORY

apologetic, meek, shy person: MILQUETOAST

apparatus that functions by itself: AUTOMATON

apparent, seeming: OSTENSIBLE

apparent to sight or understanding, evident, obvious: MANIFEST

apparently but not really correct: SPECIOUS

apparition of a person thought to be alive, seen just before or after his death: WRAITH

apparition or ghost: SPECTER

apparitions or images in a series, as in a dream: PHANTASMAGORIA

appeal earnestly, direct, command: ADJURE

appeal to prejudice, not reason: AD HOMINEM

appealing to emotions: AFFECTIVE

appear or come into view as through a mist often ominously: LOOM

appearance: SEMBLANCE

appearance, aspect: GUISE

appearance, manner: MIEN

appearance-improving: COSMETIC

appearance of truth: VERISIMILITUDE

appearance or aspect that is false in order to deceive: GUISE

appearance or look of a thing: PHYSIOGNOMY

appearance or manifestation of a deity, a showing forth: EPIPHANY

appearing in various passages in a book: PASSIM

appeasable, forgiving: PLACABLE

appease, pacify: PLACATE

appease, win good will: PROPITIATE

appease or satisfy by deceit, put off by lies or evasion: FOB

appeasement gift or bribe: SOP

append: SUBJOIN

appendix to a will: CODICIL

appetite so great as to be pathological: BULIMIA

appetizer in form of alcoholic drink: APERITIF

appetizer of toast and a spread: CANAPÉ

appetizers: HORS D'OEUVRES
appetizing, tasty: SAVORY
applauders hired for the purpose: CLAQUE
applause: PLAUDIT
applause outburst: OVATION
applicable, pertinent: RELEVANT
appoint or preempt: CO-OPT
appointment or secret meeting, as of lovers: TRYST
appointment to meet, meeting place: RENDEZVOUS
apprehension, doubt, qualm: MISGIVING
apprentice, beginner: NOVICE
approach game or prey in a stealthy manner: STALK
approachable: ACCESS
appropriate, just right: PAT
appropriate, applicable: RELEVANT
appropriate or pirate the ideas, writings, music, etc., of another: PLAGIARIZE
appropriate or seize beforehand: PREEMPT
appropriateness, fitness: EXPEDIENCY
approval: APPROBATION
approval, support, encouraging look: COUNTENANCE
approve, permit, ratify: SANCTION
approved status granted an academic institution: ACCREDITATION
approximately: CIRCA
apt, well chosen, agreeable in manner or style: FELICITOUS
Arabian hooded cloak: BURNOOSE
Arabian kerchief worn over head and shoulders: KAFFIYEH
Arabian sleeveless garment: ABA
Arabic or decimal system of counting: ALGORISM
arbitrary, overbearing: HIGHHANDED
arbor or walk with a latticework roof: PERGOLA
arch that is narrow and acutely pointed: LANCET ARCH
archeological excavation: DIG
architectural movement promoting synthesis of painting, sculpture and technology: BAUHAUS
architectural projecting block: DENTIL
architecture order of Greece characterized by fluted columns and simple capitals: DORIC
architecture order of Greece characterized by ornate, bell-shaped capitals: CORINTHIAN
architecture order of Greece characterized by scrolls on the capitals: IONIC

arctic, frigid: HYPERBOREAN
ardent, extremely fervid: PERFERVID
ardent, passionate: TORRID
ardent, violent, impetuous: VEHEMENT
ardor, intensity of emotion: FERVOR
area of authority or competency: BAILIWICK
arena for horse shows, circuses: HIPPODROME
arguable, open to question: DISPUTABLE
argue earnestly or debate: CONTEND
argue earnestly with someone about the inadvisability of some action: EXPOSTULATE
argue or contend about trifling matters: STICKLE
argue or dispute noisily: WRANGLE
argue or oppose: CONTROVERT
argue over terms or prices: HIGGLE
arguer who takes wrong side perversely: DEVIL'S ADVOCATE
argument: POLEMIC
argument in which one of the premises or the conclusion is not stated but implied: ENTHYMEME
argumentation, debate: FORENSICS
argumentative: AGONISTIC
argumentative: ERISTIC
argumentative, contentious: DISPUTATIOUS
aristocrat, member of the upper classes: PATRICIAN
arm or leg stiffness or cramp: CHARLEY HORSE
aromatic substances in a ball: POMANDER
around, about, approximately: CIRCA
arouse anger or bitterness: RANKLE
arouse interest or curiosity: INTRIGUE
arouse, startle, thrill: ELECTRIFY
arousing comment, as a piece of furniture or art: CONVERSATION PIECE
arrange or organize: COLLOCATE
arrangement according to time of occurrence: CHRONOLOGY
arrangement of parts: CONFIGURATION
arrangement of parts in abnormal or irregular fashion, as parts of the body: HETEROTAXIS
arrangement of parts that is harmonious and elegant: CONCINNITY
arrangement or plan of a book, TV show, etc.: FORMAT
arrangement or progression that is orderly or gradual: GRADATION
arrest made by citizen who sees a crime: CITIZEN'S ARREST

arrive at or reach a port: FETCH

arrogance arising from overbearing pride or passion: HUBRIS

arrogance or conceit characterizing one's ways or attitudes: OVERWEENING

arrogant: RODOMONTADE

arrogant: SUPERCILIOUS

arrogant, domineering: IMPERIOUS

arrogant, forward: PRESUMPTUOUS

arrogant assertion of beliefs: DOGMATIC

art, music or literature schools that seek to produce moods through quick glimpses of subject: IMPRESSIONISM

art and literary movement that tries to exhibit the workings of the subconscious mind: SURREALISM

art cult that rejected conventions: DADA

art for art's sake: ARS GRATIA ARTIS

art of curvilinear designs, now characterized as campy: ART NOUVEAU

art of everyday realism by U.S. Group: ASHCAN SCHOOL

art of good eating: GASTRONOMY

art or literature of a cheap, popular or sentimental quality: KITSCH

art work painted directly on a wall: MURAL

art work consisting of arrangement of flat materials pasted on a surface: COLLAGE

artery walls thickened: ATHEROSCLEROSIS

artful moves or strokes: MANEUVERS

artful strategy, cunningness, craftiness: FINESSE

article or book presenting facts on a subject: TREATISE

articulate clearly and distinctly: ENUNCIATE

artificial, affected: FACTITIOUS

artificial, counterfeit: POSTICHE

artificial part of body: PROSTHESIS

artificial manner: AFFECTATION

artificially elegant style of speech or writing: EUPHUISM

artillery or cannon, military material: ORDNANCE

artist or writer who doesn't sell his services exclusively to one employer: FREE LANCE

artistic small article: OBJET D'ART

artistically thought-of ordinary object: OBJET TROUVE

artless, candid, sincere: GUILELESS

artless, unaffected, simple, candid: NAIVE

arts movement that departs from reality to reproduce inner experience: EXPRESSIONISM

ash gray: CINEREOUS

ashamed, degraded, sneaky: HANGDOG

aside directed to a person or thing: APOSTROPHE

assistant: COADJUTOR

assistant or attendant: ACOLYTE

ask for humbly, pray earnestly for something: SUPPLICATE

ask questions, examine: INTERROGATE

aspect, phrase or side of a person or subject: FACET

aspersion: SLUR

assault from behind with intent to rob: MUG

assembling of separate parts into a whole: SYNTHESIS

assembly place: AGORA

assent: ACQUIESCENCE

assertion of something made by the negation of its opposite: LITOTES

assimilation of thoughts or facts that is gradual: OSMOSIS

assist: ABET

assistance or money furnished to advance a venture: GRUBSTAKE

assistant or servant, as of a magician or scholar: FAMULUS

associate closely with someone: FRATERNIZE

associate on close terms: HOBNOB

association, fellowship: SODALITY

association of individuals to negotiate some business: SYNDICATE

assume as a fact: POSIT

assume to be true: POSTULATE

assumed name or identity: INCOGNITO

assumptions based on evidence at hand or facts already known: EXTRAPOLATION

assumption provisionally accepted as basis for reasoning or argument: HYPOTHESIS

assure, guarantee: VOUCH

astound, confound: FLABBERGAST

astrologers' chart of position of planets and stars for fortune telling: HOROSCOPE

astringent: ACERB

at once, immediate: INSTANTER

at the home of: CHEZ

at this time: HEREAT

athlete's leap over a high horizontal bar

with the aid of a long pole: POLE VAULT

athletic, sturdy body structure: MESOMORPHIC

athletic club, gymnast association: TURNVEREIN

athletic contest in which each contestant participates in five events: PENTATHLON

athletic contest of ten field and track events in all of which each contestant participates: DECATHLON

athletically vigorous: STHENIC

atmosphere beginning at a height of about seven miles: STRATOSPHERE

atmosphere of a place or situation: AMBIENCE

atmosphere or influence that is unwholesome or noxious: MIASMA

atmospheric and weather phenomena, as a science: METEOROLOGY

atom splitting: NUCLEAR FISSION

atomic bomb: A-BOMB

atomic particle carrying a positive charge: PROTON

atomic particle carrying no charge: NEUTRON

atone for, make amends for: EXPIATE

atonement shown for wrongdoing: PENANCE

atoning: PIACULAR

atrocious, beyond decency: OUTRAGEOUS

atrocious, odious, wicked, evil: HEINOUS

atrocious, wicked: FLAGITIOUS

attach the property of a person so it can be used to pay a debt: GARNISHEE

attachment of one thing to another: APPURTENANCE

attachment to a thing or a person: FIXATION

attack, dispute or challenge the truth or validity of: IMPUGN

attack that is swift and sudden, usually in war: BLITZKRIEG

attack that is violent: ONSLAUGHT

attack with scathing criticism: FLAY

attempting: CONATION

attendant who arranges details of journey for travelers: COURIER

attendants, retainers or followers in a group: ENTOURAGE

attendants of a person of rank, escort: RETINUE

attentive: ASSIDUOUS

attentive to every detail: CIRCUMSPECT

attitudes and character of a community or individual: ETHOS

attract, cause or make likely: INVITE

attractive, pleasing: PREPOSSESSING

attractive, sweet, engaging: WINSOME

attractive in a flashy way: MERETRICIOUS

attractive photographically: PHOTOGENIC

attribute to another without just reason: ARROGATE

auction or sale that is public: VENDUE

audacity, brassiness: CHUTZPAH

audacity, boldness, impudence: EFFRONTERY

aura, halo: NIMBUS

auspices: AEGIS

auspicious, favorably disposed: PROPITIOUS

austere: ASTRINGENT

austere person: ASCETIC

authenticity lacking: APOCRYPHAL

authoritative, urgently necessary, unavoidable: IMPERATIVE

authoritative because of rank or office: EX CATHEDRA

authority or power that is absolute or supreme: IMPERIUM

authority shared: COLLEGIALITY

authorization: FIAT

authorize, empower: WARRANT

author's assumed name: NOM DE PLUME

auto driving contest: RALLY

automatic, lifeless: MECHANICAL

automatic response to a stimulus: TROPISM

automaton, mechanical man: ROBOT

automobile adjusted or re-equipped for quick starts and high speed: HOT ROD

automobile engine that works on rotary combustion: WANKEL ENGINE

automobile of standard make modified for racing: STOCK CAR

automobile with convertible design but with a rigid top: HARDTOP

auxiliary: ADMINICLE

auxiliary: ANCILLARY

avarice, greed: CUPIDITY

avenging, punitive: VINDICATORY

average, moderately good: RESPECTABLE

avert or prevent: OBVIATE

avoid, turn aside, ward off: PARRY

avoid or escape: ELUDE

avoid or outwit: CIRCUMVENT

avoidable: EVITABLE

away from the center: CENTRIFUGAL

awesome, ominous: PORTENTOUS
awesome or fearsome: FORMIDABLE
awesome or imposing: AUGUST
awaiting, until: PENDING
awkward: UNGAINLY
awkward, askew, awry: SPLAY
awkward, boorish: UNCOUTH
awkward, clumsy: GAUCHE
awkward, incompetent, clumsy: INEPT
awkward, slouching movement: LOP

awkward fellow, clown, boor: LOUT
awkward or complicated situation, predic-
    ament: PLIGHT
awkward or inexperienced person on
    board a ship: LANDLUBBER
awkward rustic: BUMPKIN
ax- or hatchet-shaped: DOLABRIFORM
axiomatic, terse, pithy: SENTENTIOUS
axis common to loudspeakers or transmis-
    sion lines: COAXIAL

B

baby delivery by abdominal surgery: CAESAREAN SECTION

baby delivery, childbirth: PARTURITION

back country, remote area, inland region: HINTERLAND

back of horse, ox or deer, between shoulder blades: WITHERS

back of the neck: NAPE

back out of an agreement, revoke: RENEGE

backbone creatures: VERTEBRATES

backer of a·cause: PROPONENT

backward looking, turning or bending: RETROVERSION

backward movement: RECOIL

backward movement, reversion: REGRESSION

backward moving, tending to recede: RECESSIVE

backward reading of a word or sentence is the same as forward reading: PALINDROME

backward reasoning, from consequence to antecedent, considered a logical fallacy: HYSTERON PROTERON

backward tending, worsening, declining: RETROGRADE

backward writing that is readable in a mirror: MIRROR WRITING

bacon or pork slice used for larding meat: LARDON

bad, evil, repulsive: VILE

bad breath: HALITOSIS

bad check: KITE

bad handwriting or spelling: CACOGRAPHY

bad in a conspicuous fashion, glaring, flagrant: EGREGIOUS

bad job: BOTCH

bad luck: AMBSACE

bad money drives out good: GRESHAM'S LAW

bad morally: UNSAVORY

badge or sign of devotion consisting of two small pieces of cloth worn about the neck by members of religious orders: SCAPULAR

bad-tempered: ATRABILIOUS

bad-tempered: CANTANKEROUS

bad-tempered, spiteful: SPLENETIC

bad-tempered outburst: TANTRUM

bag of perfumed powder: SACHET

bag used by sailors for carrying personal belongings: DITTY BAG

bag worn strapped across the shoulders used for carrying supplies: KNAPSACK

bag worn over one shoulder: HAVERSACK

baggage, supplies and equipment carried by an army: IMPEDIMENTA

bagpipe's shrill sound: SKIRL

bait, allurement, enticement: GUDGEON

balance: EQUILIBRIUM

balance, counteract or compensate for something else: OFFSET

balance or counterbalance: EQUIPONDERATE

balcony, window or porch with an excellent view, in Spanish architecture: MIRADOR

baldness: ALOPECIA

baldness, especially on top of the head: CALVITIES

balk, move restlessly sidewise or backward: JIB

balky, fretful, jittery: RESTIVE

ball game in which players hit a ball against a wall by striking it with their hands: HANDBALL

ball of small size: PELLET

ballet dancer, female: BALLERINA

ballet dancer, male: DANSEUR

ballet dancer who performs only in groups: FIGURANT

ballet dancer who ranks between the so-

loists and the corps de ballet: CORY-
PHEE
ballet dancer's whirling on the toes: PIR-
OUETTE
ballet dancing position on tiptoe: POINTE
ballet leap upward with dancer activating
legs in air: ENTRECHAT
ballet's principal female dancer: PRIMA
BALLERINA
ballet's principal male dancer: PREMIER
DANSEUR or DANSEUR NOBLE
ball's horizontal twist or spin: ENGLISH
ban or curse: ANATHEMA
banal, trite, commonplace remark: PLATI-
TUDE
band or group: COHORT
bandage, bound with a band: FASCIATE
bandage used to compress an artery to
stop the flow of blood: TOURNIQUET
banish, exile: RELEGATE
bankrupt, insufficient funds: INSOLVENT
banned, forbidden: TABOO
banner fixed to a crosspiece rather than a
pole: GONFALON
banter: CHAFF
banter, flippant talk or writing: PERSIFLAGE
banter, jesting: RAILLERY
bar, upright and forming the principal support: STANCHION
bar serving food and drink: BRASSERIE
bar used to prevent a vehicle from slipping
backward on an incline: SPRAG
barefooted, as certain religious orders:
DISCALCED
barely begun: INCHOATE
bargain, at a good bargain: A BON MARCHÉ
bargain or argue about terms: HAGGLE
baring parts of the body for sexual stimu-
lation of oneself: EXHIBITIONISM
bark or yelp: YAWP
barrel maker: COOPER
barrel stave: LAG
barren, bleak: STARK
barren, fruitless, sterile: INFECUND
barren, insipid, dry, lacking interest,
naive: JEJUNE
barren, said of cows infertile for a period:
FARROW
barren, unfruitful: STERILE
barren or weak: EFFETE
barrier made up of strong stakes: PALISADE
barrier to keep out disease: CORDON SANI-
TAIRE
base, degraded, vile: SORDID
base, dishonorable, degraded: IGNOBLE

base, weak, wretched: CAITIFF
base something on known facts or conditions: PREDICATE
baseball home run hit when there is a runner on every base: GRAND SLAM
baseball pitcher strikes out a batter: FAN
baseball pitcher who replaces another:
RELIEFER or RELIEVER
baseball barely deflected by the bat: FOUL
TIP
baseball decision by a player to try to put
out man already on base rather than
the batter: FIELDER'S CHOICE
baseball diamond space within the four
base lines: INFIELD
baseball fly hit in fielding practice by a
batsman who tosses the ball up and
strikes it as it descends: FUNGO
baseball hard hit so that it travels in an approximately horizontal trajectory:
LINE DRIVE
baseball hit on which the batter reaches
third base: TRIPLE
baseball hit that allows the batter to touch
all bases and score a run: HOME RUN
or HOMER
baseball infielder stationed between second and third bases: SHORTSTOP
baseball out made when a runner, forced
from his base by a teammate's hitting
the ball, fails to reach the next base
before the ball is caught there:
FORCE-OUT
baseball pitch by a right-hander that
curves right or by a left-hander that
curves left: SCREWBALL
baseball pitch that curves only slightly:
SLIDER
baseball pitch that curves sharply downward as it approaches home plate:
SINKER
baseball pitch that the catcher cannot
handle, thereby allowing a runner to
advance: WILD PITCH
baseball play in which a man on base
starts running with the pitch and the
batter is obligated to strike at the ball
to protect him: HIT-AND-RUN PLAY
baseball play in which a runner is caught
off base by a sudden throw: PICKOFF
baseball play in which the batter tries to
bunt the ball to allow a man on third
to score: SQUEEZE PLAY
baseball play in which three players are
put out: TRIPLE PLAY

baseball play in which two players are put out: DOUBLE PLAY

baseball player able to bat both left-handed and right-handed: SWITCH HITTER

baseball player who is used as a substitute in different positions: UTILITY PLAYER

baseball retirement of a batter with three strikes: STRIKEOUT

baseball slang for a long hit: CLOUT

baseball term for catching fly balls in practice: SHAGGING

baseball term for division of the game during which each team has a turn at bat: INNING

baseball term for fly ball or bunt that results in an out, but enables a base runner to advance: SACRIFICE

baseball term for fly ball that falls between the infield and the outfield for a base hit: TEXAS LEAGUER

baseball term for hit ball that rolls or bounces along the ground: GROUND BALL or GROUNDER

baseball term for hitting the ball lightly without swinging the bat: BUNT

baseball term for lefthanded pitcher: SOUTHPAW

baseball term for illegal pitched ball, that is wetted on one side with saliva: SPITBALL

baseball term for not swinging at a pitched ball: TAKE

baseball term for pitcher's illegal motion: BALK

baseball term for play in which a base runner trapped between two bases is put out: RUNDOWN

baseball term for obscure minor league: BUSH LEAGUE

baseball term for pen where pitchers warm up: BULLPEN

baseball term for catcher's error in failing to catch a pitch, thus allowing man on base to advance: PASSED BALL

baseball term for weakly hit ball: BLOOPER

baseless: UNFOUNDED

baseness, vileness, depravity: TURPITUDE

basic: ABECEDARIAN

basic, inherent in, fundamental: ORGANIC

basic unity in ecology, including both organisms and environment: ECOSYSTEM

basis, fundamental principle: HYPOSTASIS

basis for a discussion or conclusion: PREMISE

basket, usually large and covered: HAMPER

basket of fruit done in sculpture: CORBEIL

basketball free throw: FOUL SHOT

basketball moved by bouncing it with the hand: DRIBBLE

basketball shot made with one hand from close to the basket: LAYUP

basketball shot made by a player in the air during a jump: JUMP SHOT

bath: ABLUTION

bathing suit for women that is brief and two-piece: BIKINI

batter cake that is crisp and baked in a griddle: WAFFLE

battle formation: DEPLOYMENT

battle that is great or decisive: ARMAGEDDON

battle-ax with two sharp edges: TWIBIL

bawl, shout, exclaim loudly: VOCIFERATE

bay or stream leading into the land from a larger body of water: INLET

bay window: ORIEL

beach bathhouse: CABANA

beam going from wall to wall: CROSSBEAM

beam resting horizontally upon the walls of a building and supporting the ends of joists: SUMMER

beam-emitting device that amplifies and concentrates light waves: LASER

beams placed parallel and horizontally from wall to wall: JOISTS

bearable: TOLERABLE

beard on the chin: GOATEE

beard that is short and pointed: VANDYKE

beastlike in form: THERIOMORPHIC

beat, cudgel: FUSTIGATE

beat, overcome: DRUB

beat, thrash severely or punish: TROUNCE

beat at which the hand of the conductor is raised: UPBEAT

beat rapidly, flutter, quiver: PALPITATE

beat soundly: BELABOR

beat with the fists: PUMMEL

beating with a stick: BASTINADO

beautiful buttocks: CALLIPYGIAN

beauty: PULCHRITUDE

beauty, as a subject of study: ESTHETICS

because of this: HEREAT

become known, leak out: TRANSPIRE

become or make better: AMELIORATE

becoming sour: ACESCENT

bed, grade, layer: STRATUM

bed cover that is quilted: COMFORTER

bed of straw that lies on the floor: PALLET

bedridden the person is not: AMBULATORY

bedsore: DECUBITUS

bedspread or quilt: COUNTERPANE

bed-wetting: ENURESIS

beef cattle male: STEER

beef cut from the loin end ahead of the rump: SIRLOIN

beef marinated in vinegar before cooking: SAUERBRATEN

beef tenderloin, lean and thick, broiled: FILET MIGNON

beehive, especially one made of straw: SKEP

beehives: APIARY

beer or ale and ginger ale mixed: SHANDYGAFF

before noon: ANTEMERIDIEM

before now, previously: HERETOFORE

before the Flood: ANTEDILUVIAN

beforehand opinion: PRECONCEIVE

beg: CADGE

beg something of: SUPPLICATE

beg urgently, entreat: IMPLORE

beget, produce: PROCREATE

beggar or sponger: SCHNORRER

begging: MENDICANT

begin, commence: INAUGURATE

begin, commence, originate: INITIATE

beginner: ABECEDARIAN

beginner: FLEDGLING

beginner, apprentice: NOVICE

beginner, recent convert: NEOPHYTE

beginner, novice: TYRO

beginning, commencement: CONCEPTION

beginning, start: INCEPTION

beginning a series of lines or sentences with same word or phrase: ANAPHORA

beginning affixed to a word: PREFIX

beginning to appear, coming into existence: INCIPIENT

beginnings, earliest stages of development: INCUNABULA

behave (oneself): DEMEAN

behavior or deportment: DEMEANOR

behavior that is seemly and proper: DECOROUS

behead: DECAPITATE

behind: BUTTOCKS

behind: DERRIÈRE

behind, after, later: POSTERIOR

behold: VOILA

being, objective existence of something in the mind, actual being: ENTITY

belch: ERUCT

belief, doctrine or principle maintained as true by a person or a group: TENET

belief in a god: THEISM

belief in one god without denying the existence of others: HENOTHEISM

belief in something with too little evidence: CREDULITY

belief or opinion contrary to established doctrine: HERESY

beliefs or opinions held to be true and necessary: DOGMA

believability: CREDIBILITY

believable, apparently true but open to doubt: PLAUSIBLE

belittle: DISPARAGE

belittle, detract: DEROGATE

belittle: DEPRECIATE

belittle, put down: DISPARAGE

belittle, speak disparagingly: POOH-POOH

bell casting and ringing: CAMPANOLOGY

bell ringing variations: CHANGE RINGING

bell rung at morning, noon and night: ANGELUS

bell shaped woman's hat: CLOCHE

bell signal, alarm: TOCSIN

bell sounded slowly and at regular intervals: TOLLING

bell tolling, especially one announcing a death: KNELL

bell tower, especially one that is not part of a building: CAMPANILE

belligerent's right to use or destroy neutral's property: ANGARY

bells ringing: TINTINNABULATION

bells rung by hammers operated from a keyboard: CARILLON

belly, big and prominent: PAUNCH

belly button: NAVEL

belly button: UMBILICUS

belt buckle's tonguelike part: TANG

belt or cord put around the waist: CINCTURE

bench, upholstered and without arms: BANQUETTE

benches without roof at sporting event: BLEACHERS

bend, contort, twist: WRITHE

bend, curve in and out: SINUATE

bend, misrepresent, twist: DISTORT

bend the knee, as in worship: GENUFLECT

bendable, flexible: PLIABLE

bending, curved or bent part: FLECTION

bending easily, graceful, limber: LITHE

bending of light or heat ray as it moves from one medium to another: RE-FRACTION

bending or winding, unsteady, wavering: FLEXUOUS

beneath, below: NETHER

beneath one's dignity: INFRA DIG

beneficial: SALUTARY

beneficiary or recipient of a legacy: LEGATEE

benefit owed because of status: PERQUISITE

bent backward: RETROFLEX

bent like a hook: UNCINATE

berate, upbraid, scold severely: OB-JURGATE

beseeching: SUPPLIANT

beset by a difficult situation: HARDSET

beset or surround: BELEAGUER

beside the (real) point: ACCIDENTAL

bespangled with fine stars: STELLULAR

best, most distinguished: ELITE

best in given field: ARISTOCRACY

best moment, most critical time: PSY-CHOLOGICAL MOMENT

best quality, highest priced: GILT-EDGED

bestow, make known, disclose: IMPART

bet on races in which those backing winners share in the total wagered: PARIMUTUEL

betrayal: SELLOUT

betterment: MELIORATION

betterment of the world: MELIORISM

betting on a choice that has little chance of winning: LONG SHOT

betting on winners in two races: DAILY DOUBLE

betting the winnings of a previous race on a later one: PARLAY

between: INTERVENING

between acts: ENTR'ACTE

between the devil and the deep blue sea: DILEMMA

between the lines: INTERLINEAR

bevel a surface: CHAMFER

bewilder, amaze, stun: STUPEFY

bewilder, dumbfound, perplex: NONPLUS

bewilder, muddle, obscure: OBFUSCATE

bewildered: BEMUSED

bewildered, tense, worried, agitated, crazed: DISTRAUGHT

bewildered, uncertain, puzzled: PER-PLEXED

beyond the lawful powers of, forbidden: ULTRA VIRES

beyond words: INEFFABLE

bias, prejudice: PRECONCEPTION

bias or partiality preconceived: PREDILEC-TION

biased: TENDENTIOUS

biased, favoring one party, prejudiced: PARTIAL

biblical interpretation: HERMENEUTICS

bids entered simultaneously for the same stock are resolved by a flip of a coin: MATCHED AND LOST

big belly: PAUNCH

Big Board: NEW YORK STOCK EXCHANGE

big toe: HALLUX

bigoted, narrow-minded, obstinate: HIDE-BOUND

bigotry: INTOLERANCE

big, thick-skinned animals with hooves: PACHYDERMS

biggest portion (originally the whole thing): LION'S SHARE

bill for merchandise sent or services rendered: INVOICE

billiard ball caused to recoil after impact: DRAW

billiard shot in which the ball first strikes the cushion: BRICOLE

billiard shot in which the cue ball strikes two others in succession: CAROM

billiard stroke in which the cue is held perpendicularly: MASSÉ

bind one's arm to render helpless: PINION

biological classification that is a sub-division of a genus: SPECIES

biological deterioration of a strain or type, especially of man: DYSGENIC

bird cage, usually large: AVIARY

bird group terms and terms for young—see "creature terms"

bird study: ORNITHOLOGY

bird's rump or part that holds the tail feathers: UROPYGIUM

birth, buttocks first: BREECH DELIVERY

birth by abdominal surgery: CAESAREAN SECTION

birth control governing the number and spacing of offspring: PLANNED PAR-ENTHOOD

birthmark: NEVUS

biscuit baked on a griddle and served with butter: SCONE

biscuit for army and navy use that is hard and crackerlike: HARDTACK

bishop who acts as assistant or auxiliary to another bishop: SUFFRAGAN

bishopric, bishops collectively: EPIS-COPATE
bishop's geographical area of jurisdiction: DIOCESE
bit, scrap: SNIPPET
biting: ASTRINGENT
biting, caustic: PUNGENT
biting, sarcastic: CAUSTIC
biting, sharp, keen: INCISIVE
biting taste, manner, speech, nature: ACRID
bitter: ACERB
bitter: ACRIMONIOUS
bitter, rancorous: VIRULENT
bitter taste, manner, speech, nature: ACRID
bitterness: ASPERITY
bizarre, fantastic: GROTESQUE
black: JET
black alloy used in cut-in decorations in metal: NIELLO
black and blue: LIVID
black and blue mark, bruise: ECCHYMOSIS
black and white, light and shade: CHIAROSCURO
black letter type: OLD ENGLISH
black magic, fortune telling, sorcery: NEC-ROMANCY
blacken, disparage, defame: DENIGRATE
blackness, darkness: NIGRESCENCE
blacks in America of African descent: AFRO-AMERICAN
blacksmith's workshop: SMITHY
bladder examination: CYSTOSCOPY
bladder inflammation: CYSTITIS
blame: CENSURE
blame, charge with fault: INCULPATE
blame, criticize, find fault with: REPRE-HEND
blame, reprove, censure: REPROACH
blame, rebuke, disapproval: REPROOF
blame is mine: MEA CULPA
blamed person to whom mistakes of others are attributed: SCAPEGOAT
blameless: IRREPROACHABLE
blameless, faultless: UNIMPEACHABLE
blameworthy: CULPABLE
bland, dull, tasteless, flat: INSIPID
blank, gap: LACUNA
blank, fixed, uncomprehending: GLASSY
blank check: CARTE BLANCHE
blank leaf at beginning or end of a book: FLYLEAF
blasphemous: IMPIOUS
bleach or dry in the sun: INSOLATE
bleak, barren: STARK

bleeding condition caused by absence of a clotting factor: HEMOPHILIA
bleeding in large quantities: HEMORRHAGE
blemish or stain: MACULATION
blend: AMALGAM
blend, combine: INTERLACE
blend and reconcile, as various philosophies: SYNCRETIZE
blend or fuse together: COALESCE
blending of two vowels generally pronounced separately: SYNERESIS
blending together as of variant readings of a text: CONFLATION
blessing: BENEDICTION
blind alley: CUL DE SAC
blind persons, printing method for: BRAILLE
blindly devoted: IDOLATROUS
blindness or impaired vision for blue and yellow: TRITANOPIA
bliss, release from care and pain: NIRVANA
blister-producing: VESICANT
blind spot: SCOTOMA
block, hinder, stop, impede: OBSTRUCT
block, shut or close off: OCCLUDE
block or obstruct: STYMIE
block or stone on which a column or statue stands: PLINTH
block that projects (architecture): DENTIL
blockhead: CLODPATE, CLODPOLL
blockhead: JACKASS
blockhead, stupid person: DOLT
blood clot in the heart or blood vessel: THROMBOSIS
blood clotting: COAGULATION
blood infection: SEPTICEMIA
blood poisoning: TOXEMIA
blood relationship: CONSANGUINITY
bloody: SANGUINARY
bloody slaughter: CARNAGE
blossom, bloom forth, flower: EFFLORESCE
blossoming: FLORESCENCE
blossoming, late: SEROTINOUS
blotch, spot, streak: MOTTLE
blouselike garment gathered at the waist: TUNIC
blow in puffs: WHIFFLE
blow to back of the neck in boxing: RAB-BIT PUNCH
blue: RISQUÉ
blue appearance of skin, due to lack of oxygen in blood: CYANOSIS
blue blindness: TRITANOPIA
blundering, clumsy: MALADROIT
blunt, direct: POINT-BLANK

blunt, dull, insensible: OBTUSE

blurred piece of print, blemish or spot: MACKLE

blurring or softening colors or lines in a painting or drawing: SCUMBLE

bluster or bragging talk: GASCONADE

board with handle underneath used to hold plaster or mortar: HAWK

boards arranged for nailing together into barrels or boxes: SHOOK

boaster: GASCON

boastful, bragging: RODOMONTADE

boastful defiance: BRAVADO

boastful or bullying speech: FANFARONADE

boastfully vain: VAINGLORIOUS

boasting soldier: SWASHBUCKLER

boasting that is ostentatious: JACTITATION

boasting that is pretentious: BRAGGADOCIO

boat, flat-bottomed with battened sails, used by Chinese: JUNK

boat, narrow and light, for racing: SCULL

boat basin for pleasure craft: MARINA

boat for fishing: SMACK

boat framework that extends beyond the rail: OUTRIGGER

boat or ship term for upper edge of craft's side: GUNWALE, GUNNEL

boat race or series of boat races: REGATTA

boat, small and flat-bottomed, used along the rivers and coasts of China and Japan: SAMPAN

boat that drags a net across a fishing bank: TRAWLER

boat that services another at sea: TENDER

bodily attributes or elements: CORPORAL, CORPOREAL

bodily disorders caused by mental or emotional conditions: PSYCHOSOMATIC

bodily pleasures or place that provides them: FLESHPOT

bodily processes that continuously build up and break down protoplasm: METABOLISM

body, as distinguished from the soul: SOMATIC

body, having preoccupation with: CARNAL

body of mean summoned to assist a peace officer: POSSE

body stealer: RESURRECTIONIST

bog, marsh: MORASS

bog, swamp, backwater: SLOUGH

bog down, sink in mud: MIRE

boil down, condense: DECOCT

boil gently: SIMMER

boil partly: PARBOIL

boiling, agitated condition: CALDRON

boisterous, unruly: OBSTREPEROUS

bold, dauntless, fearless: INTREPID

bold, indecent, self-assertive: IMMODEST

bold, saucy, brazen, shameless: IMPUDENT

boldness, audacity, impudence: EFFRONTERY

boldness, daring, audacity: HARDIHOOD

bomb or grenade consisting of a bottle containing flammable liquid: MOLOTOV COCKTAIL

bomb that explodes into jagged pieces: FRAGMENTATION BOMB

bombastic: TUMID

bombastic, high-flown: INFLATED

bombastic, grandiloquent: TURGID

bombastic, pompous: GRANDILOQUENT

bombastic, ornate, florid, showy: FLAMBOYANT

bombastic, pretentious: FUSTIAN

bond, connection, link: NEXUS

bond, tie that connects: LIGAMENT

bond often lacking a specific pledge of assets: DEBENTURE

bond issue that may be redeemed by issuer before maturity: CALLABLE

bond issued by a company with a reputation for showing a profit: GILT-EDGED

bond not having owner's name registered with issuing company and payable to any holder of the bond: BEARER BOND

bond of union: VINCULUM

bond on which principal and interest are guaranteed by a company other than the issuer of the bond: GUARANTEED BOND

bond value, as it appears on the security: FACE VALUE

bone and muscle branch of surgery: ORTHOPEDICS

bone at lower end of spine: COCCYX

bone-forming process: OSSIFICATION

bones united by muscles: SYSSARCOSIS

book bound in paper rather than cloth or leather: PAPERBACK

book bound in stiff cover as distinguished from paperback: HARD-COVER BOOK

book carrying various versions of a text: VARIORUM

book containing rules of spelling, punctuation, typography, used by editors: STYLEBOOK

book cover lining, especially when it is ornamental: DOUBLURE

book installment prior to publication: FAS-
CICLE

book jacket matter that touts the volume:
BLURB

book lover and collector: BIBLIOPHILE

book of daily prayers and offices for ca-
nonical house: BREVIARY

book or article on a single subject: MONO-
GRAPH

book or list of lessons for church service:
LECTIONARY

book or Bible peddler: COLPORTEUR

bookbinding leather: SKIVER

bookbinding style characterized by gilded
ornamentation: GROLIER

bookbinding with leather on the spine and
corners and cloth or paper on the
sides: HALF BINDING

bookmaker's advantage in the betting odds
he creates: VIGORISH

bookplate, from the library of: EX LIBRIS

books of an author or on a given subject
listed: BIBLIOGRAPHY

books or other writings on unusual topics,
often pornography: CURIOSA

books printed before 1500 A.D.: IN-
CUNABULA

boor, clown, awkward fellow: LOUT

boorish: UNCOUTH

boot covering the leg to the knee in front,
but cut lower in back: WELLINGTON
BOOT

boot of sealskin or reindeer skin worn by
Eskimos: MUKLUK

booth, newsstand, bandstand usually
lightly constructed and open: KIOSK

booty, loot: PILLAGE

booty, money: PELF

booty, stolen goods, etc.: PLUNDER

border on: ABUT

border or contrasting edge: LIMBUS

bore or displease: PALL

bored, dull, or depressed state of mind:
DOLDRUMS

boredom, discontent or weariness: ENNUI

boring, tedious: WEARISOME

boring, wearisome: TEDIOUS

born of the same parents as another:
GERMAN

born out of wedlock: MISBEGOTTEN

born with: INHERENT

borrower's property or securities pledged
to insure repayment of a loan: COL-
LATERAL

borrowing stock expected to decline in

order to sell it at a higher price:
SHORT SALE

botany as a descriptive study: PHY-
TOGRAPHY

botch a job: BUNGLE

both hands used equally well: AMBIDEX-
TROUS

both sexes united in one person: AN-
DROGYNOUS

bother, disturb: INCOMMODE

bother, fluster, fuss: POTHER

bother, inconvenience, trouble: DISCOM-
MODE

bottle for vinegar or oil: CRUET

bottle of glass that is decorative and used
for wine: DECANTER

bounce, jolt, shake up and down: JOUNCE

bound or consecrated by vow or promise:
VOTARY

bound with a band, bandage: FASCIATE

boundary, restriction: PALE

boundary between the shore and the
ocean: STRAND LINE

boundary line of a figure or area: PERIME-
TER

bountiful, lavish, generous: MUNIFICENT

bow decoration on a ship: FIDDLEHEAD

bow decoration on a ship in the form of a
carved figure: FIGUREHEAD

bow of a stringed instrument made to rebound slightly: SPICCATO

bowel stimulant, cathartic: PURGATIVE

box with feinting movements and light
blows: SPAR

boxer belonging to lightest weight class,
weighing 112 pounds or less: FLY-
WEIGHT

boxer weighing up to 126 pounds or a
wrestler up to 134 pounds: FEATH-
ERWEIGHT

boxer or wrestler weighing between 127
and 135 pounds: LIGHTWEIGHT

boxer or wrestler weighing between 136
and 147 pounds: WELTERWEIGHT

boxer or wrestler weighing between 147
and 160 pounds: MIDDLEWEIGHT

boxer or wrestler weighing between 161
and 175 pounds: LIGHT HEAVY-
WEIGHT

boxer or wrestler weighing over 175
pounds: HEAVYWEIGHT

boxer's deformed ear: CAULIFLOWER EAR

boxing: PUGILISM

boxing and matters pertaining to boxing:
FISTIC

boxing term for a victory in a fight halted by the referee: TECHNICAL KNOCK-OUT

boxing victory based on points when there has been no knockout: DECISION

boy used in sodomy: CATAMITE

brag about: VAUNT

bragging, blustering: RODOMONTADE

bragging, boastful: THRASONICAL

bragging talk or bluster: GASCONADE

braid: PLAIT

braid that is narrow and flat, woven in a herringbone effect: SOUTACHE

brain examination that traces changes in electric potential: ELECTROENCEPH-ALOGRAM (EEG)

brain inflammation: ENCEPHALITIS

brain-lacking: ANENCEPHALOUS

brains, intellect: GRAY MATTER

brake in which friction pads press on disc that is part of wheel: DISC BRAKE

branch, offshoot: RAMIFICATION

branch or spread out, diverge: DIVARICATE

branched: RAMOSE

brand new, original condition, unused: MINT CONDITION

brave, staunch: YEOMANLY

brave, steadfast: UNFLINCHING

brave, strong, determined: STALWART

brave, warlike, disciplined: SPARTAN

bravery pretended: BRAVADO

brawl: AFFRAY

brawl, fight, conflict, uproar: FRAY

brawl marked by roughness, free-for-all: DONNYBROOK

brazen, shameless, bold, saucy: IMPUDENT

brazen audacity: CHUTZPAH

brazenly display or parade: FLAUNT

bread, usually braided, eaten by Jews on holiday: HALLAH or CHALLAH

bread made of cornmeal, eggs, milk and shortening, baked soft enough to be served with a spoon: SPOON BREAD

bread that is baked yellow then sliced and toasted: ZWIEBACK

break, as in electric service: OUTAGE

break, tear apart forcibly: REND

break apart: RUPTURE

break away, separate from: DISSOCIATE

break of a relationship: RIFT

break in continuity: INTERREGNUM

break in continuity to give an episode occurring earlier: FLASHBACK

break off from an association, or separate from an association: DISSOCIATE

break off relations with: DISAFFILIATE

break or pause in a line of verse: CAESURA

break or split, especially in layer: SPALL

break out or erupt afresh: RECRUDESCE

break up a group into small dissenting factions: BALKANIZE

break up or separate into parts, analyze: RESOLVE

breakable, brittle, fragile: FRANGIBLE

breakdown or collapse that is sudden and ruinous: DEBACLE

breakfast, late, or luncheon: DÉJEUNER

breaking of a law or a pledge: INFRACTION

breaking off in the middle of a sentence without completing the idea: APOSIO-PESIS

breaking or rushing in: IRRUPTION

breast of a woman: POITRINE

breast or chest: PECTORAL

breast removal surgery: MASTECTOMY

breast separation line in a woman: CLEAVAGE

breathe: RESPIRE

breathe noisily, as a dog following a scent: SNUFFLE

breathe or blow into or upon: INSUFFLATE

breathing difficulty caused by swelling in some parts of the body: EMPHYSEMA

breathing that is labored: DYSPNEA

breeches loose above the knees, tight below: JODHPURS

breed, multiply by natural reproduction: PROPAGATE

breed rapidly, swarm, teem: PULLULATE

breeding of special races or strains of animals and plants: STIRPICULTURE

brewing process of fermentation, as a branch of chemistry: ZYMURGY

bribe or procure one to commit perjury: SUBORN

bribe or something given as appeasement: SOP

bribery acceptable, corrupt: VENAL

brick that is sun dried: ADOBE

bride's outfit: TROUSSEAU

bridge bid that exceeds the preceding bid by more than the minimum: JUMP BID

bridge hand with no card higher than nine: YARBOROUGH

bridge victory consisting of the winning of all thirteen tricks in a round of play: GRAND SLAM

bridgelike framework for holding the rails of a traveling crane: GANTRY

brief, concise, terse: LACONIC
brief and meaningful, terse, concise: SUC-
CINCT
brief general view of a work: SYNOPSIS
bright, brilliant: INCANDESCENT
bright, intense, clear: VIVID
bright, rational, clear, easily understood:
LUCID
bright idea: BRAINSTORM
brighten by rubbing: FURBISH
brilliance, radiance, splendor: RE-
FULGENCE
brilliance of action or effect: ECLAT
brilliant, ostentatious oratory: PYROTECH-
NICS
brilliant, speedy, dazzling: METEORIC
brilliant in a light and playful fashion:
LAMBENT
brilliant or dashing performance: BRAVURA
brilliantly wise or intelligent: LUMINOUS
brim in front of a cap to shade the eyes:
VISOR
brine for pickling: SOUSE
bring about, accomplish: EFFECT
bring forth, originate: SPAWN
bring on oneself: INCUR
bring something about quickly: PRECIPI-
TATE
bring together: RALLY
bring up or train: NURTURE
bring up partly digested food: REGURGI-
TATE
brisk, cheerful: CHIPPER
brisk, dashing, self-confident, stylish,
lively: JAUNTY
briskly, lively, quickly, in music: VIVACE
bristly: SETACEOUS
bristly or spiny: ECHINATE
British Parliament member who is not a
party leader: BACKBENCHER
British record of proceedings in Parliament: HANSARD
broad in tastes or understanding: CATHO-
LIC
broad jump: LONG JUMP
broadcaster who coordinates reports: AN-
CHOR MAN
broadheaded: BRACHYCEPHALIC
broadside or leaflet distributed free:
THROWAWAY
broken, incomplete: FRAGMENTARY
broken bit of earthenware: POTSHERD
broken down: DILAPIDATED
broken down, decrepit: FLEA-BITTEN
broken-hearted: INCONSOLABLE

broken off piece: CANTLE
broken piece of pottery: SHARD
broken up into incidents, disjointed: EPI-
SODIC
broker holding securities in his own name
rather than in the name of his customer: STREET NAME
brokerage house that is fraudulent:
BUCKET SHOP
brokers' broker: SPECIALIST
brokers on the floor of the stock exchange
handling transactions for other brokers: TWO-DOLLAR BROKER
bromide, trite expression: CLICHÉ
bronze or silver gilt: VERMEIL
brook or creek: ARROYO
brothel: BORDELLO
brothers or sisters: SIBLINGS
browbeat, bully, cow: INTIMIDATE
browbeat, torment, rant, bully, bluster:
HECTOR
brown paper used for bags and wrapping:
KRAFT
brown or reddish brown pigment or pictures done in this pigment: SEPIA
bruise by blow or impact: CONTUSE
bruise or black-and-blue mark: ECCHY-
MOSIS
Brussels resident: BRUXELLOIS
brutish, stupid, foolish, unmoved: INSEN-
SATE
bubble, ripple, heave: POPPLE
bubbling over with enthusiasm or excitement: EBULLIENT
Buddhist concept of birth-death-rebirth
cycle: SAMSARA
Buenos Aires native: PORTEÑO
buffet meal consisting of Scandinavian
hors d'oeuvres: SMORGASBORD
buffet or sideboard, usually without legs:
CREDENZA
buffoon, clown: MERRY ANDREW
bugle call in the military indicating good
night or marking a military burial:
TAPS
build up something with parts taken from
other things: CANNIBALIZE
building construction as an art or science:
TECTONICS
building of many stories: HIGH-RISE
bulging: PROTUBERANT
bulky, lumbering: PONDEROUS
bulky, of great volume: VOLUMINOUS
bulletin board for actors in a theater:
CALLBOARD

bullets, missiles, rockets, etc., science of: BALLISTICS

bullfight: CORRIDA

bullfight horseman who pricks the bull's neck with a lance: PICADOR

bullfighter who kills the bull: MATADOR

bullish, like a bull: TAURINE

bully, browbeat, torment: HECTOR

bully, cow, browbeat: INTIMIDATE

bulwark, fortification: RAMPART

bump, strike against: JAR

bump or lump, protuberance: KNURL

bun or knot of hair at the back of the head, worn by women: CHIGNON

bungled action: MUFF

bungling, clumsy, or domineering: HEAVY-HANDED

bungling, inept person: SCHLEMIEL

buoyancy, elasticity: RESILIENCE

buoyant, optimistic, cheerful: SANGUINE

burden: MILLSTONE

burden, discouraging or oppressive thing: INCUBUS

burdens, drawbacks: IMPEDIMENTA

burdensome: ONEROUS

bureau of drawers, often with a mirror: CHIFFONIER

burglar's crowbar: JIMMY

burial mound: TUMULUS

burial vault: SEPULCHER

burlesque imitation of a serious literary or musical work: PARODY

burlesque or imitation that is grotesque: TRAVESTY

burlesque rigmarole: AMPHIGORY

burn quickly with great heat and light: DEFLAGRATE

burn the midnight oil in writing or studying: LUCUBRATE

burn tissue: CAUTERIZE

burn up, cremate: INCINERATE

burning, caustic: VITRIOLIC

burning fiercely: CONFLAGRANT

bursting or breaking in: IRRUPTION

bury, inter: INHUME

business that may hire nonunion workers, who are required to become union members by a specified time: UNION SHOP

businessman who assumes full control and risk of an enterprise: ENTREPRENEUR

bustle, excitement, fluster: POTHER

bustle about, rush pell-mell: HURRY-SCURRY

busybody: QUIDNUNC

butterfly or moth: LEPIDOPTERAN

buttocks: DERRIÈRE

buttocks: FUNDAMENT

buttocks: NATES

buttocks that are fat, especially in women: STEATOPYGIA

buttress joined to a wall some distance away: FLYING BUTTRESS

buy or sell order for securities good only for the day on which it is entered: DAY ORDER

buy up goods for reselling at a profit: FORESTALL

buy up with the aim of selling at a higher price: REGRATE

buyer beware: CAVEAT EMPTOR

buying and selling the same stock simultaneously in two different cities to realize a profit: ARBITRAGE

buying and selling volume of stocks relatively low: THIN MARKET

buying or selling sacred things: SIMONY

buying securities at stated intervals by the dollars' worth: MONTHLY INVESTMENT PLAN

by the very fact: IPSO FACTO

by-product, new application, incidental result: SPIN-OFF

C

cabal: CAMARILLA

cabal, intriguing group: JUNTA

cable, wire or rope used to steady or secure something: GUY

cable or rope for mooring or towing: HAWSER

cafe or restaurant that provides entertainment: CABARET

cage, usually large, for live birds: AVIARY

Cairo (Egypt) resident: CAIRENE

cajole: BLANDISH

cake, small and made of unsweetened batter: CRUMPET

cake made of butter and eggs, with fruit or nuts added: TORTE

cake made of sugar, eggs, and flour, containing no shortening and beaten very light: SPONGE CAKE

calamity: CATASTROPHE

calculating device with counters moving up and down on rods: ABACUS

calculator of risks and premiums for insurance: ACTUARY

calendar used in most of the world: GREGORIAN CALENDAR

California gold miner: ARGONAUT

calfskin or lambskin that is untanned: KIP

call, summon or draw forth: EVOKE

call in question, dispute, challenge: OPPUGN

call or whistle derisively: CATCALL

call to troops for service, review, etc.: MUSTER

call together, as a meeting: CONVOKE

call upon for aid, protection, witness: INVOKE

callow, immature, but opinionated: SOPHOMORIC

calm: DISPASSIONATE

calm, peaceful, tranquil: PLACID

calm down, quiet, abate: SUBSIDE

calm, quiet, serene: TRANQUIL

calm, serene, idyllic: HALCYON

calm, serene, unmoved: IMPASSIVE

calm, unruffled: IMPERTURBABLE

calm, untroubled, tranquil: SERENE

calmness, composure, even-temper: EQUANIMITY

Cambridge (Mass.) resident: CANTABRIGIAN

Cambridge (U.K.) resident: CANTABRIGIAN

camel with one hump: DROMEDARY

camera lens that records 180-degree field of vision: FISH-EYE LENS

camp, temporary, usually without shelter: BIVOUAC

can or cup that is small: CANNIKIN

cancel, recall, rescind, annul: REVOKE

cancer of the blood: LEUKEMIA

cancer-causing substance: CARCINOGEN

cancerous growth: CARCINOMA

candelabrum with seven branches used in the Jewish religion: MENORAH

candid, sincere, artless: GUILELESS

candidate almost unknown who wins a nomination or election: DARK HORSE

candidate list: SLATE

candidate put forward as a cover for another person: STALKING HORSE

candied or sugared, iced, frozen: GLACÉ

candlemaker: CHANDLER

candlestick that is branched: CANDELABRUM

candlestick that is branched, rotating firework: GIRANDOLE

canine tooth: CUSPID

cannibals: ANTHROPOPHAGI

cannon or artillery, military materiel: ORDNANCE

cannon with a relatively high angle of fire: HOWITZER

canoe that is covered except for an opening for the paddler: KAYAK

canopy or large tent, summerhouse: PAVILION

canopy over a pulpit or bed: TESTER

canopy used in religious processions: BALDACHIN

cant, lingo: JARGON

cantankerous: CROTCHETY

canvas sheet stretched on a frame and used for acrobatics: TRAMPOLINE

cap, flat and round: BERET

cap cover with long rear flap: HAVELOCK

cap of felt with a tassel, worn by Moslem men: TARBOOSH

cap that is square and stiff and worn by clergy: BIRETTA

capable of working, as a plan; able to live: VIABLE

caper, antic: DIDO

caper, antic: GAMBADO

caper, prance about: TITTUP

capital letters in type: UPPER CASE

capital that is hardly adequate used in starting a business: SHOESTRING

caprice, whim, fanciful humor: WHIMSY

capricious, willful: WAYWARD

caption or explanatory description on an illustration, chart or map: LEGEND

capture or seize: CORRAL

Caracas resident: CARAQUENO

card game called twenty-one: VINGT-ET-UN

card game series in which the series is terminated when one side has won two games: RUBBER

card game state in which a winner has made more than double his opponent: LURCH

card game that breaks a tie between players: RUBBER

card of a suit that outranks other suits during the playing of a hand: TRUMP

cards left on the table after the deal: TALON

carefree: FOOTLOOSE

carefree, light-hearted, gay: ROLLICKING

carefree, unconcerned, lighthearted: INSOUCIANT

carefree, worry-free: SANS SOUCI

carefree existence, drink and play: BEER AND SKITTLES

careful, checking every detail: CIRCUMSPECT

careful, frugal, cautious: CHARY

careful, scrupulous observance of forms: PUNCTILIOUS

careful, wise: JUDICIOUS

careful about what one says, prudent, tactful: DISCREET

careful and diligent: PAINSTAKING

carefully, cautiously: GINGERLY

carefully and delicately made: WROUGHT

careless, reckless: DEVIL-MAY-CARE

careless, reckless, weak: FECKLESS

careless, negligent: REMISS

careless or untidy person: SLOVEN

carelessly done: SLIPSHOD

caress or touch lightly as with the lips or make gentle contact, as two billiard balls: KISS

cargo cast overboard by an imperiled ship: JETSAM

carp or raise trivial objections: CAVIL

carpet of velvety texture: WILTON

carriage with hood and with high seat for horse driver: CABRIOLET

carried away by foolish love: INFATUATED

carrier of microorganisms: VECTOR

carry away wrongfully: ABDUCT

carry, haul, drag: SCHLEP

carry or move gently, float: WAFT

carry through, put into effect: IMPLEMENT

carry through or accomplish something: TRANSACT

carve, engrave, cut into: INCISE

carved design beneath the surface: INTAGLIO

carved ivory, stone, or shells: SCRIMSHAW

carving or engraving, especially on gems: GLYPTICS

case or example: INSTANCE

cash in a prize coupon, etc.: REDEEM

cash lacking: ILLIQUID

cash payment that must be made by customer when he uses his broker's credit for purchase of a security: MARGIN

cask holding half a barrel: KILDERKIN

cassock worn by Roman Catholic priest: SOUTANE

cast off, as dead skin: SLOUGH

cast off or discard a previously favored sweetheart: JILT

cast out an evil spirit by prayers or incantations: EXORCISE

cast out matter or refuse as from a volcano: EJECTA

casting or molding of footprints, etc., for

use in criminal investigation: MOU-
LAGE
castle-like in structure: CASTELLATED
castrate, geld, weaken, make effeminate:
EMASCULATE
castrated animal, especially a horse:
GELDING
castrated man or youth: EUNUCH
castrated rooster: CAPON
casual, indiscriminate, especially sexually:
PROMISCUOUS
casual, minor, secondary: INCIDENTAL
casualties sorted to fix priorities for treatment: TRIAGE
cat, particularly an old female one: GRI-
MALKIN
cat family: FELINE
catch up with or get ahead of, as a ship:
FOREREACH
catching: INFECTIOUS
Catholic Church list of forbidden books:
INDEX EXPURGATORIUS
catlike cry, long and plaintive cry: WAUL
cat's eye: CHATOYANT
Catskill and White Mountain hotels that
provide entertainment: BORSCHT CIR-
CUIT
cattle food: PROVENDER
cattle herder: COWBOY, COWHAND, COW-
PUNCHER
cattle movement to more suitable pastures:
TRANSHUMANCE
caught in the act: IN FLAGRANTE DELICTO
caught in the act: RED-HANDED
cause, bring about: INDUCE
cause a result creditable or discreditable:
REDOUND
cause and effect theory in philosophy,
especially of human behavior: DE-
TERMINISM
cause or make likely, attract: INVITE
cause something abruptly or unexpectedly:
PRECIPITATE
cause that produces a result: FACTOR
cause to effect, prior to: A PRIORI
causes and origins as subjects of study:
ETIOLOGY
caustic: ACRIMONIOUS
caustic, biting: PUNGENT
caustic, burning: VITRIOLIC
caustic, cutting, sarcastic: MORDANT
caustic, mercilessly severe, withering:
SCATHING
cautious: WARY
cautious, frugal, careful: CHARY

cautious, moderate, opposed to change:
CONSERVATIVE
cautious checking of every detail: CIR-
CUMSPECT
cautiously, carefully: GINGERLY
cautiously shrewd: CANNY
cave explorer: SPELUNKER
cave formation, cone-shaped, that is built
up on the floor: STALAGMITE
cave formation, long and tapering, that
hangs from the roof: STALACTITE
cave man: TROGLODYTE
cave or fall in, sink, collapse, fail:
FOUNDER
caves, as a subject of study: SPELEOLOGY
cavities in the skull leading into nasal cavities: SINUSES
cease-fire, armistice: TRUCE
ceiling decorated with a painted or carved
design: PLAFOND
celebrate, make merry, delight (in): REVEL
celebrity, fame: RENOWN
celestial, heavenly: SUPERNAL
celestial, sublime, superior, fiery: EM-
PYREAL
cellar or underground shelter used during
cyclones or tornadoes: CYCLONE
CELLAR
cells; study of their structure, organization
and function: CYTOLOGY
cement or plaster used to surface walls:
STUCCO
cemetery for paupers: POTTER'S FIELD
censor by deleting offensive passages:
BOWDLERIZE
censor by removing obscene or otherwise
objectionable material: EXPURGATE
censorship that is exaggerated: COM-
STOCKERY
censure, blame, rebuke: REPROACH
censure, scold, reproach: UPBRAID
censure or rebuke severely: REPRIMAND
censure vehemently: INVEIGH
center in common: CONCENTRIC
center of attraction: CYNOSURE
centerless: ACENTRIC
central essential element, core: NUCLEUS
central point, hub, navel: OMPHALOS
century, era, period: SIÈCLE
century and a half: SESQUICENTENNIAL
century's end, especially the end of the
19th century; also decadence: FIN DE
SIÈCLE
ceremonial procession: CORTEGE
ceremonial washing of hands: ABLUTION

ceremonies commemorating the founding of a city or university or the consecration of a church: ENCAENIA

ceremony that is pretentious or hypocritical: MUMMERY

certain: APODICTIC

certain: COCKSURE

certain, accurate: UNERRING

certain, unavoidable: INEVITABLE

certain, unquestionable: INDUBITABLE

certainly, without doubt: SANS DOUTE

certificate acknowledging debt: DEBENTURE

certificate entitling the holder to receive shares of stock, money, etc.: SCRIP

chain hanging from woman's belt to hold keys or purse: CHATELAINE

chain of colored paper, ribbon or flowers hung in loops: FESTOON

chain or closely connected series: CATENA

chain of things or events: CONCATENATION

chair of wood, with spindle back and slanting legs: WINDSOR CHAIR

chair with high back and side pieces: WING CHAIR

challenge: THROW DOWN THE GAUNTLET

challenge, dispute or attack the truth or validity of: IMPUGN

challenge the honesty or validity of: IMPEACH

chamberpot in a low chair or cabinet: COMMODE

chance occurrence: HAPPENSTANCE

change appearance of: TRANSFIGURE

change form or quality: TRANSMUTE

change in the form, character or appearance: METAMORPHOSIS

change in vowel for changed tense, etc.: ABLAUT

change into a different shape: TRANSMOGRIFY

change one substance into another: TRANSUBSTANTIATE

change opinion completely: ABOUT-FACE

change or movement that is constant: FLUX

change or vary often and in irregular manner: FLUCTUATE

change personal convictions by coercion: BRAINWASH

change places, alternate: INTERCHANGE

change plans of someone by persuasion: DISSUADE

change sides, apostatize: TERGIVERSATE

changeable: AMBIVALENT

changeable, erratic: INCONSISTENT

changeable, fickle: MUTABLE

changeable, inconstant: FICKLE

changeable, lively, clever: MERCURIAL

changeable, unstable: LABILE

changeable into different forms or shapes: PROTEAN

changeable luster: CHATOYANT

changeable person: CHAMELEON

changes in price that can be absorbed by the market in a particular security: LIQUIDITY

changes in series of plant or animal formations: SERE

changes or variations occurring irregularly, as of fortune: VICISSITUDES

changing rapidly and intricately: KALEIDOSCOPIC

channel for water, as under a road: CULVERT

chant: INTONE

chanted, nonmetrical hymn: CANTICLE

chanted formula or magic words: INCANTATION

chapel for private prayer: ORATORY

character, mark or stamp that is distinctive: IMPRESS

character and attitudes of a community or individual: ETHOS

characterization, often disparaging, of a person or thing: EPITHET

characterless: INVERTEBRATE

characterless, not distinctive: NONDESCRIPT

charcoal pencil or a sketch or drawing done in charcoal: FUSAIN

charge a public official with a crime or misdemeanor: IMPEACH

charge with a crime, accuse: INDICT

charge, fixed, that is added to bill at cabarets, hotels, clubs for entertainment or service: COVER CHARGE

charged, filled: FRAUGHT

charging of a wrongdoing or fault, accusation: IMPUTATION

charity, alms: ELEEMOSYNARY

charity case, a very poor person: PAUPER

charity to aid mankind: PHILANTHROPY

charlatan, vendor of quack medicines: MOUNTEBANK

charlatanism: SCIOLISM

charm: AMULET

charm: ENAMOR

charm as if by magic: BEWITCH

charm or amulet: TALISMAN

charm or divert: BEGUILE
charm or talisman: GRIGRI
chart containing lines representing changes in value: GRAPH
chary, stingy, economical: SPARE
chasm or fissure, as in a glacier: CREVASSE
chastise or rebuke severely: CASTIGATE
chat, talk idly: SCHMOOZE
chat or gossip: CONFABULATE
chat or informal conversation: CAUSERIE
chatter, talk senselessly: PRATE
chauvinist: JINGO
cheap, flashy dress or ornamentation: FRIPPERY
cheap, poor quality: SCHLOCK
cheap, sensational talk: CLAPTRAP
cheap, shoddy, poorly made: SLEAZY
cheap, trashy, measly: CHINTZY
cheap and showy: BRASSY
cheap and showy: TAWDRY
cheap and showy, designed merely to sell: CATCHPENNY
cheap red wine: VIN ORDINAIRE
cheat: BAMBOOZLE
cheat, dawdle, or pass time: DIDDLE
cheat, outwit: EUCHRE
cheat, swindle: ROOK
cheat, trick: HOODWINK
cheat, trick, deceive: FINAGLE
cheat a stranger: BUNCO
cheat or deceive in a petty way: COZEN
cheat or extort: GOUGE
cheat or defraud a person: MULCT
cheated or fooled easily: GULLIBLE
cheater, quibbler: PETTIFOGGER
check or restrain, as an impulse: INHIBIT
check or stop the flow of: STANCH
check stub, or stub of money order kept as record: COUNTERFOIL
checkered or plaid pattern of dark lines on a light ground: TATTERSALL
cheerful: BLITHE
cheerful: BUOYANT
cheerful, brisk: CHIPPER
cheerful, buoyant, optimistic: SANGUINE
cheerful, gay: JOCUND
cheerful, lively, urbane: DEBONAIR
cheerful, optimistic: ROSEATE
cheerful willingness: ALACRITY
cheese and crumbs crust: AU GRATIN
cheese, melted and cooked, often with beer or ale added, and served on toast or crackers: WELSH RABBIT
cheese, Italian, that is hard and is sprinkled on spaghetti or soup: PARMESAN

chess term for a draw resulting when a player can make no move without placing his king in check: STALEMATE
chest of drawers, high and often with a mirror: CHIFFONIER
chest of drawers, on short legs, about table height: LOWBOY
chest of drawers, usually in two sections, the lower on legs: HIGHBOY
chew noisily or munch: CHAMP
chewy, as spaghetti: AL DENTE
chewing food thoroughly as an aid to good health: FLETCHERISM
chicken, few months old: SPRING CHICKEN
chicken and leeks soup: COCK-A-LEEKIE
chicken pox: VARICELLA
chicken stewed in wine: COQ AU VIN
chicken stewed Italian style: CHICKEN CACCIATORE
chief commodity of a place or region: STAPLE
chief of a political party: SACHEM
chief or leader: COCK OF THE WALK
child murder: INFANTICIDE
child murder by a parent: FILICIDE
child prodigy: WUNDERKIND
child with extraordinary talent: PRODIGY
child who because of neglect spends his time in the streets: GUTTERSNIPE
childbirth, delivery: PARTURITION
childbirth pangs: TRAVAIL
childbirth ritual among primitive people in which father of newly born goes through motions as if he had given birth: COUVADE
childish, trivial, silly: PUERILE
childish talk: PRATTLE
children's diseases and hygienic care, as a study: PEDIATRICS
child's relation to parents: FILIAL
chilling: FRIGORIFIC
china or porcelain that is very thin and delicate: EGGSHELL CHINA
Chinese use of needles in medical practice: ACUPUNCTURE
chivalry: KNIGHT-ERRANTRY
chuckles of glee: CHORTLE
church architecture and decoration: ECCLESIOLOGY
church area behind the altar: RETROCHOIR
church area under jurisdiction of a bishop: DIOCESE
church rule by prelates: PRELACY
churchman of high rank: PRELATE
choice: OPTION

choice, excellence or exceptional quality: VINTAGE

choice must be made between two equally undesirable alternatives: DILEMMA

choice of what is offered or nothing: HOBSON'S CHOICE

choke to death: STRANGLE

choose, elect: OPT

choose with care: HAND PICK

chord's notes played in quick succession: ARPEGGIO

Christmas display of stable, scene of Jesus' birth: CRÈCHE

chronology as estimated by growth rings on trees: DENDROCHRONOLOGY

cigar, long and slim: PANATELA

cigar, long, slender and inexpensive: STOGIE

cigar, strong and dark: MADURO

cigar, tapering at both ends: PERFECTO

cigar, cut square at both ends: CHEROOT

circle boundary: CIRCUMFERENCE

circle or persons having an interest or interests in common: COTERIE

circle with locked arms formed by dancers in this Rumanian and Israeli folk dance: HORA

circle's circumference in relation to its diameter: PI

circling back to the original problem results after its solution raises other problems: VICIOUS CIRCLE

circular, revolving or whirling motion: GYRAL

circular graph divided into proportionate sections: PIE CHART

circulate, permeate: DIFFUSE

circumference, especially the waist: GIRTH

circumlocution, wordiness: PERIPHRASIS

cite for proof or example: ADDUCE

citizenship bestowal, freeing from slavery: ENFRANCHISEMENT

city area where vice and corruption flourish: TENDERLOIN

civic or a town resident: OPPIDAN

civil liberties advocate: LIBERTARIAN

civil magistrate or officer representing a government: SYNDIC

civilian clothes, especially those worn by one who usually wears a uniform: MUFTI

civilians arming spontaneously in times of military emergency: LEVY EN MASSE

civilities: AMENITIES

civility: COMITY

claim, require: POSTULATE

claim on property in payment of or as security for a debt: LIEN

claim without right: ARROGATE

clairvoyance, telepathy: CRYPTESTHESIA

clam: QUAHOG

clam of the littleneck variety only larger: CHERRYSTONE

clam that is the young of the quahog: LITTLENECK

clannish set: CLIQUE

clarify, enlighten, illuminate, light up: IRRADIATE

clarify, explain: INTERPRET

clarinet's lowest register: CHALUMEAU

class, sort, kind: ILK

class or group in society: CASTE

classic, venerable, time-honored: VINTAGE

classification laws and principles: TAXONOMY

clattering or rattling noise: BRATTLE

clauses in a sentence without connectives between them: PARATAXIS

claw, hoof, nail: UNGUIS

clay pottery: CERAMICS

clean, correct, flawless: IMMACULATE

clean slate: TABULA RASA

clear of blame or accusation, acquit: EXONERATE

cleanse or wipe off: DETERGE

cleansing agent: ABLUENT

clear, bright, intense: VIVID

clear, comprehensible: INTELLIGIBLE

clear, definite, straightforward, outspoken: EXPLICIT

clear, easily understood, rational, bright, shining: LUCID

clear, lucid, understandable: PERSPICUOUS

clear, rounded, full voice: OROTUND

clear, transparent, lucid, pure: LIMPID

clear, understandable: PELLUCID

clear, understandable in one way only: UNEQUIVOCAL

clear and resounding: CLARION

clear of accusation: VINDICATE

clear the throat audibly: HAWK

clearing area in a fog bank: FOGDOG or SEADOG

clearing in the woods: GLADE

clergyman's salary paid out of church revenues: PREBEND

clerical cap that is square and stiff: BIRETTA

clerical garb that is loose and white and has wide sleeves: SURPLICE clerical or professional worker: WHITE COLLAR

clever, skillful, inventive: INGENIOUS

clever man, thinker: SOPHIST

clever remark: BON MOT

cliché: BROMIDE

clicking pieces for keeping time to music, especially Spanish: CASTANETS

cliff at the rim of a plateau: SCARP

cliff on the side of a hill: SCAR

cliff projecting into the water: HEADLAND

cliff that extends a distance: PALISADES

cliff's edge, dangerous situation: PRECIPICE

climax: APOGEE

climax in coitus: ORGASM

climb, as a tree, by clasping it with the arms and legs: SWARM

clinging, retentive: TENACIOUS

clinging closely: OSCULANT

clique: CAMARILLA

clique or group: FACTION

close association, confidential friendship: INTIMACY

close but not touching: CONTIGUOUS

close off, block or shut up: OCCLUDE

close one's eyes to something as if it had not happened: CONDONE

close one's eyes to wrongdoing: CONNIVE

close quarters, close contact: HAND-TO-HAND

close together, jammed: CHOCKABLOCK

closed or secret session: IN CAMERA

closed session to consider confidential business: EXECUTIVE SESSION

closed to others' opinions or beliefs: INTOLERANT

closed to outside influence, incapable of being passed through: IMPERVIOUS

closemouthed, reserved: TACITURN

closeness: PROPINQUITY

clot formation causing dead tissue: INFARCTION

cloth containing an intricate design that usually includes loops ending in curlicues: PAISLEY

cloth laid on the lap of a bishop officiating at a mass or ordination: GREMIAL

cloth of yellowish brown: KHAKI

clothe richly: CAPARISON

clothed negligently or partly: DISHABILLE

cloud formation, dense, usually white, with domed top and horizontal base, seen in fair weather: CUMULUS

cloud of rounded mass appearing before a thunderstorm: THUNDERHEAD

cloud streamers, or wisps of precipitation: VIRGA

cloud study, as a branch of meteorology: NEPHOLOGY

clouds, long and fibrous, supposed to foretell a storm: MARE'S TAIL

clouds in a fine, whitish veil, giving a hazy appearance: CIRROSTRATUS

clouds in a mass of fleecy globular cloudlets: CIRROCUMULUS

clouds in large globular masses, disposed in waves, groups or bands: STRATOCUMULUS

clouds in a white wispy tufts or bands across the sky: CIRRUS

cloudy: TURBID

cloudy, foggy, obscure, indefinite: NUBILOUS

cloudy or overcast: LOWERY

clown, buffoon: MERRY ANDREW

cloying, oversweet or rich: LUSCIOUS

clumsily done: BOTCHED

clumsy, awkward, heavy in appearance or movement: LUMBERING

clumsy, awkward, incompetent: INEPT

clumsy, blundering: MALADROIT

clumsy, boorish, awkward: GAUCHE

clumsy, bungling, or domineering: HEAVY-HANDED

clumsy, labored: PONDEROUS

clumsy, lacking skill: INAPT

clumsy, stupid person: CLODHOPPER

clumsy in handling things: BUTTERFINGERS

clumsy job: BUNGLE

clumsy rustic: BUMPKIN

clump along pompously: GALUMPH

clump or tuft, as of grass or hair: TUSSOCK

coal mining by stripping off soil rather than sinking a shaft: STRIP MINING

coarse, abusive in language: SCURRILOUS

coarse, loud, rough in sound: RAUCOUS

coarse, unrefined, natural: EARTHY

coarse food: ROUGHAGE

coarsely or vulgarly joking: RIBALD

coat lapel: REVERS

coat of which the sleeves are in one piece up to the collar: RAGLAN

coat or covering, as of a seed: TEGMEN

coats of arms, genealogies, etc.: HERALDRY

coax or flatter to persuade: WHEEDLE

coax with flattery: CAJOLE

cock less than a year old: COCKEREL
coddle: COCKER
coddle or pamper: COSHER
code deciphering: CRYPTANALYSIS
coded writing: CRYPTOGRAPHY
codfish that is young: SCROD
coercion, compulsion: DURESS
coercive measures taken to force a country
   to comply with demands: SANCTIONS
coffee, black: CAFE NOIR
coffee, small cup of: DEMITASSE
coffee or coffee-flavored: MOCHA
coffee with milk: CAFE AU LAIT
coffin of stone: SARCOPHAGUS
coffin-supporting framework: CATA-
   FALQUE
coherence lacking: DISJOINTED
coiled: TORTILE
coiled spirally: HELICOID
coin a word: MINT
coin or medal space for date, place of
   coining, etc.: EXERGUE
coined money: SPECIE
coins, medals, etc., as a study: NUMIS-
   MATICS
cold in the head: CORYZA
cold sore: HERPES LABIALIS
coil up intricately: CONVOLUTE
coincidence: CONJUNCTION
collapse, fail, sink: FOUNDER
collapse inward violently: IMPLODE
collar or cord used in executions: GAR-
   ROTE
colleague or fellow member: CONFRERE
collect, gather or store as in a granary:
   GARNER
collect, incorporate, make part of a whole:
   EMBODY
collected excerpts from literary works:
   ANALECTS
collection during a religious ceremony:
   OFFERTORY
collection of choice extracts for instruction
   in a language: CHRESTOMATHY
collection of poems, stories, etc.: AN-
   THOLOGY
collection of things, mass, heap:
   CONGERIES
collection of works and roles of a performance or company: REPERTORY
collection or cluster that is heterogeneous:
   CONGLOMERATE
collective farm in Soviet Union: KOLKHOZ
collective farm or settlement in Israel:
   KIBBUTZ

collector or connoisseur of works of art:
   VIRTUOSO
college enrollment: MATRICULATION
color blindness: ACHROMATOPSIA
color blindness: DALTONISM
color blindness to one of the three primary
   colors: DICHROMATIC
color or tint uniform throughout:
   ISOCHROOUS
color slightly: TINGE
color study: CHROMATICS
colored differently in different parts: PAR-
   TICOLORED
coloring matter: PIGMENT
colorless, pale: PALLID
colors changing in different lights: VER-
   SICOLOR
colors of the rainbow in shifting hues and
   patterns: IRIDESCENCE
column in form of a female figure:
   CARYATID
columns that are regularly spaced: COL-
   ONNADE
collusion in a lawsuit to get share of matter sued for: CHAMPERTY
combative: PUGNACIOUS
combination of circumstances of events:
   CONJUNCTURE
combination of two or more substances:
   AMALGAM
combine, blend and reconcile, as various
   philosophies: SYNCRETIZE
combustible substance that will ignite with
   a spark: TINDER
come forth into the open, emerge: DE-
   BOUCH
come between, especially as a barrier: IN-
   TERPOSE
come into office or dignity: ACCEDE
come into view or appear as through a
   mist often ominously: LOOM
comedian who is the star: TOP BANANA
comedy that is broad or exaggerated:
   FARCE
comedy that is loud and crude: SLAPSTICK
comfort in grief: SOLACE
comic antics: HARLEQUINADE
coming from without, unrelated to the
   matter at hand: EXTRANEOUS
coming in continually as of people or
   things: INFLUX
coming into a country not one's own: IM-
   MIGRANT
coming into existence, beginning to appear: INCIPIENT

coming together, or a crowd: CONCOURSE
command, order, forbid: ENJOIN
command level: ECHELON
commandeer a plane in transit: HIJACK
commence, begin: INAUGURATE
commence, originate, begin: INITIATE
commencement headgear with a flat, square top: MORTARBOARD
commendation: PLAUDIT
commendatory: LAUDATORY
comment that is not binding, a remark made in passing: OBITER DICTUM
comment-arousing object: CONVERSATION PIECE
commentary, explanatory note: GLOSS
commerce, communication, exchange: INTERCOURSE
commissions and other costs of distribution included in the price paid by the purchaser of securities: LOAD
commit or do something, as a crime or hoax: PERPETRATE
committee consisting of all members of a legislative body: COMMITTEE OF THE WHOLE
committee formed for specific purpose: AD HOC COMMITTEE
common, vulgar: PLEBEIAN
common, widely practiced: PREVALENT
common people, masses: HOI POLLOI
common people, pertaining to: DEMOTIC
common people's language: VULGAR
common rather than literary language: VERNACULAR
common run, ordinary people: RUCK
common sense: MOTHER WIT
common stock earnings as affected by bond interest and preferred stock dividends: LEVERAGE
common to the masses: VULGAR
commonplace: TOLERABLE
commonplace, banal, trite remark: PLATITUDE
commonplace, basic: BREAD-AND-BUTTER
commonplace, dull: STODGY
commonplace, ordinary, simple: EXOTERIC
commonplace, trite idea or expression: CLICHÉ
commonplace, trite statement: PLATITUDE
commonplace, uninspired, unimaginative: PROSAIC
commotion: TURBULENCE
commotion, fluster, bustle: POTHER
communication, exchange, commerce: INTERCOURSE

communication of minds in other than normal sensory means: TELEPATHY
communication system for immediate, direct exchange in an emergency: HOT LINE
communication system that is secret and usually person to person: GRAPEVINE
Communist emblem: HAMMER AND SICKLE
compact, agreement, pledge: COVENANT
companionship: SODALITY
company that uses its capital to invest in other companies: INVESTMENT TRUST
compare critically, as writings or facts: COLLATE
comparison implied in a figure of speech: METAPHOR
compatible, congenial: SIMPATICO
compel or force to go: HALE
compelling, fascinating: IRRESISTIBLE
compensate, make up, offset: COUNTERVAIL
compensate, pay back: REIMBURSE
compensate, pay for: REMUNERATE
compensate, repay in kind: REQUITE
compensate, right a wrong: REDRESS
compensate for or counteract something else: OFFSET
compensation for injury to the feelings: SOLATIUM
compensation for loss or damage, exemption from penalties or liabilities: INDEMNITY
compete: VIE
competent legally to take care of one's own affairs: SUI JURIS
competition or rivalry: CONTENTION
competitive: EMULOUS
complacent, self-satisfied: SMUG
complain: CARP
complain, find fault: CRAB
complain, fret: REPINE
complaining, whining: QUERULOUS
complaint, grievance: PLAINT
complaint receiver in government, consumer organizations, etc.: OMBUDSMAN
complement or mate to another: COUNTERPART
complete, absolute: UNMITIGATED
complete, absolute, full: PLENARY
complete, entire: INTEGRAL
complete confidence: CERTITUDE
completely organized and active: FULL-FLEDGED
completeness: INTEGRITY

complex, subtle, highly intellectual: METAPHYSICAL

compliant, manageable: TRACTABLE

complicate, confuse, entangle: EMBRANGLE

complicate, disconcert, hamper: EMBARRASS

complicated, involved, puzzling: INTRICATE

complicated or confused state of affairs: IMBROGLIO

complicated or refined in design: SOPHISTICATED

complicated situation, predicament: PLIGHT

complication, intertwining, entanglement: INVOLUTION

comply, either in fact or only apparently: TEMPORIZE

comport (oneself): DEMEAN

compose or write out: REDACT

composure, coolness: SANG-FROID

composure, even-temper, calmness: EQUANIMITY

composure, serenity, self-assurance: POISE

comprehension or awareness independent of the senses: ESP (EXTRASENSORY PERCEPTION)

compressed: ANGUSTATE

compulsive, excessive preoccupation with a thought or feeling: OBSESSION

compulsory service: CONSCRIPTION

computer design and apparatus: HARDWARE

computer information delivered in printed form: PRINTOUT

computer information that is fed into the apparatus: INPUT

computers and human nervous system under study: CYBERNETICS

conceal, pretend, dissemble: DISSIMULATE

conceal, disguise, feign, make a false show of: DISSEMBLE

concealed: ABSTRUSE

concealed, secret or sheltered: COVERT

concealing language: AESOPIAN LANGUAGE

concealment by a public official of an offense or crime, or wrongdoing by such an official: MISPRISION

concealment of one's real activities or designs: COVER-UP

conceit, egotism: EGO

conceit or arrogance characterizing a person's ways of attitudes: OVERWEENING

conceited, arrogant: BUMPTIOUS

conceited, boastful: VAINGLORIOUS

concentration of psychic energy upon a person, idea, fantasy: CATHEXIS

concerned: SOLICITOUS

concerning, in the matter of: IN RE

conciliate, win over: PROPITIATE

conciliate opposing sides: MEDIATE

concise: TERSE

concise, terse, brief: LACONIC

concise, terse, meaningful: SUCCINCT

concise summary or abstract: PRECIS

conclude or accept from evidence: INFER

conclude or suppose from incomplete evidence: CONJECTURE

conclusion in a sentence that emerges from the PROTASIS, or condition: APODOSIS

concretize, make real: REIFY

concurrent: SIMULTANEOUS

condemn: CENSURE

condemn, prohibit, outlaw: PROSCRIBE

condemn or denounce: DECRY

condense: ABBREVIATE

condense: ABRIDGE

condense, boil down: DECOCT

condescend: DEIGN

condescend to, grant or permit: VOUCHSAFE

condition existing at a particular time: STATUS QUO

condition or stipulation: PROVISO

condition set forth in a clause that leads to APODOSIS, or conclusion: PROTASIS

conditional transaction authorized for when, as and if a security is issued: WHEN ISSUED

cone or pyramid with top sliced off: FRUSTUM

conference: POWWOW

conference of opposing sides, talk: PARLEY

conference or conversation that is formally arranged: COLLOQUY

confidence lacking, timidity, shyness: DIFFIDENCE

confidential friendship, close association: INTIMACY

confidential or private, as a conversation: TÊTE-À-TÊTE

confine, imprison: INCARCERATE

confine, surround, enclose within walls, imprison: IMMURE

confine or detain, as during war: INTERN

confined without means of communication: INCOMMUNICADO

confining or checking item, as a rope: TETHER

confinement that is forced, imprisonment: DURANCE

conflicting, mismated, discordant: INCOMPATIBLE

conflicting tendencies: AMBITENDENCY

conforming, done in accordance with: PURSUANT

conforming or agreeing: CONGRUENT

conformity forced ruthlessly: PROCRUSTEAN

confuse, defeat the plans of, frustrate: DISCOMFIT

confuse, divert: DISTRACT

confuse, mix up: DISORIENT

confuse, muddle: EMBROIL

confuse, obscure, bewilder: OBFUSCATE

confuse, upset, frustrate: DISCONCERT

confuse or mix up, as ideas or things: CONFOUND

confused: ADDLED, ADDLE-BRAINED, ADDLEHEADED, ADDLEPATED

confused, disjointed: INCOHERENT

confused, disorderly situation, from military slang acronym "situation normal, all fouled [not sic] up": SNAFU

confused, random: INDISCRIMINATE

confused, vague: HAZY

confused and hurried: HELTER-SKELTER

confused condition, mess: MARE'S NEST

confused mixture, medley: FARRAGO

confused or complicated state of affairs: IMBROGLIO

confused or meaningless talk: GALIMATIAS

confused state: TURBIDITY

confusion, hodgepodge: KATZENJAMMER

confusion that is noisy: BEDLAM

congenial, compatible: SIMPATICO

congratulate: FELICITATE

congratulation on a witty retort or a successful point made: TOUCHÉ

conjunctions omitted: ASYNDETON

connect like links of a chain: CATENATE

connect with a crime or fault: IMPLICATE

connection, bond, link: NEXUS

connive or conspire: COLLUDE

connoisseur: MAVEN, MAVIN

connoisseur, collector of works of art: VIRTUOSO

conscious of oneself as being observed by others, ill at ease: SELF-CONSCIOUS

conscious perception: APPERCEPTION

consciously or deliberately done: WITTINGLY

consciousness: SENTIENCE

consecrate, make holy: HALLOW

consecrated or bound by vow or promise: VOTARY

consent: ACCEDE

consent given passively: SUFFERANCE

consent quietly: ACQUIESCE

consequence: AFTERMATH

consequence: SEQUELA

consequence or result that is normal: COROLLARY

conservative, almost reactionary workers: HARD HATS

conservative, reactionary: RIGHTIST

conservative in beliefs, especially in politics: TORY

conservative or old-fashioned person: FOGY

conservative person: MOSSBACK

consider as real: HYPOSTATIZE

consider carefully, think about, reflect: PONDER

consign to an obscure place or inferior position: RELEGATE

consistency brought about, as in ideas: RECONCILED

consolation in grief: SOLACE

conspicuous, striking, standing out: SALIENT

conspicuous public position: LIMELIGHT

conspiracy, plot, secret and underhanded activity: INTRIGUE

conspire, connive: COLLUDE

conspire, scheme: MACHINATE

constant: INVARIABLE

constant movement or change: FLUX

constantly cause irritation, rankle: FESTER

constipated: COSTIVE

construction material of plaster and fiber that is temporary: STAFF

contact at a single point or along a line: TANGENT

contagious disease that breaks out suddenly and affects many individuals at the same time: EPIDEMIC

contain or include: COMPRISE

container: RECEPTACLE

container, usually metal, for tea, spices: CANISTER

container of miscellaneous things: CATCHALL

container's weight deducted to find weight of contents: TARE

contemplation of the navel: OMPHALO-SKEPSIS

contemporary: COEVAL

contemptible, trivial, petty: PALTRY

contemptible, vile: DESPICABLE

contemptuous sound: BRONX CHEER

contend or argue about trifling matters: STICKLE

contentious, argumentative: DISPUTATIOUS

contentment or smugness: COMPLACENCY

contest in which each player engages every other player: ROUND ROBIN

contest won without much opposition: WALKAWAY

continue unchanged, abide: SUBSIST

continuing, lasting a long time: CHRONIC

continuing, undecided: PENDING

continuing throughout the year or lasting a long time: PERENNIAL

continuing without interruption: INCESSANT

continuity interrupted to give an episode occurring earlier: FLASHBACK

continuous, pitiless: RELENTLESS

continuum of four dimensions—three of space plus time: SPACE-TIME

contraceptive intrauterine device: LOOP

contraceptive medication for women: PILL (THE PILL)

contraceptive or anti-infection sheath for the penis: CONDOM

contraceptive pessary: DIAPHRAGM

contract obligating a person to work for another for a period: INDENTURE

contracted: ABBREVIATED

contradict, deny, oppose: GAINSAY

contradict, repudiate, deny: DISAFFIRM

contradiction, inconsistency: DISCREPANCY

contradictory-appearing statement that is really true: PARADOX

contradictory terms combined in one phrase: OXYMORON

contradictory thoughts or attitudes: AMBIVALENCE

contrary, nonconforming: PERVERSE

contrary to: ATHWART

contrast: ANTITHESIS

contrast by reverse parallelism in phraseology: CHIASMUS

contrition: PENITENCE

control and communication as they apply to the operation of complex machines and functions of human organisms: CYBERNETICS

control artfully: MANIPULATE

controlled course of living: REGIMEN

conventional, proper: ORTHODOX

conventional person uninformed about culture or aesthetics: PHILISTINE

conversational: COLLOQUIAL

conversation about unimportant things: SMALL TALK

conversation or conference that is formally arranged: COLLOQUY

conversation that is informal, chat: CAUSERIE

conversational wit: REPARTEE

convert, transform: RESOLVE

convert by intensive indoctrination: BRAINWASH

convert into a different shape: TRANSMOGRIFY

convert or try to convert a person to one's religion: PROSELYTE

convert the energy of instinctual drives into socially acceptable manifestations: SUBLIMATE

convincing: COGENT

convincing, influential: POTENT

convulsive: SPASMODIC

convulsive seizure, as in pregnancy or childbirth: ECLAMPSIA

cook gently: CODDLE

cookery, or the kitchen: CULINARY

cooking, its style and quality: CUISINE

cooking pot that is airtight and prepares food quickly under pressure: PRESSURE COOKER

cool, casually indifferent: NONCHALANT

coolness, composure: SANG-FROID

coop or pen for small animals: HUTCH

cooperative, working together: SYNERGETIC

cooperate secretly: COLLUDE

coordinator of a broadcasting team: ANCHOR MAN

copy, duplicate made by the originator: REPLICA

copy in form, as a legislative bill: ENGROSS

copy or reproduction that is exact: FACSIMILE

copying device made up of four rods in parallelogram shape: PANTOGRAPH copying process employing electrostatic attraction: XEROGRAPHY

copyright or patent has run out: PUBLIC DOMAIN

cord or belt worn around the waist: CINCTURE

cord or metal collar used in executions: GARROTE

cordlike decoration used on clothes: PIPING

corduroy ridge: WALE

core, central or essential element: NUCLEUS

core group: CADRE

cornmeal dough ball fried in deep fat: HUSH PUPPY

cornstalks: STOVER

corporation embracing companies in unrelated industries: CONGLOMERATE

corporation that holds securities of another corporation that it normally controls: HOLDING COMPANY

corporation's total amount of securities issued: CAPITALIZATION

corporeal, physical: SOMATIC

corpulent, very fat: OBESE

correct or change a literary work, especially after scholarly study: EMEND

correctable or reformable: CORRIGIBLE

correctness of judgment, uprightness: RECTITUDE

corrode or corrupt: CANKER

corrosive, caustic: ESCHAROTIC

corrupt: ADULTERATE

corrupt: PERVERT

corrupt, invalidate, debase: VITIATE

corrupt, morally degraded: SCROFULOUS

corrupt, pervert: DEPRAVE

corrupt, rotten: PUTRID

corrupt, seduce, deprave: DEBAUCH

corrupt, sinful: PECCANT

corrupt, subject to bribery: VENAL

corrupt, undermine the morale: SUBVERT

costs of transaction included in the price paid by a purchaser of securities: LOAD

costs or continuous operating expenses of a business: OVERHEAD

cottage cheese: SMEARCASE

cottage or duplex apartment: MAISONETTE

couch or sofa, upholstered and without back or arm rests: DIVAN

couch without arms or back: OTTOMAN

couchlike chair with elongated seat to support legs: CHAISE LONGUE

cough drop: TROCHE

cough up (phlegm): HAWK

couldn't care less: APATHETIC

counterbalance: EQUIPONDERATE

countercharge: RECRIMINATION

counterfeit, artificial: POSTICHE

counterfeit, illegitimate: SPURIOUS

counterpart: OBVERSE

counting time in reverse: COUNTDOWN

countries that are underdeveloped and belong to neither the communist nor the capitalist bloc: THIRD WORLD

country home, Russian: DACHA

country person who is awkward: BUMPKIN

courage, initiative, shrewd common sense: GUMPTION

courage, pluck, spirit: METTLE

courage inspired by alcohol: DUTCH COURAGE

courageous, valiant: METTLESOME

course for advanced study: SEMINAR

court clerk who is chief: PROTHONOTARY

court command that a thing be done: MANDAMUS

court engaged in arbitrary or illegal procedures: STAR CHAMBER

court has it under consideration: SUB JUDICE

court official's cry to obtain silence: OYEZ

court order to appear and testify: SUBPOENA

court that is unauthorized and irregular: KANGAROO COURT

court writ ordering production of documents or other evidence: SUBPOENA DUCES TECUM

courteous, gallant, generous: CHIVALROUS

courtesy: COMITY

courtly or gallant man: CAVALIER

court-martial in the field for an offense committed during operations: DRUMHEAD COURT-MARTIAL

cover or suffuse with a liquid or color: PERFUSE

coverall worn by paratroops, mechanics, etc., or a woman's similar lounging garment: JUMP SUIT

covered with matted woolly hair: TOMENTOSE

covered with matted woolly masses: FLOCCULENT

covering or outer coating, especially a natural covering: INTEGUMENT

cow, not fertile: FARROW

cow, young and not yet having produced a calf: HEIFER
coward: POLTROON
coward or sneak: DASTARD
cowardly: CRAVEN
cowardly, unfaithful: RECREANT
cowardly, weak: PUSILLANIMOUS
cowardly or timid: CHICKEN-HEARTED or CHICKEN-LIVERED
cowboy's leather trousers: CHAPS
co-worker: COADJUTOR
coy, shy, modest, reserved: DEMURE
crablike: CANCROID
crack, cleft, chink: CREVICE
crack, small space: INTERSTICE
cracked or fissured, chinky: RIMOSE
crackle or rattle: CREPITATE
cracklings: GREAVES
cracks that intersect, as in glazed pottery: CRAZE
craft, cunning: SLEIGHT
craftiness, cunning: WILE
craftsman: ARTIFICER

crafty, foxlike, sly: VULPINE
crafty, insincere: DISINGENUOUS
cramp or muscle pain: MYALGIA
cramped, uncomfortably small: INCOMMODIOUS
cranky, stubborn: PERVERSE
crashing noisily, as waves: PLANGENT
crave, yearn, desire: HANKER
craven, mean-spirited person: POLTROON
craving: APPETENCE
crawl face downward, lie prostrate: GROVEL
craze for irrational interest in one thing: MONOMANIA
craze, obsession: MANIA
crazed: DISTRAUGHT
crazy: CRACKBRAINED
crazy: HAYWIRE
crazy, absurd: COCKAMAMIE
creating ill will or dislike: INVIDIOUS
creation that turns on its creator: FRANKENSTEIN'S MONSTER
creative, original: PROMETHEAN

CREATURE TERMS

Creature	Group	Male	Female	Young
antelope	herd	buck	doe	kid
ass	herd, drove, pace	jack	jenny	colt, foal
badger	cete	boar	sow	
bear	sloth			cub
beaver				kitten
bee	swarm, hive	drone	queen	
boar	sounder			squeaker, calf
buffalo	herd	bull	cow	
camel	herd, flock	bull	cow	foal, calf, colt
cat	kindle (young), clowder, cluster	tom	she-cat, queen (fancy breed)	kitten
cattle	herd, drove	bull	cow	calf, heifer (female)
chicken	brood, flock	rooster, cock	hen	chicken, pullet (f) cockerel (m)
cod			codling, sprag	
crane	herd			
crow	murder			
deer	herd	buck, stag	doe	fawn

Creature	Group	Male	Female	Young
dog	pack, kennel	hound	bitch	puppy, whelp
duck	team (in flight) paddling (in water)	drake	duck	duckling
eagle	convocation			eaglet
eel	swarm			elver
elephant	herd	bull	cow	calf
elk	gang	bull	cow	calf
ferret	business	dog	bitch	
finch	charm			
fish (general)	shoal, school, run			fry
frog	army			
fox	earth, skulk	vix	vixen	cub
giraffe	herd			
goat	flock, herd, tribe	billy	nanny (colloq)	kid
goose	flock, skein (on the wing), gaggle (on water)	gander	goose	gosling
grouse	covey (family), pack (larger group)			
gull	colony			
hare	drove, trace	buck	doe	leveret
hawk	flight			eyas
heron	siege			
herring	army, glean, shoal			
hippopotamus				calf
horse	herd, stable	stallion	mare	colt, foal
hummingbird	charm			
jay	band			
kangaroo	troop			joey
lark	exaltation			
leopard	leap	leopard	leopardess	
lion	pride, flock, troop	lion	lioness	cub
lobster			hen	chicken lobster
mackerel	shoal			spike, blinker, tinker
monkey	troop, tribe			
moose		bull	cow	calf
mouse	nest			
mule	barren, rake			
nightingale	watch			
owl				owlet
otter		dog	bitch	
ox	herd, drove			
parrot	flock			
partridge	covey			squeaker
peafowl	muster	peacock	peahen	
pheasant	nye (young), brood			
pigeon	flight, flock			squab, squealer, squeaker

Creature	Group	Male	Female	Young
pig	herd	boar	sow	pig, farrow, shote
polecat		hob	jill	
porpoise	school			
quail	bevy			
raven	unkindness			
rhinoceros	crash			
seal	crash, herd, pod			cub
sheep	flock	ram	ewe	lamb
sparrow	host			
squirrel	dray			
starling	chattering			
stork	mustering			
swallow	flight			
swan	herd, wedge	cob	pen	cygnet
swine	sounder	boar	sow	
tiger		tiger	tigress	cub
toad	knot			
trout	hover			
turkey	flock	tom	hen	poult
turtle	bale			
whale	herd, school, gam, pod	bull	cow	calf
wolf	herd, rout, pack	dog wolf	bitch	whelp, cub
wren	herd			
zebra	herd			foal, colt

credit amount that may legally be advanced by brokers to customers for purchase of securities: REGULATION T

credit for an achievement: KUDOS

credits in film or TV show that move vertically on screen: CRAWL

credulous, unaffected, simple, candid, artless: NAIVE

creek or stream: KILL

cremate, burn up: INCINERATE

crescent or crescent-shaped: MENISCUS

cricket, to deflect a ball by a slight turn of the bat: DRAW

cricket over, or period, in which no runs are scored: MAIDEN OVER

crime, criminals and prisons as a study: PENOLOGY

crime, proof of a: CORPUS DELICTI

crime or concealment of an offense by a public official: MISPRISION

crime such as murder, rape, arson or burglary: FELONY

crime study: CRIMINOLOGY

criminal, evildoer: MALEFACTOR

cringe fondly, toady: FAWN

crisis or conflict between two opposing political groups: CONFRONTATION

crisis or critical situation: CONJUNCTURE

criterion or standard for testing the qualities of something: TOUCHSTONE

critic or adviser who is frank and severe: DUTCH UNCLE

critical: CAPTIOUS

critical, demanding immediate action, urgent: EXIGENT

critical, harsh remark: BRICKBAT

critical to an excessive degree, hard to please: HYPERCRITICAL

critical year or period: CLIMACTERIC

criticism: ANIMADVERSION

criticism or difficulties from both sides: GANTLET

criticism that is bitter or malicious: DIATRIBE

criticism that is petty: QUIBBLE

criticism that is severe: STRICTURE

criticize, as if by perforation: RIDDLE

criticize, find fault with, rebuke, blame: REPREHEND

criticize angrily, caustically: VITRIOLIC

criticize sharply: SCARIFY
cross bearer: CRUCIFER
cross from one side to another: TRANS-VERSE
cross in form of an x, intersect: DECUSSATE
cross shaped: CRUCIATE
cross shaped: CRUCIFORM
cross threads in cloth: WEFT
cross with circle behind crossbeam: CELTIC CROSS
cross woman, old-fashioned in dress: FRUMP
crossbreed: INTERBREED
cross-country race along a course containing obstacles: STEEPLECHASE
cross-country runner: HARRIER
cross-country skiing run: LANGLAUF
crossed the equator by ship: SHELLBACK
cross-eyed condition: STRABISMUS
cross-fertilization: XENOGAMY
crouch or shrink in servility: CRINGE
crowbar used by burglars: JIMMY
crowd: RUCK
crowd, or a coming together: CONCOURSE
crowd, or a flocking together: CONFLUENCE
crowd or push roughly, shake up, elbow, shove: JOSTLE
crowded, densely populated: IMPACTED
crowded dwelling: WARREN
crown or headband: DIADEM
crownlike, jeweled headdress worn by women: TIARA
crucially important, essential: PIVOTAL
crude: INDELICATE
crude, lacking polish: INURBANE
crude, unrefined, rough: UNCOUTH
cruel, stubborn: TRUCULENT
cruel, vicious, inhuman: FELL
cruel exercise of power: TYRANNY
cruel or hideous being: OGRE
cruel or wantonly pitiless person: HELLKITE
crumbly or pulverizable: FRIABLE
crusade or fanatic campaign: JIHAD
crush, subdue utterly, silence: SQUELCH
crushable or crumbly: FRIABLE
cry, wail, whimper: PULE
cry loudly, scream, bawl: SQUALL
cry or whine with low, broken sounds: WHIMPER
cry that is long and plaintive, like a cat's: WAUL

cuddle: SNUGGLE
cuddle, snuggle for comfort: NESTLE
culminating point: SOLSTICE
culminating or highest point: ZENITH
cultivate deliberately the confidence or favor of others: INGRATIATE
cultivation capability, of land: ARABLE
cultural change in one society being affected by culture of another: ACCULTURATION
cunning, craft: SLEIGHT
cunning, craft, deceit: GUILE
cunning, craftiness: WILE
cunning, ingenious, intricate: DAEDAL
cunning, treacherous, wily: INSIDIOUS
cunningness, artful strategy, craftiness: FINESSE
cup for drinking, large, often with a cover: TANKARD
cup holder of filigreed metal, for a hot coffee cup: ZARF
cup or glass filled to the brim: BUMPER
cup or glass for measuring liquor: JIGGER
curative, healing: THERAPEUTIC
curb about a hatchway or skylight to keep out water: COAMING
cure-all, remedy for all ailments: PANACEA
curious to an offensive degree: INQUISITORIAL
curling, to play the stone gently: DRAW
curse, call down a calamity: IMPRECATE
curse, denounce violently: EXECRATE
curse against someone, slander, calumny: MALEDICTION
curse or ban: ANATHEMA
cursing: BLASPHEMY
curtain at rear of stage: BACKDROP
curtain in a doorway: PORTIÈRE
curve, especially inward: INCURVATE
curve in and out, bend: SINUATE
curve pattern that circles around a central point or in either direction around an axis: SPIRAL
curved or bent part, bending: FLECTION
curved wall or screen usually containing pictures: CYCLORAMA
curving inward: CONCAVE
curving outward: CONVEX
custard or other easily digested dish: FLUMMERY
custodian, superintendent, in charge of a museum or similar institution: CURATOR
customary practice, habit: WONT

custom-made (British): BESPOKE

customs or folkways of a social group: MORES

cut, scratch: SCOTCH

cut across, divide: INTERSECT

cut expenses: RETRENCH

cut into, carve, engrave: INCISE

cut off by ecclesiastical authority: EX-COMMUNICATE

cut or mark the edge of border with notches: INDENT

cut or notch carved out by a saw or ax: KERF

cut or part into two sections: DICHOT-OMIZE

cut or split into long thin pieces: SLIVER

cut or trim the branches as from a tree: LOP

cut out, excise: EXSCIND

cut the top or end from: TRUNCATE

cut up or stir the surface, as of topsoil: SCARIFY

cutlet, especially veal: SCHNITZEL

cutoff of operation or service by accident: OUTAGE

cutting, intersecting: SECANT

cutting, splitting: SCISSION

cutting off: ABSCISSION

cutting teeth, teething: DENTITION

cyclone in the western Pacific: TYPHOON

cynical, sneering, scornful: SARDONIC

D

dabbler with a superficial interest in an art or science: DILETTANTE

dagger mark, double, in printing (‡): DIESIS

dagger or sword with wavy-edged blade: KRIS

daily: DIURNAL

daily expense allowance: PER DIEM

daily occurrence: QUOTIDIAN

daily prayers said by Catholic clergy: BREVIARY

dainty, elegant or affectedly prim: MINC-ING

dainty, oversensitive: FASTIDIOUS

dam placed in a stream to divert the water, as in irrigation: WEIR

damage as if by perforation: RIDDLE

damage or destruction done deliberately to obstruct a cause: SABOTAGE

damage to a person's reputation done through a false or malicious written statement or graphic representation: LIBEL

damages awarded in excess of actual loss: EXEMPLARY DAMAGES

damaging or destruction of property willfully: VANDALISM

damnation, hell: PERDITION

damp, moist: HUMID

dance in which couples form sets in squares: SQUARE DANCE

dance in which the performer's shoes sharply accentuate the rhythm with the toes and heels: TAP DANCE

dance like a slow polka: SCHOTTISCHE

dance movement in which a couple swing round with hands joined: POUSETTE

dance of Rumanians and Israelis in which dancers lock arms in a circle: HORA

dance of Slavs in which a man performs the prisiadka, a step in which from a squatting position each leg is kicked out alternately: KAZATSKY

dancer: TERPSICHOREAN

dancing art: CHOREOGRAPHY

dancing mania, characteristic of a nervous disorder: TARANTISM

dancing muse: TERPSICHORE

dandified man or one who dresses over-fastidiously: FOP

dandruff: FURFUR

dandruff or similar scales shed by the skin: SCURF

dandy, fop, man who dresses flashily: DUDE

danger: JEOPARDY

danger on both sides: BETWEEN SCYLLA AND CHARYBDIS

danger sign, warning, especially in zoology: SEMATIC

danger that is imminent: SWORD OF DAM-OCLES

dangerous speed: BREAKNECK

dangerous to society: PESTILENT

daring, audacity, impudence, boldness: HARDIHOOD

dark: APHOTIC

dark, gloomy: CIMMERIAN

dark, gloomy: TENEBROUS

dark, gloomy, infernal: STYGIAN

dark, obscure, misty: MURKY

dark complexioned, dusky: SWARTHY

dark and threatening, as the weather: LOWERING

dark appearance or dark pigmentation: MELANOID

dark shape or profile with a light background: SILHOUETTE

darkened or tinged with brown, as a part of an insect's wing: INFUSCATE

dash, enthusiasm, vivacity: ÉLAN

dash, spirited style: PANACHE

dash, vigor: VERVE

dashing, gay, smart: RAKISH

dashing, large, vigorous, swift: SPANK-ING

dashing, self-confident, stylish, lively, brisk: JAUNTY

date on which a loan or bond comes due: MATURITY

daughter's sexual attachment to her father: ELECTRA COMPLEX

dauntless, fearless, bold: INTREPID

dawdle, waste time: DILLYDALLY

dawdle, waste time: PIDDLE

dawdle, pass time, cheat: DIDDLE

dawn: COCKCROW

day blindness: HEMERALOPIA

day by day account of events: CHRONOL-OGY

day or month added to the calendar: IN-TERCALARY

day when night and day are of equal length, marking start of spring or autumn: EQUINOX

daydreaming: musing: REVERIE

daydreaming tendency: AUTISM

days and nights are equal at these times, March 21 and September 21: VERNAL EQUINOX AND AUTUMNAL EQUINOX

daytime rather than nighttime: DIURNAL

dazzling, brilliant, swift: METEORIC

dazzling, shining with brilliance, vividly bright: RESPLENDENT

dead, extinct: DEFUNCT

dead; say nothing but good about them: DE MORTUIS NIL NISI BONUM

dead at birth: STILLBORN

dead or rotten flesh: CARRION

dead person: DECEDENT

deaden, paralyze with fear: PETRIFY

deadlocked situation: STALEMATE

deadly, fatal: LETHAL

deadly, injurious malicious: PERNICIOUS

deadly to both sides of a group: INTER-NECINE

deaf mute alphabet: DACTYLOLOGY

dealer or trader: MONGER

dealing with people or situations delicately and without giving offense: TACT

death: DEMISE

death, resurrection, immortality, as a subject of study: ESCHATOLOGY

death anniversary observed by Jews: YAHRZEIT

death blow or mortal blow: COUP DE GRACE

death investigation: INQUEST

death omen: KNELL

death only apparent not real: ANABIOTIC

death that is painless and peaceful: EU-THANASIA

deathly looking: CADAVEROUS

debase: ADULTERATE

debase, corrupt, invalidate: VITIATE

debase oneself as from fear or servility: GROVEL

debatable or so hypothetical as to be without significance: MOOT

debate or argue earnestly: CONTEND

debate, argumentation: FORENSICS

debate that is formal: DISPUTATION

debauched, immoral: DISSOLUTE

debt-acknowledging certificate: DEBEN-TURE

debt acknowledgment that is non-negotiable and usually exchangeable for goods or services: DUE BILL

debt or liability extinguished gradually, as by installment payments: AMORTIZED

decay, rot: PUTREFY

decay or decline as in art or morals: DE-CADENCE

decayed: CARIOUS

decayed, neglected, shabby: DILAPI-DATED

deceit, cunning, craft: GUILE

deceit, dishonest dealing: INDIRECTION

deceitful: MENDACIOUS

deceitful, treacherous: DOUBLE-DEALING

deceitfulness, trickery, double-dealing: DUPLICITY

deceitfulness, trickery, rascality: KNAVERY

deceive: BEGUILE

deceive, cheat, trick: FINAGLE

deceive, mislead: EQUIVOCATE

deceive or cheat in a petty way: COZEN

deceiver: IMPOSTOR

deception, trickery: HOCUS-POCUS

deception or pretended blow meant to distract: FEINT

deceptive, pretended, sham: FEIGNED

deceptive explanation designed to cover up a defect or a fault: GLOSS

deceptively appearing to be true or correct: SPECIOUS

decided previously by judicial authority: RES JUDICATA

deciding statement: CLINCHER

deciding vote: CASTING VOTE

decimal system of counting: ALGORISM

decision maker in a dispute: ARBITER

decisive, final, absolute, positive: PER-EMPTORY

declare relevant and operative, as a law: INVOKE

declare solemnly: ASSEVERATE

decline or decay as in art or morals: DE-CADENCE

declining, worsening, going backward: RETROGRADE

declining market: BEAR MARKET

decoding: CRYPTANALYSIS

decorate, dress up: TITIVATE

decorate, ornament: EMBELLISH

decorate an initial page or word of a manuscript with designs or bright colors: ILLUMINATE

decorate lavishly as with jewels: INCRUST, ENCRUST

decorate or dress up with showy ornaments: PRANK

decorate or enrich with engraved or inlaid work: ENCHASE

decorated with material embedded flush with the surface: INLAID

decorative horizontal strip, as along the top of a wall: FRIEZE

decorative plan of a room: DECOR

decree: RESCRIPT

decree, command or prohibition: EDICT

decree, establish: ORDAIN

decree, law: STATUTE

decree that is official and arbitrary: UKASE

dedicate or sign a book for presentation: INSCRIBE

dedicatory words or lines at the end of a poem: ENVOY

deduce by logical methods: RATIOCINATE

deduction, conjecture: INFERENCE

deduction, discount: REBATE

deduction, inference: ILLATION

deductive reasoning: SYNTHESIS

deductive reasoning formula: SYLLOGISM

deep in intellect or feeling: PROFOUND

deep involvement: IMMERSION

deep red or purplish red: CARMINE

deep-rooted, firmly established: IN-GRAINED

deep-sea chamber: BATHYSPHERE

deeply established habits: SECOND NATURE

deer meat: VENISON

deer's tail: FLAG

defamation that is spoken: SLANDER

defame, dishonor: SMIRCH

defame, disparage, blacken: DENIGRATE

defame, disparage, despise: VILIPEND

defame, revile: VILIFY

defame, say malicious things: TRADUCE

defame, traduce: MALIGN

defamatory and abusive words: OBLOQUY

defeat, nullify, prevail over: OVERRIDE

defeat but with great losses: CADMEAN VICTORY, PYRRHIC VICTORY

defeat by cleverness: OUTWIT

defeat by skillful maneuver: CHECKMATE

defeat the plans or purposes of, frustrate, vanquish: DISCOMFIT

defeat suffered abruptly: REBUFF

defeat utterly: DRUB

defeated officeholder with some time to remain in office: LAME DUCK

defect existing at birth: CONGENITAL DEFECT

defendable, maintainable: TENABLE

defense or justification: APOLOGIA

defense system that is a form of jujitsu: JUDO

defenseless, cannot be defended, as an attitude: UNTENABLE

defensive tactic: PARRY

defer, put off, postpone: WAIVE

defiance of established doctrine: HERESY

defiant in an aggressive way: TRUCULENT

deficiency: INSUFFICIENCY

defile, besmirch, soil: SULLY

defile, dirty: POLLUTE

definite, clear, straightforward, outspoken: EXPLICIT

definitive, judicial, established by decree: DECRETORY

deflect, turn aside, distract, amuse, entertain: DIVERT

deformation of the earth's crust, forming mountains, continents: DIASTROPHISM

defraud or cheat a person: MULCT

defy, scoff, mock, jeer: FLOUT

degrade: DEMEAN

degraded, base, dishonorable: IGNOBLE

degraded, morally debased: SCROFULOUS

degraded, sneaky, skulking: HANGDOG

degree of personal excellence: CALIBER

degree or range of occurrence: INCIDENCE

degree or strength of some feeling, quality, action: INTENSITY

deification: APOTHEOSIS

deign to grant or permit: VOUCHSAFE

dejected: CHAPFALLEN

dejected: DISPIRITED

dejected: INCONSOLABLE

dejected, depressed: CRESTFALLEN

dejected, gloomy, saddened: DISCONSOLATE

dejection of spirits, hopelessness: DESPONDENCY

dejection or despair: SLOUGH OF DESPOND

delay, hinder, put obstacles in the way of: IMPEDE

delay, hinder, slow: RETARD

delay,·postponement, interval of relief or rest: RESPITE

delay, temporary: ABEYANCE

delay authorized in some specific activity: MORATORIUM

delayed reaction to a joke or unusual situation: DOUBLE TAKE

delaying: DILATORY

delete obscene or otherwise objectionable material: EXPURGATE

deletion, erasure: EXPUNCTION

deliberate decision: VOLITION

deliberately or consciously done: WITTINGLY

delicate, flimsy substance: GOSSAMER

delicately and carefully made: WROUGHT

delicious, sometimes sweet in excess, cloying: LUSCIOUS

delight, give unusual pleasure, entertain: REGALE

delight (in), celebrate, make merry: REVEL

delightful, entrancing: RAVISHING

deliver up or surrender an accused individual to another state or country: EXTRADITE

delusions of persecution or grandeur: PARANOIA

demand for a customer to put money or securities with his broker: MARGIN CALL

demand or summons: REQUISITION

demand rigorously, require as a matter of justice: EXACT

demanding constant hard work: EXACTING

demanding insistently: IMPORTUNATE

demolish, level to the ground: RAZE

demon that takes possession of a living person: DYBBUK

demon-possessed: DEMONIAC

demonstrable: APODICTIC

demonstrate convincingly, show clearly: EVINCE

denounce, condemn: DECRY

denounce violently, curse: EXECRATE

dense, incomprehensible: IMPENETRABLE

dentistry branch that is devoted to gums and bones supporting the teeth: PERIODONTICS

dentistry that strives to prevent and correct tooth irregularities: ORTHODONTICS

denunciation: REPROBATION

denunciation, loud and violent: FULMINATION

denunciation or accusation that is violent: INVECTIVE

denunciation or threat, especially from a divine source: COMMINATION

denunciatory speech: TIRADE

deny, repudiate: DISAFFIRM

deny, oppose, contradict: GAINSAY

deny oneself something: ABSTAIN

deny or renounce one's own rights, etc.: ABNEGATION

depart suddenly: ABSCOND

dependable, firm: STAUNCH

dependency: APPANAGE

dependent on luck: ALEATORY

deportment, or manner in which one bears oneself: DEMEANOR

deposit eggs or roe: SPAWN

deprave, corrupt, seduce: DEBAUCH

depravity, baseness, vileness: TURPITUDE

depreciatory or derogatory: PEJORATIVE

depressed, bored, or dull state of mind: DOLDRUMS

depressed, dejected: CRESTFALLEN

depressed, downhearted: DISPIRITED

depressed, gloomy, dusky: SOMBER

depressed mood: FUNK

depressing, unhappy: DOWNBEAT

deprive as a punishment: AMERCE

deprive as of rights or possessions, strip as of clothes: DIVEST

deprive of, strip, rob: DESPOIL

deprive of rights or privileges, as of a citizen's right to vote: DISFRANCHISE

deputy, agent, substitute: VICAR

deranged mentality: ABERRATION

deride, sneer, laugh coarsely, jeer: FLEER

derisive or mocking speech or manner: JEER

derisive sound: BRONX CHEER

derivations and development of words, as a study: ETYMOLOGY

derogatory or depreciatory: PEJORATIVE

descendant, offspring: SCION

descent of an individual traced from a certain ancestor: GENEALOGY

describe, portray, paint, or draw: LIMN

description of a person, as of a criminal for identification: SIGNALMENT

desecrate, pollute: PROFANE

desert, change sides: TERGIVERSATE

deserted, wretched, abandoned, cheerless: FORLORN

deserter, traitor: RENEGADE

desertion of faith or principles: APOSTASY

deserved or suitable, as a punishment: CONDIGN

design cut on a gem: GLYPTOGRAPH

design in nature, as studied in cosmology: TELEOLOGY

design in relief, as in metal: REPOUSSÉ

design or shape that doesn't adhere to any rigid pattern: FREE-FORM

desire: APPETENCE

desire, crave, yearn: HANKER

desire, feel the need for or the lack of: DESIDERATE

desire or lust for something belonging to another: COVET

desolate or saddened through loss: BEREAVED

despair or dejection: SLOUGH OF DESPOND

despise, defame, disparage: VILIPEND

despise, scorn: CONTEMN

despotic subordinate governor: SATRAP

despotism: ABSOLUTISM

destroy completely, wipe out: OBLITERATE

destroy or kill a large proportion of: DECIMATE

destroy or weaken the affection of: DISAFFECT

destroy utterly, pull up by the roots, uproot, erase: ERADICATE

destroy wholly, root out: EXTIRPATE

destroyer of images, or of venerated objects or ideas: ICONOCLAST

destruction, mutilation or alteration, especially of a legal document: SPOLIATION

destruction, ruin: HAVOC

destruction of great scope, especially by fire: HOLOCAUST

destruction or extermination of an entire people or national group: GENOCIDE

destructive force that is slow and irresistible: JUGGERNAUT

detached, isolated: INSULAR

detached, unbiased: OBJECTIVE

detail, declare, state: EXPOUND

detailed examination or discussion: CANVASS

detain or confine, as during war: INTERN

detective (humorous use): HAWKSHAW

deter or alter the plans of someone by persuasion: DISSUADE

detergent: ABLUENT

deteriorated, rickety: RAMSHACKLE

deterioration, biologically, of a strain or type, especially of man: DYSGENIC

determined, brave, strong: STALWART

determined, resolved, unflinching: RESOLUTE

detest: ABHOR

detestable, revolting, abominable: EXECRABLE

detestation: ABHORRENCE

detract, take away from: DEROGATE

detraction: DISPARAGEMENT

develop, sit on and hatch eggs: INCUBATE

develop or work out gradually: EVOLVE

develop to the utmost, make the most of: OPTIMIZE

developed or advanced more rapidly than is usual: PRECOCIOUS

deviating from normal rule: ANOMALOUS

deviating from the right way: ABERRANCE

deviating from what is generally accepted: PERVERSE

deviation: ABERRATION

deviation from the main current: EDDY

deviation from the normal: PERVERSION

devil, in Moslem countries: SHAITAN

devilish: CLOVEN-HOOFED

devious: AMBAGIOUS

devious: TORTUOUS

devise, think out carefully: EXCOGITATE

devise or make up: CONCOCT

devitalize, sap the strength of, weaken: ENERVATE

devoted: ASSIDUOUS

devoted blindly: IDOLATROUS

devotee: AFICIONADO

devotee of a particular pursuit, enthusiast: VOTARY

dexterity or skill in manipulation: SLEIGHT

dexterous: ADROIT

diagonal: CATER-CORNERED

diagonal or oblique line: BIAS

diagram showing a sequence of operations for a program or process: FLOW CHART

diagram, synopsis or summary, as of a process: SCHEMA

diagrams, charts, drawings, etc., used as explanatory matter: GRAPHICS dialect, especially one that is crude: PATOIS

dialect of a region that has become the language of a larger area: KOINE

dialect or jargon mixed with English: PIDGIN ENGLISH

dialogue: INTERLOCUTION

diameter-measuring instrument: CALIPERS

diametrically opposed: ANTIPODAL

dictatorial, imperious: PEREMPTORY

dictionary compiling: LEXICOGRAPHY

die without having made a will: INTESTATE

differ in opinion: DIVERGE

difference: DISSIMILITUDE

difference, as of opinion: DIVERGENCE

difference of opinion, discord, quarrel: DISSENSION

differences in outlook between individuals: PERSONAL EQUATION

different: DIVERSE

different, dissimilar, distinct: DISPARATE

different directions, move in: DIVERGE

differing: DISSIDENT

differing, not all alike: HETEROGENEOUS

differing in names that show a relationship: HETERONYMOUS

difficult, stubborn, unruly: INTRACTABLE

difficult and interminable: SISYPHEAN

difficult or puzzling, as a problem: STICKLER

difficult position: QUAGMIRE

difficult situation: MORASS

difficult to accomplish: HERCULEAN

difficult to deal with: SCABROUS

difficult to understand: ABSTRUSE

difficulties or criticism from both sides: GANTLET

diffuse or scatter, as if by sowing: DISSEMINATE

diffusion of a fluid through a membrane: OSMOSIS

dig out the facts: PLUMB

dig up a corpse or some buried thing: EXHUME

digest or summary: CONSPECTUS

digestion that is good: EUPEPSIA

dignified, well-bred air: DISTINGUÉ

digress, wander or stray from the subject: DIVAGATE

digression: APOSTROPHE

digressive, rambling: EXCURSIVE

digs, study of: ARCHEOLOGY

diligent, constant, working steadily: SEDULOUS

diligent and careful: PAINSTAKING

dim, obscure, pertaining to twilight: CREPUSCULAR

diminish: ABATE

diminish or lessen: DWINDLE

dimming of lights: BROWNOUT

dimple or small depression: FOSSETTE

dinner menu with each item having a separate price: A LA CARTE

dinner menu with a complete meal at a set price: TABLE D'HÔTE

dinner precooked and frozen in an aluminum-foil tray: TV DINNER

dining hall in a college or monastery: REFECTORY

dip into liquid for pickling: SOUSE

dip lightly or suddenly into water, as a bird does: DAP

diphtheria test: SCHICK TEST

diplomatic, prudent, wise: POLITIC

diplomatic etiquette: PROTOCOL

direct, blunt: POINT-BLANK

direct, plain: FLAT-FOOTED

direct into set channels: CANALIZE

direct opposite: ANTITHESIS

directed firmly, unwavering, steadfast: INTENT

direct relationship, freedom from intervention: IMMEDIACY

direction or sense of direction lost or mixed up: DISORIENTATION

dirge, funeral hymn: EPICEDIUM

dirge, funeral song: THRENODY

dirty, defile: POLLUTE

dirty, foul, appearing neglected: SQUALID

dirty, squalid: SORDID

disable: INCAPACITATE

disadvantage: DRAWBACK

disadvantage imposed on contestants of superior ability in a contest or race: HANDICAP

disagree: DISSENT

disagreeable, offensive: UNSAVORY

disagreeable, ugly, unpleasant in appearance: ILL-FAVORED

disagreement: DISSIDENCE

disagreement, quarreling: AT LOGGERHEADS

disappear by degrees, vanish gradually: EVANESCE

disappointment over one's own acts: CHAGRIN

disapproval: ANIMADVERSION
disapprove, plead against: DEPRECATE
disarrayed or partly dressed: DISHABILLE
disaster that brings violent change: CATA-CLYSM
disavow a former belief: RECANT
disbelief or denial of purpose in existence or in customary institutions: NIHILISM
disbelieving, doubting: INCREDULOUS
discard or cast off a previously favored sweetheart: JILT
discard something that hampers: JETTISON
discerning, perceptive, keen: PERSPICA-CIOUS
discernment, wisdom: SAGACITY
discharge of repressed emotions: CA-THARSIS
discharge suddenly and quickly, exclaim: EJACULATE
disciplinarian of extreme militaristic severity: MARTINET
disciplinary action that is swift: CRACK-DOWN
disclose, bring to light, reveal: EXHUME
disclose, make known, bestow: IMPART
disclose, reveal, give vent to: UNBOSOM
disclose, reveal, tell: DIVULGE
disclosure in a trial or hearing that a defendant is compelled to make: DIS-COVERY
disconcert, impede, complicate: EMBAR-RASS
disconcerted by some occurrence: ABASHED
disconnect: UNCOUPLE
disconnected, lacking in coherence: DIS-JOINTED
disconnected, separate: DISCRETE
discontent or illness, a chronic feeling of either: DYSPHORIA
discord, quarrel, difference of opinion: DISSENSION
discord, harsh disagreement: DISSONANCE
discordant: ABSONANT
discordant, harsh sound: JANGLE
discordant, conflicting, mismated: IN-COMPATIBLE
discordant sound: CACOPHANY
discourage: DISHEARTEN
discourteous or rude manner: INCIVILITY
discover with the eye, discern, observe: DESCRY
discovery and investigation as a way of learning: HEURISTICS
discriminate or distinguish: SECERN

discriminating taste in food and drink: GOURMET
discussion or series of remarks: DESCANT
discussion that is informal and rambling: CRACKER-BARREL
disdainful, arrogant: SUPERCILIOUS
disease breaking out suddenly and affecting many individuals at the same time: EPIDEMIC
disease correction by manipulation of parts of the body: OSTEOPATHY
disease moving from one part of the body to another: METASTASIS
disease of the intestine usually caused by eating undercooked pork: TRICHI-NOSIS
disease-preventing treatment: PROPHY-LAXIS
disease treatment effected by producing incompatible conditions: ALLOPATHY
diseases and their nature, as a branch of medicine: PATHOLOGY
diseases classified and described: NOSOG-RAPHY
disembowel or remove vital part of: EVIS-CERATE
disentangle, free from entanglement: EX-TRICATE
disgrace, infamy: OBLOQUY
disgrace attached to a person or group: STIGMA
disgraceful: INGLORIOUS
disgraceful, shocking, notorious: FLA-GRANT
disgracing, abusive: OPPROBRIOUS
disguise, feign, conceal, make a false show of: DISSEMBLE
disguise or shelter: COVERTURE
disguise to avoid recognition: INCOGNITO
disguise to blend with environment: CAM-OUFLAGE
disgust or dislike in the extreme, abhorrence: LOATHING
disgusting, offensive, hateful, repugnant: ODIOUS
disgusting, offensive, stinking, noxious: NOISOME
dish, deep and covered, for serving soup: TUREEN
dish made light by adding beaten egg whites: SOUFFLÉ
dish of chopped meat, eggs, onions, anchovies: SALMAGUNDI
disharmony in a relationship: RIFT
disheveled, untidy: UNKEMPT

dishonesty, deceitfulness, trickery: KNAVERY

dishonesty, lack of integrity: IMPROBITY

dishonor, defame: SMIRCH

dishonorable: IGNOMINIOUS

dishonorable, degraded, base: IGNOBLE

disinterested, free from bias, fair: IMPARTIAL

disjoint, dislocate: LUXATE

disjointed, broken up into separate incidents: EPISODIC

disjointed, confused: INCOHERENT

dislike of debate, argument, or reasoning: MISOLOGY

dislike or disgust in the extreme, abhorrence: LOATHING

dislocate, throw out of joint: LUXATE

dismayed: AGHAST

dismiss in disgrace: CASHIER

dismissal or leavetaking: CONGÉ

disobedient: INSUBORDINATE

disobedient, insolently so: CONTUMACIOUS

disobedient, stubborn, rebellious: RECALCITRANT

disorder, confusion: HUGGER-MUGGER

disorder, destruction or carnage, scene of: SHAMBLES

disorder and inertness as an irreversible tendency of a system: ENTROPY

disorder resulting from lack of leader or plan: ANARCHY

disordered, jumbled, topsy-turvy: HIGGLEDY-PIGGLEDY

disorderly, boisterous, rude: RAMBUNCTIOUS

disorderly, loud: RAUCOUS

disorderly, wild haste: PELL-MELL

disown, reject, refuse to accept: REPUDIATE

disparage, defame, blacken: DENIGRATE

disparage, treat with contempt: VILIPEND

disparaging term used to describe something inoffensive: DYSPHEMISM

dispel, waste, squander: DISSIPATE

display ostentatiously: FLOURISH

display or parade brazenly or gaudily: FLAUNT

displease or bore: PALL

dispose of, make unnecessary: OBVIATE

dispose of a matter quickly: DISPATCH

dispose of by fraud or trickery: FOB

dispose of swiftly: MAKE SHORT SHRIFT OF

dispose quickly of a matter: DISPATCH OR WITH DISPATCH

disposition, tendency, leaning: PROCLIVITY

dispossession that is unlawful: DISSEIZIN

disproportionate, inadequate: INCOMMENSURATE

disprove, demonstrate an error: REFUTE

dispute: ALTERCATION

dispute, challenge, attack the truth or validity of: IMPUGN

dispute, challenge, call in question: OPPUGN

disregard, forgetfulness: OBLIVION

disregard, neglect: SLIGHT

disregard for the rules or for fact to achieve artistic effect: POETIC LICENSE

disreputable, ill-tempered, perverse woman, hussy: JADE

disreputable, tawdry, vulgar: RAFFISH

disrespect toward one to whom deference is due: LESE MAJESTY

disrespectful, insulting: INSOLENT

dissension, disagreement, lack of harmony: DISCORD

dissenter: RECUSANT

dissimilar, distinct, different: DISPARATE

dissimilar, unrelated, unlike: HETEROGENEOUS

dissolute, lustful: WANTON

distance around: CIRCUMFERENCE

distance light travels in a vacuum in one year: LIGHT-YEAR

distance measured by determination of angles: TELEMETRY

distance of an eighth of a mile: FURLONG

distance of 3,280.8 feet: KILOMETER

distant, unknown region: ULTIMA THULE

distended, swollen: TURGID

distinct, different, dissimilar: DISPARATE

distinct, separate, disconnected from others: DISCRETE

distinctive mark: CACHET

distinguish or discriminate: SECERN

distinguished: PRESTIGIOUS

distinguished, dignified, well-bred: DISTINGUÉ

distinguished, renowned: ILLUSTRIOUS

distinguishing characteristic, facial contour or feature: LINEAMENT

distort, misapply: PERVERT

distort, pervert: WREST

distorted vision or view: ASTIGMATISM

distortion of shape: ANAMORPHISM

distract, amuse, entertain: DIVERT

distract, turn aside, deflect: DIVERT

distress, cause of: BANE
distress, pain, suffering, anguish: TRAVAIL
distress or disturb the mind or feelings painfully: HARROW
distribute or divide in proportion: PRORATE
district of a city in which a minority lives: GHETTO
distrust or hatred of mankind: MISANTHROPY
distrustful: ASKANCE
disturb, alarm, upset: PERTURB
disturb, bother: INCOMMODE
disturb, trouble, inconvenience: DISCOMMODE
disturb or ruffle: DISTEMPER
disturb the mind or feelings painfully, distress: HARROW
disturb the smoothness of: RUFFLE
disturbance, civil disorder: DISTEMPER
disturbance of the peace: AFFRAY
ditch or moat artificially created: FOSSE
dive in which one does a back flip and plunges into the water head first and facing the board: HALF GAINER
dive down suddenly, as a whale when harpooned: SOUND
diverge, spread apart or branch out at a wide angle: DIVARICATE
divergency, inconsistency: DISCREPANCY
diverse, varied to a great degree: MULTIFARIOUS
diversify or vary by adding something different: INTERLARD
diversity of sources used: ECLECTIC
divert, confuse: DISTRACT
diverted by thought, preoccupied: BEMUSED
divide, separate, part: DISSEVER
divide or shape a voting area to advance the interests of one political party: GERRYMANDER
divide by cutting or passing across: INTERSECT
divide into opposing groups or views: POLARIZE
divide into two sections: DICHOTOMIZE
divide or distribute in proportion: PRORATE
divide or spread out into divisions: RAMIFY
divided in half: DIMIDIATE
dividend, either regular or scheduled, that has been omitted: PASSED DIVIDEND
dividend on stock, paid in securities instead of cash: STOCK DIVIDEND
divination by means of figures formed when particles of earth are thrown down at random: GEOMANCY
divination by use of a divining rod: RHABDOMANCY
divinatory, mystical or magical arts: OCCULT
divine or supernatural intervention in human affairs: THEURGY
division: SCISSION
division of a church or other organization into factions: SCHISM
dizziness: VERTIGO
dizzy, whirling, spinning: VERTIGINOUS
do or commit something, as a crime or hoax: PERPETRATE
do away with, as a law or a right: ABROGATE
do penance, be humbled: GO TO CANOSSA
doctor serving apprenticeship in a hospital: INTERN
doctor who treats animals: VETERINARIAN
doctor's auxiliary or assistant: PARAMEDIC
doctrine, belief or principle maintained as true by a person or a group: TENET
doctrine that all life is sacred: AHIMSA
doctrine that holds reality has existence independent of the mind: OBJECTIVISM
doctrines held to be true and necessary: DOGMA
document accrediting an envoy to a foreign power: LETTER OF CREDENCE
document wholly in the handwriting of the person whose signature it bears: HOLOGRAPH
dodge, avoid: SIDESTEP
dodge or device to avoid unpleasantness: SUBTERFUGE
dogmatic, arrogant, haughty, pompous: PONTIFICAL
dogmatic or unproved assertion: IPSE DIXIT
doll made of wood representing spirit ancestors of Pueblo Indians: KACHINA
dollar per share of stock: POINT
domain: DEMESNE
domain of authority: BAILIWICK
dome, or roof that is rounded: CUPOLA
dominant, prevalent: REGNANT
dominate thoughts, engross: PREOCCUPY
domination of one state over another or leadership: HEGEMONY
domineering, arrogant: IMPERIOUS
domineering, overwhelming: OVERBEARING

done beyond recall, accomplished fact: FAIT ACCOMPLI

done or said for effect or as a formality: GESTURE

done with great effort: LABORED

doomed to failure: FORLORN HOPE

door, entrance: PORTAL

door divided horizontally so that either half can be opened separately: DUTCH DOOR

door or window part, above the opening and supporting structure above it: LINTEL

doorkeeper of a building: CONCIERGE

doorway curtain that replaces a door: PORTIERE

doorway or window drapery that covers only top half of opening: LAMBREQUIN

doorway side post: JAMB

dormant: LATENT

dots of many colors used as a method of painting: POINTILLISM

dots or hyphens in a horizontal row serving to guide the eye across a page: LEADER

dots or shadings used in photoengraving: BENDAY

dots over the second of two adjacent vowels to indicate it is pronounced separately (ö): DIERESIS

dots used to indicate the omission of words: SUSPENSION POINTS

dotted pattern woven into fabric: SHARKSKIN

double, two or paired: BINARY

double dagger symbol used in printing (‡): DIESIS

double dealer: AMBIDEXTER

double dealing, trickery: DUPLICITY

double image, blot: MACKLE

double meaning: AMBIGUOUS

double meaning, ambiguous, uncertain in origin or character, dubious: EQUIVOCAL

double meaning attributable to grammatical looseness: AMPHIBOLOGY

double or become doubled: GEMINATE

double or twofold: DUPLE

double pulse beat with each heartbeat: DICROTIC

double tablet, picture or carving, often depicting a religious subject: DIPTYCH

double vision: DIPLOPIA

doubling of a syllable or sound in a word: REDUPLICATION

doubling the stakes in gambling, to recover previous losses: MARTINGALE

doughnut in elongated, twisted shape: CRULLER

doubt, qualm, apprehension: MISGIVING

doubter: SKEPTIC

doubtful: DUBIOUS

doubtful state: DUBIETY

doubtfulness: INCERTITUDE

doubting, disbelieving: INCREDULOUS

doubting, resisting, ignoring attitude: NEGATIVISM

dowdy, sometimes ill-tempered woman: FRUMP

down in spirits, dejected: DISPIRITED

down in the dumps, down in the mouth: DOLDRUMS

down in the mouth: CHAPFALLEN

down to earth, practical rather than speculative: PRAGMATIC

downcast: DISPIRITED

downhearted, depressed: DISPIRITED

downy, covered with soft fine hair: LANUGINOUS

dowry, woman's marriage portion: DOT

drab, frumpish, not smartly dressed: DOWDY

draft: CONSCRIPTION

drag in the mud, lag, follow slowly: DRABBLE

drag or haul: SCHLEP

drapery or board across the top of a window: VALANCE

draw, paint, engrave with dots instead of lines: STIPPLE

draw a line around: CIRCUMSCRIBE

draw back, as claws: RETRACT

draw forth, call, or summon: EVOKE

draw forth, evoke, bring to light: ELICIT

draw or scribble aimlessly: DOODLE

draw or a tie, as in a game: STANDOFF

drawback, burden: IMPEDIMENTA

drawing a conclusion, based on reasoning from general to particular: DEDUCTION

drawing to create the illusion of depth and distance while keeping the proper proportions: FORESHORTEN

drawing together, reconciliation: RAPPROCHEMENT

drawn-out speech or writing: LONGWINDED

dread, abnormal and persistent, of a particular thing: PHOBIA (and see listing under that word)

dreaded or hated object or person: BÊTE NOIRE

dream interpreter: ONEIROCRITIC

dreamer or visionary: FANTAST

dreamlike, visionary: HYPNAGOGIC

dreamy repose caused by smoking narcotics: KEF

dregs of wine or liquor: LEES

dregs or lees, refuse grain from breweries and distilleries: DRAFF

drench or stain, especially with blood: IMBRUE

dress fussily: PRIMP

dress hanging straight from the shoulders: CHEMISE

dress showily, primp: PREEN

dress up or decorate: TITIVATE

dressed negligently or partially: DISHABILLE

dressing in garments of the opposite sex, a compulsion to do so: TRANSVESTITISM

dressing room for a woman: BOUDOIR

dressmaker, male: COUTURIER

dribbling of saliva: SLAVER

drink: IMBIBE

drink, given to: BIBULOUS

drink and play, carefree existence: BEER AND SKITTLES

drink greedily or to excess: GUZZLE

drink heartily: QUAFF

drink of mild nature to wash down hard liquor: CHASER

drink or eat greedily, gorge: INGURGITATE

drink sparingly: ABSTEMIOUS

drink that is drugged: MICKEY FINN

drinkable: POTABLE

drinking bowl or its contents: JORUM

drinking cup or goblet: MAZER

drive a sharp stake through: IMPALE

drive away, dispel: DISSIPATE

drive off, dispel, scatter: DISPERSE

drive away or remove, as by scattering: DISPEL

drive back, ward off: REPEL

drive or force to action, urge on: IMPEL

drive out of hiding: FERRET

drivel, incoherent talk: MAUNDER

driving force: IMPETUS

driving too closely behind another vehicle: TAILGATING

droop, hang loosely: LOLL

droop, weaken: FLAG

droop gradually, pine, weaken: LANGUISH

droop or hang down loosely: LOP

drop heavily and clumsily, flop: FLUMP

drop of liquid, in pharmacy: GUTTA

drop or plunge straight down: PLUMMET

dropping of sounds or letters from the middle of a word: SYNCOPE

dropping a sound at the end of a word: APOCOPE

dropping the initial letter or sound in a word: APHERESIS

dropping to earth of particles after a nuclear explosion: FALLOUT

drowning as a form of execution: NOYADE

drowsy: SOMNOLENT

drudge, one who hires himself out to do routine or tedious work: HACK

drug salesman: DETAIL MAN

drug that is incapable of doing harm or good: ADIAPHOROUS

drug that overcomes effects of sedatives: ANALEPTIC

drug withdrawal: COLD TURKEY

drugs as a science: PHARMACOLOGY

drum: TAMBOUR

drum, small and double-headed, with a wire string across the bottom: SNARE DRUM

drum in the form of a hollow hemisphere with a parchment top: KETTLEDRUM

drum or tap monotonously: THRUM

drum or trumpet signal for a parley: CHAMADE

drumbeat with two sticks striking almost simultaneously: FLAM

drumhead with jingles in its rim: TAMBOURINE

drumlike: TYMPANIC

drumming continuously: TATTOO

drunk: BESOTTED

drunk: INEBRIATED

drunkard: TOPER

drunken, gluttonous: CRAPULENT

drunken revelry: BACCHANAL

drunk-making: INTOXICANT

dry: BRUT

dry, lacking interest, naive, barren, insipid: JEJUNE

dry or roast by exposing to heat: TORREFY

dry up, make thirsty: PARCH

dry up or out: EXSICCATE

drying: SICCATIVE

dryness: XERIC

dualism in theology, belief in two co-equal gods: DITHEISM

dubious use of ploys to gain an advantage: GAMESMANSHIP

dueling sword with sharp point and no cutting edge: EPEE

dull: LACKLUSTER

dull, commonplace: STODGY

dull, depressed or bored state of mind: DOLDRUMS

dull, heavy, lethargic: LOGY

dull, inactive, sluggish: TORPID

dull, insensible, not acute: OBTUSE

dull, lifeless, insipid, flat: VAPID

dull, light-resistant: OPAQUE

dull, mediocre, prosaic: PEDESTRIAN

dull, monotonous: HUMDRUM

dull, ordinary, uninspired: PROSAIC

dull, tasteless, flat, bland, vapid: INSIPID

dull, trite: BANAL

dull, zestless: PERFUNCTORY

dull or become stupid: HEBETATE

dulled from overindulgence, worn-out, exhausted, sated: JADED

dullness, apathy, sluggishness: LETHARGY

dullness, stagnation, weakness, fatigue, dreaminess, spiritlessness: LANGUOR

dullness, yawning: OSCITANCY

dupe or tool: CAT'S-PAW

dumbfound, perplex, bewilder: NONPLUS

duplicate: DITTO

duplicate of a work made by the originator, close copy: REPLICA

duplication of a word for rhetorical effect: GEMINATION

durable, binding: INDISSOLUBLE

durable, permanent: PERDURABLE

durable products such as automobiles, refrigerators, furniture: HARD GOODS

dusky, dark complexioned: SWARTHY

dusky, gloomy, depressed: SOMBER

dusty, powdery: PULVERULENT

dwarf, midget: HOMUNCULUS

dwell or stay temporarily: SOJOURN

dwelling: ABODE

dwelling, house, home, abode: DOMICILE

dwelling that is wretched and small, shed: HOVEL

dying work, as of a writer or composer: SWAN SONG

E

eager curiosity or excitement: AGOG
eager for food in quantity: VORACIOUS
ear deformed by blows: CAULIFLOWER EAR
ear diseases, as a study: OTOLOGY
ear reception: AURAL
earache: OTALGIA
earliest stages of development, beginnings: INCUNABULA
earlike projections for holding something, as a pot or kettle: LUGS
early edition of a newspaper: BULLDOG EDITION
early in the morning: MATUTINAL
early morning: COCKCROW
earnest, warm, glowing: FERVENT
earnestly appeal: ADJURE
earnings of common stock as affected by bond interest and preferred stock dividends: LEVERAGE
ears ringing: TINNITUS
earth inhabitant: TELLURIAN
earth study of materials, their structure and characteristics: GEOGNOSY
earthenware, glazed, usually blue and white: DELFT
earthenware piece in broken condition: POTSHERD
earthly: TERRESTRIAL
earthquake: TEMBLOR
earthquake measuring scale: RICHTER SCALE
earthquake phenomena, as a science: SEISMOLOGY
earth's physical structure, as a science: GEOLOGY
earth's structure and the forces that change it, as a scientific study: TECTONICS
earth's surface above sea level treated as a science: HYPSOGRAPHY

easily: HANDILY
easily achieved, ready or quick in performance, skillful: FACILE
easing, as of discord, between nations: DETENTE
easterly wind in Mediterranean regions: LEVANTER
eastern hemisphere: ORIENT
easy mark: GULL
easy to approach: AFFABLE
eat, especially with someone: BREAK BREAD
eat greedily: ENGORGE
eat ravenously: GUTTLE
eat or drink greedily, gorge: INGURGITATE
eat sparingly: ABSTEMIOUS
eat voraciously or gluttonously: GOURMANDISE
eater and drinker with discriminating taste: GOURMET
eater of much food: TRENCHERMAN
eater to excess: GOURMAND
eating as an art: GASTRONOMY
eating at the same table: COMMENSAL
eating implements: CUTLERY
eating or wearing away of a substance: CORROSION
eating to excess: GLUTTONOUS
eating many foods: POLYPHAGIA
eats all kinds of food both animal and vegetable: OMNIVOROUS
ebb, flowing back: REFLUX
ebbing, flowing back: REFLUENT
eccentric or queer: CRANKY
eccentric, irregular, nonconforming: ERRATIC
ecclesiastical council: SYNOD
ecclesiastical cutting of one off from fellowship of a church: EXCOMMUNICATION

ecclesiastical property transferred to laymen: IMPROPRIATED

echo, response: REPLICATION

echoic as pertaining to words: ONOMATOPOEIC or ONOMATOPOETIC

echoing loudly: REBOANT

ecology, basic unit including both organisms and environment: ECOSYSTEM

ecology—nonavailable water of the soil: ECHARD

ecology—plant adjustment to a new habitat: ECESIS

ecology—soil rather than climate as an affective factor: EDAPHIC

ecology—zone wherein two different species contend for dominance: ECOTONE

ecology of plant and animal communities: SYNECOLOGY

economic self-sufficiency: AUTARKY

economic union of Belgium, Netherlands and Luxembourg: BENELUX

economic union of Western Europe: COMMON MARKET

economical, chary, stingy: SPARE

economy or thrift in managing: HUSBANDRY

economy spur of governmental expenditures financed by borrowing: DEFICIT FINANCING

ecstasy of a religious nature: THEOPATHY

edge of fabric so woven as not to ravel: SELVAGE

edge of paper that resembles the ragged edge of handmade paper: DECKLE EDGE

edge or outer part: PERIPHERY

edge that slopes: BEVEL

edging, selvage, strip, as of cloth: LIST

edging decorated with a series of indentations: ENGRAILED

edging of small loops of ribbon or thread: PICOT

edible: ESCULENT

edit: REDACT

edit prudishly: BOWDLERIZE

editing of a text by reference to varying manuscripts: RECENSION

editor of manuscripts in newspaper or publishing house: COPY EDITOR

educated people or individuals collectively: INTELLIGENTSIA

eel fishing by putting bait into the eels' hiding places: SNIGGLING

eel-shaped: ANGUILLIFORM

eerie, strange, weird, unnatural: UNCANNY

efface, destroy completely: OBLITERATE

effect, result: RAMIFICATION

effect that balances another effect: COUNTERPOSE

effective: POTENT

effective, moving, working: OPERATIVE

effective at a specified past time: RETROACTIVE

effeminate: EMASCULATED

effeminate, sexless: EPICENE

efficacy, potency: VIRTUE

efficient quickness: DISPATCH

eggs baked with crumbs in a buttered dish: SHIRRED EGGS

eggs cooked and served on toast spread with anchovy paste: SCOTCH WOODCOCK

eggs laid at one time: CLUTCH

egg white: ALBUMEN

egg-white glaze: GLAIR

egg yolk: VITELLUS

eight tones above or below a given one: OCTAVE

eight-year period: OCTENNIAL

elaborate, speak or write more fully: EXPATIATE

elasticity, buoyancy: RESILIENCE

elate or excite to a degree of frenzy: INTOXICATE

elated: COCK-A-HOOP

elderly woman of dignified bearing and wealth: DOWAGER

eldest or senior member of a group: DOYEN

elect, choose: OPT

election held between regular ones: BY-ELECTION

election that finally decides: RUN-OFF

electioneer on a political trip: STUMP

electric strength, unit that measures: AMPERE

electromotive force measured in volts: VOLTAGE

electronic devices without moving parts or heated elements: SOLID STATE

electronic solid-state device that controls flow of current without use of a vacuum: TRANSISTOR

element that causes a thing to be what it is: FACTOR

elemental, original, primitive: PRIMORDIAL

elementary: ABECEDARIAN

elementary: RUDIMENTARY

elementary instruction: PROPAEDEUTIC

elephant in a state of sexual frenzy: MUST
elephant keeper and driver, in India: MA-HOUT
elevator for conveying food from floor to floor: DUMBWAITER
eleven-sided figure: HENDECAGON
elf or sprite: PIXIE
elite group within an organization: CADRE
elk, large North American deer: WAPITI
emaciate, become thin: MACERATE
emaciated: TABETIC
emaciated, haggard, hollow-eyed, gloomy, desolate: GAUNT
emaciation: MARASMUS
emanate, exude: EFFUSE
emanation: EFFLUX
emanation, especially foul-smelling exhalation from decaying matter: EFFLU-VIUM
emancipate, liberate, free: MANUMIT
emasculate: CASTRATE
embarrassed: ABASHED
embarrassing occurrence: CONTRETEMPS
embarrassment at what one has done himself: CHAGRIN
embed a material such as gold or ivory into a surface so as to form a decorative pattern: INLAY
embellish, as ornamental lines or figures: FLOURISH
embellish a speech or writing with quotations, etc.: LARD
embellishment: GARNITURE
embezzle, steal funds, especially public funds: PECULATE
embezzle or misappropriate: DEFALCATE
embitter: ACERBATE
embitter: ENVENOM
embitter, stir enduring ire: RANKLE
embodiment of an attribute or a quality in a person: PERSONIFICATION
embroidery at the ankle of a sock or stocking: CLOCK
embroidery that is rich: ORPHREY
emerge, come forth into the open: DE-BOUCH
emergency or temporary as applied to a ship's rigging: JURY-RIGGED
emergency program that has top priority: CRASH PROGRAM
emotion, subjective aspect of: AFFECT
emotional in appeal: AFFECTIVE
emotional for effect, theatrical: HIS-TRIONIC
emotional intensity, ardor: FERVOR

emotional or mental block: INHIBITION
emotional or sentimental, tearfully so: MAUDLIN
emotional shock, injury: TRAUMA
emotionless: APATHETIC
employer who is excessively demanding: SLAVE DRIVER
employer's barring employes from work until they accept his terms: LOCKOUT
employes tend to rise to their level of incompetence: PETER PRINCIPLE
employment of more workers than needed: FEATHERBEDDING
empower, authorize: WARRANT
emptiness: VACUITY
empty compliment or flattery: FLUMMERY
empty tomb: CENOTAPH
enact, establish, decree: ORDAIN
enamel-and-metal work: CLOISONNÉ
enamel- or lacquer-ornamented metalware: TOLE
enchantress who changed men into swine: CIRCE
enclose within walls, imprison, confine, surround: IMMURE
encourage: ABET
encourage: HEARTEN
encouragement, exhortation: HORTATORY
encroach, infringe: IMPINGE
end a parliamentary session: PROROGUE
end, cease: SURCEASE
end, termination: EXPIRY
end of the world: CRACK OF DOOM
end-of-the-world battle between good and evil: ARMAGEDDON
end or withdraw by plan: PHASE OUT
end unexpectedly: ABORT
ending of debate in parliamentary procedure: CLOSURE, CLOTURE
ending of one or more syllables affixed to a word: SUFFIX
ending section of a book or a play that adds commentary or explanation: EPILOGUE
endless: INTERMINABLE
endless and difficult: SISYPHEAN
endowment: APPANAGE
endowment or gift, as of a church: PAT-RIMONY
ends touching: ABUTTING
endurance, vigor, strength: STAMINA
endurance test: MARATHON
endurance test, painful experience: OR-DEAL
energetic, in music: VIGOROSO

energy, enthusiasm: VERVE

energy and matter, as a science: PHYSICS

energy or force held as the basis for phenomena of the universe: DYNAMISM

enfeebled, worn out by age or use: DECREPIT

engine mounted on the rear of a small boat: OUTBOARD MOTOR

English dessert consisting of spongecake soaked in wine and topped with jam, custard and whipped cream: TRIFLE

engrave, cut into, carve: INCISE

engraver of precious stones: LAPIDARY

engross, dominate thoughts: PREOCCUPY

engross, involve deeply: IMMERSE

engrossed intensely: RAPT

engulf, overpower, submerge: WHELM

enigmatic, mysterious: INSCRUTABLE

enigmatic, prophetic: ORACULAR

enjoyment: DELECTATION

enjoyment of possessions: FRUITION

enlarge: AGGRANDIZE

enlarge a hole: REAM

enlarge excessively, increase unduly, puff up: INFLATE

enlargement: AMPLIFICATION OR AMPLIATION

enlarging, growing, waxing: INCRESCENT

enlighten, benefit, uplift: EDIFY

enlighten, illuminate, light up, make clear: IRRADIATE

enmity, malice: RANCOR

enormous, hideous: MONSTROUS

enormous, unwieldy, ponderous: ELEPHANTINE

enormous, vast: PRODIGIOUS

enrage, anger: INCENSE

enraged, angry: IRATE

enroll or register in a college or university as a candidate for a degree: MATRICULATE

entangle, complicate, confuse: EMBRANGLE

entangle, intertwine, involve: IMPLICATE

entanglement, complication, intertwining: INVOLUTION

enter office or dignity: ACCEDE

enter without leave or invitation: INTRUDE

entertain, amuse, distract: DIVERT

entertain, delight, give unusual pleasure: REGALE

enthusiasm, dash, vivacity: ÉLAN

enthusiasm, energy: VERVE

enthusiasm, zest: GUSTO

enthusiast: AFICIONADO

enthusiastic, fervent: ZEALOUS

enthusiastic or excited, bubbling: EBULLIENT

entice by flattery or guile, draw, cajole: INVEIGLE

entire range of anything: GAMUT

entirely: TOUT À FAIT

entirely, altogether: IN TOTO

entrance, going in: INGRESS

entrance hall, lobby: FOYER

entrance or gate: PORTAL

entreating earnestly and humbly: SUPPLIANT

entreaty or appeal for assistance: INVOCATION

entreaty or prayer in behalf of others: INTERCESSION

entry: ACCESS

envelope markings used instead of stamps: INDICIA

environment, setting: MILIEU

environment in relation to organisms: ECOLOGY

environmental distinctiveness: AMBIENCE

epidemic among animals: EPIZOOTIC

episode that is minor: INCIDENT

epithet or title substituted for proper name: ANTONOMASIA

equal before the law, or in ability or social position: PEER

equal in size: COMMENSURATE

equal intervals of time: ISOCHRONAL

equal number of parts: ISOMEROUS

equal or equivalent: TANTAMOUNT

equal political power in a government: ISOCRACY

equality, social and political: EGALITARIAN

equality in dimensions or measurements: ISOMETRIC

equality in rank, power, condition, etc.: PARITY

equality of racial and ethnic groups: INTEGRATION

equilibrium of an organism: HOMEOSTASIS

equipment, gear, personal effects: PARAPHERNALIA

equivalent or equal: TANTAMOUNT

equivocate, be evasive: TERGIVERSATE

equivocate, lie: PREVARICATE

era, period, century: SIÈCLE

eradicate, dislocate, uproot: DERACINATE

erase, delete: EXPUNGE

erase, destroy utterly, pull up by the roots, uproot, erase: ERADICATE erase, rub out, cancel, obliterate: EFFACE

erection of the penis as a persistent pathological condition: PRIAPISM

ermine in its brown summer coat: STOAT

erratic, unexpected: WAYWARD

erring, wicked: PERVERSE

erroneous name: MISNOMER

erroneous placement of something in time: ANACHRONISM

erroneous or misleading: FALLACIOUS

error in reading or speaking lines: FLUFF

error in speaking that is thought to disclose a person's true thinking: FREUDIAN SLIP

errorless, faultless, flawless: IMPECCABLE

errors in a list: ERRATA

escape from the law by secret departure: ABSCOND

escape or avoid: ELUDE

escort, attendants of a person of rank: RETINUE

essence of a legal complaint or accusation: GRAVAMEN

essence of something: QUIDDITY

essence of something in concentrated form: QUINTESSENCE

essence or abstract quality of anything: DISTILLATION

essential, indispensable: SINE QUA NON

essential, whole: INTEGRAL

essential, inherent: INTRINSIC

essential element: INHERENT

essential qualities of anything: DISTILLATION

essential source of life, actions, energy: ANIMA

essential theme or part, gist: PITH

established firmly, deep-rooted: INGRAINED

established firmly by long continance: INVETERATE

established rule or principle: CANON

esteem, high regard: REPUTE

estimate based on a guess: GUESSTIMATE

estimate from evidence at hand, project on the basis of facts already known: EXTRAPOLATE

estranged, alienated: DISAFFECTED

eternity or period of time that is incalculable: EON

ethical consequences of all one's acts (Buddhism and Hinduism): KARMA

ethics or science of moral obligation: DEONTOLOGY

etiquette in diplomacy: PROTOCOL

Eucharist as given just before death: VIATICUM

eulogy or praise formally delivered: ENCOMIUM

European Economic Community: COMMON MARKET

evangelist preacher: REVIVALIST

evasion of main point by stressing a trivial point: QUIBBLE

evasion of painful emotions or unacceptable impulses by adjusting behavior or mental attitude: DEFENSE MECHANISM

evasive action to gain time: TEMPORIZATION

even on the same line or with a margin: FLUSH

even beat as in music or speech: CADENCE

evening prayers or services: VESPERS

evening star: HESPERUS

evergreen: INDECIDUOUS

every two weeks: BIWEEKLY

everyday speech, popular, accepted: VULGATE

everything included: OVERALL

everywhere at once: UBIQUITOUS

everywhere present simultaneously: OMNIPRESENCE

evidence that a defendant is compelled to disclose in a trial or hearing: DISCOVERY

evidence that if unrefuted establishes the fact alleged: PRIMA FACIE EVIDENCE

evident, manifest, obvious: PATENT

evident, obvious, plainly apparent: MANIFEST

evident, open, unconcealed: OVERT

evil, repulsive, flagrantly bad: VILE

evil, vile: NEFARIOUS

evil, wicked, odious, atrocious: HEINOUS

evil eye protection: AMULET

evil notoriety: INFAMY

evil person: SHAITAN

evildoer, criminal: MALEFACTOR

evildoer, villain: MISCREANT

evoke, draw forth, bring to light: ELICIT

evolution of any animal or plant group: PHYLOGENY

exact, accurate: PRECISE

exact, honest: SCRUPULOUS

exact, precise, accurate: NICE

exact, scrupulous observance of forms: PUNCTILIOUS

exact copy or reproduction: FACSIMILE

exact words of the original: LITERAL

exaggerate a narrative with fictitious details: EMBROIDER

exaggerated sense of buoyancy and vigor: EUPHORIA

exaggeration or overstatement intended for effect and not to be taken seriously: HYPERBOLE

exalting human to divine status: APOTHEOSIS

examination of something that has already happened: POST-MORTEM

examination of tissue removed from a living organism: BIOPSY

examination or discussion that is detailed: CANVASS

examine carefully: SCRUTINIZE

examine or analyze minutely, sift: WINNOW

example or case: INSTANCE

examine by feeling or touching: PALPATE

examine or read thoroughly, scrutinize: PERUSE

examine or scrutinize carefully: TRAVERSE

example of excellence: PARAGON

example or model: PARADIGM

excavation for archeological purposes: DIG

excavations, study of, as history: ARCHEOLOGY

exceed, excel: OUTSTRIP

exceed a limit: TRANSCEND

excel: TRANSCEND

excel, beat, surpass: TRUMP

excel, exceed: OUTSTRIP

excellence exemplified: PARAGON

excellence or exceptional quality, choice: VINTAGE

excellent or fine: COPESETIC

exercises to promote grace and health: CALISTHENICS

excerpts or selections from literary works: ANALECTS

excess, abundance beyond need: SUPERFLUITY

excess in eating or drinking: SURFEIT

excess word or phrase: PLEONASM

excessive: INORDINATE

excessive, unrestrained: WANTON

excessive or insincere: FULSOME

excessive beyond usual limits: EXORBITANT

excessive or extreme: INTEMPERATE

excessively: UNDULY

exchange, as ideas: INTERCHANGE

exchange by two countries of concessions: RECIPROCITY

exchange of something for something else: QUID PRO QUO

excite, enliven, stimulate: QUICKEN

excite, exhilarate, intoxicate: INEBRIATE

excite, rouse to action, stimulate: GALVANIZE

excite, stimulate, raise the spirits of: ELATE

excite, stimulate, sharpen: WHET

excite or elate to a degree of frenzy: INTOXICATE

excited, confused, hasty: HECTIC

excited to a feverish pitch: FRENETIC

excitement that is great and intense: WHITE HEAT

exciting or producing similar reactions in others: INFECTIOUS

exclaim, discharge suddenly and quickly: EJACULATE

exclaim loudly, shout, bawl: VOCIFERATE

exclamation, often profane: EXPLETIVE

exclamation, usually one word: INTERJECTION

exclude, make impossible, shut out: PRECLUDE

exclude, shut out: OSTRACIZE

exclude from sacraments and solemn services, as in the Roman Catholic Church: INTERDICT

exclusive control of a product or service: MONOPOLY

exclusive set: CLIQUE

excrement: FECES

excrete waste matter: DEFECATE

excusable, pardonable, as a fault: VENIAL

excuse or exempt, as from a regulation: DISPENSE

excuse or reason for being: RAISON D'ETRE

excuse or try to excuse from blame: EXTENUATE

excuse that clears from censure, criticism or suspicion: EXCULPATION

excuse that is not quite honest: SALVO

execute or attack with a cord or metal collar, which is tightened: GARROTE

exemption as from a rule or law: DISPENSATION

exemption from local law granted to members of the diplomatic corps: DIPLOMATIC IMMUNITY

exemption from obligation or penalty, resistance to harmful influence or disease: IMMUNITY

exemption from penalties or liabilities, compensation for loss or damage: INDEMNITY

exemption or freedom from punishment, harm or unpleasant consequences: IMPUNITY

exhausted, helpless, lying flat: PROSTRATE

exhibit in which modeled figures are set in a naturalistic foreground, which blends into a painted background: DIORAMA

exhibition or parade that is spectacular: PAGEANT

exhilarate, excite: INEBRIATE

exhortation, encouragement: HORTATORY

existing, surviving: EXTANT

exit, or going out: EGRESS

exiled person: EXPATRIATE

expand, grow, increase step by step: ESCALATE

expand, stretch out, swell: DISTEND

expand, widen, swell: DILATE

expand a business by increasing the variety of its products: DIVERSIFY

expanding with age: ACCRESCENCE

expectorated matter: SPUTUM

expedient and wise: POLITIC

expedition or journey: SAFARI

expenditures limited or regulated, as by law: SUMPTUARY

expense account: SWINDLE SHEET

expenses or continuous costs of operating a business: OVERHEAD

expense allowance for each day: PER DIEM

experience alone as the source of knowledge: EMPIRICISM

experiment subject: GUINEA PIG

expert: ADROIT

expert: MAVEN, MAVIN

expert in matters of art and taste: CONNOISSEUR

expert on recorded music: DISCOPHILE

expertness, manual skill: HANDINESS

explain, make clear: INTERPRET

explain actions or thoughts on rational grounds, which may not be the real motives: RATIONALIZE

explain away: GLOZE

explain away: RESOLVE

explain or interpret: EXPLICATE

explainer or promoter: EXPONENT

explanation that is detailed: EXPLICATION

explanation of a word, passage or work: EXEGESIS

explanatory description or caption on a chart, map or illustration: LEGEND

explanatory note, commentary: GLOSS

explicit, most accurate and complete: DEFINITIVE

explode suddenly and with violence: DETONATE

exploration of enemy positions: RECONNAISSANCE

explosive effect: BRISANCE

explosive force of a thousand tons of TNT: KILOTON

explosive sounds, or throwing off small particles as by frying meat: SPLUTTER

explosive that is trinitrotoluene: TNT

expose actual or alleged corruption: MUCKRAKE

expose to the sun as for bleaching: INSOLATE

exposure to risk to achieve some end: BRINKMANSHIP

express by gestures: GESTICULATE

expurgate: BOWDLERIZE

extemporize: AD LIB

extend, spread out: SPLAY

extended to great subtleness: FINE-DRAWN

extension: AMPLIFICATION or AMPLIATION

extent, scope, range: PURVIEW

extenuate, alleviate: PALLIATE

extermination or destruction of an entire people or national group: GENOCIDE

extinct or dead: DEFUNCT

extinguish or satisfy thirst: QUENCH

extirpate, uproot, dislocate, eradicate: DERACINATE

extort: EXACT

extort or swindle to get goods or money: FLAY

extra day in leap year: BISEXTILE

extra something given beyond obligation: LAGNIAPPE

extra vowel inserted into word: ANAPTYXIS

extract or passage, especially from the Bible: PERICOPE

extraneous, superfluous: SUPEREROGATORY

extraordinary happening: PHENOMENON

extrasensory perception of distant objects: TELESTHESIA

extravagance as in entertaining or in style of living: LUCULLAN extravagance to impress: CONSPICUOUS CONSUMPTION

extravagant, pompous: HIGHFALUTIN

extravagant, wasteful, lavish: PRODIGAL

extravagant ornamentation: BAROQUE

extravagantly praise: ADULATE

extreme or excessive: INTEMPERATE

extrinsic: ADVENTITIOUS

exude, emanate: EFFUSE

exult over another's bad luck: GLOAT

eye, make eyes at suggestively: OGLE

eye disease marked by pressure within the eyeball: GLAUCOMA

eye disorder in which both eyes cannot be focused simultaneously on the same spot: STRABISMUS

eye examination to determine response to light and shadow: SKIASCOPY

eye examiner: OPTOMETRIST

eye for an eye, a tooth for a tooth: RETALIATION

eye in which the iris is light-colored: WALLEYE

eye or sight: OCULAR

eye sees an object double: DIPLOPIA

eyebrows bushy and prominent: BEETLE-BROWED

eyeglass dealer: OPTICIAN

eyeglasses that grip the bridge of the nose: PINCE-NEZ

eyeglasses with handle into which they may be folded: LORGNETTE

eyeglasses with three-part lenses: TRIFOCALS

eyeglasses with two-part lenses: BIFOCALS

eyelet of metal: GROMMET

eyes, as a medical study: OPHTHALMOLOGY

eyes dark and velvety: SLOE-EYED

eyes see what appear to be specks or threads: MUSCAE VOLITANTES

F

fable or tale with a moral: APOLOGUE

fabric edge so woven as not to ravel: SELVAGE

fabric gathered in parallel rows: SHIRRING

fabric piece, usually triangular, inserted in a garment for roomier fit: GUSSET

fabric sample: SWATCH

fabric surface of velvet, plush or corduroy: PILE

fabric with a soft pile: VELOUR

fabric with fibers that make the surface fuzzy: NAPPED

fabric woven with a dotted pattern: SHARKSKIN

fabrication, fiction: FIGMENT

face or facial expression: VISAGE

face that is pale and sallow: WHEYFACE

face to face: VIS-À-VIS

face upward, lying on the back: SUPINE

face-down lying position: PRONE

face-to-face meeting: CONFRONTATION

facial contour or feature, distinguishing characteristic: LINEAMENT

facial expression indicative of pain or annoyance: GRIMACE

facial features regarded as clues to character: PHYSIOGNOMY

facile, too glib: PAT

facilitate, quicken, speed up: EXPEDITE

facing toward one: OBVERSE

factual condition as distinguished from legal condition: DE FACTO

fail, sink, collapse: FOUNDER

fail disastrously: COME A CROPPER

fail to carry out a mission: ABORT

fail to keep a promise: RENEGE

failure in duty, willful omission or neglect: DERELICTION

failure or neglect to meet an obligation: DEFAULT

failure that is complete or humiliating: FIASCO

failure to realize one's intentions: MISCARRIAGE

faint, hidden, unclear: OBSCURE

fair, disinterested: IMPARTIAL

fair, impartial: UNBIASED

fair, impartial, reasonable: EQUITABLE

fairness, impartiality, justness: EQUITY

fairy, elf, goblin: SPRITE

faithful devotion to obligations: FIDELITY

faithful follower: MYRMIDON

faithful forever: SEMPER FIDELIS

faithfulness, obligation owed, loyalty: FEALTY

falconry term for the short strap on each leg of a hawk, used for attaching a leash: JESS

fall or cave in, sink, collapse, fail: FOUNDER

fall straight down, plunge: PLUMMET

fall that is heavy: CROPPER

fall upon, strike against: IMPINGE

falling behind, slow; a straggler: LAGGARD

falling objects always roll to the most inaccessible spot: BERNSTEIN'S FIRST LAW

falling off or shedding as petals, leaves, fruit: DECIDUOUS

false, artificially invented, not real: FICTITIOUS

false, fraudulently invented: TRUMPED-UP

false, not genuine: SPURIOUS

false, ridiculous or self-contradictory statement: PARADOX

false appearance, pretense: GUISE

false conception or deceptive appearance: ILLUSION

false charges: ASPERSIONS

false front: FACADE

false pathos: BATHOS

false sentimentality: MAWKISHNESS

false step, mistake, error especially in etiquette: FAUX PAS

false story circulated for political purposes: ROORBACK

false story or rumor: CANARD

falsehood: FABRICATION

falsehood, deception, humbug, sham: FLAM

false or malicious written statement or graphic representation that damages a person's reputation: LIBEL

falsetto and normal chest tones alternated in song: YODEL

falsify or misrepresent: BELIE

fame, celebrity: RENOWN

familiar phrase or person that represents a type: BYWORD

family name: COGNOMEN

family name: PATRONYMIC

family or branch of a family: STIRPS

family or kindred, collectively: COUSINRY

family tree, descent of an individual from a certain ancestor: GENEALOGY

famous: RENOWNED

famous, distinguished: ILLUSTRIOUS

fan: AFICIONADO

fanatic, partisan to excess: ZEALOT

fanatical, raging: RABID

fanatical enthusiast, one possessed by evil spirits: ENERGUMEN

fanciful humor, caprice: WHIMSY

fanciful idea or notion that emerges suddenly: WHIM

fanciful thought or expression: CONCEIT

fancy trappings, finery: REGALIA

fanfare, as of trumpets: FLOURISH

fan-shaped structure: FLABELLUM

fantastic: CHIMERICAL

farewell: ADIEU

farewell: VALE

farewell drink: STIRRUP CUP

farewell speech: VALEDICTORY

farm on which vegetables are grown for market: TRUCK FARM

farm operated cooperatively: COLLECTIVE

farming: HUSBANDRY

farming or rural affairs: GEORGIC

farseeing: PRESCIENT

farsightedness as an abnormal condition of the eye: HYPERMETROPIA

farsightedness that accompanies aging: PRESBYOPIA

farthest possible point: ULTIMA THULE

fascinate, beguile: INTRIGUE

fascinating, enchanting: IRRESISTIBLE

fashionable: DE RIGUEUR

fashionable, wealthy people: JET SET

fast time in music: ALLEGRO

fasten firmly: RIVET

fasten or tie together: COLLIGATE

faster than the speed of sound: SUPERSONIC

fastidious, overly exacting: FINICKY

fasting or other ascetic practices to keep from sinning: MORTIFICATION

fat: ADIPOSE

fat, very stout: OBESE

fat and red-faced: BLOWZY

fat and short person: SQUAB

fat of hogs in melted form: LARD

fat or fleshy: CORPULENT

fatal, deadly,: LETHAL

fate: KISMET

fatigue, spiritlessness, dreaminess, dullness, stagnation: LANGUOR

father of newly born child in primitive tribes going through motions as if he had given birth, such as going to bed: COUVADE

fatherly: PATERNAL

fatlike substance: LIPOID

fats of beef or mutton, used in making soap and candles: TALLOW

fats that limit cholesterol level: POLYUNSATURATED

fatten: BATTEN

fatty buttocks, especially in women: STEATOPYGIA

fatty substance linked to atherosclerosis: CHOLESTEROL

faucet or valve used to drain off water or air: PETCOCK

fault in character that is minor: FOIBLE

fault or trivial sin: PECCADILLO

faultfinder: MOMUS

faultfinding: CAPTIOUS

faultfinding: CENSORIOUS

faultfinding: QUERULOUS

faultfinding, berating: VITUPERATION

faultless, blameless: UNIMPEACHABLE

faultless, flawless, errorless: IMPECCABLE

faulty or illogical reasoning: PARALOGISM

favorable, mild, gentle: BENIGN

favorably disposed, auspicious gracious: PROPITIOUS

favoring one party, prejudiced, biased: PARTIAL

favoritism shown to relative in jobs: NEPOTISM

fawn upon someone: ADULATE

fawn, cower: CRINGE

fawning, servile, overly obedient: OBSEQUIOUS

fawning, servile person: TOADY

fear, abnormal and persistent, of a particular thing: PHOBIA (and see listing under that word)

fear, amazement or panic that is sudden and paralyzing: CONSTERNATION

fear-inspiring, formidable: REDOUBTABLE

fear of losing sexual power: APHANISIS

fearful, timid: TIMOROUS

fearful anxiety: TREPIDATION

fearful feeling that something is about to happen: PRESENTIMENT

fearful or timid, trembling: TREMULOUS

fearless, bold, dauntless: INTREPID

fearsome or awesome: FORMIDABLE

feast, picnic or pleasure trip: JUNKET

feather beginning to pierce the skin: PINFEATHER

feathers on the neck of a rooster or pigeon or hairs on the neck of a dog: HACKLES

feces, waste matter from bowels: EXCREMENT

federal funds appropriated to help an official with his constituents: PORK BARREL

federally regulated amount of credit that a bank may extend to a customer for the purchase of stock: REGULATION U

fee paid to obtain the services of an attorney or a consultant: RETAINER

feebleminded: ANILE

feebleminded person: AMENT

feed, support, rear, train: NURTURE

feed or fodder for cattle: STOVER

feed or supply to excess: SURFEIT

feeding on other animals, exploiting others: PREDATORY

feeding on vegetables, plant-eating: HERBIVOROUS

feeding through a stomach tube: GAVAGE

feel about with the hands, grope, sprawl, flounder: GRABBLE

feel of a place or situation: AMBIENCE

feel or examine by touching: PALPATE

feeling sharing or emotion sharing with another: EMPATHY

feign, conceal, disguise, make a false show of: DISSEMBLE

fellow member or colleague: CONFRERE

fellowship: CAMARADERIE

fellowship, association: SODALITY

female and male sexual organs in one individual: HERMAPHRODITES

female demon: SUCCUBUS

female external genitals: PUDENDUM

female figure forming a column or pillar: CARYATID

female line of kinship: ENATE

female line or maternal branch of family: DISTAFF SIDE

female opera singer of note, prima donna: DIVA

female professional singer: CANTATRICE

female singer in the principal position: PRIMA DONNA

femininity, womanhood: MULIEBRITY

fence of rails crossed at ends so that the fence zigzags: WORM FENCE

fence made up of strong stakes: APLISADE

fence or wall placed in a ditch so as not to interfere with the view: HA-HA

fermentation, as in brewing: ZYMOLYSIS

ferocious, stubborn, defiant: TRUCULENT

fertile: PROLIFIC

fertile, fruitful: FERACIOUS

fertile, fruitful, prolific: FECUND

fertilize, saturate, permeate: IMPREGNATE

fervid to an extreme, ardent: PERFERVID

fester, form pus: SUPPURATE

fetus killed: FETICIDE

fetus that is malformed, monstrosity: TERATISM

fetus's lodging place within the mother before birth: PLACENTA

feud, usually a blood feud, involving families: VENDETTA

fever: PYREXIA

feverish: FEBRILE

feverishly excited: FRENETIC

feverless: AFEBRILE

few words his mark: LACONIC

fewer words than the original: ABRIDGMENT

fewness, small quantity: PAUCITY

fickle: INCONSTANT

fickle: SKITTISH

fickle, changeable: MUTABLE

fickle, frivolous, shallow: FLIGHTY

fickle, unstable, fleeting, transient: VOLATILE

fickle person, variable thing: WEATHERCOCK

fickleness, lightness, gaiety that is inappropriate, frivolity: LEVITY

fiction, fabrication: FIGMENT

fictitious: MYTHICAL

fictitious name, pen name: PSEUDONYM

fidgety, unruly, restless: RESTIVE

field near a stable where horses are exercised: PADDOCK

fiendish: DEMONIAC

fierce, harsh: FELL

fierce, malicious, unruly: VICIOUS

fierce, wild, unsociable: FAROUCHE

fifth of a gallon, especially of liquor: FIFTH

fight, brawl or dispute that is noisy: FRACAS

fight, conflict, uproar, brawl: FRAY

fight among people that is confused and noisy: MELEE

fighter in an independent raiding band: GUERRILLA

fighting in public: AFFRAY

fighting over words, verbal contention: LOGOMACHY

fighting with an imaginary foe: SCIAMACHY

figure of speech, figurative language: TROPE

figure of speech endowing inanimate things with human qualities: PERSONIFICATION

figure of speech implying a comparison: METAPHOR

figure of speech or construction in which a word modifying two or more words acquires different meanings: SYLLEPSIS

figure of speech in which a word modifying two others relates correctly to one of them: ZEUGMA

figure of speech in which an assertion is made by the negation of its opposite: LITOTES

figure of speech in which an attribute or an associated term is substituted for the name of the thing itself: METONYMY

figure of speech in which contradictory ideas are combined: OXYMORON

figure of speech in which normal order of things or events is reversed: HYSTERON PROTERON

figure of speech in which two nouns joined by "and" are used instead of noun and modifier: HENDIADYS

figure of speech that describes an event as

happening before it could have happened: PROLEPSIS

figure of speech that makes a comparison by use of "as" or "like": SIMILE

filled, laden: FRAUGHT

film director or maker with personal style: AUTEUR

film documentary close to reality: CINÉMA VÉRITÉ

film of part of a television series used for trial purposes: PILOT FILM

film of tiny size for reproducing texts, pictures, etc.: MICROFILM, MICROFICHE

filtering action: LEACH

filth or indecency in art or literature: COPROLOGY

filthy or foul sediment: FECULENCE

final contestant of a team: ANCHORMAN

final deciding election: RUN-OFF

final lines of a poem, usually a dedication: ENVOY

final unraveling or solution in a plot: DENOUEMENT

finalism, final causes as studied in cosmology: TELEOLOGY

financial: FISCAL

fine change or gradation in meaning: NUANCE

fine or excellent: COPESETIC

fine point of behavior or etiquette: PUNCTILIO

fine point or subtlety: NICETY

finery, fancy trappings: REGALIA

finger: DIGIT

finger beside the little finger: RING FINGER

finger snap or quick tap with the nail of a finger that has been snapped: FILLIP

fingerless: ADACTYLOUS

fingerprint: DACTYLOGRAM

fingerprint ridge: WHORL

fingertip infection that is painful: WHITLOW

finicky, fussy: NIGGLING

finish used to coat fabrics, paper or other surfaces: SIZE

fire-breathing monster, part goat, lion and serpent: CHIMERA

firecracker that burns with a spitting sound before exploding: SQUIB

firefighter who parachutes into or near a forest fire: SMOKE JUMPER

fireflies' fire: LUCIFERIN

firelike: IGNEOUS

fireplace or furnace floor: HEARTH

fireplace support for wood: ANDIRON
fireproof: INCOMBUSTIBLE
fireworks: PYROTECHNICS
fireworks that rotate, branched candle-stick: GIRANDOLE
firm, dependable: STAUNCH
firm, durable: INDISSOLUBLE
firm, hard, obdurate: FLINTY
firm, solid, forthright: FOURSQUARE
firm, unshakable: IMPREGNABLE
firm foundation of anything: HARDPAN
firm in chewing, as spaghetti: AL DENTE
firmly established by long continuance: INVETERATE
firmly faithful, unwavering: STEADFAST
first, original, principal: PRIMAL
first in rank: PREMIER
first mention or suggestion: BROACH
first principle or fundamental: RUDIMENT
fish, as a branch of zoology: ICHTHYOL-OGY
fish basket used by anglers: CREEL
fish cured by splitting and drying in the air, without salting: STOCKFISH
fish eggs, especially in masses: SPAWN
fish group terms—see "creature terms"
fish or hunt illegally: POACH
fish resembling a sardine: SPRAT
fishing by dragging a hook and line near the surface: TROLLING
fissure or chasm, as in a glacier: CRE-VASSE
fissured or cracked, chinky: RIMOSE
fit of bad temper: TANTRUM
fit together, unify, bring together into a whole: INTEGRATE
fitness or agreement: CONGRUITY
fitting, as to proportion: COMMENSURATE
five-line stanza: CINQUAIN
five-year period: LUSTRUM
fix in place: IMMOBILIZE
fix the eyes or attention of: RIVET
fix upon a sharp stake: IMPALE
fixed, blank, uncomprehending: GLASSY
fixed, unchangeable: INFLEXIBLE
fixed amount, as of work to be done in a specified time: STINT
fixed idea: IDÉE FIXE
fixed in one place: STABILE
fixed price for a whole meal: PRIX FIXE
flabby, intellectually or morally: INVER-TEBRATE
flag fixed to a crosspiece rather than a pole: GONFALON

flagrant, glaring, conspicuously bad: EGREGIOUS
flaming, flaring: IGNESCENT
flaming, said of food served flaming with ignited brandy or other liquor: FLAMBÉ
flaring, flaming up: IGNESCENT
flash like lightning: FULGURATE
flashy, cheap dress or ornamentation: FRIPPERY
flat, bland, dull, tasteless,: INSIPID
flat, broad piece: SLAB
flat, dull, lifeless, insipid: VAPID
flat, knifelike instrument for spreading, as plaster or cake icing: SPATULA
flat and open country: CHAMPAIGN
flatter or coax to persuade: WHEEDLE
flatter or wheedle: BLANDISH
flatter servilely: ADULATE
flatterer who is servile, parasite: SYCO-PHANT
flattery contrived as a means of per-suasion: SNOW JOB
flattery or empty compliment: FLUMMERY
flatulence remedy: CARMINATIVE
flavor, taste: SAPOR
flavor-enhancing chemical: MONOSODIUM GLUTAMATE
flavor or odor imbued in a substance: TINCTURE
flawless, errorless, faultless: IMPECCABLE
flawless, warranting no criticism: UNEX-CEPTIONABLE
fleet of large merchant ships: ARGOSY
fleeting, transient, fickle, unstable: VOLA-TILE
fleeting, transitory: EVANESCENT
fleeting, quickly passing: FUGACIOUS
flesh-eating mammals: CARNIVORES
fleshly: CARNAL
fleshy or fat: CORPULENT
fleshy part below the lower jaw: JOWL
flexible, bendable: PLIABLE
flexible, easily changed: SUPPLE
flexible, pliable: MALLEABLE
flickering, radiating softly: LAMBENT
flighty, haughty: HOITY-TOITY
flighty, giddy, foolish: HAREBRAINED
flimsily built: JERRYBUILT
flimsy, delicate, thin: TENUOUS
flimsy, delicate substance: GOSSAMER
flippant, light style of writing or talk: PERSIFLAGE
flippantly humorous, jesting: FACETIOUS

flirt or act in a trifling manner: COQUET

float, carry or move gently: WAFT

floating cylinder or boat to support a temporary bridge: PONTOON

floating objects on a body of water: FLOTSAM

floating or swimming: NATANT

floating wreckage: FLOTSAM

flocking together, a crowd: CONFLUENCE

flood, pertaining to, especially the flood at the time of Noah: DILUVIAL

flood of the tide in an estuary: EAGRE

flood or overwhelm with abundance or excess: INUNDATE

floodlight used in making motion pictures: KLIEG LIGHT

floors of inlaid woodwork: PARQUETRY

florid, overelaborate: ROCOCO

florid, showy, bombastic, ornate: FLAMBOYANT

florid, showy, excessively ornamented: ORNATE

flounder, splash: SLOSH

flourish at the end of a signature: PARAPH

flourish or mark after a signature: RUBRIC

flow of water beneath and opposite to the surface current: UNDERTOW

flower, bloom forth, blossom: EFFLORESCE

flower and ornamental plant culture: FLORICULTURE

flowering, flourishing: INFLORESCENCE

flowerless: ANANTHOUS

flowers, in a bunch: BOUQUET

flowery, excessively ornate: FLORID

flowery, metaphorical: FIGURATIVE

flowery speech or writing: EUPHUISM

flowing and sweet sounding: MELLIFLUOUS

flowing back, ebb: REFLUX

flowing back, ebbing: REFLUENT

flowing in: INFLUENT

flowing or a discharge: FLUX

flowing out: EFFLUENCE

flowing together: CONFLUENCE

fluctuate, swing back and forth: OSCILLATE

flushed, ruddy: FLORID

fluster, excitement, bustle: POTHER

flute with eleven finger holes and a plug, or fipple, near the mouthpiece: RECORDER

fluted or crimped ornamentation, as along the edge of fabric: GOFFER

flutter, beat rapidly: PALPITATE

flying, able to fly: VOLANT

flying men's nervous disorder: AERONEUROSIS

foam, scum, froth: SPUME

fodder, food suitable for horses and cattle: FORAGE

fodder or feed for cattle: STOVER

fog containing ice particles: POGONIP

fog or mist: BRUME

foggy, misty, indefinite: NUBILOUS

foil, frustrate, obstruct: THWART

fold of cloth doubled back and pressed flat: PLEAT

folded backward, also to reply, to reproduce itself or oneself: REPLICATE

folded fanlike: PLICATED

foliage that has fallen in a forest: DUFF

folk singers' meeting for a public performance: HOOTENANNY

folkways or customs of a social group: MORES

follies or vices attacked by ridicule or wit: SATIRE

follow closely upon something: SUPERVENE

follower or favorite who behaves servilely: MINION

followers, retainers or attendants in a group: ENTOURAGE

followers or companions in a group: COHORT

following, as an effect or conclusion: CONSEQUENTIAL

following in time: SUBSEQUENT

fond of one's wife to excess or submissive to her: UXORIOUS

fond of others' company: GREGARIOUS

food: ALIMENT

food: NUTRIMENT

food, cheap and popular among Southern blacks: SOUL FOOD

food, especially choice food: VIAND

food, means of support, livelihood: SUSTENANCE

food expert: EPICURE

food for body or mind: ALIMENT

food prepared by highly skilled chefs: HAUT CUISINE

food reheated: RECHAUFFÉ

food suitable for horses or cattle, fodder: FORAGE

food that is coarse: ROUGHAGE

fooled or cheated easily: GULLIBLE

foolhardiness, heedlessness: TEMERITY

foolish, flighty, giddy: HAREBRAINED

foolish, idiotic, stupid: FATUOUS

foolish, stupid, brutish, unmoved: INSEN-SATE

foolish, talkative person: BLATHERSKITE

foolish appearance given to something or someone: STULTIFIED

foolish love, unreasoning passion: INFATUATION

foolish or excessive affection: DOTAGE

foolish or senseless talk: DRIVEL

foolishly wasteful, involved procedure: RIGMAROLE

foot and toenail treatment: PEDICURE

foot race 26 miles long: MARATHON

foot section above the arch between the ankle and the toes: INSTEP

foot that is flat and turned out: SPLAYFOOT

foot treatment: PODIATRY

football area between goal line and end line where a touchdown may be scored: END ZONE

football defensive player stationed just behind the linemen: LINEBACKER

football field corner at goal line: COFFIN CORNER

football illegality consisting of blocking from behind an opponent who is not carrying the ball: CLIPPING

football kick in which ball is dropped, then kicked, as it bounces up from ground: DROP KICK

football kicked after being dropped from the hands but before touching the ground: PUNT

football line parallel to the goal line along which teams take positions at start of play: LINE OF SCRIMMAGE

football lineman between the guard and the end: TACKLE

football maneuver in which one back hands the ball to another: HANDOFF

football mass play after the ball has been snapped by the center: SCRIMMAGE

football offensive formation with the quarterback behind the center and the fullback behind him flanked by the halfbacks: T FORMATION

football official supervising at the sidelines: LINESMAN

football pass that moves parallel to the passer's goal line rather than forward: LATERAL PASS

football place kick that starts play at the

beginning of each half or following a touchdown: KICKOFF

football play in which a player grounds the ball behind his own goal line after it has been moved there by an opponent: TOUCHBACK

football play in which the ball is thrown toward the opponent's goal: FORWARD PASS

football player, one of a pair who with the quarterback and fullback make up the backfield: HALFBACK

football player stationed behind the quarterback: FULLBACK

football player who calls the signals: QUARTERBACK

football players behind the linemen: BACKFIELD

football players providing protection for the ball carrier: INTERFERENCE

football score of six points made by touching the ball down behind the opponent's goal line: TOUCHDOWN

football scoring of one or two extra points after a touchdown: CONVERSION

football term for a member of the backfield stationed far out before the ball is put in motion: SLEEPER

football term for a player's touching the ball to the ground behind his own goal line at the cost of two points: SAFETY

football term for being ahead of the ball before it is snapped by the center: OFFSIDE

football term for charging the opposing quarterback by rushing through the line: RED-DOG

football term for putting the ball in play: SNAP

footprint or other trace of a wild animal: SPOOR

footstool, usually upholstered: HASSOCK

for example, or, by way of example: E.G. (EXEMPLI GRATIA)

forbid a person to have or do something: INTERDICT

forbidden: VERBOTEN

forbidden, banned: TABOO

forbidden, beyond the lawful powers of: ULTRA VIRES

force, use of: DURESS

force of destruction that is slow and irresistible: JUGGERNAUT force one's thoughts or self upon others: INTRUDE

force oneself, or one's opinion, on someone else: OBTRUDE

force or compel to go: HALE

force or drive to action, urge on: IMPEL

force or pack down by repeated pressure: TAMP

force or spirit from within that guides: NUMEN

force that balances another force: COUNTERPOISE

force that is overpowering or coercive: FORCE MAJEURE

force that sets a body in motion: IMPETUS

force unjustly: EXACT

forced feeding: GAVAGE

forced labor, particularly for repairing roads: CORVÉE

forces at work in any field: DYNAMICS

forcible separation: AVULSION

foreboding: PREMONITION

foreboding: PRESENTIMENT

forever: AD INFINITUM

forefather, earliest ancestor: PRIMOGENITOR

forefather or source: PROGENITOR

forefinger: INDEX FINGER

forehead just above the nose and between the eyebrows: GLABELLA

foreknowledge: PRESCIENCE

forerunner, preliminary: PRECURSOR

foreshadow: ADUMBRATE

foreshadow, warn: PORTEND

foresight, prudent economy: PROVIDENCE

foreskin: PREPUCE

forests of a certain region and their characteristics: SILVA

foretell: VATICINATE

foretell, indicate beforehand: PROGNOSTICATE

foreteller of events: SOOTHSAYER

foretelling by omens: AUGURY

foretelling the future, prophecy: DIVINATION

forethought: CALCULATION

forgetfulness, disregard: OBLIVION

forgetfulness, oblivion: LETHE

forgivable, as sins: REMISSIBLE

forgiveness: ABSOLUTION

forgiving, appeasable: PLACABLE

forgo, relinquish, give up: WAIVE

fork with three broad tines, one sharp: RUNCIBLE SPOON

forked, branching: FURCATE

forked twig or branch popularly thought to be effective in finding underground water: DIVINING ROD

form, shape, outline: FIGURATION

form a point of view beforehand: PRECONCEIVE

form lacking or indefinite: AMORPHOUS

form only: PRO FORMA

formal in an artificial way, pompous: STILTED

formation in ranks or steps as with troops, fleets or airplanes: ECHELON

formed into a rounded mass: GLOMERATE

formed or fashioned: WROUGHT

former: QUONDAM

formidable, fear-inspiring: REDOUBTABLE

formless: INCHOATE

forsaking one's faith, party or principles: APOSTASY

forte, one's occupation for which he is particularly suited: MÉTIER

forthright, firm, solid: FOURSQUARE

fortification, bulwark: RAMPART

fortified place: BASTION

fortnightly: BIWEEKLY

fortune telling, sorcery, black magic: NECROMANCY

fortune telling from the lines of the palm: PALMISTRY

fortuneteller, sorceress: SIBYL

forward, overconfident, arrogant: PRESUMPTUOUS

fossil study or examination of prehistoric forms of life: PALEONTOLOGY

foul or filthy sediment: FECULENCE

foul-smelling: MEPHITIC

foundation of stones thrown together: RIPRAP

foundation or basic facilities of a community: INFRASTRUCTURE

four, group of four: TETRAD

four-dimensional continuum—three of space plus time: SPACE-TIME

four-year period: QUADRENNIUM

foxlike, sly, crafty: VULPINE

fracas, rough-and-tumble clash: SCRIMMAGE

fragment, as of pottery: SHARD

fragments or particles separated from rock masses by erosion or glaciers: DETRITUS

fragments or selections from literary works: ANALECTS

fragrant, suggestive of something: REDO-LENT

fragrant odor: ODOROUS

frame of mind: DISPOSITION

frame of mind: POSTURE

framework like a bridge for holding the rails of a traveling crane: GANTRY

framework or structure: FABRIC

frank, innocent, simple, naive, straightforward: INGENUOUS

fraudulent or tricky action: JOCKEYING

fraudulently invented, false: TRUMPED-UP

freakish, strange: OUTLANDISH

freckle: LENTIGO

free, emancipate, liberate: MANUMIT

free and easy, offhand: CAVALIER

free from blame, prove innocent: EXCULPATE

free from bondage or restraint: EMANCIPATE

free from fever: AFEBRILE

free from slavery, admit to citizenship: ENFRANCHISE

free of charge: GRATIS

free will denied or minimized in regard to human behavior: DETERMINISM

freedom from restrictions: LATITUDE

freedom or exemption from punishment, harm or unpleasant consequences: IMPUNITY

free-for-all, brawl marked by roughness: DONNYBROOK

freight train's rear car: CABOOSE

French for good day: BON JOUR

French for good evening: BON SOIR

French working girl, especially one with free and easy manners: GRISETTE

frenzied, raging: MADDING

frequent visitor to a place: HABITUÉ

frequently occurring: PREVALENT

fresh, springlike, youthful: VERNAL

fret, complain: REPINE

fretful, jittery, balky: RESTIVE

fried rapidly with little fat: SAUTÉ

friend who is exceedingly close to one: ALTER EGO

friendly: AFFABLE

friendly: AMICABLE

friendly and solicitous toward guests: HOSPITABLE

friendship or loyalty weakened or destroyed: DISAFFECTION

frighten with threats: INTIMIDATE

frightened, panicky mood: FUNK

frightened easily: SKITTISH

frightful: HORRENDOUS

frigid, arctic: HYPERBOREAN

fringed: LACINIATE

frisk about, frolic: DISPORT

frisk about or prance: CAVORT

frivolity, fickleness, lightness, gaiety that is inappropriate: LEVITY

frivolous, impulsive, irresponsible: FLIGHTY

frivolous, restless, superficial: YEASTY

frolic, skip or leap about: GAMBOL

frolic or amuse oneself, frisk about: DISPORT

frolic with hilarity: SKYLARK

front or primary side of something, such as a coin: OBVERSE

froth, foam, scum: SPUME

frozen, icy: GELID

frugal, careful, cautious: CHARY

frugal, chary, stingy: SPARE

fruit-bearing: FRUITION

fruit-eating: FRUGIVOROUS

fruitful: PROCREANT

fruitful, fertile: FERACIOUS

fruitful, fertile, prolific: FECUND

fruitful, inventive, productive: PREGNANT

fruitless, unsuccessful: INEFFECTUAL

fruits stewed in syrup: COMPOTE

frustrate, confuse, defeat the plans of: DISCOMFIT

frustrate, obstruct, foil: THWART

frying pan, of iron and with a long handle: SPIDER

fulfillment: FRUITION

full, absolute, complete: PLENARY

full, overflowing: TEEMING

full, rounded voice: OROTUND

full, sated, amply supplied: REPLETE

full attendance, as in a legislative body: PLENUM

full length: IN EXTENSO

full moon after the harvest moon: HUNTER'S MOON

full of meaning: PREGNANT

full power conferred: PLENIPOTENTIARY

fuller statement, addition for fuller explanation: EPEXEGESIS

fullness of a container lacking by this amount: ULLAGE

full-sounding, loud: SONOROUS

fumble, bungle, misplay: FOOZLE

fumbler who drops things: BUTTERFINGERS

fun, quip, playfulness: JEST

fun that is noisy and rough: HORSEPLAY
fund invested so that its gradual accumulations will pay a debt: SINKING FUND
fundamental, basic, inherent in: ORGANIC
fundamental principle, basis: HYPOSTASIS
funeral hymn, dirge: EPICEDIUM
funeral hymn, lament: DIRGE
funeral pile: PYRE
funeral rites: OBSEQUIES
funeral song, dirge: THRENODY
funnier than average: UPROARIOUS
fur, or other covering of a mammal: PELLAGE
fur hat worn by hussars, etc.: BUSBY
furious, enraged: LIVID
furiously angry, maddened: HORN-MAD
furnace floor or fireplace: HEARTH
furnace or oven for baking or drying bricks, pottery, cement: KILN

furnish, supply: PURVEY
furtive: CLANDESTINE
furtively move about: SKULK
fuse or blend together: COALESCE
fuss, commotion in a relatively simple situation: TSIMMES
fuss over something trivial: FOOFARAW
fussy, old-fashioned person: FUDDY-DUDDY
fussy, overprecise, finicky: NIGGLING
fussy, precise, overly fastidious, exacting: FINICKY
futile, unsuccessful: UNAVAILING
futile endeavor: WILD-GOOSE CHASE
future event referred to as if it had already happened: PROLEPSIS
future generations: POSTERITY
fuzzy or hairy, in botany: COMATE

G

gad about, walk about idly or aimlessly: TRAIPSE

gadget or device, the name of which is forgotten: DINGUS

gaiety: JOLLITY

gaiety or merriment that is exuberant and noisy: HILARITY

gaiety that is inappropriate, frivolity, fickleness, lightness: LEVITY

gallant, courteous, generous: CHIVALROUS

gallant or courtly man: CAVALIER

gallery or portico that is arcaded and built into the side of a building: LOGGIA

gallows: GIBBET

gambling or luck as a cause or reason: ALEATORY

gambling system in which one doubles the stakes to recover previous losses: MARTINGALE

game in which one team fails to score: SHUTOUT

game of ball, popular in Latin America, played with a curved basket fastened to the arm: JAI ALAI

gangrenous: SPHACELATE

gap, blank: LACUNA

gap, opening, break or interruption of continuity: HIATUS

gap in a mountain through which a torrent passes: FLUME

gape, stare stupidly: GAWK

gaping or expanse of open mouth: RICTUS

garden cultivation: HORTICULTURE

garden for quiet pleasure: PLEASANCE

garment, one piece and tight-fitting, worn by acrobats and dancers: LEOTARD

garment like a skirt worn by both sexes in the Malay Archipelago: SARONG

garment of one piece often worn over regular clothes: COVERALL

garment with no sleeves, worn by Arabs: ABA

garment worn by an official or a clergyman: VESTMENT

garments that dry quickly after washing and need no ironing: DRIP-DRY

garments that need no ironing after washing: WASH-AND-WEAR

gas in the intestine: FLATUS

gash, cut: INCISION

gasoline that vaporizes at a relatively low temperature: HIGH-TEST

gate controlling flow of water into canal lock: HEAD GATE

gate that revolves to admit passengers after deposit of fare: TURNSTILE

gateway or porch, covered, at the entrance of a building: PORTE-COCHÈRE

gather or store, as in a granary; accumulate: GARNER

gather sheets of manuscript into a unified whole: COLLATE

gathered into a mass: AGGLOMERATE

gathering of people, animals or things: CLUTCH

gauge or pattern used to copy something accurately, as in woodworking: TEMPLATE

gaunt, pale, ghastly: CADAVEROUS

gaunt, wild or worn look, as from fatigue, hunger or anxiety: HAGGARD

gay, carfree, light-hearted: ROLLICKING

gay, cheerful: JOCUND

gay, puckish, strange: FEY

gay, smart, dashing: RAKISH

gear, equipment, personal effects: PARAPHERNALIA

geld, weaken, castrate, make effeminate: EMASCULATE

gem cutting, engraving or polishing: LAPIDARY

gem measurement: CARAT

gem that is cut in oblong shape: BAGUETTE

gems, as a study: GEMOLOGY

genealogies, armorial bearings, etc.: HERALDRY

general epidemic, widespread, universal: PANDEMIC

general idea, vague concept: NOTION

general pardon: AMNESTY

general store: EMPORIUM

general to particular, as in reasoning: DEDUCTION

generalization to particular instances: A PRIORI

generous: BOUNTEOUS

gemerous, bountiful, lavish: MUNIFICENT

generous, high-minded, great of soul: MAGNANIMOUS

generous in giving or spending: LAVISH

gentle, mild, favorable: BENIGN

gentle, reproof: ADMONITION

geometry that deals with three-dimensional figures: SOLID GEOMETRY

germ killer: GERMICIDE

German for "so long": AUF WIEDERSEHEN

German prisoner-of-war camp: STALAG

German song: LIED

gestures without words: PANTOMIME

get by begging: CADGE

get rid of, shed: SLOUGH

get something from a person by violence or threats: EXTORT

getting even with someone: REPRISAL

ghastly, sepulchral: CHARNEL

ghost: REVENANT

ghost believed to cause sounds: POLTERGEIST

ghost or apparition: SPECTER

ghostly double of someone not yet dead: DOPPELGANGER

ghostly or weird: EERIE

gibberish: GALIMATIAS

gibberish, speech that is confused or meaningless: JARGON

gibe or witty remark: QUIP

giddy, flighty: HOITY-TOITY

giddy, flighty, foolish: HAREBRAINED

gift given at start of new year or new venture: HANDSEL

gift of money, tip: GRATUITY

gift that is small and comes from one who can barely afford it: WIDOW'S MITE

gift to a beggar: HANDOUT

gifts bestowed liberally: LARGESS

gigantic, strong, having power to great proportions: HERCULEAN

gigantic unidentified water beast: LEVIATHAN

gilt of bronze or silver: VERMEIL

gin or vodka mixed with bouillon as a cocktail: BULLSHOT

gin or vodka mixed with dry vermouth as a cocktail: MARTINI

gin or vodka mixed with water and sweetened lime juice: GIMLET

girl (Spanish): MUCHACHA

girls in a group: BEVY

gist, essential theme or part: PITH

give and take: BANDY

give back: RETROCEDE

give cause for just complaint: AGGRIEVE

give grudgingly: STINT

give off or send forth as light or heat: EMIT

give out, distribute: DISPENSE

give to another in a will: BEQUEATH

give up: ABDICATE

give up, abandon, yield: RELINQUISH

give up, relinquish, forgo: WAIVE

give up conditionally: CAPITULATE

give up or turn over something to someone: CONSIGN

give up rights, etc.: ABNEGATE

give up something: CEDE

give up something as a penalty: FORFEIT

give vent to, reveal, disclose: UNBOSOM

given without requirement of payment or return: GRATUITOUS

giver of benefits or favors: BENEFACTOR

giving or spending generously: LAVISH

giving up or resigning an office: DEMISSION

glaciers, as a scientific study: GLACIOLOGY

glance at, read quickly: SCAN

glance over or read hastily: SKIM

glandular secretion that is internal: ENDOCRINE

Glasgow resident: GLASWEGIAN

glass, broken or refuse, which is gathered for remelting: CULLET

glass or cup filled to the brim: BUMPER

glass or cup for measuring liquor: JIGGER

glass showcase, as for art objects: VITRINE

glass that is colored and used in mosaics: SMALTO

glasses with three lenses: TRIFOCALS

glasses with two lenses: BIFOCALS

glassware with embedded ornaments of colored glass: MURRHINE GLASS

glassy: VITREOUS

glaze made of raw egg white: GLAIR

gleeful chuckles: CHORTLE
glib, talkative, speaking fluently: VOLU-
BLE
glib and swift talk: PATTER
glide or skim over water: SKITTER
glide or slide, as a snake: SLITHER
gliding, sinuous motion: UNDULATION
glitter: SPANGLE
glitter, flash, sparkle: SCINTILLATE
globular: CONGLOBATE
gloomy, dark: CIMMERIAN
gloomy, dark: TENEBROUS
gloomy, dejected: DISCONSOLATE
gloomy, depressed, murky: SOMBER
gloomy, desolate, haggard: GAUNT
gloomy, grave, morose: SATURNINE
gloomy, ill-humored, sullen: MOROSE
gloomy, infernal, dark: STYGIAN
gloomy, melancholy: SEPULCHRAL
gloomy, peevish: DYSPEPTIC
gloomy, saddened, dejected: DIS-
CONSOLATE
gloomy, stern, morose, ill-tempered:
DOUR
Gloria Patri, Gloria in excelsis Deo: DOX-
OLOGY
glorification: APOTHEOSIS
glorify, idealize: TRANSFIGURE
glory of the world thus passes away: SIC
TRANSIT GLORIA MUNDI
gloss producing machine, used on paper
or fabric: CALENDER
glove part uniting back and front parts of
adjacent fingers: FOURCHETTE
glowing: LUMINOUS
glowing or luminous with heat: INCAN-
DESCENT
glum, resentfully morose: SULLEN
glut, offer more than enough: SATIATE
gluttonous or drunken: CRAPULENT
go about, roam in search of diversion:
GALLIVANT
go in peace: VADE IN PACE
go without sleep, keep vigil: WATCH
goad, incite, foment, provoke, spur on to
some drastic action: INSTIGATE
goat or sheep newly born: YEANLING
goatlike, lustful: HIRCINE
go-between: INTERMEDIARY
go-between: INTERNUNCIO
goblet or large drinking cup: MAZER
God as the uncaused creator of all things:
FIRST CAUSE
God conceived as having human characteristics: THEANTHROPISM

God evidenced in every feature of the universe: PANTHEISM
God's existence denied: ATHEISM
God's existence questioned: AGNOSTICISM
going before, preceding: PREVENIENT
going in, entrance: INGRESS
going or traveling from place to place:
ITINERANT
going out, or exit: EGRESS
gold-colored alloys used in cheap jewelry
and ornaments: ORMOLU
Golden Fleece searchers with Jason:
ARGONAUTS
golf course obstacle or trap: HAZARD
golf play in which the ball goes into the
hole on the drive from the tee: HOLE
IN ONE
golf shot, short and lofted, made in approaching the green: CHIP SHOT
golf situation in which an opponent's ball
lies on the green in a direct line between a player's ball and the hole:
STYMIE
golf stroke on the green to move the ball
into or near the hole: PUTT
golf term for one stroke over par on a
hole: BOGEY
golf term for one stroke under par on a
hole: BIRDIE
golf term for two strokes under par on a
hole: EAGLE
golf term indicating ball on the green on a
line perpendicular to line of approach: HOLE-HIGH
golfer's shouted warning that the ball is
about to be hit: FORE
good breeding: SAVOIR-VIVRE
good deed (Hebrew): MITZVAH
good living: CAKES AND ALE
good luck piece: AMULET
good nature: BONHOMIE
good or benevolent spirit: EUDEMON
good things of life: AMENITIES
goodbye: ADIEU
goodbye (Spanish): HASTA LA VISTA or
HASTA LUEGO or HASTA MAÑANA
good-natured, polite remark: PLEAS-
ANTRY
goodness, moral excellence: VIRTUE
goods accumulated as a reserve: STOCK-
PILE
goods paid for by dealer only after they've
been sold: ON CONSIGNMENT
goods sold in a miscellany collection to a
retailer: JOB LOT

goods that may not be imported or exported: CONTRABAND
goof or social blunder: FAUX PAS
goose flesh: HORRIPILATION
gospel-spreading through preaching and revival meetings: EVANGELISM
gossip: BRUIT
gossip carelessly: BANDY
gossip or chat: CONFABULATE
gourmet, sensualist: EPICURE
gout: PODAGRA
government administration by inflexible officials: BUREAUCRACY
government by a few: OLIGARCHY
government by holy men: HAGIARCHY or HAGIOCRACY
government by men only: PATRIARCHY
government by priests or members of the clergy: HIEROCRACY
government by the military: STRATOCRACY
government by the old: GERONTOCRACY
government by the rich: PLUTOCRACY
government by women or a woman: GYNARCHY
government council, local or national, in the Soviet Union: SOVIET
government expenditures financed by borrowing in order to increase productivity and consumption: DEFICIT FINANCING
government in which people as a whole control production and distribution of goods: COLLECTIVISM
government or authority shared jointly by two men: DUUMVIRATE
governmental organization of a state or society: POLITY
government publication on a relatively less important subject: WHITE PAPER
government seizure, usually sudden and often accompanied by violence: COUP D'ETAT
government with absolute power: AUTARCHY
government-must-go theory: ANARCHISM
government's unlimited authority: ABSOLUTISM
gown, loose and flowing, gathered from the neckline: MUUMUU
graceful, slender young woman: SYLPH
graceful, smooth, expressive: FLUENT
graceful in bending, bending easily, limber: LITHE
graceful structure or movement: EURYTHMIC

gracious: BENIGNANT
gracious gesture: BEAU GESTE
gradation or subtle change in meaning: NUANCE
grade, layer, bed: STRATUM
gradual reduction and extinction of debt or liability, as by installment payments: AMORTIZATION
graduation address: BACCALAUREATE
graduation speech of farewell: VALEDICTORY
grain that has been or is to be ground, meal: GRIST
grammatical change of construction within a sentence: ANACOLUTHON
grammatical or syntactical violation: SOLECISM
grammatical system consisting of a set of rules for producing sentences: GENERATIVE GRAMMAR
grammatical term for possessive case: GENITIVE
grammatical theory that holds that all sentences are kernel sentences or transformations of them in accordance with transformational rules: TRANSFORMATIONAL GRAMMAR
grammatically analyze a sentence by giving form, function and syntactical relationship of its words: PARSE
grand, stately, impressive: IMPOSING
grand jury report on an offense based on its own knowledge and with no indictment: PRESENTMENT
grand or imposing: GRANDIOSE
grandiloquent: TURGID
grant with condescension: VOUCHSAFE
grape cultivation for wine: VINICULTURE
grape growing: VITICULTURE
grape refuse after pressing, from which brandy is distilled: MARC
graph in form of a circle divided into proportionate sections: PIE CHART
graphic symbol representing an object or idea: IDEOGRAPH
grasping, greedy: RAPACIOUS
grasping, holding: PREHENSION
grass in second growth after regular cutting, usually tall and rank: FOG
grass or hay in its second growth; aftermath: ROWEN
grass-covered land, turf: SWARD
grass-eating: GRAMINIVOROUS
grassland or open country of South Africa: VELDT

gratify or yield to one's desires: INDULGE

grating, shrill: STRIDENT

gratuity, something extra given: LAGNIAPPE

grave, gloomy, morose: SATURNINE

grave robber: GHOUL

grave robber, of bodies: RESURRECTIONIST

graveyard shift in newspaper work: LOBSTER SHIFT

gravy in natural form included: AU JUS

gray or graying hair: GRIZZLED

gray- or white-haired, ancient, venerable: HOARY

grayish, often with a mottled appearance: GRISEOUS

grease or oil something: LUBRICATE

greasy, slippery feeling: UNCTUOUS

great of soul, generous, high-minded: MAGNANIMOUS

great style: BRAVURA

great work, masterpiece: MAGNUM OPUS

greed, avarice: CUPIDITY

greedy: COVETOUS

greedy: INSATIABLE

greedy, grasping: RAPACIOUS

greedy, insatiable, immoderate: VORACIOUS

greedy, rapacious person: HARPY

Greek architecture characterized by elaborateness: CORINTHIAN

Greek architecture characterized by ornamental scrolls on capitals: IONIC

Greek architecture characterized by simplicity and plain capitals on columns: DORIC

Greek monster with head and trunk of man, body and legs of horse: CENTAUR

green, grassy: VERDANT

green coating on bronze or copper: PATINA

green crops for animal fodder: SOILAGE

green pigment in plant cells involved in photosynthesis: CHLOROPHYLL

greenish: VIRESCENT

greenish-yellow: LUTEOUS

greeting: SALUTATION

greeting in the Orient consisting of a low bow with the right palm at the forehead: SALAAM

grief or sorrow, to cause: AGGRIEVE

grief or weeping that is false: CROCODILE TEARS

grievance: GRAVAMEN

grievance, complaint: PLAINT

grieve or sympathize with someone: CONDOLE

grim, severe, strict: STARK

grin, laugh: RISUS

grind or scrape harshly, cut, pierce: GRIDE

grinding of teeth, especially during sleep: BRUXISM

gritty like sand: SABULOUS

groggy: PUNCH-DRUNK

grooved, striped: STRIATED

grooved timber, in which wings of a stage set slide: COULISSE

grooved with long, rounded channels: FLUTED

ground, as of a region or territory: TERRAIN

ground plan of a building or other structure: ICHNOGRAPHY

ground that is solid and unbroken: HARDPAN

group arranged by rank: HIERARCHY

group of girls: BEVY

group of persons sharing same interest or interests: COTERIE

group of two or more business concerns for a venture: CONSORTIUM

group or clique: FACTION

group spirit: ESPRIT DE CORPS

group with common interests living together: COMMUNE

grow, increase, expand step by step: ESCALATE

growing, waxing, enlarging: INCRESCENT

growing along the ground, lying down: DECUMBENT

growing old, aging: SENESCENT

growing or coming together: CONCRETION

growing plants in solutions rather than in soil: HYDROPONICS

growing white: ALBESCENT

growing with age: ACCRESCENCE

growth arrested: ATROPHY

growth on a field, as of corn: STAND

growth rings on trees as means of determining approximate dates of past events: DENDROCHRONOLOGY

growth that is gradual: ACCRESCENCE

gruesome, horrible, ghastly: MACABRE

gruff or irritable person, usually elderly: CURMUDGEON

grumble, complain: GROUSE

guarantee: WARRANTY

guarantee, assure: VOUCH

guarantee, promise: STIPULATE

guard, watchman, keeper: WARDER

guard against, hinder or prevent in advance: FORESTALL

guard line, as of men or ships enclosing an area: CORDON

guardian, trustee: FIDUCIARY

guarding and watching carefully: WARY

guess: CONJECTURE

guess correctly, surmise: DIVINE

guessing game, based on pantomimed actions: CHARADES

guide or interpreter for travelers in the Near East: DRAGOMAN

guide who explains to tourists: CICERONE

guidebook: BAEDEKER

guidebook, manual: HANDBOOK

guidebook for travelers: ITINERARY

guiding or animating spirit from within: NUMEN

guiding principle or example; star used as guide in navigation: LODESTAR

guilt feeling: COMPUNCTION

guilt feeling, self-reproach: REMORSE

guilt or wrongdoing implied: INCRIMINATION

Gulf State inhabitant, Spanish American or West Indian of European descent: CREOLE

gullibility: CREDULITY

gully that is deep and dry: ARROYO

gum inflammation: GINGIVITIS

gunfire that sweeps across the length of a trench or a troop of men: ENFILADE

gush forth, squirt: SPURT

gush or spurt of liquid from a narrow orifice: JET

gushing, overdemonstrative: EFFUSIVE

gut reaction, deeply felt: VISCERAL

gutter or channel of a street: KENNEL

gymnast association, athletic club: TURNVEREIN

gymnastics to promote grace and health: CALISTHENICS

gypsy: TZIGANE

H

habit, customary practice: WONT

habits deeply established: SECOND NATURE

habitual or hardened in a particular character or opinion: INVETERATE

habitual or usual way of reacting: DISPOSITION

habituated, accustomed or used to: WONT

habitue or inhabitant: DENIZEN

hack, mangle, cut unskillfully: HAGGLE

hack writers: GRUBSTREET

hades: ACHERON

hag: CRONE

hag, hateful old woman: HARRIDAN

hag who is ugly and malicious: BELDAM

haggard, hollow-eyed, gloomy, desolate, emaciated: GAUNT

hair covering that is matted and woolly: TOMENTOSE

hair covering that is soft like velvet: VELUTINOUS

hair growing to a point on the forehead: WIDOW'S PEAK

hair of a woman: TRESSES

hair remover: DEPILATORY

hair sticking up: COWLICK

hair that is woolly or crispy: ULOTRICHOUS

hairdo in which the hair is bound by a ribbon in back and hangs loosely below it: PONYTAIL

hairdresser (male): COIFFEUR

hairs in the nostrils: VIBRISSA

hairy: HIRSUTE

hairy or fuzzy, in botany: COMATE

half, portion, share: MOIETY

half-breed, mixed origin: HYBRID

half-man, half-horse monster of Greek mythology: CENTAUR

half turn made by horse with rider: CARACOLE

Halifax resident: HALIGONIAN

hallucination-causing or mind-intensifying: PSYCHEDELIC

halo: AUREOLE

halo: GLORIOLE

halo, aura: NIMBUS

halved: DIMIDIATE

ham, spicy and thin: PROSCIUTTO

ham that is smoked or cured: GAMMON

hammered or stamped, as the figure or design on a coin: INCUSE

hand down, transmit, grant in will: BEQUEATH

hand measure, with the thumb and little finger extended: SPAN

hand over or give up something to someone: CONSIGN

handbag, small, used by women: RETICULE

handbook or manual: ENCHIRIDION

handcuff, fetter, shackle: MANACLE

handle, especially of a knife, sickle, sword: HAFT

handle or move skillfully: MANIPULATE

handrail supported by balusters: BALUSTRADE

hands on hips: AKIMBO

handsome man: ADONIS

handwriting art: CHIROGRAPHY

handwriting or spelling that is bad: CACOGRAPHY

handwriting or type that resembles it: SCRIPT

handwritten by the signer: HOLOGRAPH

hang around, waste time, loiter: DAWDLE

hang down or droop loosely: LOP

hang loosely, droop: LOLL

hanger-on: CAMP FOLLOWER

hanging in a loose position: PENSILE

hanging in a swinging position: PENDULOUS

hanging on in spite of difficulties: TENA-
CIOUS

haphazard: RANDOM

happen, take place: SUPERVENE

happen or come into being as a final outcome: EVENTUATE

happening at the same rate: SYNCHRONOUS

happening or event: INCIDENT

happiness, relaxation, well-being: EU-
PHORIA

happiness or well-being as found in the
life of moderation: EUDEMONIA

happy and healthy: EUPEPTIC

happy condition: SEVENTH HEAVEN

happy, optimistic: UPBEAT

harangue, abusive denunciation: DIATRIBE

harangue that is lengthy: SCREED

harass or annoy with taunts or questions:
HECKLE

harass with persistency: IMPORTUNE

harass, worry: CHEVY

hard, cruel, obdurate: FLINTY

hard legendary mineral: ADAMANT

hard or impossible to explain, as of something causing wonder: UNCANNY

hard shelled: TESTACEOUS

hard, stony: PETROUS

hard to believe, amazing: INCREDIBLE

hard to express: JE NE SAIS QUOI

hard to grasp: ELUSIVE

hard to handle because of size, strength or
difficulty: FORMIDABLE

hard to please: FASTIDIOUS

hard to please, excessively critical: HY-
PERCRITICAL

hard to understand: ABSTRUSE

harden, become rigid: OSSIFY

harden, deaden, paralyze with fear: PET-
RIFY

hardened, unfeeling: INDURATE

hardhearted, stubborn, pitiless: OBDURATE

hardness: CALLOSITY

harm the reputation of: DISCREDIT

harmful, injurious: NOCUOUS

harmful, unwholesome: NOXIOUS

harmful, mischievous: MALEFICENT

harmful, noxious: VIRULENT

harmful with intent, spiteful: MALICIOUS

harmless: INNOCUOUS

harmless: INNOXIOUS

harmless substance given to comfort a patient or as a test control: PLACEBO

harmonious or pleasing in sound, smooth:
EUPHONIOUS

harmonious relationship, accord: RAPPORT

harmony, in sympathy: EN RAPPORT

harmony and elegance in arrangement of
parts: CONCINNITY

harmony restored: RECONCILED

harpsichord or small piano: SPINET

harsh: ACERB

harsh, caustic, withering: SCATHING

harsh, discordant sound: JANGLE

harsh, fierce: FELL

harsh, high sound: STRIDENT

harsh, merciless: INCLEMENT

harsh, pitiless: RELENTLESS

harsh, stern: ASTRINGENT

harsh cry or sound like a donkey's:
BRAY

harsh sound: CACOPHANY

harshness: ASPERITY

haste, turmoil, excitement: HECTIC

hasten, hurry: HIE

hastening the tempo, in music: STRIN-
GENDO

hasty, rash, impulsive: IMPETUOUS

hasty or impulsive actions or speech:
HALF-COCKED

hat, round and close-fitting: TOQUE

hat with brim turned up to form three
sides: TRICORN

hat with broad brim turned up at the sides:
SHOVEL HAT

hatchet- or ax-shaped: DOLABRIFORM

hate, deep enmity: RANCOR

hated or dreaded object or person: BÊTE
NOIRE

hateful, repugnant, loathsome, disgusting,
offensive: ODIOUS

hatred: ANIMUS

hatred of men: MISANDRY

haughty, arrogant: CAVALIER

haughty, arrogant, pompous, dogmatic:
PONTIFICAL

haughty person: BRAHMIN

haughty person who sets great store by
social status, wealth, etc.: SNOB

haul, drag, carry: SCHLEP

haunt, place to which one often returns:
PURLIEU

Hawaiian feast with entertainment: LUAU

Hawaiian salutation: ALOHA

hay fever: POLLENOSIS

hay or grain raked into a long ridge or
pile: WINDROW

haystack with the top fashioned to protect
interior from rain: RICK

hazy, misty, vague, unclear: NEBULOUS

head cold: CORYZA

head enlargement caused by excess of fluid in cranium: HYDROCEPHALUS

head of a human joined to animal body: ANDROCEPHALOUS

head of the line: VAN

head that is broad: BRACHYCEPHALIC

head to foot: CAP-A-PIE

headache on one side as in migraine: HEMICRANIA

headband or crown: DIADEM

headdress, crownlike and jeweled, worn by women: TIARA

headdress of Moslems consisting of wound cloth: TURBAN

headland, high land extending into the sea: PROMONTORY

headless: ACEPHALOUS

healing: SANATIVE

healing, curative: THERAPEUTIC

health-conscious person unduly anxious about illness: VALETUDINARIAN

health or spirits: FETTLE

health resort: SANITARIUM

health that is sound and vigorous, robust: HALE

healthful: SALUBRIOUS

healthy and happy: EUPEPTIC

heap, mass or collection of things: CONGERIES

heard by someone but not positively known to be true: HEARSAY

hearing diminution that accompanies aging: PRESBYCUSIS

heart attack: CORONARY THROMBOSIS

heart attack factor, according to experimental evidence: CHOLESTEROL

heart examination that traces changes in electric potential: ELECTROCARDIO-GRAM (EKG)

heart rhythm disturbance: EXTRASYSTOLE

heart-shaped: CORDIFORM

heartbeat abnormality, with double pulse beat: DICROTIC

heartbeats that are weak and irregular: FI-BRILLATION

heartburn: PYROSIS

heart's regular contraction: SYSTOLE

heat and cold sensitivity: THERMES-THESIA

heat causing or producing: PYROGENIC

heat energy employed after nuclear fusion: THERMONUCLEAR

heat measurement: CALORIMETRY

heat or light ray bent in passage from one medium to another: REFRACTION

heat or warmth producing, like a mustard plaster: CALEFACIENT

heat producing: CALORIFIC

heat-producing medical treatment: DIA-THERMY

heat that is oppressive or overpowering: SWELTERING

heavenly, celestial: SUPERNAL

heavens, sky: FIRMAMENT

heavy, clumsy, awkward in appearance or movement: LUMBERING

heavy shoe: BROGAN

hedge or wall set low in a ditch so as not to obstruct the view: HA-HA

heedless, inattentive: UNAWARE

heedlessness, foolhardiness: TEMERITY

heel-stamping Spanish dance, flamen-colike: ZAPATEADO

height, instrument for measuring: ALTIM-ETER

height of power, exuberance: HEYDAY

held notes, prolonged tempo, in music: SOSTENUTO

held or sustained, in music: TENUTO

helicopter landing place: HELIPORT

hell: INFERNO

hell: NETHER WORLD

helmet worn as protection against the sun: TOPEE

help: ABET

help: ADMINICLE

helpful person or rescuer: SAMARITAN

helping to make possible: CONDUCIVE

helpless, ineffective: IMPOTENT

helplessness, ineffectiveness: IMPOTENCE

hen that has been spayed: POULARD

hence: ERGO

herald or announcement of the coming of something or someone: HARBINGER

heraldic blue banner with three fleurs-de-lis of gold: ORIFLAMME

heraldic vertical band through the middle of the shield: PALE

heraldic white or silver: ARGENT

heraldry device placed above the shield in a coat of arms: CREST

heraldry position of a beast reared on its hind legs: RAMPANT

heraldry term for animal walking with a forepaw raised: PASSANT

heraldry term for a square table set diagonally, displaying arms of a deceased person: HATCHMENT

heraldry term for design with many small figures: SEMÉ

heraldry term for division of the quarter usually on the dexter side: CANTON

heraldry term for left: SINISTER

heraldry term for sitting with the forelimbs upright: SEJANT

heraldry term for two coats of arms placed side by side on an escutcheon: IMPALE

heraldry term for vertical bands of alternating colors: PALY

here and there in a book: PASSIM

heredity study to improve quality of humans: EUGENICS

hermaphroditic: ANDROGYNOUS

hermit: ANCHORITE

hero as a rogue in fiction: PICARESQUE

hesitancy or uneasiness regarding a question of moral right: SCRUPLE

hesitate, take exception, object: DEMUR

hesitate in speaking: HAW or HEM AND HAW

hesitating: IRRESOLUTE

hidden: ABSTRUSE

hidden, profound: RECONDITE

hidden, unclear, faint: OBSCURE

hidden goods or articles: CACHE

hidden or secret: ARCANE

hidden or unknown difficulty: JOKER

hidden tendency: UNDERCURRENT

hide or obscure: CAMOUFLAGE

hideous, enormous: MONSTROUS

hideous or cruel being: OGRE

hiding of one's real activities or designs: COVER-UP

hiding place for goods or articles: CACHE

hieroglyphics key: ROSETTA STONE

high, harsh sound: STRIDENT

high and mighty: HAUGHTY

high birth or rank: AUGUST

high fashion: HAUT COUTURE

high level land: PLATEAU

high on a hill or mountain, said of a house or stronghold: AERIE

high or culminating point: SOLSTICE

high priest, prelate: HIERARCH

high regard, esteem: REPUTE

high society: HAUT MONDE

high spirits or elated: COCK-A-HOOP

high voice above natural register: FALSETTO

higher price on a stock transaction than the preceding transaction price: UP TICK, PLUS-TICK

highest bid to buy and lowest offer to sell a given stock at a given time: QUOTATION

highest grade, usually said of diamonds and pearls: FIRST WATER

highest honors attending graduation: SUMMA CUM LAUDE

highest in kind, quality, or degree: SUPERLATIVE

highest in rank: PARAMOUNT

highest or culminating point: ZENITH

highest point: APOGEE

highest point: PINNACLE

highest point, topmost stone: CAPSTONE

highest point of anything, zenith: MERIDIAN

highest priced or best quality: GILT-EDGED

high-minded, great of soul, generous: MAGNANIMOUS

high-pressure peddling by phone of stocks of dubious value: BOILER ROOM

high-wire acrobat: AERIALIST

high-wire walker: FUNAMBULIST

highway interchange with overpass and curved ramps: CLOVERLEAF

hill or small round mound: KNOLL

hilly, moundy: TUMULOSE

hinder, block or guard against in advance: FORESTALL

hinder, impede, crowd with useless additions: ENCUMBER

hinder, interfere with the movements of, impede: HAMPER

hinder, put obstacles in the way of, retard: IMPEDE

hinder, slow, delay: RETARD

hinder or obstruct: CRIMP

hindrance, impediment: TRAMMEL

Hindu ascetic philosophy that involves deep meditation: YOGA

Hindu mythology triad of Brahma, Vishnu and Siva: TRIMURTI

Hindu system of exercises practiced in the Yoga discipline: YOGA

Hindu women's garment consisting of a long piece of fabric artfully wound about the body: SARI

hint, imply: INTIMATE

hint, notion, slight suggestion, vague idea: INKLING

hint, sly intimation: INSINUATION

hint, suggestion, insinuation, usually derogatory: INNUENDO

hint at, signify: IMPLY

hired applauders: CLAQUE

hissing sound: SIBILANT
history study based on excavations: ARCHEOLOGY
hit and rebound: CAROM
hit repeatedly: PELT
hit repeatedly with the fists: PUMMEL
hit sweepingly along the side: SIDESWIPE
hives, nettle rash: URTICARIA
hoarding riches: AVARICE
hoax: SPOOF
hobos' section of a city: SKID ROW
hockey enclosure to seat players removed as a penalty: PENALTY BOX
hockey foul of touching opponent's body with stick held in both hands: CROSS-CHECK
hockey term for illegal entry of opponent's zone ahead of the puck: OFFSIDE
hockey term for moving the puck with light taps of the stick: DRIBBLE
hockey term for starting play by dropping the puck between the sticks of two opposing players: FACE OFF
hocus-pocus, sleight of hand, trickery: LEGERDEMAIN
hodgepodge, confusion: KATZENJAMMER
hodgepodge, hash: GALLIMAUFRY
hodgepodge, medley: MÉLANGE
hoggish, piggish, swinish: PORCINE
hold back from something: ABSTAIN
hold forth, discuss: DESCANT
hold someone by binding the arms: PINION
holding, as of land or a term of office: TENURE
holding of an office: INCUMBENCY
holding together: COHERENT
hole drilled through the ocean floor: MOHOLE
hole in a paved road: POTHOLE
holiday spent in activity similar to one's regular work: BUSMAN'S HOLIDAY
holiness or righteousness pretended: SANCTIMONIOUS
hollow in a wall, as for a bust, statue or the like: NICHE
holy men forming the government: HAGIARCHY or HAGIOCRACY
holy oil: CHRISM
holy water basin: STOUP
homage, respect, reverence: OBEISANCE
home: ABODE
home, house or dwelling: DOMICILE
homeless, roaming: NOMADIC
homeless, wandering youngster: GAMIN

homeless person forced by a war, to live in a foreign country: DISPLACED PERSON
homeless wanderer: WAIF
homeless rover, vagabond: VAGRANT
homesickness that is severe: NOSTALGIA
homosexual male: URANIST, URNING
homosexual female: LESBIAN
homosexuality, especially among males: URANISM
honest, conscientious: SCRUPULOUS
honest, morally proper: UPRIGHT
honest, straightforward dealing: PLAIN-DEALING
honest, upright: INCORRUPT
honesty: VERACITY
honesty, probity: INTEGRITY
honeylike, semifluid, sticky: VISCOUS
honor with festivities: FETE
honorable, respectable; in good usage: REPUTABLE
honored for excellence in one's achievements: LAUREATE
honors awarded according to property owned, as a form of government: TIMOCRACY
honors included, as at graduation: CUM LAUDE
hood and mask worn at masquerades: DOMINO
hooded: COWLED
hooded cloak: BURNOOSE
hoof, nail, claw: UNGUIS
hook at the end of the pole for landing large fish: GAFF
hooked or curved: AQUILINE
hooklike: UNCIFORM
hoot, wail, howl: ULULATE
hope with little or no expectation of getting what is desired: FORLORN HOPE
hopeless, incapable of being reformed: INCORRIGIBLE
hopeless plight: CHANCERY
hopelessness, dejection of spirits: DESPONDENCY
hormone of male sex: ANDROSTERONE
horn overflowing with fruit, vegetables, grain: CORNUCOPIA
horn that is low-pitched, especially one used on ships to signal alarms: KLAXON
horn-bereft animal: POLLARD
hornlike or horny: CORNEOUS
horrible fancy: CHIMERA
horrified: AGHAST

horse breed notable for its trotters and pacers: STANDARDBRED

horse command word meaning to turn left: HAW

horse of light tan with ivory-colored mane and tail: PALOMINO

horse of medium size used for ordinary driving or riding: HACKNEY

horse race in which any entry is subject to purchase at a previously set price: CLAIMING RACE

horse race in which the competitors are selected far in advance: FUTURITY

horse race with only one starter: WALK-OVER

horse racing information sheet: DOPE SHEET

horse racing term for designated weight carried by a horse in a handicap race: IMPOST

horse that has been castrated: GELDING

horse that is male and uncastrated: STALLION

horse that races well on a muddy track: MUDDER

horse whose coloring is permeated whth gray or white: ROAN

horse-drawn two-wheeled vehicle for one person: SULKY

horselike mythical animal with one horn: UNICORN

horse's lifting of a forefoot and the opposite hind foot without moving forward or backward: PIAFFER

horses or horsemanship: EQUESTRIAN

horses or oxen in a matched pair: SPAN

horses used for heavy work: PERCHERONS

horse-training term for a gait in which a horse moves partly sidewise: VOLT

hospital department in which outpatients are treated: POLICLINIC

hospital or ship for the treatment of contagious diseases: LAZARETTO

hostile, antagonistic: INIMICAL

hostile, inharmonious, incongruous: DISSONANT

hostile, resisting, antagonistic: REPUGNANT

hostile behavior: BELLICOSITY

hostile feeling: ANIMUS

hot, scorched: TORRID

hot days of July and August: DOG DAYS

hotel designed to accommodate motorists: MOTEL

hotel system in which the price includes room, service and meals: AMERICAN PLAN

hotel system of charging for room and service without meals: EUROPEAN PLAN

hourly: HORAL

house with a view: BELVEDERE

house with each floor half a story above or below the adjacent one: SPLIT-LEVEL

household: MÉNAGE

household gods: LARES AND PENATES

howl, hoot, wail: ULULATE

hubbub, turmoil: HURLY-BURLY

huge: TITANIC

huge or powerful thing or creature: LEVIATHAN

human attributes ascribed to inanimate things: PATHETIC FALLACY

human attributes ascribed to inanimate things in figurative speech: PERSONIFICATION

human embodiment: INCARNATION

human emotions or passions attributed to gods or objects: ANTHROPOPATHY

human form or characteristics ascribed to something not human: ANTHROPOMORPHISM

human improvement through control of environment: EUTHENICS

human improvement through control of factors that affect heredity: EUGENICS

human knowledge as a subject of study, cognition: EPISTEMOLOGY

human shaped: ANDROID

humanly made object or art: ARTIFACT

humble and earnest entreating: SUPPLIANT

humiliate: ABASE

humorous: WAGGISH

humpback, curvature of the spine: KYPHOSIS

hundredfold: CENTUPLE

hunger that is continuous: BULIMIA

hungry, greedy: ESURIENT

hungry in a wild or greedy way: RAVENOUS

hunt or fish illegally: POACH

hunted creature: QUARRY

hurl from a height: PRECIPITATE

hurried and confused: HELTER-SKELTER

hurry: POSTHASTE

hurry, hasten: HIE

hurry off, run: SCAMPER

hurtful: DELETERIOUS

hurtful to the feelings in a sharp way: POIGNANT

hurtle through air: CATAPULT

husband of a reigning female sovereign: PRINCE CONSORT

husband of an unfaithful wife: CUCKOLD

husband or wife: CONSORT

husband who murders his wife: UXORICIDE

husbandly excessive fondness for or submissiveness to wife: UXORIOUS

husk, shell or pod: SHUCK

hussy: JADE

hybrid offspring of a stallion and a female ass: HINNY

hymn for the dead: REQUIEM

hymn or verse in praise of God: DOXOLOGY

hyprocrisy: PHARISAISM

hypocrisy: SANCTIMONY

hypocrite: AMBIDEXTER

hypocrite: TARTUFFE

hypocrite: WHITED SEPULCHER

hypocrite who is fawning and scheming: URIAH HEEP

hypocritical, insincere: PECKSNIFFIAN

hypocritical, pretentious or ostentatious ceremony: MUMMERY

hypocritical behavior: DISSEMBLANCE

hypocritical pious expressions: CANT

hypothetical, academic, debatable: MOOT

hysterical outburst or rage: CONNIPTION

I

I am at fault: MEA CULPA

I came, I saw, I conquered: VENI, VIDI, VICI

ice game, in which heavy stones are slid toward a goal: CURLING

iced or chilled beverages as a dessert: FRAPPÉ

icy, frozen: GELID

increase power, rank or wealth: AGGRANDIZE

increasing the number of shares of a company by dividing the outstanding shares: SPLIT

idea conference: BRAINSTORMING

idealize, glorify: TRANSFIGURE

identification card: ID CARD

identifying oneself with other persons or objects: INTROJECTION

idiocy: AMENTIA

idiom, language, speaking style: PARLANCE

idiot: AMENT

idiotic, inane, stupid: FATUOUS

idle, dormant: FALLOW

idle, lazy: OTIOSE

idle, unoccupied: VACUOUS

idle chatter; also a discussion: PALAVER

idle talk: PRATE

idle tramp who is subject to arrest: VAGRANT

idler, do-nothing: FAINEANT

idyllic, serene, calm: HALCYON

if anything can go wrong, it will: MURPHY'S LAW

if you please; please: S'IL VOUS PLAÎT

ignorant: BENIGHTED

ignoring the complexity of problems, oversimplifying them: SIMPLISTIC

ignorance: NESCIENCE

ignorance pretended to expose errors of opponent's argument: SOCRATIC IRONY

ill will, spitefulness: RANCOR

ill temper, spitefulness, peevishness: SPLEEN

ill-assorted, incongruous: DISSOCIABLE

ill-disposed, wishing evil toward others: MALEVOLENT

illegal bargain made in a lawsuit to get share of matter sued for: CHAMPERTY

illegal commerce in goods that may not be exported or imported: CONTRABAND

illegal influencing of a judge or jury: EMBRACERY

illegitimate, counterfeit: SPURIOUS

ill-humored, cross, gloomy: SULKY

ill-humored, sullen, gloomy: MOROSE

illiterate, uneducated: UNLETTERED

illiterate who is unable to learn to read: FUNCTIONAL ILLITERATE

ill-natured or rude person: CHURL

illness, disorder: DISTEMPER

illness or discontent, a chronic feeling of either: DYSPHORIA

illness or disorder of mind or body: DISTEMPER

illness that is slight: INDISPOSITION

illogical or faulty reasoning: PARALOGISM

ill-starred: STAR-CROSSED

ill-tempered or peevish: BILIOUS

illusion of reality, in art or decoration: TROMPE L'OEIL

illusion that a new experience has happened before: DÉJÀ VU

illustrate a book already in print with illustrations from another book: GRANGERIZE

illustrative: EXEMPLARY

illustrious, shining: SPLENDENT

image: EIDOLON

image in the mind, specter: PHANTASM

image, likeness, picture, usually an object of veneration: ICON

image, likeness, representation, usually crudely done of a disliked person: EFFIGY

images in works of art studied to determine thematic significance of the subject: ICONOGRAPHY

imaginable, possible, secular: EARTHLY

imaginary, assumed, supposed: HYPOTHETICAL

imaginary, flimsy: INSUBSTANTIAL

imaginary, unrealistic: VISIONARY

imaginary grotesque monster: CHIMERA

imaginary or visionary semblance: SIMULACRUM

imaginative resources: INGENUITY

imagined symptoms as part of anxiety about one's health: HYPOCHONDRIA

imitate, look or act like someone or something: SIMULATE

imitate in attempt to equal or surpass: EMULATE

imitation, especially in literature and art: MIMESIS

imitation by a word of some sound: ECHOIC

imitation of a literary or musical work, meant humorously: PARODY

imitation marble: SCAGLIOLA

imitation or burlesque that is farcical: TRAVESTY

imitation or reproduction of the original: ECTYPE

immature: CALLOW

immature, callow but opinionated: SOPHOMORIC

immature, inexperienced: UNFLEDGED

immediate: INSTANTANEOUS

immediately: TOUT DE SUITE

immediately, at once: INSTANTER

immediately following this: HEREUPON

immoral, debauched: DISSOLUTE

immoral man, roué: RAKE

immortality: ATHANASIA

immovable: ADAMANT

immune, resistant: INSUSCEPTIBLE

immune to injury, unconquerable: INVULNERABLE

immunity to disease, as a study: IMMUNOLOGY

immunize by an injection: INOCULATE

impair, spoil: VITIATE

impair secretly, weaken by degrees: UNDERMINE

impart gradually: INSTILL

impartial, fair: UNBIASED

impartial, fair, reasonable: EQUITABLE

impartial, unbiased: DISINTERESTED

impartial, objective: DISPASSIONATE

impartiality, justness, fairness: EQUITY

impassioned: FERVID

impassive, unfeeling: STOLID

impassive, unaffected by pain or pleasure: STOICAL

impede, block, hinder, stop: OBSTRUCT

impede, disconcert, complicate: EMBARRASS

impede, hinder, obstruct, crowd with useless additions: ENCUMBER

impede, restrain, interfere with the movements of: HAMPER

impediment, hindrance: TRAMMEL

impending, threatening: IMMINENT

imperious, dictatorial: PEREMPTORY

impetuous: BRASH

impetuous, ardent, violent: VEHEMENT

impetus of a body in motion: MOMENTUM

implant ideas or opinions: INSEMINATE

implicate: INVOLVE

implication of a word, an expression or a text: CONNOTATION

implied, not directly stated: TACIT

imply, hint: INTIMATE

imply or give the appearance of fact, often falsely: PURPORT

important: CONSEQUENTIAL

important, essential: PIVOTAL

important, highly regarded: PRESTIGIOUS

important, outstanding feature: HIGHLIGHT

important person: HIGH MUCK-A-MUCK

important person in a group: KINGPIN

impose, introduce or insert fraudulently: FOIST

imposing, awesome: AUGUST

imposing, pretentiously grand: GRANDIOSE

impossible to extricate oneself from, impossible to disentangle or undo: INEXTRICABLE

impress on the mind, instill: INCULCATE

impressive, grand, stately: IMPOSING

imprison: INCARCERATE

imprison, confine, surround enclose within walls: IMMURE

imprisonment, forced confinement: DURANCE

improbable person or event introduced to untangle a story plot: DEUS EX MACHINA

improper: UNSEEMLY

improper, unseemly: UNTOWARD

improve: AMELIORATE

improvements to property: CAPITAL EXPENDITURE

improvise: AD LIB

improvised: EXTEMPORANEOUS

improvised musical passage: CADENZA

improvised to fill a need temporarily: STOPGAP

imprudent: IMPOLITIC

imprudent, unwise: INDISCREET

impudence: CHUTZPAH

impudence, boldness, audacity: EFFRONTERY

impudent young woman: BAGGAGE

impudently or ostentatiously display: FLAUNT

impulse that is creative: AFFLATUS

impulsive, hasty, rash: IMPETUOUS

impulsive or hasty action or speech: HALF-COCKED

impulsive without forethought: SPONTANEOUS

impure, to make: ADULTERATE

in name alone, not in fact: NOMINAL

in on a secret: PRIVY

in opposition to: ATHWART

in place of: LIEU

in the matter of, concerning: IN RE

in the morning, early: MATUTINAL

in wine there is truth: IN VINO VERITAS

inability to understand or use objects: APRAXIA

inactive, indolent, listless: SUPINE

inactive, settled, seated a great part of the time: SEDENTARY

inactive sluggish, dull: TORPID

inactive, still, placid: QUIESCENT

inactive for a period, especially winter: HIBERNATING

inadequate, disproportionate: INCOMMENSURATE

inadequate, not quite enough: SCANT

inadvertent or random action, accidental homicide: CHANCE-MEDLEY

inane or idle thing: VACUITY

inanimate objects possess souls, as a belief: ANIMISM

inappropriate, at odds with, unsuitable: INCONGRUOUS

inappropriate, out of place: MALAPROPOS

inattentive, heedless: UNAWARE

inborn: INHERENT

inborn: INNATE

incantation used to conjure an evil spirit: INVOCATION

incarnation of a quality or idea: AVATAR

incapable of being passed through: IMPERVIOUS

incapable of being transferred or removed: INALIENABLE

incautious, thriftless, rash: IMPROVIDENT

incense ingredient: TACAMAHAC

incentive, motivating force: IMPETUS

incentive, stimulus: FILLIP

incident or controversy attracting wide attention: CAUSE CÉLÈBRE

incidental result, by-product, new application: SPIN-OFF

incised carving: INTAGLIO

incite, foment, provoke, spur on, goad to some drastic action: INSTIGATE

incite, instigate, stir up: FOMENT

inclination, tendency, bent: PROPENSITY

inclination or slope of countryside: VERSANT

inclination or tendency: BENT

incline downward, be of greater weights: PREPONDERATE

incline linking different levels: RAMP

include or embrace: COMPRISE

include or take in as a part of the whole: INCORPORATE

incoherent, rapid talk: GIBBERISH

incoherent talk: GABBLE

income in dollars of individuals adjusted to take account of inflation: REAL INCOME

incompetence tends to be the level achieved by the promotion of employes: PETER PRINCIPLE

incompetent, clumsy, awkward: INEPT

incomplete, broken: FRAGMENTARY

incomprehensible, dense: IMPENETRABLE

incongruity, lack of harmony: DISSONANCE

incongruous, ill-assorted: DISSOCIABLE

inconsistency, contradiction: DISCREPANCY

inconsistent or opposed, antagonistic: REPUGNANT

inconstant, changeable: FICKLE

inconvenience, bother, trouble: DISCOMMODE

incorporate, collect, make part of a whole: EMBODY

incorrect though popular idea of the origin of a word: FOLK ETYMOLOGY

increase, addition, something added or gained: INCREMENT

increase, grow, expand step by step: ESCALATE

increase unduly, puff up, enlarge excessively: INFLATE

increasing, enlarging, growing: INCRESCENT

incriminate: INCULPATE

incriminating position: RED-HANDED

indecency or pornography in art or literature: COPROLOGY

indecent: UNSEEMLY

indecent, bold, self-assertive: IMMODEST

indecent, risqué: SCABROUS

indecisive: VACILLATING

indefinable something: JE NE SAIS QUOI

indefinite, misty, foggy: NUBILOUS

indefinite or vague: INTANGIBLE

indention of all lines of a paragraph except the first, as in the format of this entry: HANGING INDENTION

independent: AUTONOMOUS

independent, needing no help: SELF-SUFFICIENT

independent, particularly in politics: MUGWUMP

independent and supreme authority: SOVEREIGN

independent in resources: SUBSTANTIVE

independent of an original or main body or group: SPLINTER

independent of outside control: AUTONOMOUS

index to words in a particular book: CONCORDANCE

Indiana resident: INDIANIAN, HOOSIER

indicate, point out, signify: DENOTE

indifference, dullness, stagnation, weakness, fatigue, spiritlessness: LANGUOR

indifference to pleasure or pain: STOICAL

indifferent: APATHETIC

indifferent, apathetic: PHLEGMATIC

indifferent, apathetic, lackadaisical: LISTLESS

indifferent, uncaring: POCOCURANTE

indifferent in a casual way, cool: NONCHALANT

indigenous: ABORIGINAL

indigenous, native: ENCHORIAL

indignity: AFFRONT

indirect, not obvious: SUBTLE

indirect, slanted: OBLIQUE

indirect and unexpected stroke: BRICOLE

indirect mention: ALLUSION

indirect method of proceeding: AMBAGE

indirect or roundabout: CIRCUITOUS

indirect words used to say something: PERIPHRASTIC

indiscretions of youth: WILD OATS

indiscriminate, especially sexually: PROMISCUOUS

indispensable, without which not (nothing): SINE QUA NON

indispensable, essential, whole: INTEGRAL

indispensable, required: REQUISITE

indisputable: APODICTIC

indisputable, unquestionable: INCONTESTABLE

individuals or items chosen in the expectation they will be representative of a whole group: RANDOM SAMPLE

indoctrination that is coercive: BRAINWASHING

indolent, irresponsible individual: LOTUS-EATER

indolent, listless, inactive: SUPINE

induce or bribe one to commit perjury: SUBORN

indulgence that is excessive: DISSIPATION

industrial worker: BLUE COLLAR

indwelling: IMMANENCE

inebriate: INTOXICATE

ineffective, lazy, useless: FAINEANT

ineffectual, useless: OTIOSE

ineffectual person: WEAK SISTER

inequality, unlikeness: DISPARITY

inertness and disorder as an irreversible tendency of a system: ENTROPY

inevitable, unavoidable: INELUCTABLE

inevitability: FATALISM

inexperienced: CALLOW

inexperienced: VERDANT

infallible authority, wise person: ORACLE

infamy, disgrace: OBLOQUY

infantile concept of a parent or loved one persisting in the adult: IMAGO

infer from incomplete evidence: CONJECTURE

inference or deduction: ILLATION

inference resulting from concealment or misrepresentation of facts: SUBREPTION

inferior, paltry, pitiable: SORRY

inferior in any way: SUBORDINATE

inferior in rank: SUBALTERN

inferior quality: SHODDY

inferior substitute: ERSATZ

inferior to an appalling degree: EXECRA-BLE

infernal, dark, gloomy: STYGIAN

infinitive in which an adverb intervenes between the "to" and the verb: SPLIT INFINITIVE

inflamed, sore: IRRITATED

inflated, bombastic, as a style of speech: TURGID

inflated, overloaded: PLETHORIC

inflated, pompous: TUMID

inflated, pretentious: OVERBLOWN

inflation designed by government to bring back a former price structure: RE-FLATION

inflection of words: ACCIDENCE

inflexible, rigid: HARD-SHELL

inflict or enforce in an arbitrary fashion: IMPOSE

inform: APPRISE

informal noisy gathering: CLAMBAKE

informal word or phrase: COLLOQUIALISM

informed, acquainted with facts: AU FAIT

informed on current things: AU COURANT

informer for the police: STOOL PIGEON

ingenious, cunning, skillful: DAEDAL

ingenious, refined: SUBTLE

inhabitant or habitue: DENIZEN

inharmonious, incongruous, hostile: DIS-SONANT

inharmonious: DISSONANCE

inherent: INNATE

inherent, essential: INTRINSIC

inhuman, cruel, vicious: FELL

initial, beginning: INCEPTIVE

initial letter or sound dropped in the development of a word: APHERESIS

initial letter or sound the same in a series of words: ALLITERATION

initial letters of a series of words combined to form a word: ACRONYM

initial letters of lines forming a word: ACROSTIC

initiate someone by subjecting him to pranks and humiliating horseplay: HAZE

inject or add certain elements: INCORPO-RATE

injection under the skin: HYPODERMIC

injured or victimized by one's plans to injure another: HOIST BY ONE'S OWN PETARD

injured feeling, resentment: UMBRAGE

injurious: DELETERIOUS

injurious, deadly, malicious: PERNICIOUS

injurious, harmful: NOCUOUS

injurious, unwholesome: NOXIOUS

injury, damage: LESION

injury, harmful action, ill service: DISSER-VICE

injury or emotional shock that is severe: TRAUMA

ink blot test used to analyze personality: RORSCHACH TEST

inland region, remote area, back country: HINTERLAND

inlet of sea between steep cliffs: FIORD

inlet of the sea or mouth of a river where tide and current meet: ESTUARY

inmost parts as in a house of worship: PENETRALIA

inn or hostelry: CARAVANSARY

innards, internal organs such as stomach, heart, lungs: VISCERA

inner force that animates or guides: NUMEN

innkeeper: BONIFACE

innocence, peace and simplicity portrayed as associated with rural life: PASTO-RAL

innocence-proving: EXCULPATORY

innocent young woman: INGÉNUE

innumerable, vast indefinite number: MYRIAD

insanity: ALIENATION

insatiable, immoderate, greedy: VORA-CIOUS

inscribe or adorn with names or symbols: BLAZON

inscription on a tomb or monument: EPI-GRAPH

inscriptions, scribblings or drawings on walls: GRAFFITI

insect study: ENTOMOLOGY

insensible, blunt, dull: OBTUSE

insert, as an additional day in the calendar: INTERCALATE

insert, throw in between other things, introduce abruptly: INTERJECT

insert an organ within the body: IMPLANT

insert unacknowledged addition in order to falsify a text: INTERPOLATE

insertion, as in a wooden joint, to hide a bad fitting or to replace a broken piece: DUTCHMAN

insertion of a sound or letter into a word: EPENTHESIS

insertion of a word between the parts of a compound word: TMESIS

insertion of one thing into another: IN-
TROMISSION
insertion sign in typewritten or printed
matter (^): CARET
inside exclusive group: CLIQUE
inside of a curved surface: CONCAVITY
inside talk of a special group: CANT
insider, one in the know: COGNOSCENTE
insignia that is V shaped: CHEVRON
insignificant, trifling, tiny: MINUTE
insignificant, unimportant, trifling: PETTY
insignificant amount: IOTA
insignificant or trifling size or amount:
NEGLIGIBLE
insincere, ambiguous: LEFT-HANDED
insincere, crafty: DISINGENUOUS
insincere, hypocritical: PECKSNIFFIAN
insincere or excessive: FULSOME
insincere religious or moralistic talk: CANT
insincere sympathy: BATHOS
insinuation, hint, suggestion, usually derogatory: INNUENDO
insipid, dry, lacking interest, naive, barren: JEJUNE
insipid, flat, dull, lifeless: VAPID
insolent: BRASSY
insolence, rudeness: IMPERTINENCE
insolent or rebellious: CONTUMACIOUS
insolent treatment: AFFRONT
inspection of one or a few typical things
out of many, to insure quality: SPOT
CHECK
inspire, activate, lead, as a group: SPARK-
PLUG
inspire with ideas: IMBUE
install, as an official: INAUGURATE
install or place in office formally: INVEST
installment ceremony: INVESTITURE
instantly: IN A TRICE
instigate, incite, stir up: FOMENT
instigate an evil act: SUBORN
instill, impress on the mind: INCULCATE
institute legal proceedings: PROSECUTE
instruct in doctrines, principles or systems
of belief: INDOCTRINATE
instructional, boringly pedagogical: DI-
DACTIC
instrument similar to the xylophone:
MARIMBA
instrument that is long and tubular with a
curving stem: BASSOON
instrument to measure diameter of thickness: CALIPERS
insubstantial, nonmaterial, spiritual: IN-
CORPOREAL

insult, affront: INDIGNITY
insult openly: AFFRONT
insulting: ABUSIVE
insulting, disrespectful: INSOLENT
insulting rudeness in speech: CONTUMELY
insurance risk and premium calculator:
ACTUARY
insurrection: INSURGENCE
intact: INVIOLATE
intangible: IMPALPABLE
integrity, honesty: PROBITY
integrity lack, dishonesty: IMPROBITY
intellect, brains: GRAY MATTER
intellectual activity: NOETIC
intellectual quickness, keenness: ACUMEN
intellectual perception of something unknowable through the senses: NOU-
MENON
intemperance: DISSIPATION
intensify: AGGRANDIZE
intensify or elevate: HEIGHTEN
inter, bury: INHUME
interbreeding of races: MISCEGENATION
interest not compounded but computed on
the original principal alone: SIMPLE
INTEREST
interesting and agreeable: SAPID
intermediate point between two extremes,
sometimes an average: MEAN
interminable and difficult: SISYPHEAN
internal organs, innards, such as stomach,
heart, lungs: VISCERA
internal rhyme, in which a word within a
line of verse rhymes with the final
word of the line: LEONINE RHYME
internal-examining machine: FLUORO-
SCOPE
International Criminal Police Organization: INTERPOL
interpret or explain: EXPLICATE
interpretation, especially of the Bible:
HERMENEUTICS
interpretation of a word, passage or work:
EXEGESIS
interpretation of words, spiritual and mystical: ANAGOGE
interpretation or performance of a text,
role, etc.: RENDITION
interpreter or guide for travelers in the
Near East: DRAGOMAN
interrupted, broken: DISCONTINUOUS
interruption, as of electric service: OUT-
AGE
interruption or break in continuity: IN-
TERREGNUM

interruptions, insertions, additions in a discourse, process or series: INTERPOLATIONS

intersect, cross in form of an x: DECUSSATE

intersecting, cutting: SECANT

intertwining, entanglement, complication: INVOLUTION

interval between events or activities, recess: INTERMISSION

intervene in behalf of another or to mediate: INTERCEDE

interweave: PLEACH

intestinal: ENTERIC

intestinal disease usually caused by eating undercooked pork: TRICHINOSIS

intestinal inflammation: COLITIS

intestinal waves of contraction that push the contents outward: PERISTALSIS

intimate friend: ALTER EGO

intimate relation: A DEUX

intimately: CHEEK BY JOWL

intricate: INVOLVED

intricate, skillful, cunning, ingenious: DAEDAL

intriguers, cabal: JUNTA

intriguing secret group: CABAL

introduce, impose, insert fraudulently: FOIST

introduce abruptly, throw in between other things: INTERJECT

introduce additions, comments, interruptions into a discourse or process: INTERPOLATE

introduce ideas or opinions into the mind of: INOCULATE

introduce or bring in something new: INNOVATE

introduce some new element into: INJECT

introduce subtly and gradually: INSINUATE

introduction, as to a field of study: ISAGOGE

introduction or preface: PREAMBLE

introduction to a book or thesis: PREFACE

introduction to an art or science: PROPAEDEUTIC

introductory remark, foreword: PROLEGOMENON

introductory statement, preface: PROEM

intrude, meddle in the affairs of others: INTERLOPE

intrude gradually, make inroads, trespass, advance beyond proper limit: ENCROACH

intrude oneself or one's opinion on someone else: OBTRUDE

intuitive, emotional: VISCERAL

intuitive knowledge, direct awareness: IMMEDIACY

invalid: VALETUDINARIAN

invalidate, debase, corrupt: VITIATE

invasion, raid: INCURSION

invasion that is sudden: IRRUPTION

invent, produce, perform without previous thought or preparation: IMPROVISE

invent a word: MINT

invent details to compensate for loss of memory: CONFABULATE

invent or make up as a story or a lie: FABRICATE

invented, false, not real: FICTITIOUS

inventive, clever, skillful: INGENIOUS

inventive, fruitful, productive: PREGNANT

inversion of the structure of the second of two parallel clauses: CHIASMUS

inverted order of words: ANASTROPHE

inverted ''v'' placed under a line to indicate insertion: CARET

investigate or search for information: DELVE

investigation, officially done, of the beliefs and activities of individuals: INQUISITION

investigation and discovery as a way of learning: HEURISTICS

invigorate, cheer up, pep up, stimulate: EXHILARATE

inviolable, as an oath: STYGIAN

inviting attack, vulnerable: PREGNABLE

involve, entangle, intertwine: IMPLICATE

involve in trouble: EMBROIL

involve necessarily or naturally: IMPLY

iota: TITTLE

involved, complicated, puzzling: INTRICATE

involved, foolishly wasteful procedure: RIGMAROLE

invulnerable, unfeeling: IMPASSIBLE

inward violent collapse: IMPLOSION

iridescence: OPALESCENCE

iridescence, especially on pottery: REFLET

iridescent: VERSICOLOR

iridescent, pearl-like: NACREOUS

iridescent, resembling a peacock's tail: PAVONINE

Irish pronunciation: BROGUE

iron for pressing clothes that is pointed at both ends: SADIRON

irony: ANTIPHRASIS

irregular: ANOMALOUS
irregular, eccentric, nonconforming: ERRATIC
irregular, occasional: SPORADIC
irregularity: ABNORMALITY
irrelevance: IMPERTINENCE
irrelevant: INAPPOSITE
irrelevant remark: NON SEQUITUR
irreligious, unbelieving: HEATHEN
irresistibly attractive: BEWITCHING
irresponsible, reckless, wild: HARUM-SCARUM
irreverent: IMPIOUS
irreverent remarks about God or sacred things: BLASPHEMY
irritability or excitability in any part of the body to an abnormal degree: ERETHISM
irritable, quick-tempered: IRASCIBLE
irritable, unruly, cranky, rebellious: FRACTIOUS
irritable or gruff person, usually elderly: CURMUDGEON
irritableness, peevishness: PETULANCE
irritate: ACERBATE
irritate, embitter: RANKLE
irritate or upset: RUFFLE
irritated or angry state: SNIT
irritating, annoying: VEXATIOUS
is it not so? (German): NICHT WAHR?

islamic prophet or messiah expected before the end of the world: MAHDI
island or reef especially one of coral, low and beside a coast: KEY
islands, chain of: ARCHIPELAGO
Isle of Man native: MANXMAN
isn't it so?: N'EST-CE PAS?
isolate: INSULATE
isolate a thought: PRESCIND
isolated, detached: INSULAR
isolated, private room: SANCTUM
isolated, separated: SPORADIC
Israeli and Rumanian folk dance in which dancers lock arms in a circle: HORA
Israeli collective farm or settlement: KIBBUTZ
Israeli Constituent Assembly: KNESSET
Israeli native: SABRA
Italian dessert containing layers of different ice creams: SPUMONI
Italian frothy dessert made of eggs, sugar, and wine: ZABAGLIONE
Italian small eating place: TRATTORIA
itemized list of securities held by a person or an institution: PORTFOLIO
items too small or too numerous to be separately specified: SUNDRIES
ivory, bone, or shells ornamented by cutting or carving: SCRIMSHAW

J

jabbering: BLITHERING

jacket that binds the arms to the body to restrain a violent person: STRAIT-JACKET

jammed, close together: CHOCK-A-BLOCK

Japanese American of the third generation: SANSEI

Japanese art of paperfolding: ORIGAMI

Japanese broad sash with a bow in the back: OBI

Japanese classical drama: NO

Japanese dish of thinly sliced meat and vegetables usually cooked rapidly at the table: SUKIYAKI

Japanese play on popular or comic themes: KABUKI

Japanese ritual suicide by disembowelment: HARA-KIRI

Japanese stringed musical instrument: KOTO

Japanese suicidal air attack: KAMIKAZE

Japanese syllabic writing: KANA

Japanese translucent paper screen used as a partition or door: SHOJI

Japanese verse form: HAIKU or HOKKU

Japanese wrestling system that uses size and strength of an opponent against him: JUJITSU

jar, in which moisture is retained, for storing cigars and tobacco: HUMIDOR

jar or pot, broad-mouthed and of earthenware: OLLA

jargon: ARGOT

jargon or vocabulary of a profession or class: LINGO

jaundice: ICTERUS

jaunty, gay, dashing: RAKISH

jaw, pertaining to: GNATHIC

jazz that is loud and improvised: BARREL-HOUSE

jeer, defy, scoff, mock: FLOUT

jeer, deride, sneer, laugh coarsely: FLEER

jeer or reproach sarcastically: TAUNT

jeer, taunt: GIBE

jelly-making substance: PECTIN

jerky, unsteady movement: JIGGLE

jesting, flippantly humorous: FACETIOUS

jesting, playful: JOCOSE

jesting, teasing talk: RAILLERY

Jesus' saying not found in Bible: AGRAPHA

jewelers' or watchmakers' magnifying glass: LOUPE

jewelers' weights system: TROY

jewels set so closely as to hide metal: PAVÉ

Jewish boy's coming-of-age ceremony at 13: BAR MITZVAH

Jewish civil and religious law and commentaries thereon: TALMUD

Jewish dietary standards observed: KOSHER

Jewish girl's coming-of-age ceremony: BAS (or BAT or BATH) MITZVAH

Jewish greeting: SHALOM

Jewish law and literature, also the Pentateuch: TORAH

Jewish leather cases containing Scriptural passages that are placed on the forehead and left arm during morning prayers: PHYLACTERIES

Jewish marriage broker: SCHATCHEN

Jewish mourning prayer: KADDISH

Jewish New Year: ROSH HASHANA

Jewish observance of mourning period: SIT SHIVA

Jewish Passover feast commemorating the exodus from Egypt: SEDER

Jewish school or college: YESHIVA

Jewish scroll in a small tube that is affixed to a doorpost: MEZUZA

Jewish seven-day period of mourning: SHIVA

Jews' dispersion: DIASPORA
Jews of Spanish or Portuguese descent:
    SEPHARDIM
jittery, balky, fretful: RESTIVE
joined together: CONJUNCTIVE
joint formed in carpentry: MITER
joint government or authority shared by
    two men: DUUMVIRATE
jointed: ARTICULATED
joke, mischief: WAGGERY
joke, mock: JAPE
joker: WAG
joker, wag: FARCEUR
jolt, bounce, shake up and down: JOUNCE
jolting of the neck or base of the brain, as
    in an automobile crash: WHIPLASH
jot: TITTLE
journey, usually short and for pleasure:
    JAUNT
journey made for safety or as an escape:
    HEGIRA
journey or expedition: SAFARI
journey or laborious trip: TREK
joy of living: JOIE DE VIVRE
joy to the utmost, ecstasy: RAPTURE
joyful, triumphant: JUBILANT
joyful, vigorous, vital, spirited: EXUBER-
    ANT
jubilant, triumphant, joyful: EXULTANT
judge: ADJUDICATE
judge: ARBITER
judge's private room in court: CAMERA
judgment lacking: INJUDICIOUS

judicial, definitive, established by decree:
    DECRETORY
judicial order requiring one to take, or re-
    frain from, certain action: INJUNC-
    TION
jug, narrow-necked and often enclosed in
    wickerwork: DEMIJOHN
jug or mug in form of an old man wearing
    a three-cornered hat: TOBY
jug or pitcher with wide mouth: EWER
juice of grapes or other fruit that is unfer-
    mented: MUST
juicy: SUCCULENT
July and August hot sultry days: DOG DAYS
jumbled, topsy-turvy, disordered: HIG-
    GLEDY-PIGGLEDY
jumbled heap: AGGLOMERATE
jumpy, shy: SKITTISH
jurors summoned to fill vacancies: TALES
jury of twelve selected after each party
    strikes a given number of names from
    a panel: STRUCK JURY
just right, appropriate: PAT
justice, prudence, temperance and forti-
    tude: CARDINAL VIRTUES
justice that is ideal with the good re-
    warded and the evil punished: POETIC
    JUSTICE
justify: VINDICATE
justify, sufficient grounds for: WARRANT
juvenile, trivial, silly: PUERILE
juxtaposition of words, one to explain the
    other: APPOSITION

K

keen, acute as in pleasure or pain: EXQUI-SITE

keen, cutting, acute, sharp: INCISIVE

keen, discerning, perceptive: PERSPICACIOUS

keen, discriminating: SUBTLE

keen, incisive: TRENCHANT

keenly desirous, as for food: SHARP-SET

keenness of mind: ACUMEN

keep back, suppress: STIFLE

keep vigil, go without sleep: WATCH

keeper, guard, watchman: WARDER

kept man: GIGOLO

kerchief worn by Arabs over head and shoulders: KAFFIYEH

kerchief worn on head: BABUSHKA

kettledrums: TIMPANI

key to hieroglyphics: ROSETTA STONE

kidnap: ABDUCT

kidney bean and other edible beans: HARICOT

kidney disease: NEPHRITIS

kidney removal by surgery: NEPHRECTOMY

kill by choking: STRANGLE

kill or destroy a large portion of: DECIMATE

killing action: QUIETUS

killing of a human being by another: HOMICIDE

killing of a king: REGICIDE

killing of a legislative bill by a chief executive: VETO

killing of one's brother or one's countrymen: FRATRICIDE

kind disposition: BENIGN

kind, sort, class: ILK

kind or type, as in art of literature: GENRE

kindly disposed, auspicious: PROPITIOUS

King Arthur's legendary court site: CAMELOT

king-killing: REGICIDE

king's deputy who rules a country, colony, etc.: VICEROY

kinship, nearness: PROPINQUITY

kissing: OSCULATION

kitchen utensil with small holes through which potatoes and other foods are pressed: RICER

knack: INSTINCT

knapsack: RUCKSACK

knee inflammation: HOUSEMAID'S KNEE

knee tendon: HAMSTRING

kneel on one knee, as in worship: GENUFLECT

knickknacks: BRIC-A-BRAC

knife with blade at right angles to the handle: FROE

knife with blade folded in that springs open when a button is pressed: SWITCH-BLADE KNIFE

knife-sharpening stone: WHETSTONE

knife that is swordlike: SNICKERSNEE

knife with a handle at each end: DRAWKNIFE

knitted fabric, machine made: TRICOT

knitted to follow the contour of the leg or body: FULL-FASHIONED

knitting stitch that gives a ribbed appearance: PURL

knob, knot, or swelling: NODE

knobby: TOROSE

knock about or cuff: BUFFET

knock-kneed: VALGUS

knot or bun of hair worn by women at the back of the head: CHIGNON

knot that forms a loop having no free ends: HARNESS HITCH

known or able to be known, characterized by awareness: PRESENTATIVE

knowing all things, all-knowing: OMNISCIENT

knowing or perceiving: COGNITION

knowing something before it occurs: PRE-
SCIENCE

knowledge, skill: EXPERTISE

knowledge derived from sense perception:
PERCEPT

knowledge of something without conscious attention or reasoning: INTU-
ITION

knowledge of the right thing to say or do:
SAVOIR-FAIRE

knowledge or cognition as a subject of
study: EPISTEMOLOGY

knowledge or familiarity of a subject:
CONVERSANT

knowledge that is superficial: SCIOLISM

knowledgeable: GNOSTIC

L

"l" pronounced like "r" or "w," or "r" pronounced like "w": LALLATION

label someone as infamous: BRAND

labored, clumsy: PONDEROUS

laborer on river vessels or on the waterfront: ROUSTABOUT

labor, toil: TRAVAIL

lace in which patterns are held together by connecting threads rather than by a net ground: GUIPURE

lack, scarcity, famine: DEARTH

lack of energy: ANERGY

lack of power or ability, impotence: IMPUISSANCE

lackadaisical: LANGUID

lackadaisical, indifferent, apathetic: LISTLESS

lacking animation, weak, listless: LANGUID

lacking any easing: UNMITIGATED

lacking common measure or standard of comparison: INCOMMENSURABLE

lacking fulfillment, unsuccessful: MANQUÉ

lacking particular character, not distinctive: NONDESCRIPT

lacking understanding: PURBLIND

ladder hung over the side of a ship: ACCOMMODATION LADDER

lady's maid: ABIGAIL

lag, follow slowly, drag in the mud: DRABBLE

lamb chunks broiled on a skewer: SHASHLIK

lamb or other meat chunks skewered and broiled with tomatoes, onions, peppers: SHISH KEBAB

lambskin or calfskin that is untanned: KIP

lament, woeful tale, complaint: JEREMIAD

lamentation or mourning in verse or song: ELEGY

lamentation or wailing for the deceased: KEEN

lamp with light directed upward by a bowl reflector: TORCHIER

land, usually a narrow piece, extending into a body of water and connecting two larger land masses: ISTHMUS

land between hills, especially along a river: INTERVALE

land cultivation based on scientific principles: AGRONOMY

land extending in a narrow point from the shore into the water: SPIT

land extending into the sea, the high point of it: PROMONTORY

land or soil capable of being cultivated: ARABLE

land or water vehicle or creature: AMPHIBIAN

land projecting into water: PENINSULA

land strip plowed or cleared to prevent spread of fire: FIREBREAK

land tenure or distribution: AGRARIAN

landing of a plane using only electronic signals: INSTRUMENT LANDING

landing of a spacecraft on water: SPLASHDOWN

landlord who lets slum dwellings run down: SLUMLORD

language, as a science or a study: LINGUISTICS

language, idiom, speaking style: PARLANCE

language, usually hybrid, that is used as a common speech by people having different tongues: LINGUA FRANCA

language invented for international use: ESPERANTO

language lacking sincere meaning or intention: RHETORIC

language or grammatical forms that are customary: USAGE

language mixture: POLYGLOT

language native to an area, common rather than literary language: VERNACULAR

language study that assumes a formal system of signs and examines their nature and arrangement: STRUCTURAL LINGUISTICS

language that conceals: AESOPIAN LANGUAGE

language that is deliberately ambiguous and deceptive (Orwell coinage): NEWSPEAK

language, informal and substandard, that consists of coined words and new meanings of existing words: SLANG

language theory that stresses tagmemes, the smallest meaningful grammatical forms: TAGMEMICS

language's smallest meaningful unit: MORPHEME

lapel of a coat: REVERS

large, as capital letters: MAJUSCULE

large groups involved: MACROSCOPIC

large system regarded as a unity: MACROCOSM

lasso, lariat: RIATA

last, often inferior, remnant: RUMP

last part or remnant, usually of no further use: FAG END

last stage of any journey or project: HOMESTRETCH

last syllable of a word: ULTIMA

lasting a short time, transitory, fleeting: EPHEMERAL

lasting condition, sometimes specifically for life: PERPETUITY

lasting or continuing a long time: CHRONIC

lasting through the year: PERENNIAL

late blossoming: SEROTINOUS

latest fashion or word: DERNIER CRI

Latin American term for a foreigner, especially an American or Englishman: GRINGO

latitude, additional space for freedom of action: LEEWAY

laugh at with contempt: DERIDE

laugh immoderately or noisily: CACHINNATE

laughable or having the power to laugh: RISIBLE

laughing: RIANT

laughter in a loud boisterous burst: GUFFAW

laughter that is uproarious and irrepressible: HOMERIC LAUGHTER

launch at high speed: CATAPULT

lavish, copious, generous: PROFUSE

lavish, bountiful: MUNIFICENT

lavish, overflowing: EXUBERANT

law derived from custom, usage or court opinions: COMMON LAW

lavish, wasteful, extravagant: PRODIGAL

law, especially of a municipal body: ORDINANCE

law and its administration, as a science: JURISPRUDENCE

law based on usage rather than legislation: UNWRITTEN LAW

law of locality not applied to foreign diplomats: DIPLOMATIC IMMUNITY

laws to protect investors against securities frauds: BLUE SKY LAWS

law that limits the time during which a particular legal action may be brought: STATUTE OF LIMITATIONS

law violation less serious than a felony: MISDEMEANOR

lawbreaker whose violations are habitual: SCOFFLAW

lawful: LICIT

lawful act performed in an unlawful way: MISFEASANCE

lawless confusion: ANARCHY

lawmaker, particularly a wise one: SOLON

lawsuit: LITIGATION

lawyer, not highly competent, who deals with small cases: PETTIFOGGER

lawyer expelled from the profession: DISBARRED

lawyer who is unethical or deceitful: SHYSTER

layer, bed, grade: STRATUM

lazy: SHIFTLESS

lazy: SLOTHFUL

lazy, idle: INDOLENT

lazy, useless, futile: OTIOSE

lazy person: SLUGGARD

lazy person, idler: FAINÉANT

lead, inspire, activate, as a group: SPARKPLUG

lead astray: DELUDE

lead-colored: LIVID

leader of a group that follows sheeplike: BELLWETHER

leader of singing in church: PRECENTOR

leader or chief: COCK OF THE WALK

leader or one who sets an example: FUGLEMAN

leader who appeals to prejudices and passions: DEMAGOGUE

leaderless: ACEPHALOUS

leaders of new movements: AVANT GARDE

leadership or domination of one state over another: HEGEMONY

leadership person lacking real power: FIGUREHEAD

leadership quality that captures imagination and inspires loyalty: CHARISMA

leading character in a drama or a cause: PROTAGONIST

leading to: CONDUCIVE

leafy: FOLIATE

leak out, become known: TRANSPIRE

lean, thin: SPARE

lean body structure: ECTOMORPHIC

leaning, lying down, reclining: RECUMBENT

leaning, usually toward something objectionable: PROCLIVITY

leaning, weighing or resting upon something: INCUMBENT

leaning or bent, liking, tendency: INCLINATION

leap year's extra day, Feb. 29: BISSEXTILE

learn the facts, fathom: PLUMB

learned, scholarly: ERUDITE

learned person: PUNDIT

learned person, scholar: SAVANT

learned response: CONDITIONED REFLEX

learner: ABECEDARIAN

learning, branch of: DISCIPLINE

learning or teaching through discovery and investigation: HEURISTICS

least amount possible: AMBSACE

leather produced by some process not using tanning liquor: TAW

leather used for bookbinding: SKIVER

leatherlike: CORIACEOUS

leave one country to settle in another: EMIGRATE

leaves own country to live elsewhere: EMIGRANT

leavetaking or dismissal: CONGÉ

leaving one's faith, party or principles: APOSTASY

lecherous, lewd, obscene: SALACIOUS

lecherous man: SATYR

lecherous or malicious look: LEER

lecture, sermonize: PRELECT

lecture briefly setting forth details: BRIEFING

lecture with diagrams made on blackboard: CHALK TALK

lecturer, tutor, teacher without faculty rank: DOCENT

left- and right-handed: AMBIDEXTROUS

left side as opposed to right side or dexter, especially in heraldry: SINISTER

left side of a vessel as one faces forward: PORT

left-hand page of a book: VERSO

left-handed: SINISTRAL

leftover: REMNANT

leftover part, remainder: RESIDUE

leg or arm stiffness or cramp: CHARLEY HORSE

legs kicked out alternately from a squatting position in this Slavic folk dance by a male: KAZATSKY

legal arrangement by which diplomatic corps members are exempt from local law: DIPLOMATIC IMMUNITY

legal questions to which medical knowledge is applied: MEDICAL JURISPRUDENCE

legal right to use and profit from the property of another: USUFRUCT

legally based; by law: DE JURE

legislative body's calling to account of an administrative official: INTERPELLATION

legislative receptacle, figuratively, for bills to be taken up at a future time: HOPPER

legs far apart: ASTRIDE

leisurely gait: AMBLE

lender who charges illegal rates of interest: LOAN SHARK

lengthened toward the poles: PROLATE

lenient: INDULGENT

lenient, tolerating unusual freedom: PERMISSIVE

lens used in movies or TV that adjusts rapidly for close-up or distance shots while holding focus: ZOOM LENS

less severe, more moderate, milder: MITIGATED

less than one would expect: NOMINAL

lessen: ABATE

lessen: ABRIDGE

lessen in quality or value, make worse: IMPAIR

lessen or diminish: DWINDLE

lessen the guilt or odiousness of an offense: EXTENUATE

lessening of productivity in proportion to increase in expenditure: DIMINISHING RETURNS

lessening of speed: RETARDATION
let go, give up: RELINQUISH
let it stand, as a direction used in proof-reading: STET
lethargy: HEBETUDE
letter, long and formal: EPISTLE
letter delivered from same postoffice at which it was posted: DROP LETTER
letter or sound inserted into a word: EPENTHESIS
letter that each member of a group signs: ROUND ROBIN
letters in early Greek and Latin manuscripts resembling rounded modern capitals: UNCIAL
letting business act without regulation: LAISSEZ FAIRE
level land with few or no trees: SAVANNA
level of command: ECHELON
level to the ground, demolish: RAZE
lewd, grossly ribald: ITHYPHALLIC
lewd, lustful: LECHEROUS
lewd, sexually aroused: RANDY
lewd, obscene, lecherous: SALACIOUS
lewd, sexually abandoned: LICENTIOUS
lewd or dissipated person: DEBAUCHEE
lewd or lascivious: LUBRICOUS
lewd or wanton: CYPRIAN
liability or debt gradually extinguished, as by installment payments: AMORTIZED
liability to conviction and punishment: JEOPARDY
liable or possible: CONTINGENT
liable to err, be misled or deceived: FALLIBLE
liable to injury, attack, or criticism: VULNERABLE
liberal or radical political figure: LEFTIST
liberal or unorthodox in attitudes or beliefs: LATITUDINARIAN
liberate, free, emancipate: MANUMIT
lie: FABRICATION
lie: PREVARICATE
lie, equivocate: PALTER
lie, humbug, sham: FLAM
lie or lean in a relaxed manner: LOLL
lie that is trivial and told to be polite or spare someone's feelings: WHITE LIE
life and matter viewed as inseparable: HYLOZOISM
life insurance policy in which the payment is double the face value in case of accidental death: DOUBLE INDEMNITY
life is generated from living organisms only: BIOGENESIS

life is like that: C'EST LA VIE
lifeless, automatic: MECHANICAL
lifeless state: ABIOSIS
life-manifesting: VITAL
life-size drawing or illustration: MACROGRAPH
lift up your hearts: SURSUM CORDA
lifting to test weight or gauge: HEFT
light, according to wavelengths: SPECTRUM
light, airy, spiritual: ETHEREAL
light and frothy dish fixed in that condition by adding beaten egg whites: SOUFFLÉ
light and shade, black and white: CHIAROSCURO
light beam passes over a surface for television or other production: SCAN
light emitted by a substance after exposure to some form of energy: PHOSPHORESENCE
light meal: COLLATION
light or heat ray bent in passage from one medium to another: REFRACTION
light thrown by a candle on one square foot of surface one foot away: FOOT-CANDLE
light wind: CAT'S-PAW
light-admitting but not transparent: TRANSLUCENT
lighthearted: BUOYANT
lighthearted, carefree, unconcerned: INSOUCIANT
lighthearted, gay, carefree: ROLLICKING
lighthouse: PHAROS
lightness, gaiety that is inappropriate, frivolity, fickleness: LEVITY
lightning without thunder, in fitful play usually near horizon on hot evenings: HEAT LIGHTNING
light-producing or light-conveying: LUMINIFEROUS
light-resistant, dull: OPAQUE
light up, make clear, enlighten, illuminate: IRRADIATE
light-wave or sound-wave change that seems to accompany change in distance between source and observer: DOPPLER EFFECT
like it or not: WILLY-NILLY
likeness, image, representation, usually crudely done of a disliked person: EFFIGY
likeness in sound: ASSONANCE
likening one thing to something else in a

figure of speech using "like" or "as": SIMILE

liking, tendency, trend, leaning or bent: INCLINATION

liking for something: PENCHANT

limber, bending easily and gracefully: LITHE

limit freedom: TRAMMEL

limit or range, as of power or action: TETHER

limited as by human or natural conditions: FINITE

limited, narrow, provincial: PAROCHIAL

limitless: AD INFINITUM

limitless or vast: INFINITE

limits: AMBIT

line, as of men or ships, enclosing an area: CORDON

line over a vowel indicating long sound: MACRON

line that slants, used in printing or writing: VIRGULE

linear markings: STRIATION

lined: LINEATE

linen for a household: NAPERY

lines that make up a page, an article, an ad, etc.: LINAGE

linger or walk aimlessly: LOITER

lingo, cant: JARGON

linguistical study of the structure of words: MORPHOLOGY

link, connection, bond,: NEXUS

linked things or events: CONCATENATION

lion-like: LEONINE

lip deformity consisting of a cleft, usually on the upper lip: HARELIP

liplike: LABIATE

liqueurs served in layers: POUSSE-CAFÉ

liquid measure of about 63 gallons: HOGSHEAD

liquid medicine: POTION

liquid poured ceremonially, as in honor of a deity: LIBATION

liquor mixed with water, soda, ginger ale, etc. and served in a tall glass: HIGHBALL

liquor quantity, a fifth of a gallon: FIFTH

list, with definitions, of technical, obscure or foreign words of a work or field: GLOSSARY

list of acknowledgments in film or TV show: CREDITS

list of acknowledgments in film or TV show that moves vertically on screen: CRAWL

list of articles on hand with description and quantity of each: INVENTORY

list of candidates: SLATE

list of goods being shipped: WAYBILL

list of merchandise sent or services rendered; including price to purchaser: INVOICE

list of names: ROSTER

list of securities held by a person or an institution: PORTFOLIO

list of supplications, with a fixed response after each: LITANY

listen: HARK

listen in at a college class: AUDIT

listless: LACKADAISICAL

listless, inactive, indolent: SUPINE

listless, lacking animation, weak: LANGUID

listless discontent or weariness, boredom: ENNUI

literal translation of word or construction from one language to another: LOAN TRANSLATION

literary club: ATHENEUM

literary composition in a mixture of languages: MACARONIC

literary effort that is labored and pedantic: LUCUBRATION

literary study or scholarship: PHILOLOGY

literary work that is short, depicting something subtly: VIGNETTE

literature: BELLES-LETTRES

literature or art of a cheap, popular or sentimental quality: KITSCH

lithe, pliant, supple, agile: LISSOME

little universe: MICROCOSM

live in distressing conditions: LANGUISH

live or reside in, occupy as a home: INHABIT

live passively, monotonously, dully: VEGETATE

live together: COHABIT

live well at another's expense: BATTEN

lively, active, spirited: VIVACIOUS

lively, aggressive: FEISTY

lively, brisk, dashing, self-confident: JAUNTY

lively, changeable, volatile: MERCURIAL

lively, cheerful, urbane: DEBONAIR

lively, energetic: VIBRANT

lively, quickly, briskly, in music: VIVACE

lively, racy: PIQUANT

lively, saucy: PERT

lively in one's behavior: TITTUP

lively or playful movement in music: SCHERZO

lively person: GRIG

lively spirits, vivacity, gaiety, sparkle: EFFERVESCENCE

livelihood, food, means of support: SUSTENANCE

liveliness: ALACRITY

liveliness: BRIO

living together of dissimilar organisms, usually in a mutually advantageous partnership: SYMBIOSIS

liver inflammation: HEPATITIS

Liverpool resident: LIVERPUDLIAN

load a missile can lift and carry to a target: THROW-WEIGHT

loafer, spendthrift: WASTREL

loafer or idler who lives off others: DRONE

loan or prepayment of money from public funds: IMPREST

loan that may be terminated at any time: CALL LOAN

loathesome, hateful, repugnant, disgusting: ODIOUS

loathing: ABHORRENCE

lobby, entrance hall: FOYER

lobster liver, considered a delicacy: TOMALLEY

local road: VICINAL ROAD

lockjaw: TRISMUS

lodging for soldiers in a private home: BILLET

lodging place that is part-time or temporary: PIED-À-TERRE

lofty, impressive, noble, as in quality or style: SONOROUS

logic formula in which two premises are laid down and a conclusion is drawn from them: SYLLOGISM

logic, reasoning from general to particular: DEDUCTION

logical argument in examining ideas or opinions: DIALECTIC

logical rather than intuitive: DIANOETIC

loincloth or waistcloth of printed calico worn by Samoan natives: LAVA-LAVA

loiter or waste time: DAWDLE

London press: FLEET STREET

Londoner of East End: COCKNEY

long and polysyllabic, as of words: SESQUIPEDALIAN

long and wordy, tedious: PROLIX

long jump, as formerly known: BROAD-JUMP

long life: LONGEVITY

long live: VIVE

longing for something distant in time or place: NOSTALGIA

long-drawn-out explanation or narrative: MEGILLAH

longheaded: DOLICHOCEPHALIC

long-sleeved robe, sashed, worn in Mediterranean countries: CAFTAN

long-winded: DIFFUSE

long-windedness: CIRCUMLOCUTION

look, countenance, face: VISAGE

look at closely, scrutinize: SCAN

look like or act like someone or something: SIMULATE

look or appearance lacking reality: SEMBLANCE

look that implies malice, lechery or slyness: LEER

loose, not rigid: LAX

loose, weak: SLACK

loose morals: WANTON

lopsided, unsymmetrical: SKEWED

Los Angeles resident: LOS ANGELENO, LOS ANGELEAN, ANGELINO

lose heart, withdraw in fear: QUAIL

losing contender or one expected to lose: UNDERDOG

loss from sale of assets: CAPITAL LOSS

loss of an unaccented vowel at the beginning of a word: APHESIS

loss of income anticipated from eventual reduction in supply of natural resources: DEPLETION

loss of memory: AMNESIA

loss of muscular coordination: ATAXIA

loss of power of speech: APHASIA

loss of sight without organic defect: AMAUROSIS

lottery, often based on a horse race, in which all the wagers may be won by one or a few bettors: SWEEPSTAKES

loud, full-sounding: SONOROUS

loud, rough in sound: RAUCOUS

loud and abusive: THERSITICAL

loud and noisy: UPROARIOUS

loud to an extreme: STENTORIAN

loudness measure: DECIBEL

loud-voiced person: STENTOR

Louisiana descendant of the Acadian French: CAJUN

louse infestation: PEDICULOSIS

love affair that is secret or illicit: INTRIGUE

love feast: AGAPE

love insincerely (applied to a man): PHI-LANDER

love letter: BILLET-DOUX

love of mankind: ALTRUISM

love of women: PHILOGYNY

love potion: PHILTER

lover or gallant of a married woman: CI-CISBEO

lover or illicit sexual companion: PAR-AMOUR

lovers, secret meeting of: ASSIGNATION

low neckline in a dress: DECOLLETAGE

lowdown, rumor, gossip: SCUTTLEBUTT

lower: NETHER

lower in dignity or reputation: DEMEAN

lower middle class: PETITE BOURGEOISIE

lower oneself to do something: CONDE-SCEND

lower price on a stock transaction than on the preceding transaction: DOWN TICK, MINUS-TICK

lower someone in prestige or estimation: ABASE

lowering of esteem: DISPARAGEMENT

lowest point: NADIR

lowest point in an orbit: PERIGEE

low-priced stocks, selling at less than $1 a share: PENNY STOCKS

loyal: STAUNCH

loyal adherent: MYRMIDON

loyalty, obligation owed, faithfulness: FEALTY

loyalty or friendship weakened or de-stroyed: DISAFFECTION

lozenge, medicated as for a sore throat: TROCHE

lucid, clear, understandable: PERSPICUOUS

lucid, pure, clear, transparent: LIMPID

lucky discoveries made accidentally: SERENDIPITY

lucky stroke, good luck: FLUKE

ludicrous or ridiculous situation: FARCE

lukewarm: TEPID

lumbering, bulky: PONDEROUS

luminous or glowing with heat: INCAN-DESCENT

lump or bump, protuberance: KNURL

lunatic or maniac: DEMONIAC

lurch or twist from side to side: CAREEN

lust for or desire something belonging to someone else: COVET

lust or sexual desire: CONCUPISCENCE

lustful: LASCIVIOUS

lustful: LIBIDINOUS

lustful, dissolute: WANTON

lustful, lewd: LECHEROUS

lustful, amorous: RANDY

luxurious, sensual: VOLUPTUOUS

luxury-loving person: VOLUPTUARY

lying: MENDACIOUS

lying abnormally: MYTHOMANIA

lying down, growing along the ground: DECUMBENT

lying down, reclining, leaning: RECUM-BENT

lying down or reclining: COUCHANT

lying face down: PRONE

lying flat, helpless, exhausted: PROSTRATE

lying on the back, face upward: SUPINE

lying under oath: PERJURY

M

machine for giving gloss to paper or fabric: CALENDER

"madam-I'm-Adam" type of sentence: PALINDROME

maddened, furiously angry: HORN-MAD

made to order: BESPOKE

Madrid resident: MADRILENIAN, MADRILEÑO

magic: CONJURATION

magic: THEURGY

magic tricks: PRESTIDIGITATION

magic tricks: SLEIGHT OF HAND

magic word: ABRACADABRA

magic words or formula: INCANTATION

magical, mystical or divinatory arts: OCCULT

magical, occult, relating to alchemy: HERMETIC

magician: THAUMATURGE

magician or sorcerer: CONJURER

magnifying glass used by jewelers or watchmakers: LOUPE

maid to a lady, lady's maid: ABIGAIL

maiden name of a married woman: NÉE

mail sent without charge as by congressmen: FRANKED MAIL

main clause of a sentence at the beginning: LOOSE SENTENCE

main clause of the sentence at the end: PERIODIC SENTENCE

main course of a meal: ENTREE

main dish or chief item in a collection: PIÈCE DE RÉSISTANCE

main idea or substance of an argument, discussion, question: GIST

Main resident: MAINER

maintainable, defendable: TENABLE

majestic: AUGUST

make amends for, atone for: EXPIATE

make eyes at suggestively, stare at: OGLE

make faces: GRIMACE

make known, disclose, bestow: IMPART

make merry, delight (in), celebrate: REVEL

make noteworthy or call attention to: SIGNALIZE

make or become better: AMELIORATE

make outwardly real: EXTERNALIZE

make over, renovate: REVAMP

make poor or fruitless: IMPOVERISH

make specific: CONCRETIZE

make up, compensate: COUNTERVAIL

make up or devise: CONCOCT

make up or invent as a story or lie: FABRICATE

making sense: COHERENT

makeup of a book, newspaper, etc.: FORMAT

male adoption of female clothing and mannerisms: EONISM

male and female sexual organs in one individual: HERMAPHRODITE

male ballet dancer: DANSEUR

male ballet dancer who is the principal performer: PREMIER DANSEUR

male counterpart of a ballerina: DANSEUR NOBLE

male figure used as a supporting pillar: TELAMON

male figure with pointed ears, horns and goat's legs, in Greek mythology: SATYR

male flirt: PHILANDERER

male genitals subjected to oral contact: FELLATIO

male government: PATRIARCHY

male homosexual: URANIST, URNING

male line relationship: AGNATION

male of beef cattle: STEER

male sex hormone: ANDROSTERONE, TESTOSTERONE

male singer in the principal position: PRIM'ORO

male sterilization by surgery: VASECTOMY

malevolent: ILL-DISPOSED

malformation: ABNORMALITY

malice, hate: RANCOR

malice, spite: VENOM

malicious, cutting: SNIDE

malicious, fierce, unruly: VICIOUS

malicious, unprovoked, unjust: WANTON

malicious, wicked: PERNICIOUS

malicious, wishing evil toward others: MALEVOLENT

malicious or lecherous look: LEER

malicious or mean behavior: DOGGERY

malignant, as a disease: VIRULENT

malnutrition: CACHEXIA

mammals bringing forth living young: VIVIPAROUS

man about town: BOULEVARDIER

man as center: ANTHROPOCENTRIC

man hatred: MISANDRY

man in relation to environment: ANTHROPONOMY

man of great beauty: ADONIS

man supported by a woman to whom he is not married: GIGOLO

man to whom a woman is engaged: FIANCÉ

man who dresses flashily: DUDE

manage shrewdly: MANIPULATE

manage to live: SUBSIST

manageable, compliant: TRACTABLE

management or superintendance: INTENDANCE

manager, sponsor or organizer of performers for entertainment: IMPRESARIO

manager of another's affairs: PROCURATOR

Manchester native: MANCUNIAN

maneuver, especially in diplomacy: DÉMARCHE

maneuver, trick, device for obtaining advantage: STRATAGEM

maneuver by craftiness: FINAGLE

maneuver for an advantage: JOCKEY

maneuver or stratagem to outwit someone: PLOY

maneuvering, methods or management to gain an end: TACTICS

maneuvering with ploys to gain an advantage: GAMESMANSHIP

mangle, cut unskillfully, hack: HAGGLE

mangle, tear raggedly: LACERATE

manhandle, abuse, handle roughly: MAUL

mania: CACOETHES

maniac or lunatic: DEMONIAC

manias.

> (In the following listing read the words "obsession with" ahead of each entry.)

alcoholic liquor: DIPSOMANIA

animals: ZOOMANIA

ballet: BALLETOMANIA

bees: APIMANIA

birds: ORNITHOMANIA

books: BIBLOMANIA

cats: AILUROMANIA

children: PEDOMANIA

crowds: OCHLOMANIA

dancing: CHOREOMANIA

dogs: CYNOMANIA

eating: SITOMANIA

fire: PYROMANIA

fish: ICHTHYOMANIA

flowers: ANTHOMANIA

gaiety: CHEROMANIA

grandiose things: MEGALOMANIA

horses: HIPPOMANIA

ideas: IDEOMANIA

insects: ENTOMOMANIA

money: CHREMATOMANIA

nakedness: GYMNOMANIA

one subject or thing: MONOMANIA

pleasure: HEDONOMANIA

reptiles: OPHIDIOMANIA

roaming: DROMOMANIA

solitude: AUTOMANIA

speech: LALOMANIA

stealing: KLEPTOMANIA

stillness: EREMIOMANIA

travel: HODOMANIA

wealth: PLUTOMANIA

women: GYNEMANIA

manic-depressive condition that is mild: CYCLOTHYMIA

manifest, demonstrate convincingly, show clearly: EVINCE

manifest, evident, obvious: PATENT

manifestation or appearance of a deity, a showing forth: EPIPHANY

manipulation of parts of the body to correct diseases: OSTEOPATHY

mankind hater: MISANTHROPE

manlike: ANDROID

manlike apes and man: HOMINOIDS

manly vigor: VIRILITY

manner: MIEN

manner in which one bears oneself, deportment: DEMEANOR

manner of operating: MODUS OPERANDI
manner of speech: LOCUTION
mannerism, personal peculiarity: QUIRK
mannerism, quirk, habit peculiar to an individual: IDIOSYNCRASY
man's nature regarded as consisting of decisive actions rather than inner dispositions: EXISTENTIALISM
manual guidebook: HANDBOOK
manual or handbook: ENCHIRIDION
manual skill, expertness: HANDINESS
manual training system: SLOYD
manual worker: BLUE COLLAR
manuscript copier: AMANUENSIS
manuscript of a play, film, or television show: SCRIPT
manuscript sheets gathered into a unified whole: COLLATED
man-woman relationship without sexual activity: PLATONIC
many and varied forms: MANIFOLD
many-sided: VERSATILE
map making: CARTOGRAPHY
map of the earth with parallel longitude lines intersected by parallel latitude lines: MERCATOR PROJECTION
map or survey used for taxation basis: CADASTER
mapping of regions or districts: CHOROGRAPHY
mapping or charting of area in detail: TOPOGRAPHY
marble used for shooting: TAW
marginal note of explanation: SCHOLIUM
marginal, not essential: PERIPHERAL
marine animal and plant organisms that drift or float: PLANKTON
mark or mark as infamous: BRAND
mark, stamp or character that is distinctive: IMPRESS
mark between parts of a compound word: HYPHEN
mark like a hook under letter ç: CEDILLA
mark of authenticity: CACHET
mark of identification: EARMARK
mark of infamy or disgrace: STIGMA
mark or proof of genuineness or high quality: HALLMARK
mark out boundaries or limits, separate: DEMARCATE
mark out limits: CIRCUMSCRIBE
marked with lines, striped: LINEATE
marker or memorial of heaped-up stones: CAIRN

market, outdoor, for dealing in second-hand goods: FLEA MARKET
market on the decline: BEAR MARKET
market on the rise: BULL MARKET
marketable: VENDIBLE
marketplace: AGORA
markings of a spotted animal or plant: MACULATION
markings on an envelope used in place of stamps: INDICIA
marriage a man is forced into because of sexual relations with the woman: SHOTGUN WEDDING
marriage after the death or divorce of first spouse: DIGAMY
marriage between unequals in which titles and estates are not passed on to the inferior partner: MORGANATIC
marriage broker, Jewish: SCHATCHEN
marriage for the second time: DEUTEROGAMY
marriage in trial form: COMPANIONATE MARRIAGE
marriage relationship: CONJUGAL
marriage with one of lower position: MÉSALLIANCE
marriage within the group or tribe, inbreeding: ENDOGAMY
marriageable because of physical maturity: NUBILE
married male American Indian: SANNUP
married man: BENEDICT
married state: CONNUBIAL
married woman: FEME COVERT
married woman's acknowledged lover or gallant: CICISBEO
married woman's legal status: COVERTURE
marrying while still married: BIGAMY
marsh, bog: MORASS
marshy body of water: BAYOU
marshy ground, bog: QUAGMIRE
marshy low ground: SWALE
martini served with pickled onion: GIBSON
marvelous, wonderful: PRODIGIOUS
marvelous or wonderful to tell: MIRABILE DICTU
masculine, strong, sturdy: VIRILE
masculine woman: AMAZON
masculinity: VIRILITY
masculinity, aggressive virility: MACHISMO
mask for the eyes, worn at masquerades: DOMINO
masochism or sadism: ALGOLAGNIA

mass, heap or collection of things: CONGERIES

mass of things indiscriminately thrown together: AGGLOMERATE

Massachusetts resident: MASSACHUSETT-SAN, BAY STATER

massacre, especially directed against Jews: POGROM

massacre or slaughter: CARNAGE

masses: DEMOS

masses, common people: HOI POLLOI

masses, pertaining to: DEMOTIC

mast or boom on a sailboat: SPAR

master of technique: VIRTUOSO

masterpiece, great work: MAGNUM OPUS

masterstroke, sudden telling blow, brilliant stratagem: COUP

masturbation or interruption of coitus: ONANISM

matchless: INIMITABLE

matchless, unequaled: NONPAREIL

mate or complement to another: COUNTERPART

material, real, having definite shape: TANGIBLE

materialize, concretize: REIFY

maternal or female line of a family: DISTAFF SIDE

mathematical sequence in which the ratio between each two numbers is the same: GEOMETRIC PROGRESSION

mathematical term indicating parts into which the whole is to be divided: DENOMINATOR

mathematics is incapable of expressing it in rational numbers: SURD

matter and energy, as a science: PHYSICS

mattress of straw: PALLIASSE

mature: FULL-FLEDGED

maxim: APOTHEGM

maxim: AXIOM

maxim, rule, moral guide: PRECEPT

maxim, wise saying: GNOME

maze, an intricate structure: LABYRINTH

meal: REPAST

meal, particularly dinner: PRANDIAL

meal at which guests serve themselves: BUFFET

meal served in a restaurant complete at a fixed price: TABLE D'HÔTE

meal that is light: REFECTION

meal that is light and informal: COLLATION

meals and room included in hotel rate: AMERICAN PLAN

mean: PETTY

mean or malicious behavior: DOGGERY

mean or stingy practice: CHEESE-PARING

meaning, purport, general course: TENOR

meaning of language forms: SEMANTIC

meaning that is exact as stated: LITERAL

meaning that is suggested, significance: PURPORT

meaningless, merely sociable, as applied to talk: PHATIC

meaningless, worthless: NUGATORY

meaningless performance: CHARADE

meaningless speech: BALDERDASH

meaningless talk: ABRACADABRA

meanings of language forms, as a subject of study: SEMANTICS

means of support, livelihood, food: SUSTENANCE

meantime, time between periods or events: INTERIM

measure, especially by the hand, with thumb and little finger extended: SPAN

measure of length for yarn: SPINDLE

measure that is practical rather than scientifically accurate: RULE OF THUMB

measure the depth of water with, or plumb: PLUMB

measured from side to side: BREADTH

measurement of advertising space: AGATE LINE

measurement of distance by determination of angles: TELEMETRY

meat and vegetable stew and its broth: POT-AU-FEU

meat broiled on a skewer: BROCHETTE

meat chunks marinated: KEBAB

meat pie topped with mashed potatoes: SHEPHERD'S PIE

meat portion, that is small: COLLOP

mechanical man, automaton: ROBOT

mechanical way of doing something or doing it solely by memory: ROTE

meddle, intrude in the affairs of others: INTERLOPE

meddler in the affairs of others: KIBITZER

mediating factor between opposite things: TERTIUM QUID

medical auxiliary or assistant: PARAMEDIC

medical graduate serving in and living at a hospital for clinical training: INTERN

medical knowledge applied to questions of law: FORENSIC MEDICINE medical oath setting forth a code of ethics: HIPPOCRATIC OATH

medical profession symbol, wand or staff of Mercury: CADUCEUS

medical technique employing needles inserted into body: ACUPUNCTURE

medical term for the branch of medicine dealing with functions and diseases of women: GYNECOLOGY

medical-appearing substance given to comfort a patient or as a test control: PLACEBO

medicinal liquid injected into the colon as a purgative: ENEMA

medicine obtainable without prescription: OFFICINAL

medicine of one's own invention, quack medicine, cure-all: NOSTRUM

medicine that causes vomiting: EMETIC

medicine that eases irritation: ABIRRITANT

medicine that increases flow of urine: DIURETIC

medicines described and listed in a book: PHARMACOPOEIA

medieval chemistry: ALCHEMY

mediocre: INDIFFERENT

mediocre, prosaic, dull: PEDESTRIAN

meditate or ponder: RUMINATE

medium, moderate, in music: MEZZO

medley: SALMAGUNDI

medley, confused mixture: FARRAGO

medley, mixture: POTPOURRI

meek, apologetic, shy person: MILQUETOAST

meeting at the same point, simultaneous: CONCURRENT

meeting or secret appointment, as of lovers: TRYST

meeting place, meeting or appointment to meet: RENDEZVOUS

meeting to confer on a particular subject: SYMPOSIUM

melancholy: ATRABILIOUS

melancholy, gloomy: SEPULCHRAL

melancholy, pessimism, romantic world-weariness: WELTSCHMERZ

Melbourne resident: MELBURNIAN

melodic: ARIOSE

melodious, soothing, pleasant: DULCET

melodious or musical: CANOROUS

melody added to another melody: COUNTERPOINT

melting: LIQUESCENT

members or items chosen out of a group in the expectation they will be representative of the whole group: RANDOM SAMPLE

membership on a stock exchange: SEAT

memorable or prominent object in the landscape: LANDMARK

memorandum to remind one of something in the future: TICKLER

memory: RETENTION

memory aid: MNEMONIC

memory alone as a way of doing something, mechanical action: ROTE

memory blocks, speech errors or faulty actions: PARAPRAXIS

memory involving clear visualization of objects previously seen: EIDETIC IMAGERY

memory loss: AMNESIA

memory loss concerning muscular movements: APRAXIA

menacing, threatening: MINACIOUS, MINATORY

men's clothes and matters pertaining thereto: SARTORIAL

men's furnishings: HABERDASHERY

menstruation cessation: MENOPAUSE

mental age times 100 divided by chronological age: INTELLIGENCE QUOTIENT (IQ)

mental confusion: AMENTIA

mental derangement: ALIENATION

mental disorder marked by separation of thought from emotions: SCHIZOPHRENIA

mental disorders treated by study of the unconscious: PSYCHOANALYSIS

mental lapse: ABERRATION

mental or emotional block: INHIBITION

mental position, frame of mind: POSTURE

mental powers impaired: DEMENTIA

mental quickness, keenness: ACUMEN

mental telepathy: CRYPTESTHESIA

mental torpor, pathological: ACEDIA

mentally deficient person: AMENT

mentally retarded person: IMBECILE

mentally unsound: NON COMPOS MENTIS

mention of something by saying it will not be mentioned: APOPHASIS

mention or suggest for the first time: BROACH

menu with each item having a separate price: A LA CARTE

mercenary, subject to bribery: VENAL

merciless: RUTHLESS

merciless, unrelenting: IMPLACABLE

mercy killing: EUTHANASIA

merge gradually one into another: INTERGRADE

merging into one of two vowels generally pronounced separately: SYNERESIS

merited or deserved, as a punishment: CONDIGN

merriment or spirited gaiety: MIRTH

merry-go-round: WHIRLIGIG

mess, confused condition: MARE'S NEST

messenger, especially one on urgent or diplomatic business: COURIER

messiah or prohet in Islam: MAHDI

metal condition, as regards hardness and elasticity: TEMPER

metal disk or spangle: PAILLETTE

metal-and-enamel work: CLOISONNÉ

metals and alloys, as a science: METALLURGY

metalware with enameled or lacquered design: TOLE

metaphorical, flowery: FIGURATIVE

meter mixed within a poem: LOGAOEDIC

Mexican dish of hot-seasoned meat and corn, wrapped in corn husks: TAMALES

Mexican farm laborer who enters United States illegally: WETBACK

Mexican flat, round cake: TORTILLA

Mexican strong, alcoholic liquor: TEQUILA

Michigan resident: MICHIGANITE, MICHIGANDER

microscopic, small to the point of being incalculable: INFINITESIMAL

middle class: BOURGEOIS

middle number in a series of statistics: MEDIAN

middle way: VIA MEDIA

middleman handling transactions between company issuing new securities and the public: INVESTMENT BANKER

midget, dwarf: HOMUNCULUS

midway in the action rather than at the start: IN MEDIAS RES

mighty, powerful: PUISSANT

mild, gentle, favorable: BENIGN

mild or bland word substituted for one that might give offense or pain: EUPHEMISM

milder, less severe, more moderate: MITIGATED

mildly given reproof: ADMONITION

milieu: AMBIENCE

military aircraft on a single mission: SORTIE

military class in command of the government: STRATOCRACY

military court: COURT-MARTIAL

military detachment designated to do a particular job: DETAIL

military equipment and supplies: MATERIEL

military equipment of the heavy variety: HARDWARE

military headgear with visor and a flat top: KEPI

military materiel, cannon: ORDNANCE

military persecution: DRAGONNADE

military position taken on enemy side of a river, defile, etc.: BRIDGEHEAD

military science that deals with procurement, maintenance, movement, disposition of all supplies and personnel: LOGISTICS

milk included: AU LAIT

milklike: LACTESCENT

milk fermented by a bacterium: YOGURT

milk from mare or camel, fermented: KUMISS

milk's thin part that separates from solids, as in making cheese: WHEY

milky: LACTEAL

milky liquid: EMULSION

million tons of TNT as the measurement of an explosive: MEGATON

mimic, play the part of: IMPERSONATE

mind controlling matter: PSYCHOKINESIS

mineral springs treatment of disease: BALNEOLOGY

mingle in a friendly fashion with people of an enemy or conquered country: FRATERNIZE

minor, secondary, casual: INCIDENTAL

minor league of no note: BUSH LEAGUE

minority incursion into a neighborhood used to frighten homeowners into selling: BLOCKBUSTING

miracles, as a study: THAUMATOLOGY

mirage, especially as observed in the Strait of Messina: FATA MORGANA

mirror between two windows: PIER GLASS

mirror for signaling by flashes of light: HELIOGRAPH

mirror hung on horizontal pivots in a frame: CHEVAL GLASS

misapply, distort: PERVERT

misappropriate or embezzle: DEFALCATE

miscarry: ABORT
miscarry, said of animals: SLINK
miscellany: POTPOURRI
mischief, joke: WAGGERY
mischief-maker: HELLION
mischievous, harmful: MALEFICENT
misconduct of an official: MISPRISION
miser: SKINFLINT
miserable person: WRETCH
miserliness: PARSIMONY
miserly: AVARICIOUS
miserly, hard man: SCROOGE
misery, suffering: TRIBULATION
misfortune: AMBSACE
misgiving, fear: QUALM
mishaps in actions, speech, or memory: PARAPRAXIS
mislead: BAMBOOZLE
mislead: DELUDE
mislead or deceive: EQUIVOCATE
misleading talk: HUMBUG
mismated, conflicting, discordant: INCOMPATIBLE
misrepresent: BELIE
misrepresent, twist, bend: DISTORT
missile with two or more warheads aimed at separate targets: MIRV
missile's forward separable section designed to stand intense heat: NOSE CONE
missile's nose containing the explosive: WARHEAD
misstroke or misplay: FOOZLE
mist or fog: BRUME
mistake, error, false step: FAUX PAS
mistress of any fashionable household: CHATELAINE
misty, unclear, dark: MURKY
misuse of words: CATACHRESIS
miswriting of words or phrases generally caused by cerebral injury: PARAGRAPHIA
mix up, confuse: DISORIENT
mix up ingredients for a drink or a dish: CONCOCT
mixed fruits or vegetables used as dessert or salad: MACEDOINE
mixed metaphor: CATACHRESIS
mixed meter in a poem: LOGAOEDIC
mixed origin, half-breed: HYBRID
mixed-up: ADDLED, ADDLE-BRAINED, ADDLEHEADED, ADDLEPATED
mixture, medley: POTPOURRI
mixture in a society of ethnic, racial, religious, or cultural groups: PLURALISM
mixture in an artistic composition of features from various sources: PASTICHE
mixture of a confused mass of elements: MEDLEY
mixture of languages in one literary composition: MACARONIC
mob rule: OCHLOCRACY
mobile-home area: TRAILER PARK
mock, jeer, defy, scoff: FLOUT
mock, joke: JAPE
model, pattern, typical example: EXEMPLAR
model of an apparatus or structure: MOCKUP
model of the human body used to show off clothes: MANNEQUIN
model or perfect standard: PROTOTYPE
moderate, cautious, opposed to change: CONSERVATIVE
moderate, restrained: TEMPERATE
moderate tempo in music: ANDANTE
moderately good, average: RESPECTABLE
moderation produced by addition of another element: TEMPER
modest, shy, coy, reserved: DEMURE
modesty: PUDENCY
modification of the causes of a result by the result itself: FEEDBACK
moist, damp: HUMID
moisten and rub the body with oil: EMBROCATE
moisture absorbing: DELIQUESCENT
moisture measurement (in the air): HYGROMETRY
mold in which something is cast or shaped: MATRIX
moldable: PLASTIC
molding around the walls, close to the ceiling: CORNICE
molding or casting of footprints, etc., for use in criminal investigation: MOULAGE
monetary matters: PECUNIARY
money, booty: PELF
money bet or invested by supposedly knowing people: SMART MONEY
money carried by a woman on a date to let her get home alone if need be: MAD MONEY
money changing: AGIOTAGE
money given to one who helped a person

or company obtain a job or contract: KICKBACK

money in circulation lessened, resulting in a decline in prices: DEFLATION

money or assistance furnished to advance a venture: GRUBSTAKE

money paid to a person to prevent his disclosing something: HUSH MONEY

money pooled for any specific purpose: KITTY

money used for corrupt political purposes: SLUSH FUND

money-making: LUCRATIVE

mongolism: DOWN'S SYNDROME

monkey or ape: SIMIAN

monk's haircut, with the crown of the head shaved: TONSURE

monochromatic: HOMOCHROMATIC

monologue: SOLILOQUY

monstrosity, in biology: TERATISM

monstrous act, wickedness: ENORMITY

monthly: MENSAL

monument to a dead person containing no body: CENOTAPH

moo like a cow: LOW

moon's surface, as a subject of scientific study: SELENOGRAPHY

mooring rope or cable: HAWSER

moral corruption: DRY ROT

moral decline or decay: DECADENCE

moral guide, maxim, rule: PRECEPT

moral sense of right and wrong lacking: AMORPHOUS

moralizing, pedantic: DIDACTIC

moralizing, trite: SENTENTIOUS

morally bad: UNSAVORY

morally debased, degraded: SCROFULOUS

morally degraded: DEGENERATE

morally neutral: ADIAPHOROUS

morally unrestrained, unchaste: LIBERTINE

more than one wife or husband at once: POLYGAMY

more than the regular number: SUPERNUMERARY

morning call by bugle or drum signaling the time to rise: REVEILLE

morning song: MATIN

morose, gloomy, grave: SATURNINE

mortal blow or death blow: COUP DE GRACE

mortar that is thin and used to fill crevices between bricks or tiles: GROUT

mosaic pattern: TESSELLATED

mosaic piece, as of stone or glass: TESSERA

mosaic woodwork style, popular in Renaissance Italy: INTARSIA

Moscow resident: MOSCOVITE

Moses books in Bible: TORAH, PENTATEUCH

Moslem law as observed by the orthodox: SUNNA

Moslem prince or commander, especially in Arabia: EMIR

Moslem scholars: ULEMA

Moslem term for devil: SHAITAN

Moslem title of respect for one who has memorized the Koran: HAFIZ

Moslem's sacred book: KORAN

Moslems who slew during Crusades: ASSASSINS

moth or butterfly: LEPIDOPTERAN

mother as the head of the family: MATRIARCHY

mother-of-pearl shellfish: ABALONE

mother worship that is psychologically harmful: MOMISM

mother's side of the family, in kinship: ENATE

motion picture art and production: CINEMATOGRAPHY

motion picture or recording term for an uninterrupted run of a camera or recording apparatus: TAKE

motion study without reference to particular forces or bodies: KINEMATICS

motionless: STOCK-STILL

motionless, not moving: IMMOBILE

motionless with horror or awe: TRANSFIXED

motivating force, incentive: IMPETUS

motivation or reward offered for an action: INDUCEMENT

motor mounted on the rear of a small boat: OUTBOARD MOTOR

mottled, especially in white and black: PIEBALD

motto or quotation prefixed to a book: EPIGRAPH

mound, manmade, often of great size and very old: TUMULUS

mound or small round hill: KNOLL

moundy, hilly: TUMULOSE

mountain base or foot of a mountain: PIEDMONT

mountain mass of separate peaks: MASSIF

mountain nymph: OREAD

mountain range or chain: SIERRA

mountaineering term for descent of a cliff, using a rope: RAPPEL

mountains, as a study: OROGRAPHY

mournful, sad, painful: DOLOROUS

mournful, sad in a ludicrous manner: LUGUBRIOUS

mournful, sorrowful: PLAINTIVE

mournful, wretched: WOEBEGONE

mourning or lamentation in verse or song: ELEGY

mouth, opening: ORIFICE

mouth and its diseases, as a branch of medicine: STOMATOLOGY

mouth gaping, expanse of open mouth: RICTUS

move, especially in diplomacy: DÉMARCHE

move across: TRAVERSE

move ahead slowly but steadily: FORGE

move backward, withdraw: RECEDE

move designed to gain an advantage: GAMBIT

move dreamily or idly: MAUNDER

move heavily and clumsily: FLUMP

move or roll tumultuously: WELTER

move rapidly, scour, search: SKIRR

move sideways: SIDLE

move swiftly and with force: HURTLE

move the camera so as to photograph an entire scene, in movies or television: PAN

move unsteadily or irregularly at sea: YAW

move with exaggerated tosses of the body: FLOUNCE

move with rumbling noise, move clumsily: LUMBER

movement of inanimate objects without apparent external cause: TELEKINESIS

movement or change that is constant: FLUX

movements or strokes that are artful: MANEUVERS

movement or structure that is gracefully proportioned: EURYTHMIC

movie: FLICK

movie change in sound track from original language to another: DUBBING

movie device to translate dialogue from one language to another by superimposing lines on the screen: SUBTITLE

movie making: CINEMATOGRAPHY

movie showing in advance of regular showings: SNEAK PREVIEW

moving abruptly from one condition to another: TRANSILIENT

moving imperceptibly but harmfully: INSIDIOUS

moving in an emotional way, touching: POIGNANT

moving out in a different direction: DIVERGENT

moving rapidly: SPANKING

much, very much, in music: MOLTO

mud or silt deposited by flowing water: SULLAGE

muddle, bewilder, obscure: OBFUSCATE

muddle or confuse: EMBROIL

muddled, confused: TURBID

mug or jug in form of an old man wearing a three-cornered hat: TOBY

multilingual: POLYGLOT

multiply by natural reproduction, breed: PROPAGATE

mumps: PAROTITIS

munch or chew noisily: CHAMP

municipal government by elected commission: COMMISSION PLAN

mural painting using pigments mixed with waterglass: STEREOCHROMY

murder of husband by wife or wife by husband: MARITICIDE

murderous: HOMICIDAL

murmuring softly, rustling, whispering: SUSURRANT

murmuring sound, as of the wind: SOUGH

muscle and bone branch of surgery: ORTHOPEDICS

muscle pain or cramp: MYALGIA

muscle sense: KINESTHESIA

muscle spasm that pulls the head to one side: TORTICOLLIS

muscle that surrounds an opening or tube in the body and can open or close it: SPHINCTER

muscles, as a scientific study: MYOLOGY

muscular coordination loss: ATAXIA

muscular development that is light: ASTHENIC

muscular rigidity and irresponsiveness to stimuli: CATALEPSY

muscular rigidity, stupor, occasional mental agitation: CATATONIA

muscular spasm: CLONUS

muscular strengh: BRAWN

museum or library overseer: CURATOR

music at performer's pleasure: A CAPRICCIO

music by a small group, as a string quartet: CHAMBER MUSIC

music direction calling for slowness: LENTO

music direction to perform very loudly: FORTISSIMO

music lacking tonality because of disregard of key: ATONALITY

music played between stanzas of a hymn or acts of a play: INTERLUDE

music style that is smooth and flowing: LEGATO

music swelling in loudness: CRESCENDO

music tempo that is moderate: ANDANTE

music tempo that is slow: LARGO

music with fast time: ALLEGRO

musical, dramatic or ballet offering given between acts of play or opera: INTERMEZZO

musical bass instrument, large, of brass and having three to five valves: TUBA

musical brass wind instrument with coiled tube and flaring bell: FRENCH HORN

musical brass wind instrument with long, doubled-up tube: TROMBONE

musical composition for a story that is sung but not acted: CANTATA

musical composition for several male voices, having no accompaniment: GLEE

musical composition for solo instruments and orchestra: CONCERTO

musical composition in which a theme is repeated contrapuntally: FUGUE

musical composition on a religious subject for voices and orchestra: ORATORIO

musical composition suggestive of improvisation: RHAPSODY

musical composition that is playful and lively: HUMORESQUE

musical direction meaning more: PIU

musical double-reed woodwind instrument: OBOE

musical flourish: CADENZA

musical instrument in the flute category: PICCOLO

musical instrument like a piano in which strings are plucked: HARPSICHORD

musical instrument that has wooden bars of graduated length that are struck with wooden hammers: XYLOPHONE

musical instrument with double reed and low pitch: ENGLISH HORN

musical instrument with metal bars that

produce bell-like tones when struck: GLOCKENSPIEL

musical instrument with metal strings that is played with two small hammers: DULCIMER

musical notation for some stringed instruments that indicates rhythm and fingering: TABULATURE

musical note that ornaments or embellishes a more important note: GRACE NOTE

musical notes that are short and detached: STACCATO

musical or melodious: CANOROUS

musical passage ending a composition: CODA

musical passage or movement that is stately: MAESTOSO

musical piece consisting of parts of different songs: MEDLEY

musical play in a light vein: OPERETTA

musical section once considered essential to a proper performance but now often optional: OBLIGATO

musical sliding effect: GLISSANDO

musical solo composition or an exercise designed to perfect some technique: ETUDE

musical style of West Indies: CALYPSO

musical term for gradual slackening of tempo: RITARDANDO

musical term for medium, moderate: MEZZO

musical term for quick: PRESTO

musical term for slowing down gradually: RALLENTANDO

musical term for slightly, somewhat: POCO

musical term for very fast: PRESTISSIMO

musical term for very soft: PIANISSIMO

musical trembling effect caused by rapid, tiny variations in pitch: VIBRATO

musical use of syllables, as do, re, mi, etc.: SOLMIZATION

musician of eminence or a master in any art: MAESTRO

musing, daydreaming: REVERIE

muslin of a thin weave: TARLATAN

mustard plaster: POULTICE

musty, moldy, old-fashioned: FUSTY

mutilate a book by cutting out the illustrations: GRANGERIZE

mutilation, destruction or alteration, especially of a legal document: SPOLIATION

mutual: RECIPROCAL, BILATERAL
mysterious: ARCANE
mysterious: CABALISTIC
mysterious, defying understanding: IN-
    SCRUTABLE
mystery story: WHODUNIT
mystic or secret system: CABALA
mystical: ANAGOGIC
mystical poem or song: RUNE

mystical status attributed to a person, an
    institution, an activity, etc.: MYS-
    TIQUE
mystifying, secret, hidden, puzzling:
    CRYPTIC
myths explained on the premise that they
    are based on actual events: EUHE-
    MERISM

N

nag at: BADGER
nagging, petty: NIGGLING
nail, claw, hoof: UNGUIS
nail that is slender and small with a small head: BRAD
naive, insipid, dry, lacking interest, barren: JEJUNE
naive, straightforward, frank, innocent, simple: INGENUOUS
name: APPELLATION
name derived from a place, place name: TOPONYM
name of broker rather than customer used in securities holdings: STREET NAME
name of individual used for a class: ANTONOMASIA
name of one person taken by another: ALLONYM
name of person from which name of a state or institution is derived: EPONYM
name of plant or creature in common rather than scientific language: VERNACULAR
name of writer at head of article: BYLINE
name only, nominal: TITULAR
name plate, signature, trademark, etc., on a single type plate: LOGOTYPE
name replaced by title or epithet: ANTONOMASIA
nameless, anonymous: INNOMINATE
namely: VIZ
namely, to wit: SCILICET
names, terminology: NOMENCLATURE
names, as a study: ONOMASTICS
naming a parent after his or her child: TEKNONYMY
naming a thing by substituting one of its attributes or a term it suggests: METONYMY

nape: SCRUFF
nape, back of the neck: NUCHA
narcotic made from Indian hemp: HASHISH
narrow, close or small margin or space: HAIRBREADTH
narrow, limited, provincial: PAROCHIAL
narrow, unsophisticated: PROVINCIAL
narrow elevated walking space: CATWALK
narrow or limited in outlook, provincial: INSULAR
narrowed: ANGUSTATE
narrow-minded: PETTY
narrow-minded, bigoted, obstinate: HIDEBOUND
nasal tone: SNUFFLE
nation's total production of goods and services: GROSS NATIONAL PRODUCT (G.N.P.)
native, indigenous: ENCHORIAL
native language of a place: VERNACULAR
native person, animal or thing: INDIGENE
native to a given area, peculiar to a given country or people: ENDEMIC
native to a region: INDIGENOUS
native to or in a place: ABORIGINAL
natural, coarse, unrefined: EARTHY
natural, existing from birth: INBORN
natural accompaniment, attribute or endowment: APPANAGE
natural attraction: AFFINITY
natural resources diminishing in supply therefore reducing income from them: DEPLETION
natural response to stimulus: INSTINCT
natural roughness or lack of polish: AGRESTIC
natural virtues: CARDINAL VIRTUES
nauseated: QUEASY, SICKENED
nauseated or shocked easily, prudish: SQUEAMISH

navel: UMBILICUS

navel contemplation: OMPHALOSKEPSIS

near, neighboring, adjoining: VICINAL

nearly, almost: WELL-NIGH

nearness: CONTIGUITY

nearness: PROXIMITY

nearness, kinship: PROPINQUITY

nearsighted, obtuse: MYOPIC

necessarily: PERFORCE

necessary means: WHEREWITHAL

neck ailment caused by muscle contraction: TORTICOLLIS

neck or base of the brain jolted, as in an automobile crash: WHIPLASH

necklace worn high around the throat: CHOKER

neckline cut low in a dress: DECOLLETAGE

necktie, wide and soft, knotted loosely: WINDSOR TIE

necktie or scarf: CRAVAT

neck's back part: SCRUFF

need for, lack of, or desire for: DESIDERATE

needle-pricking body tissues to diagnose or remedy ills: ACUPUNCTURE

needful or right to be: BEHOOVE

negative of a statement's opposite used to express an affirmative: LITOTES

neglect, disregard: SLIGHT

neglect, overlook, disregard: PRETERMIT

neglect or failure to meet an obligation: DEFAULT

neglect or willful omission, failure in duty: DERELICTION

neglected, abandoned, unused condition: DESUETUDE

neglected, decayed, in disrepair: DILAPIDATED

negligent, careless: REMISS

negotiations between organized workers and their employers: COLLECTIVE BARGAINING

neighboring, near: VICINAL

nerve inflammation: NEURITIS

nervous excitement, anxiety, agitation: DITHER

nervous or restless movements: FIDGET

nervous system and its disorders, as a study: NEUROLOGY

nervously excited, overstrained: OVERWROUGHT

nest in high place of a predatory bird: AERIE

network: RETICULATION

network, complicated interconnection of parts: PLEXUS

network or system to catch a criminal: DRAGNET

neurotic condition caused by feelings of inferiority: INFERIORITY COMPLEX

nevertheless: NOTWITHSTANDING

new birth, revival: RENASCENCE

new convert, beginner, novice: NEOPHYTE

new life, restoration, reconstitution: REGENERATION

new movement leaders: AVANT GARDE

new word or new meaning for existing word: NEOLOGISM

New York Stock Exchange: BIG BOARD

newcomer to an organization, cult, fraternity: INITIATE

newly born: YEANLING

newly conceived, just developing: NASCENT

newly introduced element: INNOVATION

newly married man: BENEDICT

newly rich or influential, upstart: PARVENU

news correspondent who works part time for a paper elsewhere: STRINGER

newspaper or magazine listing of editors, staff and owners: MASTHEAD

newspaper section in European papers usually at the bottom of the page, where fiction is printed: FEUILLETON

newspaper with sheets half the standard size, and usually emphasizing pictures: TABLOID

newspaper work shift beginning during the late night hours: LOBSTER SHIFT

newspaper's early edition: BULLDOG EDITION

newsstand, bandstand, booth, usually lightly constructed and open: KIOSK

next: PROXIMATE

next to nothing: AMBSACE

next to the last: PENULTIMATE

niches for cinerary urns or as vaults for the dead: COLUMBARIUM

nickname: SOBRIQUET

night and day of equal length, marking start of spring or autumn: EQUINOX

night club with recorded music for dancing: DISCOTHÈQUE

night or moon blindness: NYCTALOPIA

night vigil over a body before burial: WAKE

nightmare: INCUBUS

nine inches long: SPAN
nine-day prayer recitation: NOVENA
ninefold: NONUPLE
90 to 100 years old: NONAGENARIAN
nipple's dark circular background: ARE-OLA
no fraud or trickery: ABOVEBOARD
no ifs, ands, or buts: CATEGORICAL
no let-up: CONTINUOUS
nobility's obligations (French): NOBLESSE OBLIGE
noble, lofty or impressive, as in quality or style: SONOROUS
no-contest plea in criminal case without admission of guilt: NOLO CONTEN-DERE
nodding of the head: NUTATION
noise measure: DECIBEL
noise that is clattering: BRATTLE
noise that is shrill, creaking or grating: STRIDOR
noisily crashing, as waves: PLANGENT
noisy: CLAMOROUS
noisy: VOCIFEROUS
noisy and loud: UPROARIOUS
noisy commotion of a crowd: TUMULT
noisy confusion: BEDLAM
noisy disturbance: FRACAS
noisy gaiety, boisterous merriment: HI-LARITY
noisy ghost: POLTERGEIST
nominal, in name only: TITULAR
nonconforming, contrary: PERVERSE
nonconformist: MAVERICK
nonconformist: RECUSANT
nonconformity: DISSENT
nonessential attribute: ACCIDENTAL
noninterference, especially by government in business: LAISSEZ FAIRE
nonmaterial, spiritual, insubstantial: IN-CORPOREAL
nonsense: ABRACADABRA
nonsense: AMPHIGORY
nonsense: BALDERDASH
nonsense, meaningless chatter: SKIMBLE-SCAMBLE
nonsense, worthless, rubbish: TRUMPERY
nonviolent opposition: PASSIVE RESIS-TANCE
noodles, broad and flat, served with butter or a sauce: FETTUCCINE
normal consequence: COROLLARY
North African city's crowded section: CASBAH

nose, humorous name for a large nose: PROBOSCIS
nose and its diseases, as a branch of medicine: RHINOLOGY
nosebleed: EPISTAXIS
not concrete: ABSTRACT
not inherent: ADVENTITIOUS
not moving, motionless: IMMOBILE
"not to mention . . . :" APOPHASIS
notch or cut carved out by a saw or ax: KERF
notched at the edge: SERRATED
notched or indented, as a battlement on a fortress: CRENELATED
notched pattern on edge of fabric: PINKED
notches along an edge or border, space from a margin: INDENTION
notes in music lengthened or shortened arbitrarily: RUBATO
notes in music that are short and detached: STACCATO
notes of chord played in quick succession: ARPEGGIO
notify: APPRISE
notion or fancy that emerges suddenly: WHIM
notoriety that is evil: INFAMY
notoriously bad: ARRANT
notoriously bad, odious, vile reputation: INFAMOUS
nouns linked by conjunction that express same thought as noun with modifier: HENDIADYS
nourish, rear, train: NURTURE
nourishment: ALIMENT
novel that includes actual persons under fictitious names: ROMAN À CLEF
novel that is brief and often contains a moral: NOVELLA
novice: ABECEDARIAN
novice, beginner: NEOPHYTE
novice, beginner: TYRO
noxious, harmful: VIRULENT
noxious, unwholesome atmosphere, influence, effect, etc.: MIASMA
nuclear bomb: A-BOMB
nucleus or core of a group: CADRE
nudge or touch with a slight jar, shake lightly, stimulate: JOG
null and void: DIRIMENT
null and void: INVALID
numb: TORPID
number in arithmetic from which the subtrahend is to be subtracted: MINUEND

number of members necessary for an assembly to transact business: QUORUM

number sequence in which the ratio between each two terms is the same: GEOMETRIC PROGRESSION

number symbols from 0 to 9: DIGITS

number that is divisible by two or more numbers: COMMON MULTIPLE

number the pages of a book: FOLIATE, PAGINATE

number to be subtracted from another: SUBTRAHEND

number-using computer: DIGITAL COMPUTER

numberless: MYRIAD

numerous, great numbers: MULTITUDINOUS

nun's headdress covering head, cheeks, and neck: WIMPLE

nuptial poem or song: EPITHALAMIUM

nurse who rears a child without suckling it: DRY NURSE

nutrition and its processes: TROPHIC

nutrition that is defective or perverted: DYSTROPHY

nymph dwelling in or presiding over woods and trees: DRYAD

nymph fabled to live and die in the tree which she inhabited: HAMADRYAD

oath plus written statement: AFFIDAVIT

oath taken by a prospective witness or juror: VOIR DIRE

oath taker: JURANT

obedience or servility that is excessive: OBSEQUIOUS

obedient: DUTEOUS

object made by man: ARTIFACT

object of attention: CYNOSURE

object to, hesitate, take exception to: DEMUR

object serving as a boundary mark or guide to travelers: LANDMARK

object regarded as having magical powers: FETISH

objection that is trivial: QUIDDITY

objectionable, offensive: OBNOXIOUS

objective, impartial, unbiased: DISPASSIONATE

objective, unbiased: DISINTERESTED

objectivity: DISINTEREST

obligation or penalty established by authority: IMPOSITION

obligation owed, faithfulness, loyalty: FEALTY

obligatory: INCUMBENT

obligatory: IRREMISSIBLE

obligatory, required: MANDATORY

obligingness: COMPLAISANCE

oblique direction taken: SKEW

oblique earth deposited by water: ALLUVIUM

oblique or diagonal line: BIAS

oblivion, forgetfulness: LETHE

oblivion-producing potion: NEPENTHE

oblong-shaped cut gem: BAGUETTE

obscene: SCATOLOGICAL

obscene, lecherous, lewd: SALACIOUS

obscene, vulgar: FESCENNINE

obscene talk or conduct: BAWDRY

obscure: AMBIGUOUS

obscure: INCOMPREHENSIBLE

obscure, dim, pertaining to twilight: CREPUSCULAR

obscure, muddle, bewilder,: OBFUSCATE

obscure, overshadow, surpass: ECLIPSE

obscure, unclear, misty, dark: MURKY

obscure or ambiguous saying, riddle, puzzle: ENIGMA

obscure poem or song: RUNE

obsequious, servile: SUBSERVIENT

observation and analysis of one's own thoughts and feelings: INTROSPECTION

observation area built on the roof of a house: WIDOW'S WALK

observation spot or point: COIGN OF VANTAGE

observe, discern, discover with the eye: DESCRY

obsession: IDÉE FIXE

obsession, craze: MANIA. For a listing of such conditions see "manias"

obsolete, outdated, discarded: SUPERANNUATED

obstacle: IMPEDIMENT

obstinacy: PERTINACITY

obstinate, narrow-minded, bigoted: HIDEBOUND

obstinate, sinful: UNREGENERATE

obstinate, shrewd, practical: HARDHEADED

obstinate, unmanageable: REFRACTORY

obstinately resistant: DIE-HARD

obstruct, block: STYMIE

obstruct, frustrate, foil: THWART

obstruct, hinder: CRIMP

obstruction of action through time-killing tactics: FILIBUSTER

obtain by entreaty: IMPETRATE

obtrude or force oneself or one's will on another without right: IMPOSE

obtrusive, forward, pushy: OFFICIOUS
obtuse, nearsighted: MYOPIC
obvious, manifest, evident: PATENT
occasional: SPORADIC
occult: CABALA
occupation, avocation, interest: PURSUIT
occupation, career: VOCATION
occupation for which one is suited and well equipped: MÉTIER
occupy, amuse oneself: DISPORT
occupy completely, monopolize, absorb: ENGROSS
occurring or existing at the same time: SIMULTANEOUS
occurring together: CONCOMITANT
ocean grave of the drowned: DAVY JONES'S LOCKER
ocean wave, destructive, caused by underwater earthquake: TSUNAMI
oceanic: PELAGIC
oceanic: THALASSIC
odd, freakish: WHIMSICAL
odd, unconventional: OUTRÉ
odd, wild idea: VAGARY
odious, notoriously bad, vile reputation: INFAMOUS
odor from decaying matter: EFFLUVIUM
off-color, suggestive: RISQUÉ
offense against sovereign authority, treason: LESE MAJESTY
offense given or taken: UMBRAGE
offense not so serious as a felony, in law: MISDEMEANOR
offensive, disagreeable: UNSAVORY
offensive, disgusting, stinking, noxious: NOISOME
offensive, objectionable: OBNOXIOUS
offensive because of excessiveness or insincerity: FULSOME
offer: PROFFER
offer, as money: TENDER
offhand: CASUAL
offhand, free and easy: CAVALIER
offhand, spur of the moment: IMPROMPTU
office or position that pays, but involves few or no duties: SINECURE
offices filled through political power: PATRONAGE
official approval as of a literary work: IMPRIMATUR
official arbitrary decree: UKASE
official defeated in an election but filling out an unexpired term: LAME DUCK
official who is pompous or pretentious: PANJANDRUM

official who is tyrannical: SATRAP
officials, etc., arranged by rank: HIERARCHY
offset: COUNTERBALANCE
offset, make up, compensate: COUNTERVAIL
offshoot, branch: RAMIFICATION
offspring: PROGENY
offspring, descendant: SCION
offspring of a stallion and a female ass: HINNY
offspring of parents of different racial stock: HALF-BREED
offstage waiting room for performers: GREEN ROOM
oil consecrated for use in church: CHRISM
oil or grease something: LUBRICATE
oil well from which oil spouts: GUSHER
oily: OLEAGINOUS
oily, greasy: PINGUID
oily-tongued, suave to an excess: UNCTUOUS
old, infirm, doting: SENILE
old age, senility: DOTAGE
old age, as a branch of medicine: GERIATRICS
old age weakness: CADUCITY
old-fashioned: ANTEDILUVIAN
old fashioned: DÉMODÉ
old-fashioned: PASSÉ
old-fashioned, fussy person: FUDDY-DUDDY
old-fashioned, musty, moldy: FUSTY
old-fashioned, out of step with the times, ancient, outmoded: ANTEDILUVIAN
old-fashioned or ultra-conservative person: FOGY
old maid: SPINSTER
old men forming a governing body: GERONTOCRACY
old salt, veteran sailor: SHELLBACK
Old Testament interpretation largely mystical: ANAGOGE
old-woman-like: ANILE
omelet prepared with ham, onion, and green pepper: WESTERN OMELET
omen, portent: AUGURY
omen, warning, portent: PRESAGE
omen of death: KNELL
ominous, awesome: PORTENTOUS
omission of conjunctions: ASYNDETON
omission of understood word or words: ELLIPSIS
omission of words from a sentence but leaving the meaning intact: ELISION

omit a vowel or syllable in pronunciation: ELIDE

omitting, passing over: PRETERITION

omnipresent: UBIQUITOUS

on the agenda for consideration: ON THE TAPIS

on the alert, wide-awake: ON THE QUI VIVE

on the up-and-up: ABOVEBOARD

on your mark, get set, go: ASYNDETON

one behind the other, as on a bicycle built for two: TANDEM

one-colored: MONOCHROME

one dollar per share of stock: POINT

one-eyed: POLYPHEMUS

one following another: SERIATIM

one hundred years: CENTENARY, CENTENNIAL

one husband at a time: MONANDROUS

one leg on each side of something: ASTRIDE

one-man rule with absolute power: AUTOCRACY

one of a kind, unique: SUI GENERIS

one side only: UNILATERAL

one-sided: EX PARTE

one-sided in heaviness or size: LOPSIDED

onomatopoeia: ECHOISM

ooze or trickle forth: EXUDE

open: ABOVEBOARD

open, unconcealed, evident: OVERT

open out, develop: EVOLVE

open paved area adjoining a home: PATIO

open to injury, attack, or criticism: VULNERABLE

open to question, arguable: DISPUTABLE

open to the sky, unroofed: HYPETHRAL

open-handed in giving: MUNIFICENT

opening, break or interruption of continuity, gap: HIATUS

opening, mouth: ORIFICE

opening cut in an interior wall of a church to allow those in a side aisle to see the main altar: HAGIOSCOPE

opening move in chess: GAMBIT

opening or slit in the upper part of a dress or skirt: PLACKET

opening oration at a commencement: SALUTATORY

opening performance: PREMIERE

open-minded: PERVIOUS

opera in which music is subordinated to words: SINGSPIEL

opera singer of note: DIVA

opera's verbal text: LIBRETTO

operetta form in Spain: ZARZUELA

opinion adopted beforehand: PRECONCEPTION

opinion or agreement that is general: CONSENSUS

opinion or belief contrary to established doctrine: HERESY

opinionated, but immature: SOPHOMORIC

opponent who takes wrong side perversely: DEVIL'S ADVOCATE

oppose, argue: CONTROVERT

oppose, contradict, deny: GAINSAY

oppose, thwart: TRAVERSE

oppose or protest by pleading: REMONSTRATE

opposed or inconsistent: REPUGNANT

opposed to change or progress, conservative: REACTIONARY

opposed to usual beliefs: HETERODOX

opponent, pursuer, or antagonist who is unusually tenacious: NEMESIS

opposite: POLAR

opposite or reversed in order or effect: INVERSE

opposite sides: ANTIPODAL

opposite word: ANTONYM

opposite meaning to words said sarcastically or humorously or with opposite result to what is expected: IRONY

opposite terms combined in one phrase: OXYMORON

opposition expressed: ADVERSATIVE

opposition that is nonviolent: PASSIVE RESISTANCE

opposition to human education: OBSCURANTISM

oppressive thing, burden: INCUBUS

optical device in which pictures on both sides of a card or disk appear to blend when the card is twirled: THAUMATROPE

optimistic, buoyant, cheerful: SANGUINE

optimistic, happy: UPBEAT

optimistic about rising prices, as in the stock market: BULLISH

oracular or ambiguous: DELPHIC

oral, not written, referring especially to wills: NUNCUPATIVE

oral, spoken: VIVA VOCE

oral defamatory statement: SLANDER

oral teaching: CATECHESIS

oration opening a commencement: SALUTATORY

oratory that is bombastic and artificial: DECLAMATION

orbital point farthest from the earth: APOGEE

orbital point of a celestial body or satellite that is nearest to the earth: PERIGEE

orbital point that is nearest the sun: PERIHELION

orbiting man-made body: SATELLITE

orchestra seats in a theater: PARQUET

order, command, forbid: ENJOIN

order, decree, enact: ORDAIN

order or send back: REMAND

order requiring certain action: MANDAMUS

order requiring one to take, or refrain from, a certain action: INJUNCTION

order that is positive and authoritative: FIAT

order to buy or sell at the most advantageous price: MARKET ORDER

order to buy or sell securities that is good only for the day on which it was entered: DAY ORDER

ordinary, commonplace: MUNDANE

ordinary, simple, commonplace: EXOTERIC

ordinary, uninspired, commonplace: PROSAIC

ordinary or hackneyed: BANAL

ordinary people, common run: RUCK

organ that uses reeds and resembles a harmonium: MELODEON

organic equilibrium: HOMEOSTASIS

organic whole has a reality other and greater than the sum of its parts, according to this theory: HOLISM

organisms derived asexually from a common ancestor: CLONE

organisms in relation to their environment: ECOLOGY

organizer, manager or sponsor of performers for entertainment: IMPRESARIO

organ-like instrument with steam whistles: CALLIOPE

orgy: BACCHANAL

origin: PROVENANCE

original, creative: PROMETHEAN

original, first, principal: PRIMAL

original, primitive, elemental: PRIMORDIAL

original condition, unused, brand new: MINT CONDITION

original pattern: ARCHETYPE

originate, begin, commence: INITIATE

originate, bring forth: SPAWN

ornament, decorate: EMBELLISH

ornament or mark used in typography: DINGBAT

ornament or trinket either gaudy or trifling: FALLAL

ornament resembling a twisted cable or cord: TORSADE

ornament that hangs: PENDANT

ornament the edge with a series of indentations: ENGRAIL

ornament with raised figures worked on a surface as decoration: EMBOSS

ornamental openwork usually composed of interlaced parts: FRETWORK

ornamental stand with shelves: ÉTAGÈRE

ornamentation done with tools, as on leather: TOOLING

ornamentation or style that is extravagant: BAROQUE

ornamentation with wavy lines or patterns, or with inlaying or etching, as on iron or steel: DAMASCENE

ornamented excessively: ORNATE

ornamental relief work in metal: TOREUTICS

ornamented tastelessly, showy and cheap: TAWDRY

ornate, excessively flowery: FLORID

ornate, florid, showy, bombastic: FLAMBOYANT

ornate writing: PURPLE PROSE

ornateness to excess: FROUFROU

ostentatious, affecting superiority: PRETENTIOUS

ostracize: BLACKBALL

ostracize, banish from society: SEND TO COVENTRY

O the times! O the customs!: O TEMPORA! O MORES!

out and out: ARRANT

out of action: HORS DE COMBAT

out of business: DEFUNCT

out of control: RAMPANT

out of date, not current: OBSOLETE

out of place, inappropriate: MALAPROPOS

out of proportion, not in accordance: INCOMMENSURABLE

out-of-the-blue element introduced to untangle a story plot: DEUS EX MACHINA

outbreak of violence: RAMPAGE

outburst of passion or emotion: ACCESS

outburst that is sudden and turbulent: PAROXYSM

outcast, one socially rejected: PARIAH

outcome in a plot: DENOUEMENT

outcome that is possible: EVENTUALITY

outcry, clamor, shouting: HUE AND CRY

outdated, obsolete, discarded: SUPER-ANNUATED

outdoor celebration, especially a dinner or bazaar: FETE

outdoor party: FETE CHAMPETRE

outer coating or covering, especially a natural covering: INTEGUMENT

outflow: EFFLUENT

outgoing person: EXTROVERT

outgrowth that is unnatural such as a wart: EXCRESCENCE

outlaw, condemn, prohibit: PROSCRIBE

outline: PROSPECTUS

outline, form, shape: FIGURATION

outline, trace out, describe: DELINEATE

outline of the main points of a course of study: SYLLABUS

outline or structure of something: CONFORMATION

outline sketchily: ADUMBRATE

outlying areas: PURLIEU

outmoded, old-fashioned, ancient, out of step with the times: ANTEDILUVIAN

outmost limit: JUMPING-OFF PLACE

outpatient department of hospital: POLICLINIC

outpouring, as of words: SPATE

outrageous, notorious, shocking, disgraceful: FLAGRANT

outside, not central: PERIPHERAL

outside the jurisdiction of a state or country: EXTRATERRITORIAL

outside the nature of something: EXTRINSIC

outspoken, definite, clear, straightforward: EXPLICIT

outstanding: PREEMINENT

outstanding, important feature: HIGHLIGHT

outwardly real, or made outwardly real: EXTERNALIZED

outwit, avoid: CIRCUMVENT

outwit, cheat: EUCHRE

ovary removal from a female animal: SPAY

oven or furnace for baking or drying bricks, pottery, cement: KILN

overabundance: PLETHORA

overbearing, arbitrary: HIGHHANDED

overcome, beat: DRUB

overdemonstrative: EFFUSIVE

overdo, as an argument: BELABOR

overelaborate, florid: ROCOCO

overflowing: INUNDANT

overflowing, full: TEEMING

overflowing, lavish: EXUBERANT

overflow or rise of a stream occurring suddenly: FRESHET

overlapping edges as in tiles or shingles: IMBRICATE

overloaded, inflated: PLETHORIC

overlook, disregard: PRETERMIT

overlook something as if it had not happened: CONDONE

overly polite: CEREMONIOUS

overnice, squeamish: FASTIDIOUS

overprecise, finicky: NIGGLING

overrefined in behavior, writing, etc.: PRECIOUS

overrun, occur in large numbers so as to be annoying or dangerous: INFEST

overshadow, obscure, surpass: ECLIPSE

overshadowing: ADUMBRAL

oversight: INADVERTENCE

oversimplifying problems: SIMPLISTIC

overspread, as with color: SUFFUSE

overstatement or exaggeration intended for the effect and not to be taken seriously: HYPERBOLE

overstrained, nervously excited: OVERWROUGHT

overthrow of a government, usually sudden and often accompanied by violence: COUP D'ÉTAT

overthrow or undermine: SUBVERT

overwhelming, domineering: OVERBEARING

overwhelm, swallow up: ENGULF

owned by a proprietor, protected as by patent or copyright: PROPRIETARY

ownership of securities: LONG

Oxford resident: OXONIAN

oxygen in liquid form: LOX

P

pacesetter, leader: FUGLEMAN

pacify, soothe: SALVE

pacify, appease, quiet down: MOLLIFY

pack animal, beast of burden: SUMPTER

pack or force down by repeated pressure: TAMP

packed or wedged firmly, thickly populated: IMPACTED

packing material composed of thin wood shavings: EXCELSIOR

page at start of a book: FRONTISPIECE

page in a book or magazine that is larger than page size and can be unfolded: GATEFOLD

page number in a book: FOLIO

page on the left-hand side of a book: VERSO

pages of a magazine or newspaper that face each other and include related material: DOUBLE TRUCK OR SPREAD

pain, suffering, anguish, distress: TRAVAIL

pain combating: ANALGESIC

pain free: ANALGESIA

pain inflicted on others as a source of pleasure for the inflicter: SADISM

pain relieving: ANODYNE

painful, agonizing: EXCRUCIATING

painful, sad, mournful: DOLOROUS

painful experience, endurance test: ORDEAL

painful inflammation near shoulder: BURSITIS

pains that are violent: THROES

painstaking, overly precise about details: METICULOUS

paint, engrave or draw with dots instead of lines: STIPPLE

painting, using shades of gray only, often in imitation of bas-relief: GRISAILLE

painting in water colors on wet plaster: FRESCO

painting in which pigment is applied thickly to a surface: IMPASTO

painting medium made from a mixture of water and other substances such as egg yolks or glue: TEMPERA

painting method of using varicolored dots: POINTILLISM

painting using opaque colors mixed with water and gum: GOUACHE

pair of matched horses or oxen: SPAN

pair of objects considered as a single unit: DUAD

paired, double or two: BINARY

pairs or separated into pairs: DICHOTOMIZED

pale, colorless: PALLID

pale, ghastly, gaunt: CADAVEROUS

pale, sallow face: WHEYFACE

pale and thin: PEAKED

palm of the hand: THENAR

palm of the hand, sole of the foot: VOLAR

palm off: FOB

palmistry: CHIROMANCY

paltry, pitiable, inferior: SORRY

paltry, trivial: PICAYUNE

pamper: CODDLE

pamper or coddle: COSHER

pamper or pet: COSSET

pampered, overindulged: SPOON-FED

panacea: CATHOLICON

pancakes, thin and rolled in hot orange sauce: CRÊPES SUZETTE

pancakes, thin, with filling: CRÊPES

panel of prospective jurors: VENIRE

paneled lower part of an inner wall: WAINSCOT

panic, amazement or fear that is sudden and paralyzing: CONSTERNATION

pantomime, especially in which Harlequin and clown play leading parts: HARLEQUINADE

pantomime in shadows thrown on a screen or wall: GALANTY SHOW

papal envoy who carries insignia to new cardinals: ABLEGATE

papal letter addressed to the bishops of the world: ENCYCLICAL

paper at front and back of book, one half of which is pasted to the binding: END PAPER

paper chewed into a wet wad for throwing: SPITBALL

paper cover slipped around a book: DUST JACKET

paper fastener of thin wire: STAPLE

paper in units of 480 to 516 sheets: REAM

paper mark of translucent lines or designs: WATERMARK

paper money in small amounts: SCRIP

paper of high grade with smooth surface: WIRE-WOVE

paper scrap: SCRIP

paper size, 23 by 31 inches: IMPERIAL

paper that does not carry the marks of the wire gauze on which it was laid: WOVE PAPER

paper that measures 13 by 16 inches: FOOLS-CAP

paper used by lawyers and usually measuring about 8½ x 13 inches: LEGAL CAP

paper watermarked with fine parallel lines: LAID PAPER

parade: CAVALCADE

parade of persons or animals fastened together: COFFLE

parade or display brazenly or gaudily: FLAUNT

parade or exhibition that is spectacular: PAGEANT

paradise: ELYSIAN FIELDS

paragon, unequaled: NONPAREIL

parallel lines slanting on each side of a spine: HERRINGBONE

parallelogram with oblique angles and its opposite sides equal: RHOMBOID

paralysis of one side of the body: HEMIPLEGIA

paralysis of the lower part of the body: PARAPLEGIA

paralyze with fear, harden, deaden: PETRIFY

parched, arid: TORRID

parchment or tablet in which earlier writing has been erased to make room for a new one: PALIMPSEST

pardon by a government given in general: AMNESTY

pardonable, as sins: REMISSIBLE

pardonable, excusable, as a fault: VENIAL

parent killing: PARRICIDE

parentage or line of descent: FILIATION

parents in common with another: GERMAN

parents of adopted child: ADOPTIVE PARENTS

parley so as to gain time: TEMPORIZE

part, divide, separate: DISSEVER

part of a debt or of a serial story: INSTALLMENT

part used to stand for the whole: SYNECDOCHE

partiality or bias held in advance: PREDILECTION

particle, negatively charged, that forms part of an atom: ELECTRON

particle or speck: MOTE

particular application, not general: AD HOC

particularize: INDIVIDUATE

partisan to excess, fanatic: ZEALOT

partnership of dissimilar organisms: SYMBIOSIS

partnership or company distinguished from a corporation: FIRM

part-time, amusement: DIVERSION

part-time or temporary lodging place: PIED-À-TERRE

party given in the evening: SOIREE

pass assuring the bearer protection on a journey, as in time of war: SAFECONDUCT

pass away, slip by (said of time): ELAPSE

pass imperceptibly from one shade or degree to another: GRADATE

pass through, survive, as a crisis: WEATHER

pass through tissue: TRANSPIRE

passage of ornate writing: PURPLE PROSE

passage or extract, especially from the Bible: PERICOPE

passageway, as between house and garage: BREEZEWAY

passing abruptly from one condition to another: TRANSILIENT

passing lightly from one subject to another, wandering from the point: DISCURSIVE

passing out of use, becoming obsolete: OBSOLESCENT

passion or love that is foolish or unreasoning: INFATUATION

passionate, ardent: TORRID

passive consent: ACQUIESCENCE
passive consent: SUFFERANCE
Passover book containing story of the Exodus: HAGGADAH
passport endorsement granting entry into or passage through a country: VISA
password, rallying cry: WATCHWORD
password, test word: SHIBBOLETH
pasta in the form of dumplings: GNOCCHI
pastoral or rustic: BUCOLIC
pastry shell, fried, in which food may be served: TIMBALE
pastry shell to be filled with meat or fish: VOL-AU-VENT
pastry store: PATISSERIE
path: ACCESS
path of an object moving through space: TRAJECTORY
path that is winding or circuitous: AMBAGE
patient treated at a hospital but not staying there: OUTPATIENT
patriot of an aggressive and boastful nature: JINGO
patriotism that is overzealous: CHAUVINISM
patronizing: CONDESCENDING
pattern, model example: PARADIGM
pattern, model, typical example: EXEMPLAR
pattern or gauge used to copy something accurately, as in woodworking: TEMPLATE
pause or interruption of continuity, gap, opening: HIATUS
pause temporarily or stop at intervals: INTERMIT
pay back, compensate: REIMBURSE
pay for, compensate: REMUNERATE
pay larger than normal given to a dismissed employe: SEVERANCE PAY
pay or fee for a service: EMOLUMENT
pay out: DISBURSE
pay to a clergyman from church revenues: PREBEND
paying back money originally invested: SELF-LIQUIDATING
payment, from earnings of a corporation, to be made to shareholders: DIVIDEND
payment beyond regular salary or profit: PERQUISITE
payment by each of his own meal ticket, party fee, etc.: DUTCH TREAT
payment for release of seized person or property: RANSOM

payment extorted to prevent disclosure: BLACKMAIL
payment immediately on delivery: SPOT CASH
payment in addition to salary, such as pension, insurance, etc.: FRINGE BENEFIT
peace be with you: PAX VOBISCUM
peace of mind: ATARAXIA
peace pipe: CALUMET
peaceable, showing good will: AMICABLE
peaceful, placid: PACIFIC
peaceful, tranquil, calm: PLACID
peaceful in purpose: IRENIC
pearl-like, iridescent: NACREOUS
pear-shaped: PYRIFORM
peculiar to a given country or people, native to a given area: ENDEMIC
peculiarity in behavior or speech, affectation of tyle: MANNERISM
pedantic: DIDACTIC
pedantic, dogmatic teacher: PEDAGOGUE
pedantic, moralizing: DIDACTIC
pedantic, smug, overexacting person: PRIG
pedantic literary effort: LUCUBRATION
peddle, cry goods in the street: HAWK
peddler of Bibles and other books: COLPORTEUR
peddler of food, liquor, etc. to an army: SUTLER
pedestal on which a statue or column stands: PLINTH
pedestal part between base and cornice: DADO
pedestrian who disregards traffic rules: JAYWALKER
pedigree record of thoroughbred stock: STUD BOOK
peep show, street show: RAREE SHOW
peeping Tom: VOYEUR
peevish: PETTISH
peevish, gloomy: DYSPEPTIC
peevish, ill-tempered: BILIOUS
peevishness, ill temper, spitefulness: SPLEEN
peevishness, irritableness: PETULANCE
pelt, shower, spatter: PEPPER
pen name: NOM DE PLUME
penalty in which something is given up or taken away: FORFEIT
penalty or obligation established by authority: IMPOSITION
pencil lead: GRAPHITE
penetrable, open-minded: PERVIOUS

penetrate, spread through completely: PERMEATE

penis erection as a persistent pathological condition: PRIAPISM

penis in rigid, enlarged condition: ERECTION

penis-like: PHALLIC

penis-like representation: PHALLUS

penmanship art: CHIROGRAPHY

penmanship that is beautiful: CALLIGRAPHY

penniless, poor: IMPECUNIOUS

pension, allowance, salary: STIPEND

Pentateuch, also Jewish law and literature: TORAH

people collectively, especially those outside a specific profession or occupation: LAITY

people forced by circumstances to listen: CAPTIVE AUDIENCE

people's protector or champion: TRIBUNE

pep up, cheer up, stimulate, invigorate: EXHILARATE

perceive, recognize as different: DISCERN

perceived below the threshold of consciousness: SUBLIMINAL

percentage of total that must be paid by customer when he uses his broker's credit to buy a security: MARGIN

perception after the event: HINDSIGHT

perception independent of senses: EXTRASENSORY PERCEPTION (ESP)

perception of distant objects by other than normal sensory means: TELESTHESIA

perception of one's own consciousness: APPERCEPTION

perception or knowing of a fact: COGNIZANCE

perception that has no external stimulus: HALLUCINATION

perceptive, keen, discerning: PERSPICACIOUS

perfect example: ARCHETYPE

perfection: NE PLUS ULTRA

perform, invent or produce without previous thought or preparation: IMPROVISE

perform a ceremony: SOLEMNIZE

perform the functions of an office: OFFICIATE

performance added in response to audience demand: ENCORE

performance or interpretation of a text, role, etc.: RENDITION

performer having a very small part, as in a play: WALK-ON

performer's special talent or piece of business: SHTICK

performing services for a fixed payment: STIPENDIARY

performing to win applause or approval: GRANDSTAND PLAY

perfumed powder in a bag: SACHET

peril that is imminent: SWORD OF DAMOCLES

period, century, era: SIÈCLE

period of happiness, comfort or wealth: MILLENNIUM

period of time that is incalculable, eternity: EON

period that divides some longer or periodic process: INTERLUDE

periodical of a company for its employes: HOUSE ORGAN

perjure oneself: FORSWEAR

permanent: INDELIBLE

permanent, durable: PERDURABLE

permeable through pores: POROUS

permeate, circulate: DIFFUSE

permeate, fertilize: IMPREGNATE

permeation gradually of thoughts or facts: OSMOSIS

permission given or implied by failure to prohibit: SUFFERANCE

permit, ratify, approve: SANCTION

permit with condescension: VOUCHSAFE

perplex, dumbfound, bewilder: NONPLUS

perplexing situation: QUANDARY

persecution complex: PARANOIA

persecution imposed by the military: DRAGONNADE

persevering: ASSIDUOUS

persevering, stubborn: INDOMITABLE

persistent: ASSIDUOUS

persistent, stubborn: PERTINACIOUS

persistent, tough, stubborn: TENACIOUS

persistent striving: PERSEVERANCE

persistently demand: IMPORTUNE

person, animal or plant that lives off another: PARASITE

person acting as if mechanically: AUTOMATON

person from whom a family descends: STIRPS

person from whom a nation, city, or epoch is said to derive its name: EPONYM

person moved out of a destroyed or threatened area: EVACUEE

person or thing uncommonly large or fine: SPANKER

person thought of as a perfect example: PERSONIFICATION

person with specialized knowledge, expert: COGNOSCENTE

person who buys and sells for another, on commission: BROKER

person who drops things: BUTTERFINGERS

person who enjoys good living: BON VIVANT

person who is a cultured or aristocratic snob: BRAHMIN

person who utters unheeded prophecies of disaster: CASSANDRA

personal excellence: CALIBER

personal feelings or one's mind as the source of judgment, as opposed to objective: SUBJECTIVE

personal need as motivation: BREAD-AND-BUTTER

personal property: CHATTEL

personality test made through interpretation of standard ink blots: RORSCHACH TEST

personification: PROSOPOPEIA

personified: INCARNATE

personnel reduction through retirement, etc.: ATTRITION

persons to whom secrets are confided: CONFIDANT

perspiration that is copious: DIAPHORESIS

persuadable, tractable: PLIANT

persuade one to act or speak: INDUCE

persuade or try to persuade by flattery: WHEEDLE

persuasive, insincere flattery: SNOW JOB

persuasively forceful: COGENT

pertinent, appropriate: RELEVANT

pertinent, related to what is being discussed, relevant: GERMANE

pervade, saturate, wet thoroughly: IMBUE

pervade or animate: INFORM

pester, press a debtor for payment: DUN

pessimism, melancholy, romantic world-weariness: WELTSCHMERZ

pessimistic about stock prices: BEARISH

pet name or endearing diminutive: HYPOCORISM

pet phrase: BYWORD

petitioner: POSTULANT

petty, cheap, sleazy: CHINTZY

petty, contemptible, trivial: PALTRY

petty, nagging: NIGGLING

petty, trivial: INSIGNIFICANT

petty, trivial, mean: PICAYUNE

petulant, self-important: HOITY-TOITY

phallus that is large, as in certain primitive art: ITHYPHALLIC

phantom: EIDOLON

phase, side or aspect of a person or subject: FACET

phobias

(In the following listing read the words "irrational fear of" ahead of each entry.)

air or drafts: AEROPHOBIA

aloneness: AUTOPHOBIA

animals: ZOOPHOBIA

being touched: HAPTEPHOBIA

blood: HEMOPHOBIA

burial alive: TAPHEPHOBIA

cats: AILUROPHOBIA

children: PEDOPHOBIA

cold: PSYCHROPHOBIA

contamination: MYSOPHOBIA

crowds: DEMOPHOBIA, OCHLOPHOBIA

dead bodies: NECROPHOBIA

death: THANATOPHOBIA, NECROPHOBIA

depths: BATHOPHOBIA

dogs: CYNOPHOBIA

eating: PHAGOPHOBIA

England, the English: ANGLOPHOBIA

fire: PYROPHOBIA

foreigners, strangers: XENOPHOBIA

heights: ACROPHOBIA

ideas: IDEOPHOBIA

infinity: APEIROPHOBIA

lice: PEDICULOPHOBIA

marriage: GAMOPHOBIA

men: ANDROPHOBIA

mice: MUSOPHOBIA

missiles: BALLISTOPHOBIA

movement: KINESOPHOBIA

night: NYCTOPHOBIA

noise: PHONOPHOBIA

novelty: NEOPHOBIA

number 13: TRISKAIDEKAPHOBIA

ocean: THALASSOPHOBIA

open spaces: AGORAPHOBIA

pain: ALGOPHOBIA

poison: TOXICOPHOBIA

red: ERYTHROPHOBIA

reptiles: OPHIDIOPHOBIA

sharp objects: AICHINOPHOBIA

sleep: HYPNOPHOBIA

snow: CHIONOPHOBIA

solitude: AUTOPHOBIA

speaking: LALOPHOBIA

stars: ASTROPHOBIA

thunderstorms: ASTRAPHOBIA

women: GYNOPHOBIA

phonograph record collector or connoisseur: DISCOPHILE

phonograph records catalogued: DISCOGRAPHY

photograph improvement through handwork to remove blemishes or add details: RETOUCHING

photographs attractively: PHOTOGENIC

phrase, clause or word inserted in a sentence to add explanation or comment: PARENTHESIS

phrase or put into words: COUCH

phrase or watchword of a group: SHIBBOLETH

phraseology verbal expression: LOCUTION

phraseology peculiar to a language or region and accepted though it may differ from the normal pattern: IDIOM

physically strong: POTENT

physically suitable for marriage: NUBILE

physician's training period at a hospital: RESIDENCY

piano-like instrument: CLAVICHORD

pick, sort out, select: CULL

pickle in a spicy, vinegary solution: MARINATE

picnic, pleasure trip, feast, banquet: JUNKET

picture, image, likeness, usually an object of veneration: ICON

picture or symbol representing a word, sound or object: HIEROGLYPHIC

picture painted on transparent curtains: DIORAMA

picture printed from engraving made with hard needle: DRY POINT

picture produced by superimposing different pictorial elements to make a single composition: MONTAGE

picturelike scene represented by silent and motionless persons: TABLEAU VIVANT

picturesque, pleasant: IDYLLIC

pie that is custard-like and made of cheese, bacon, etc., and served hot: QUICHE LORRAINE

piece cut or broken off: CANTLE

piece out, supplement: EKE

pier or wharf to protect a harbor or beach: JETTY

pierce through, impale: TRANSFIX

pigeon, especially when an unfledged nestling: SQUAB

pig-headed, stubborn, unyielding: OBSTINATE

piglike, swinish, hoggish: PORCINE

pigmentation deficiency: ALBINISM

pile of wood, etc., for burning a dead body: PYRE

pillage during a search: RANSACK

piles: HEMORRHOIDS

pilfer: FILCH

pillage, plunder, prey upon: DEPREDATE

pillage, ruin, wreck: RAVAGE

pillar in shape of a male figure: TELAMON

pimp: PANDER

pin someone or something with a sharp stake: IMPALE

pincers of small size: TWEEZERS

pincers or small tongs: FORCEPS

pine, weaken, droop gradually: LANGUISH

pink-eyed and white-skinned person: ALBINO

pinkie: LITTLE FINGER

pins, ribbons and other small miscellaneous articles for sale: NOTIONS

pinwheel-like firework: CATHERINE WHEEL

pipe with a tube passing through water to cool the smoke: HOOKAH

pirate: PICAROON

pirate or appropriate the ideas, writings, music, etc., of another: PLAGIARIZE

pit of the stomach: SOLAR PLEXUS

pitcher or jug with wide mouth: EWER

pitchers' practice area: BULLPEN

pithy saying: APOTHEGM

pitiable, inferior, paltry: SORRY

pitiful, causing sorrow, sad: PATHETIC

pitiless, hardhearted, stubborn: OBDURATE

pitiless, harsh: RELENTLESS

pivot about: SLUE

pivotal or pivoting on its own axis: TROCHOID

place for storing goods: REPOSITORY

place in a female mammal where young are generated and developed: WOMB

place name, or name derived from a place: TOPONYM

place of rest or shelter: HOSPICE

place or install in office formally: INVEST

place or position forces according to a plan: DEPLOY

place to stand on: POU STO

place where a crime is committed or a trial is to be held: VENUE

place where criminals, addicts, etc., are

helped to readjust to society: HALF-WAY HOUSE

plaid or checkered pattern of dark lines on a light ground: TATTERSALL

plain: UNVARNISHED

plain, clear, obvious, evident: MANIFEST

plain, direct: FLAT-FOOTED

plain, simple, rough: RUSTIC

plain devoid of forest, especially one of the extensive plains in Russia: STEPPE

plain of Arctic regions, treeless and vast: TUNDRA

plain or rolling tract of open land: WOLD

plait: PLEACH

plan, proposal, undertaking: PROJECT

plan of top priority to meet an emergency: CRASH PROGRAM

plane designed for short takeoffs and landings: STOL

plane designed for vertical takeoffs and landings: VTOL

planets shown as models or images on a circular dome: PLANETARIUM

planing tool having a blade set between two handles: SPOKESHAVE

planned deliberately, premeditated: STUDIED

planning for the future, prudence: PROVIDENCE

plant adapted to extreme changes of weather: TROPOPHYTE

plant and animal periodicity, as a study: PHENOLOGY

plant and animal structures, as a study, apart from function: MORPHOLOGY

plant eating, feeding on vegetables: HERBIVOROUS

plant growing in nutrient mineral solutions rather than in soil: HYDROPONICS

plant or animal selected as representative of a new species: HOLOTYPE

plant or animal series of changes in formation: SERE

plant or animal surviving from an earlier period or type: RELICT

plants growing in a given region: FLORA

plaster of Paris and glue mixed as a base for painting or for making of bas-reliefs: GESSO

plaster or a like wall coating: PARGET

platform, low and wheeled: DOLLY

platform or porch with steps at the entrance to a house: STOOP

platform that an orchestra conductor or a speaker stands on: PODIUM

platform that is raised and on which guests of honor or speakers are seated: DAIS

platitude: BROMIDE

plausible, but not certain: SPECIOUS

play rehearsal, usually the final one, performed exactly as play will be on opening night: DRESS REHEARSAL

play side by side: COLLOCATE

play written for reading rather than performance: CLOSET DRAMA

player in sports who is not on the regular team: SCRUB

playful, jesting: JOCOSE

playful conversation: BANTER

playful or lively movement in music: SCHERZO

playful teasing: BADINAGE

playfully leap about: CAPER

playfulness, fun, quip: JEST

plead against, disapprove: DEPRECATE

plead in protest or opposition: REMONSTRATE

pleasant tasting, savory: SAPID

pleasantness: AMENITY

please, if you please: S'IL VOUS PLAÎT

please reply: RÉPONEZ S'IL VOUS PLAÎT

pleasing: PREPOSSESSING

pleasing, attractive: WINSOME

pleasing in sound, harmonious, smooth: EUPHONIOUS

pleasurable and unpleasurable states, as a psychologic study: HEDONICS

pleasurably excited: TITILLATED

pleasure as the only good and proper goal or moral behavior: HEDONISM

pleasure at one's own suffering or pain: MASOCHISM

pleasure-loving and luxury-loving person: SYBARITE

pleasure or self-indulgence as a way of life: PRIMROSE PATH

pleasure-seeking and pain-avoiding drive of the ego: PLEASURE PRINCIPLE

pleasure trip, banquet, picnic, feast: JUNKET

pleated or plaited, as a fan: PLICATED

pleats that resemble bellows folds of an accordion: ACCORDION PLEATS

pledge, security, challenge: GAGE

pledge of securities or property as collateral for a loan: HYPOTHECATION

pledge property set aside by a borrower to insure repayment of a loan: COLLATERAL

plentiful: BOUNTEOUS

plentiful, abundant: RIFE
pliable: PLASTIC
pliable, flexible: MALLEABLE
pliant, supple, agile, lithe: LISSOME
plod, as through mud: SLOG
plot, conspiracy, secret and underhanded activity: INTRIGUE
plot to foil another: COUNTERMINE
pluck, spirit, courage: METTLE
plucking instrument's strings: PIZZICATO
plucking out, extracting forcibly, uprooting: EVULSION
plug or seal edges or crevices: CAULK
plump, rounded out: ROTUND
plume on a helmet; dash, verve: PANACHE
plunder: PILLAGE
plunder, invade for booty, raid: MARAUD
plunder, pillage, prey upon: DEPREDATE
plunder, pillage, raid: FORAY
plunder, during a search: RANSACK
plunder or destroy a city: RAPE
plunge straight down: PLUMMET
pod, husk, or shell: SHUCK
poem in which one poet mourns the death of another: MONODY
poem of a short, pastoral nature: ECLOGUE
poem of eight lines and two rhymes with two of the lines repeated: TRIOLET
poem of ten or thirteen lines with two rhymes: RONDEAU
poem of three stanzas and an envoy, the last lines of which are the same: BALLADE
poem or arrangement of words in which certain letters of each line spell a word: ACROSTIC
poem or composition in which the end letters of successive lines form a word: TELESTICH
poem or composition in which the middle letters of successive lines form a word: MESOSTICH
poem or stanza of four lines: QUATRAIN
poem retracting something stated in an earlier one: PALINODE
poem that is metrically complete: ACATALECTIC
poem usually of fourteen lines in rhymed iambic pentameter: SONNET
poet: BARD
poet without much talent: POETASTER
poetic forms, as a study: PROSODY

poetic metrical foot consisting of three syllables, the first accented, the others not: DACTYL
poetic metrical foot consisting of two equally accented syllables: SPONDEE
poetic metrical foot consisting of two syllables, the first accented: TROCHEE
poetical metrical foot consisting of two syllables, the first unaccented and the second accented: IAMB or IAMBUS
poetic metrical foot consisting of two unaccented syllables followed by one accented: ANAPEST
poetic pair of rhymed lines in iambic pentameter: HEROIC COUPLET
poetry with final lines usually in the form of a dedication: ENVOY
poetry free of conventional meter and rhyme: FREE VERSE
point made by showing contrary to be absurd: APAGOGE
point of view from which facts or matters are seen or judged: PERSPECTIVE
points on sole of shoe to prevent slipping: CALK
point or rod on which something rotates: PIVOT
point out, signify, indicate: DENOTE
pointed, sharp-edged: CULTRATE
pointless, silly, empty-headed: INANE
pointless or merely hypothetical: ACADEMIC
poison: ENVENOM
poisonous: TOXIC
poker bet made on a hand having only four cards of a suit: FOUR-FLUSH
poker game in which the first card is dealt face down, the four others face up: STUD POKER
poker hand made up of three of a kind and a pair: FULL HOUSE
poker hand of cards all of one suit: FLUSH
poker term for demanding a show of hands: CALL
police officer on a naval vessel: MASTER-AT-ARMS
police surveillance of a suspect or suspected place: STAKEOUT
polish or burnish: FURBISH
polite, good-natured remark: PLEASANTRY
polite, suave, refined: URBANE
polite behavior: AMENITIES
political candidate unexpectedly nominated: DARK HORSE

political device of altering a voting area to promote the interests of one political party: GERRYMANDER

political disorder: ANARCHY

political or governmental organization: POLITY

political party chief: SACHEM

political party meeting to select candidates, plan campaign: CAUCUS

political power to appoint to offices: PATRONAGE

politician from outside who is resented: CARPETBAGGER

politician who appeals to prejudices and passions: DEMAGOGUE

politicians' practice of trading votes and influence: LOGROLLING

politician's route in campaigning: HUSTINGS

politicking in rural districts: BARNSTORMING

politics of power: REALPOLITIK

poll tax: CAPITATION

pollens and spores, as a study: PALYNOLOGY

pollute, desecrate: PROFANE

polo time period: CHUKKER

polysyllabic, as of words: SESQUIPEDALIAN

pompous, artificially formal: STILTED

pompous, bombastic: FUSTIAN

pompous, bombastic style of speaking: GRANDILOQUENT

pompous, dogmatic, arrogant, haughty: PONTIFICAL

pompous, inflated: TUMID

pompous in speech: OROTUND

pompous person: BASHAW

pompously conceited: VAINGLORIOUS

ponder or meditate upon: RUMINATE

poor, also stingy: PENURIOUS

poor, penniless: IMPECUNIOUS

poor judgment shown: INJUDICIOUS

poor person, charity case: PAUPER

poorly made, cheap, shoddy: SLEAZY

poorly made, underdone: SLACK-BAKED

Pope's ambassador to a foreign government: NUNCIO

popular: DEMOTIC

popular, accepted, everyday speech: VULGATE

popular but incorrect idea of the origin of a word: FOLK ETYMOLOGY

populated densely, crowded: IMPACTED

population science: DEMOGRAPHY

porcelain or china that is very thin and delicate: EGGSHELL CHINA

porch or platform with steps at the entrance to a house: STOOP

porch with room held up by columns: PORTICO

pores admit fluids, air or light: POROUS

pornography: SMUT

pornography, as a study: COPROLOGY

port side of a ship: LARBOARD

portent, omen: AUGURY

portent, omen, warning: PRESAGE

portion, share, half: MOIETY

portion or serving: DOLLOP

portray, trace out, outline: DELINEATE

posing under a false name or character: IMPOSTURE

position or office that pays, but involves few or no duties: SINECURE

position specially suited to a person: NICHE

positive, arrogant assertion of opinion: DOGMATIC

positive, final, decisive, absolute: PEREMPTORY

positive, with no qualifications: CATEGORICAL

positive declaration: ASSEVERATION

possessive case in grammar: GENITIVE

possible, imaginable, secular: EARTHLY

possible but not in existence: POTENTIAL

possible or liable: CONTINGENT

possible outcome: EVENTUALITY

possession that is more trouble than it's worth: WHITE ELEPHANT

post at end of handrail of a staircase: NEWEL

postage stamp sold at an advanced price, the excess going to a charity or public service: SEMIPOSTAL

poster: PLACARD

poster or large sheet of paper with a printed message: BROADSIDE

postpone or forgo a right: WAIVE

postpone or put off habitually: PROCRASTINATE

postpone punishment or pain: REPRIEVE

posts supporting a handrail: BALUSTER

posture: STANCE

postponement, delay, interval of relief or rest: RESPITE

pot, small and made of earthenware: PIPKIN

pot or jar, broad-mouthed and of earthenware: OLLA

pot that is airtight and cooks food quickly under pressure: PRESSURE COOKER

potatoes prepared with finely sliced fried onions: LYONNAISE

potency, efficacy: VIRTUE

potential for development: SEMINAL

pottery, glazed, usually blue and white: DELFT

pottery of a very hard variety: STONEWARE

pouchlike receptacle on the abdomen of female marsupials for carrying the young: MARSUPIUM

pour or spread out in all directions: DIFFUSE

pour off a liquid without disturbing its sediment: DECANT

pouting facial expression: MOUE

poverty: INDIGENCE

powdered, demolished: PULVERIZED

powdery, dusty: PULVERULENT

power equal to a thousand watts: KILOWATT

power of great proportions, gigantic: HERCULEAN

power of thought or feeling: INTENSITY

power that is absolute: DESPOTISM

powerful, mighty: PUISSANT

powerful appearing but really ineffective: PAPER TIGER

powerful or wealthy man: NABOB

powerless: IMPUISSANT

powerless, incapable of producing the effect desired: INEFFECTUAL

powerless, worthless: NUGATORY

powerless to act or accomplish anything: IMPOTENT

practicable, workable: VIABLE

practical, not theoretical: PRAGMATIC

practical, obstinate, shrewd: HARDHEADED

practical, suitable: FEASIBLE

practical rather than scientific measure: RULE OF THUMB

practical saying: APOTHEGM

practice rather than theory: PRAXIS

praise: LAUD

praise, especially when formal and delivered publicly: EULOGY

praise extravagantly: ADULATE

praise for an achievement: KUDOS

praise in the highest terms, exalt, laud: EXTOL

praise or eulogy formally delivered: ENCOMIUM

praise that is elaborate, laudation: PANEGYRIC

prance or caper about: TITTUP

prance or frisk about: CAVORT

prank, spree, fling, reckless behavior: ESCAPADE

pray earnestly for something, ask for humbly: SUPPLICATE

pray for or call down a calamity or a curse: IMPRECATE

prayer, short and suitable to an occasion: COLLECT

prayer at the opening of a ceremony: INVOCATION

prayer consisting of a long list of supplications, with a fixed response after each: LITANY

prayer or entreaty in behalf of others: INTERCESSION

prayer shawl worn by Orthodox and Conservative Jewish men: TALLITH

prayer stand with a shelf for a book: PRIE-DIEU

prayer stool, usually folding and cushioned: FALDSTOOL

prayer that is brief: EJACULATION

prayers made on nine days: NOVENA

prayers or services in the evening: VESPERS

precarious position: SWORD OF DAMOCLES

preceding: PREVENIENT

precipice that extends a distance: PALISADES

precise, accurate, exact: NICE

precise, overly fastidious, fussy, exacting: FINICKY

pre-Christmas season: ADVENT

preconceived judgment: PARTI PRIS

predecessor, forerunner, something in advance: PRECURSOR

predetermination: FATALISM

predicament: QUANDARY

predicament, complicated situation: PLIGHT

predicament entailing a choice between two undesirable alternatives: DILEMMA

prediction, forecast: PROGNOSIS

predictor of the future: SOOTHSAYER

predisposition to certain forms of disease: DIATHESIS

preempt or appoint: CO-OPT

preface, introductory remark: PROLEGOMENON

preface, introductory statement: PROEM

preference preconceived: PREDILECTION

preferred stock on which unpaid dividends do not accrue: NONCUMULATIVE

preferred stock that is entitled to dividends beyond those stated: PARTICIPATING PREFERRED

pregnancy: GESTATION

pregnant: ENCEINTE

pregnant: GRAVID

pregnant for the first time or the mother of just one: PRIMIPARA

prejudice, bias: PRECONCEPTION

prejudiced, biased, favoring one party: PARTIAL

prejudicial appeal: AD HOMINEM

prelate, high priest: HIERARCH

prelate with highest rank in the country: PRIMATE

preliminary work for a project: SPADEWORK

prematurely born animal, especially a calf: SLINK

prematurely bring forth young: ABORT

prematurely developed: PRECOCIOUS

premeditated, deliberately designed: STUDIED

precise about details, overly painstaking: METICULOUS

preoccupation with a thought or feeling that is compulsive and excessive: OBSESSION

preoccupied: BEMUSED

preparatory work for a project: SPADEWORK

prerequisite: POSTULATE

present everywhere at once: UBIQUITOUS

present period or occasion: NONCE

present tense used to narrate a past event: HISTORICAL PRESENT

preside over, as a meeting: MODERATE

press a debtor for payment: DUN

press food, drinks, etc., on a person: PLY

pretend, dissemble, conceal: DISSIMULATE

pretend, feign: SIMULATE

pretend not to see wrongdoing: CONNIVE

pretended, deceptive, sham: FEIGNED

pretended blow or deception meant to distract: FEINT

pretending to be someone else in order to deceive: IMPOSTURE

pretending to be what one is not or better than one is, pretending to be virtuous or good: HYPOCRISY

pretense, false appearance: GUISE

pretentious, inflated: OVERBLOWN

pretentious, ostentatious or hypocritical ceremony: MUMMERY

pretentious, overdignified, self-important: POMPOUS

pretentious behavior: AFFECTATION

pretentious boasting: BRAGGADOCIO

pretentious language: CLAPTRAP

pretentious official: PANJANDRUM

pretentious or extremist person: HIGHFLIER

pretentiously grand, imposing: GRANDIOSE

pretentiousness, windy promposity: FLATULENCE

prevalent, dominant: REGNANT

prevent, avert: OBVIATE

prevent, guard against or hinder in advance: FORESTALL

prevent, render impossible, exclude: PRECLUDE

preventing sleep: AGRYPNOTIC

preventive treatment against disease: PROPHYLAXIS

previous to examination: A PRIORI

previously, before now: HERETOFORE

prey, game: QUARRY

prey upon, pillage, plunder: DEPREDATE

price at which a bond may be redeemed before it reaches maturity: REDEMPTION PRICE

price at which a person is ready to buy a security: BID

price at which a person is ready to sell a security: OFFER

price changes that can be absorbed by the market in a particular security: LIQUIDITY

price fall caused by decrease of money in circulation: DEFLATION

price last reported at which security was sold: MARKET PRICE

price level reduced to increase purchasing power but avoid deflation: DISINFLATION

price of a stock transaction higher than the preceding transaction: UP TICK, PLUS-TICK

price range of buyer and seller of a given stock at a given time: QUOTATION

price rise and fall in value of money: INFLATION

price that is the lowest at which something will be sold at an auction: UPSET PRICE

priceless: INESTIMABLE

priceless: INVALUABLE

prickly: SPINOUS

prickly heat: MILIARIA

pride, especially in someone else (Yiddish): NACHUS

priestly: SACERDOTAL

priest's forgiveness of sin, in confession: ABSOLUTION

priests or clergy in charge of government: HIEROCRACY

prima donna, female operatic singer: DIVA

primary in which people rather than delegates select candidates: DIRECT PRIMARY

primitive: ABORIGINAL

primitive, pure: PRISTINE

primitive state, reversion to: ATAVISM

primp, dress showily: PREEN

principle, belief or doctrine maintained as true by a person or a group: TENET

principal, original, first: PRIMAL

principal commodity, regularly in demand: STAPLE

print a line, paragraph, etc., in from the margin: INDENT

printed character containing two or more letters joined together: LIGATURE

printed sheets, loosely bound together: CAHIER

printer's shallow tray for holding type before it is put into a form: GALLEY

printer's term for an opening cut in a plate for the insertion of type: MORTISE

printing type group containing all the characters in one size and style: FONT

printing even with the outside margin: FLUSH

printing from a flat stone or metal plate on which the material to be printed is treated with grease that absorbs ink: LITHOGRAPHY

printing from raised surfaces: LETTERPRESS

printing machines that cast type in single characters: MONOTYPE

printing or writing with flowing lines: CURSIVE

printing ornament or symbol: DINGBAT

printing press that prints both sides of a sheet simultaneously: PERFECTING PRESS

printing press that uses webs, or rolls of paper, rather than separate sheets: WEB PRESS

printing press using curved plates and rolls of paper: ROTARY PRESS

printing process in which subjects are re-

produced by photography on plates in relief: PHOTOENGRAVING

printing process in which the impression is transferred to a rubber roller and then to the paper: OFFSET

printing, receptacle for broken or battered type: HELLBOX

printing sign (☞) to direct attention: INDEX or FIST

printing term for a blurred impression: MACKLE

printing term for part of a letter that extends downward: DESCENDER

printing term for part of a letter that extends upward: ASCENDER

printing term for thinnest of metal spaces separating letters or words: HAIR SPACE

printing type characteristic consisting of a fine line that finishes off a stroke: SERIF

printing type jumble: PI

printing type set in excess of the space available: OVERSET

printing type that is bold and somewhat fancy: OLD ENGLISH

printing type with thin light lines: LIGHTFACE

prints transferred from specially prepared paper to glass, wood: DECALCOMANIA

prisoner of captors setting terms for his release: HOSTAGE

prisoner surrendered or delivered up to the jurisdiction of another state or country: EXTRADITION

private, isolated room: SANCTUM

private or confidential, as a conversation: TÊTE-À-TÊTE

privately said, undertone: SOTTO VOCE

privilege extended to stockholders ahead of others, to buy new issues, usually at lower than market price: RIGHTS

privilege or benefit owed because of status: PERQUISITE

privilege or exemption as in right to send mail without charge: FRANK

prize that is the biggest one possible to win: JACKPOT

problem of choosing between unpleasant alternatives: DILEMMA

problem that is complicated: GORDIAN KNOT

problems pile up; solution of one raises another and leads back to the original one: VICIOUS CIRCLE

proclamation, public declaration: PRO-
NUNCIAMENTO

prod or incite: GOAD

produce, beget: PROCREATE

produce, perform or invent without previous thought or preparation: IMPRO-
VISE

producing many or much: PROLIFIC

producing or capable of producing a desired effect: EFFICACIOUS

production of goods and services by a nation: GROSS NATIONAL PRODUCT
(G.N.P.)

productive, inventive, fruitful: PREGNANT

productive, potential, germinal: SEMINAL

productive equipment owned by busi-
nesses: CAPITAL GOODS

profane or use sacrilegiously: DESECRATE

profaning or violation of anything sacred:
SACRILEGE

professional or clerical worker: WHITE
COLLAR

profile or dark shape with a light background: SILHOUETTE

profit anticipated but not yet realized on a
security still held: PAPER PROFIT

profit from sale of assets: CAPITAL GAIN

profitable: LUCRATIVE

profitable: REMUNERATIVE

profitable source: PAY DIRT

profound, hidden: RECONDITE

progress resulting from planning: TELESIS

progression by a constant quantity: ARITH-
METIC PROGRESSION

progression or arrangement that is orderly
or gradual: GRADATION

prohibit, debar, forbid a person to have or
do something: INTERDICT

prohibit, outlaw, condemn: PROSCRIBE

prohibited, unlawful: ILLICIT

prohibited by convention or tradition:
TABOO

prohibition: INJUNCTION

project on the basis of facts already
known, infer from evidence at hand:
EXTRAPOLATE

projecting part of a battle line: SALIENT

projecting structure supported at only one
end: CANTILEVER

proliferate, sprout: BURGEON

prolific, fruitful, fertile: FECUND

prolific or fond of children: PHILO-
PROGENITIVE

prologue: PROLUSION

prolonged or held, in music: SOSTENUTO

promenade or strut: CAKEWALK

prominent or memorable object in the
landscape: LANDMARK

promiscuous woman, slut: SLATTERN

promise, guarantee: STIPULATE

promotion awarded on the battlefield:
BREVET

promptness, speed: DISPATCH

pronounce with a sound omitted: ELIDE

pronounced without stress when in combination with a preceding word: EN-
CLITIC

pronunciation standards: ORTHOEPY

pronouncing "r" as "l" or vice versa:
LALLATION

proof of a crime: CORPUS DELICTI

proof of the genuineness of a document
such as a will: PROBATE

proof of printed matter used for making
corrections: GALLEY

proof or safe against attack: UNASSAILA-
BLE

propensity: APPETENCE

proper, advisable, suitable: EXPEDIENT

proper, conventional: ORTHODOX

proper, seemly in behavior: DECOROUS

proper or customary act or procedure:
FORMALITY

properness, conformity with accepted
usage: PROPRIETY

property improvements: CAPITAL EXPEN-
DITURE

property ownership as the key to political
power: TIMOCRACY

property reverting to government in absence of legal heirs: ESCHEAT

property seizure in legal proceeding: AT-
TACHMENT

property transfer: CONVEYANCE

prophesying, foretelling the future: DIVI-
NATION

prophet or messiah in Islam: MAHDI

prophetess of doom whose prophecies go
unheeded: CASSANDRA

prophetic, enigmatic: ORACULAR

prophetic, having divinatory power:
MANTIC

prophetic, inspired: PYTHONIC

prophetic, oracular: VATIC

proportionate: COMMENSURATE

proposal in outline form for a written
work or business project: PROSPECTUS

propose, suggest: PROPOUND

proposition that is demonstrably true, as in geometry: THEOREM

propriety or aptness of behavior: CONVENANCE

prosaic, dull, mediocre: PEDESTRIAN

prose that is long and tiresome: SCREED

prosperity, as a mark of the times for instance: FLUSH

prosperous or successful period: FLORESCENCE

prostitute: COCOTTE

prostitute: HARLOT

prostitute: HOOKER

prostitute: TROLLOP

prostitute catering to men of wealth or high rank: COURTESAN

prostitute who works in response to telephone calls: CALL GIRL

prostitute's agent: PIMP

prostitutes as a group: DEMIMONDE

prostitution, as of talent or office, for gain: VENALITY

protect against loss or damage: INDEMNIFY

protected against malfunctioning: FAILSAFE

protected legally by patent or copyright, owned by a proprietor: PROPRIETARY

protection against disease: PROPHYLAXIS

protective influence: AEGIS

protector of the people: TRIBUNE

protest or oppose by pleading: REMONSTRATE

protoplasm building and breaking down as continuous bodily processes: METABOLISM

prototype: ARCHETYPE

protruding: EXSERTILE

protuberance, swelling: TUBEROSITY

prove false or contradict: BELIE

prove someone or something wrong: CONFUTE

proverb: ADAGE

proverb: APHORISM

provincial, limited, narrow: PAROCHIAL

provincial, limited in outlook: INSULAR

provisions for a journey: VIATICUM

provoker of punishable acts: AGENT PROVOCATEUR

provoking, annoying person: GADFLY

provoking anger or resentment by being unjustly discriminating: INVIDIOUS

prudence: CALCULATION

prudent, diplomatic, wise: POLITIC

prudent, tactful, careful about what one says: DISCREET

prudent, wary: CANNY

prudish editing: BOWDLERIZATION

prudish, shocked or nauseated easily: SQUEAMISH

pry or break open as with a crowbar: JIMMY

prying or offensively curious: INQUISITORIAL

psychiatric disorder marked by separation of thought from emotions: SCHIZOPHRENIA

psychoanalysis patient: ANALYSAND

psychoanalyst, psychiatrist: SHRINK

psychoanalytical arrested development: FIXATION

public attention or notice: LIMELIGHT

public brawl: AFFRAY

public display: BLAZON

public forum place: AGORA

public good as the objective: PRO BONO PUBLICO

public offices offered as rewards of partisan service: SPOILS SYSTEM

public sale or auction: VENDUE

publicize officially, put into effect: PROMULGATE

publicizer of real or alleged corruption: MUCKRAKER

publisher of books at the author's expense: VANITY PRESS

publisher's trademark: COLOPHON

puckish, gay, strange: FET

pudding baked under a roast to catch the drippings: YORKSHIRE PUDDING

puff, blow in gusts: WHIFFLE

pugnacious in a disagreeable way: TRUCULENT

pull or force away by violent twist: WREST

pulsatory: SPHYGMIC

pulsing, throbbing: VIBRANT

pulverize: COMMINUTE

pulverize: TRITURATE

pulverize to fine powder: LEVIGATE

pun: PARONOMASIA

pun, double meaning: PLAY UPON WORDS

punch holes into: PERFORATE

pungent: ACRID

punish, beat or thrash severely: TROUNCE

punish, discipline: FERULE

punish by arbitrary fine: AMERCE

punishment for evil: RETRIBUTION

punishment that corresponds to the nature of the crime: TALION

punitive, avenging: VINDICATORY

punning: PARONOMASIA

pupil absent from school without permission: TRUANT

purchasing power of individuals: REAL INCOME

pure, primitive: PRISTINE

pure essential part: QUINTESSENCE

purging or purifying of emotions: CATHARSIS

purify by a sacrifice or ceremony: LUSTRATE

purify by exposure to air: AERATE

purify by washing and straining or decanting: ELUTRIATE

purify or refine: RAREFY

purifying: DEPURATIVE

purplish red: MURREY

purpose, aim, goal: INTENT

purposeful: TELIC

purposeless, haphazard: RANDOM

pursue an undertaking: PROSECUTE

pursuit, search, adventure: QUEST

push down, thrust away from: DETRUDE

push or crowd roughly, shake up, elbow, shove: JOSTLE

push out, make protrude: EXSERT

pushy, nosy, obtrusive, forward: OFFICIOUS

put down, belittle: DISPARAGE

put down, suppress forcibly: QUASH

put down by force, allay: QUELL

put in gradually by drops: INSTILL

put in or inject a comment or digression in a speech or argument: INTERPOSE

put in prison: INCARCERATE

put into words, phrase: COUCH

put off or postpone habitually: PROCRASTINATE

put out of consciousness unacceptable memories, desires and impulses: REPRESSION

putting into effect, carrying through: IMPLEMENTATION

puzzle in which the sound of a word or phrase is represented by letters, numerals, pictures: REBUS

puzzle out, interpret, understand: FATHOM

puzzled, uncertain, bewildered: PERPLEXED

puzzling, complicated, involved: INTRICATE

puzzling, secret, hidden, occult, mystifying: CRYPTIC

pyramid or cone with top sliced off: FRUSTUM

Pyrrhic victory: CADMEAN VICTORY

Q

quack medicine, cure-all, medicine of one's own invention: NOSTRUM

quack-medicine vendor, charlatan: MOUNTEBANK

quadrangular: TETRAGONAL

quail, tremble or crouch as in fear: COWER

quaint, fanciful, as in a literary work: WHIMSY

quality, goodness, moral excellence: VIRTUE

qualm, doubt, apprehension: MISGIVING

quantity that a container lacks of being full: ULLAGE

quantity that is specified: QUANTUM

quarrel: ALTERCATION

quarrel, difference of opinion, discord: DISSENSION

quarrel, wrangling: JANGLE

quarrel or argue noisily: WRANGLE

quarreling, inability to agree: AT LOGGERHEADS

quarrelsome: BELLICOSE

quarrelsome: CANTANKEROUS

quarrelsome: CONTENTIOUS

quarrelsome: DISSENTIOUS

quarrelsome: LITIGIOUS

quarrelsome: PUGNACIOUS

quarrelsome, vixenish: TERMAGANT

queenly: REGINAL

queer, eccentric: CRANKY

quench or satisfy, as a thirst: SLAKE

question, examine: INTERROGATE

question a person insistently: PLY

question and answer method of instruction: SOCRATIC METHOD

question and answer method of teaching: CATECHISM

question asked for effect and not calling for an answer: RHETORICAL QUESTION

question searchingly and at length: CATECHIZE

questionable, difficult to solve: PROBLEMATIC

questionable or suspicious: EQUIVOCAL

questionable or uncertain: DUBIOUS

questioning existence of God: AGNOSTICISM

questioning or prying characterized by harshness: INQUISITION

quibble: CAVIL

quibble, lie: PALTER

quibbler over small matters: PETTIFOGGER

quibbling: CAPTIOUS

quick disposal of a matter, as of a piece of business: DISPATCH OR WITH DISPATCH

quick efficiency: DISPATCH

quick or ready in performance, easily achieved: FACILE

quick tempo, rapidly, swiftly, in music: VELOCE

quickly, briskly, lively, in music: VIVACE

quickly or suddenly, in music: SUBITO

quickness of mind: ACUMEN

quick-tempered, irritable: IRASCIBLE

quiet, abate, calm: SUBSIDE

quiet, reserved, reluctant to speak: RETICENT

quiet consent: ACQUIESCENCE

quiet down, soothe, mitigate, pacify: MOLLIFY

quiet, make peaceful: PACIFY

quiet, serene, calm: TRANQUIL

quilt made of irregularly shaped pieces of variously colored and patterned fabric: CRAZY QUILT

quip: SALLY.

quip, fun, playfulness: JEST

quirk, habit, mannerism peculiar to an individual: IDIOSYNCRASY

quiver, flutter, beat rapidly: PALPITATE

quota for a race or class in admission to an academic institution: NUMERUS CLAUSUS

quotation or motto prefixed to a book: EPIGRAPH

quoting a person without using his exact words: INDIRECT DISCOURSE

R

"r" pronounced like "l" or "l" pronounced like "r" or "w": LALLATION

rabbit dwelling: WARREN

rabbit fur: LAPIN

rabbit stew as prepared in Germany: HASENPFEFFER

rabies: HYDROPHOBIA

race course's section farthest from spectators: BACK STRETCH

race course's straight portion forming the final approach to the finish: HOME STRETCH

race improvement study or science: EUGENICS

race on horseback along a course containing obstacles: STEEPLECHASE

races and ethnic groups, as subjects of study: ETHNOLOGY

racial and ethnic groups brought together in legal and social equality: INTEGRATION

racial equalizing: DESEGREGATION

racial segregation in South Africa: APARTHEID

racing finish so close that a camera is needed to decide the winner: PHOTO FINISH

racing gambling system in which those backing the winners share in the total wagered: PARIMUTUEL

racing gambling system in which winnings of a previous race are placed on a later one: PARLAY

rack or frame on which to dry fish, cheese, bricks, etc.: HACK

rack or platform for drying food: FLAKE

racketeers' money collector: BAGMAN

racy, stimulating: PIQUANT

radar warning system in North America: DEW LINE

radiance, splendor: EFFULGENCE

radiance, brilliance: REFULGENCE

radiance enveloping a sanctified being: AUREOLE

radiant, transparent: LUCENT

radiate, diffuse: EXUDE

radiating, star-shaped: STELLATE

radical or liberal political figure: LEFTIST

radical or liberal political position: LEFT

radio announcer who conducts a program of recorded music: DISC JOCKEY

radio or television station code letters: CALL LETTERS

radioactivity duration measure: HALF-LIFE

radio-reflecting layer of the ionosphere: HEAVISIDE LAYER

ragamuffin: TATTERDEMALION

ragged edge of handmade paper: DECKLE EDGE

raggedly dressed person, usually a child: RAGAMUFFIN

raging, fanatical: RABID

raging, frenzied: MADDING

raid, invasion: INCURSION

raid, lay waste, pillage: HARRY

raid, plunder, invade for booty: MARAUD

raid, plunder, pillage: FORAY

raiding force or member of one: COMMANDO

rail at, berate, find fault abusively: VITUPERATE

railroad building for repairing and switching locomotives: ROUNDHOUSE

railroad signal to go ahead: HIGHBALL

railway with a single track: MONORAIL

rainbow-like colors that shift: IRIDESCENCE

rainbow trout along the Pacific coast: STEELHEAD

rainfall study: HYETOGRAPHY

rainy: PLUVIOUS

rainy season that comes with the summer

wind along the Asian coast of the Pacific: MONSOON

raise trivial objections, or carp: CAVIL

raise with a rope: TRICE

raised figures worked on a surface as decoration: EMBOSSED

raised platform on which guests of honor or speakers are seated: DAIS

raised sculpture in which figures project slightly: BAS-RELIEF

rake, profligate: LIBERTINE

rake, sensualist: ROUÉ

raking gunfire: ENFILADE

rakish, vulgar: RAFFISH

ram that has been castrated: WETHER

ramble, wander from main subject: DIGRESS

rambling, aimless wandering: MEANDERING

rambling, confused: INCOHERENT

rambling, discursive, digressive: EXCURSIVE

rambling and wordy talk: GARRULITY

ramp or incline: GRADIENT

ramp with curving or spiral passageway: HELICLINE

ram's horn of ancient times still used in synagogues: SHOFAR

rancorous, bitter: VIRULENT

random, accidental: HAPHAZARD

random, confused: INDISCRIMINATE

random shot or criticism: POT SHOT

range, extent, scope: PURVIEW

range, scope: LATITUDE

range in its entirety: GAMUT

range or limit, as of power or action: TETHER

rank, spoiled-smelling: RANCID

rank formation as with troops, fleets, airplanes: ECHELON

rank in society, organization, business, etc.: PECKING ORDER

rankle, irritate, cause bitterness: FESTER

ransack and rob: RIFLE

rapid, swift: TANTIVY

rapidly, swiftly, quick tempo, in music: VELOCE

rapture or emotion that is overpowering: ECSTASY

rare person or thing: RARA AVIS

rare-book dealer: BIBLIOPOLE

rascal, rogue: RAPSCALLION

rash: BRASH

rash, hasty, impulsive: IMPETUOUS

rash, incautious, thriftless: IMPROVIDENT

rash, reckless: TEMERARIOUS

rashly, recklessly: HEADLONG

ratify, approve, permit: SANCTION

rational, clear, easily understood, bright, shining: LUCID

rationalization of matters of morals and ethics: CASUISTRY

rattle, crackle: CREPITATE

rattling or clattering noise: BRATTLE

rattle that is gourd-shaped and used to sound a rhythm: MARACA

rave, speak violently: RANT

raw cane sugar: MUSCOVADO

raw material: STAPLE

reach or arrive at a port: FETCH

react: REDOUND

reaction developed by training: CONDITIONED REFLEX

reaction in exaggerated form to a psychological defect: OVERCOMPENSATION

reaction in exaggerated form to a situation or subject: COMPLEX

reaction of a violent nature: BACKLASH

read intently or study with care: PORE

read or examine thoroughly, scrutinize: PERUSE

read or glance over hastily: SKIM

read quickly, glance at: SCAN

readily, willingly: LIEF

readiness to comply, pliancy: FACILITY

reading ability impairment: DYSLEXIA

reading ability is beyond this person: FUNCTIONAL ILLITERATE

reading ability lost: ALEXIA

reading of a word or sentence is the same backward as forward: PALINDROME

ready, easy-going, agreeable: FACILE

ready to be put into use: OPERATIONAL

real, actual: SUBSTANTIVE

real, material, having definite shape: TANGIBLE

real existence of something in the mind, actual being: ENTITY

realistic to the point of looking real, as in art or decoration: TROMPE L'OEIL

reality studied as a philosophical theory: ONTOLOGY

realization or accomplishment of things worked for: FRUITION

reappearance or fresh outbreak: RECRUDESCENCE

rear, feed, support, raise: NURTURE

rear car of freight train: CABOOSE

rear end of a boat: STERN

rear, toward the stern, on a boat: AFT

reason, think: INTELLECTUALIZE
reason by logical methods: RATIOCINATE
reason or justification for being: RAISON D'ETRE
reason earnestly with someone, remonstrate: EXPOSTULATE
reasonable, apparently true, but open to doubt: PLAUSIBLE
reasonable, practicable, suitable: FEASIBLE
reasoned, sensible: RATIONAL
reasoning as opposed to intuition in reaching conclusions: DISCURSIVE
reasoning from general to particular: DEDUCTION
reasoning that is clever but unsound: SOPHISTRY
reasoning that is faulty or illogical: PARALOGISM
reasons underlying something: RATIONALE
rebellious: INSUBORDINATE
rebellious: INSURGENT
rebellious, insolent: CONTUMACIOUS
rebellious, irritable, unruly, cranky: FRACTIOUS
rebirth, restoration, reconstitution: REGENERATION
rebound or skip of a bullet or stone after it hits a surface at an angle: RICOCHET
rebuff, reject, repel: REPULSE
rebuke, castigate, rake over the coals: KEELHAUL
rebuke, censure, blame for a fault: REPROACH
rebuke, disapproval, censure: REPROOF
rebuke, criticize, find fault with, blame: REPREHEND
rebuke or censure severely: REPRIMAND
rebuke or chastise severely: CASTIGATE
rebuke sharply, upbraid, berate: OBJURGATE
recall, cancel, rescind, annul: REVOKE
recall to mind, remember: RETRIEVE
recalling or telling of past events: REMINISCENCE
recalling past occurrences, remembering: RETROSPECTION
recalling to mind: ANAMNESIS
recant: ABJURE
recapitulation of an oration: PERORATION
receptive: HOSPITABLE
recess, time between parts of a performance or between events or activities: INTERMISSION
recess period in work: COFFEE BREAK

recipient of benefits or favors: BENEFICIARY
reckless, careless: DEVIL-MAY-CARE
reckless, careless, weak: FECKLESS
reckless, rash: TEMERARIOUS
reckless dealing: PLAY DUCKS AND DRAKES WITH
reckless ride in a stolen vehicle, ride for pleasure: JOY RIDE
recklessly, rashly: HEADLONG
reclining, leaning, lying down: RECUMBENT
recluse: ANCHORITE
recluse: TROGLODYTE
recognize as different, perceive: DISCERN
recoil: BACKLASH
recoil, resume original shape after being stretched: RESILE
recollection: ANAMNESIS
reconcile and blend, as various philosophies: SYNCRETIZE
record of happenings worth remembering: MEMORABILIA
recover: RECUPERATE
recover, pay off: REDEEM
recover, remedy the consequences of, regain, make up for: RETRIEVE
recovery of property pending a court test: REPLEVIN
rectify, compensate: REDRESS
rectum and its diseases, as a branch of medicine: PROCTOLOGY
recurrence in the mind of the same thought, experience, etc.: PERSEVERATION
recurrent: CHRONIC
recurring at regular intervals, intermittent: PERIODIC
red, especially in heraldry: GULES
red color that is dull: STAMMEL
red tape in government: BUREAUCRACY
reddening: RUBESCENT
redemption price of a bond, if it is higher than the face value: PREMIUM
red-handed: IN FLAGRANTE DELICTO
redistrict a voting area so as to advance the interests of a political party: GERRYMANDER
reduce expenses: RETRENCH
reduce in quantity or force: ABATE
reduce in rank or position: ABASE
reduce in size, lessen, belittle: MINIFY
reduce to smallest possible amount or degree: MINIMIZE
reduction of debt or liability, done gradu-

ally as by installment payments: AMORTIZATION

reduction of personnel through retirement, death, etc.: ATTRITION

redundancy: TAUTOLOGY

redundancy, use of excess words: PLEO-NASM

refine or purify: RAREFY

refine, purify, clear of waste matter: DEF-ECATE

refined, polite, suave: URBANE

refined or delicate to an extreme: FASTIDI-OUS

refined to excess: RECHERCHÉ

refinement, well-bred in one's ways: GENTILITY

reflect, think about, consider carefully: PONDER

reflecting light, shining back, bright: RE-LUCENT

reflective, serious, often melancholy: PENSIVE

refrain from: ABSTAIN

refreshments: COLLATION

refusal given bluntly: REBUFF

refuse, scorn, reject: SPURN

refuse, waste matter: DROSS

refuse scornfully, treat with contempt: DISDAIN

refuse to accept, disown, reject: REPUDI-ATE

refuse to deal with so as to punish: BOY-COTT

refuse to go forward, balk: JIB

refutation in syllogistic form: ELENCHUS

regain, as for a loss: RECOUP

regain, recover, make up for, remedy the consequences of: RETRIEVE

register or enroll in a college or university as a candidate for a degree: MATRIC-ULATE

register of deeds, etc.: CARTULARY

regret an action, feel contrite: REPENT

regret extremely: RUE

regret, plead against: DEPRECATE

regular fixed-dollar amount method of purchasing securities: MONTHLY IN-VESTMENT PLAN

regular repetition: CONTINUAL

regularly recurring, intermittent: PERIODIC

regulate, adjust, temper or soften: MODU-LATE

rehearsal: DRY RUN

reimburse: RECOUP

rein thirty or more feet long at the end of

which the horse moves for training and exercise: LONGE

reinvigorating: ANALEPTIC

reject, rebuff, repel: REPULSE

reject, drive back: REPEL

reject, refuse, scorn: SPURN

reject, refuse to accept, disown: REPUDI-ATE

reject with contempt, refuse scornfully: DISDAIN

rejection of customary belief, immortality and institutions: NIHILISM

rejoice greatly: EXULT

related on the male or father's side: AG-NATE

related or alike in meaning, significance or effect: SYNONYMOUS

related or similar in structure, position, value: HOMOLOGOUS

related superficially: TANGENTIAL

related to a subject, relevant: PERTINENT

related to what is being discussed, rele-vant, pertinent: GERMANE

relationship that is close: AFFINITY

relationships within a group, as a study: SOCIOMETRY

relaxant, sleep-producing medicine: OPIATE

release from care and pain, bliss: NIRVANA

release of repressed emotion by reliving or talking about original situation: ABREACTION

relentless: INEXORABLE

relevant, pertinent, related to what is being discussed: GERMANE

relevant, related to a subject: PERTINENT

relevant only in part: TANGENTIAL

relief design, as in metal: REPOUSSÉ

relieving irritation, soothing: DEMULCENT

religious belief rejected: ATHEISM

religious devotion: PIETY

religious ecstasy: THEOPATHY

religious literature, traditions, etc.: HIEROLOGY

religious movement based on literal accep-tance of everything in the Bible: FUNDAMENTALISM

religious offering: OBLATION

religious ritual: LITURGY

religious washing of hands: ABLUTION

relinquish, give up, forgo: WAIVE

reliquary: FERETORY

reliving a traumatic situation for release from it: ABREACTION

reluctant, unwilling: LOATH

remainder, leftover part: RESIDUE

remainder after deducting all allowances: NET

remark made in passing, comment that is not binding: OBITER DICTUM

remark or observation that is brief, clever and pointed: EPIGRAM

remarkable, strange, extraordinary: UNACCOUNTABLE

remarriage after death or divorce of first spouse: DIGAMY

remedy: TREACLE

remedy for all ailments, cure-all: PANACEA

remedy or cure for all ills: CATHOLICON

remedy that one swears by, medicine of one's own invention, quack medicine, cure-all: NOSTRUM

remedy the consequences of, get back, regain: RETRIEVE

remember, recall to mind: RETRIEVE

remembering: RETROSPECTION

remembering in complete detail: TOTAL RECALL

remind one of a mistake or fault in order to taunt or annoy: TWIT

remission of sin: ABSOLUTION

remorse: COMPUNCTION

remove, take off, as clothing: DOFF

remove attention from: PRESCIND

remove obscene or otherwise objectionable material: EXPURGATE

remove or dissociate from former habits: WEAN

remove or drive away, as by scattering: DISPEL

remove property to a distance or beyond a jurisdiction: ELOIGN

removing by surgery: ABSCISSION

renaming a parent after his or her child: TEKNONYMY

render null and void: INVALIDATE

renew, repair: RENOVATE

renew, restore to perfection: REDINTEGRATE

renounce: ABJURE

renounce: ABNEGATION

renounce, give up: RELINQUISH

renounce claim to right or power: ABDICATE

renounce or abandon emphatically: FORSWEAR

renovate, make over: REVAMP

renown or splendor of reputation: ECLAT

renowned, distinguished: ILLUSTRIOUS

renowned, important: PRESTIGIOUS

repay evil in kind, take revenge: RETALIATE

repay in kind, compensate: REQUITE

repay or pay, make up for, as a loss: RECOMPENSE

repeal: ABROGATE

repeal, revoke, abrogate: RESCIND

repeat: ITERATE

repeat, say or do over and over: REITERATE

repeat meaningless words over and over, babble: VERBIGERATE

repeated: CONTINUAL

repeated song or phrase in music: REPRISE

repeatedly appearing: RECURRENT

repel: REBUFF

repel, reject, rebuff: REPULSE

repent: RUE

repetition needlessly in different words: TAUTOLOGY

repetition of an initial sound in a series of words: ALLITERATION

repetition of last word of one sentence at beginning of next sentence or clause: ANADIPLOSIS

repetition of word or phrase: ANAPHORA

repetition of someone's words in senseless fashion: ECHOLALIA

repetition of written letters or words done unintentionally: DITTOGRAPHY

replace, supplant: SUPERSEDE

replies that are quick and witty: REPARTEE

reply, please: RÉPONDEZ S'IL VOUS PLAÎT (R.S.V.P.)

reply proving someone or something wrong: CONFUTE

reply sharply: RETORT

report of proceedings: CAHIER

reporting official for a conference or committee: RAPPORTEUR

representative of a government, as a civil magistrate or officer: SYNDIC

representative of a special interest group who tries to influence legislation: LOBBYIST

representative or symbol of something, as of a doctrine or a cause: EXPONENT

reprimand, scolding: RATING

reproach, scold, censure: UPBRAID

reproach sarcastically: TAUNT

reproduction or imitation of the original: ECTYPE

reprove mildly: ADMONISH

reptiles and amphibians, as a study: HERPETOLOGY

repudiate: ABJURE
repudiate, contradict, deny: DISAFFIRM
repudiate a former belief: RECANT
repugnant, disgusting, offensive, hateful: ODIOUS
repulsive: LOATHSOME
repulsive, evil, flagrantly bad: VILE
repulsive appearance: EYESORE
reputed, usually considered: PUTATIVE
request or entreaty that succeeds: IMPETRATION
require, claim: POSTULATE
require as a matter of justice, demand rigorously: EXACT
required, indispensable: REQUISITE
required, obligatory: MANDATORY
required by long use or custom: PRESCRIPTIVE
required earlier than something that follows: PREREQUISITE
resemblance in certain aspects of otherwise dissimilar things: ANALOGY
resembling another closely: COUNTERPART
resent another's possessions or enjoyment: BEGRUDGE
resentful, angry: IN HIGH DUDGEON
resentfully morose, glum: SULLEN
resentment, anger: DUDGEON
resentment, injured feeling: UMBRAGE
resentment, offended pride: PIQUE
reservation, excuse: SALVO
reserve accumulation of goods: STOCKPILE
reserve of unfilled orders: BACKLOG
reserved, close-mouthed: TACITURN
reserved, coy, shy, modest: DEMURE
reserved, reluctant to speak, quiet: RETICENT
residence: ABODE
resignation or giving up an office: DEMISSION
resiliency of market in a particular security in the face of changing prices: LIQUIDITY
resistance to established government: INSURRECTION
resistance to harmful influence or disease, exemption from obligation or penalty: IMMUNITY
resistant, immune: INSUSCEPTIBLE
resistant, not yielding to treatment, as a disease: REFRACTORY
resistant, unyielding: IMPREGNABLE
resistant to change, cautious, moderate: CONSERVATIVE

resisting, doubting, ignoring attitude: NEGATIVISM
resolved, unflinching, determined: RESOLUTE
resonant: SONOROUS
resounding loudly: REBOANT
resounding or echoing: RESONANT
respect, reverence or homage: OBEISANCE
respect deeply: VENERATE
respect demanded, criticism forbidden for such a person or idea: SACRED COW
respectable: SAVORY
respects paid to a dignitary such as a king: DEVOIRS
responding involuntarily to a stimulus, as an organism does: TROPISM
response developed by training: CONDITIONED REFLEX
response, echo: REPLICATION
responsibility for all one's acts (Buddhism and Hinduism): KARMA
responsive to persuasion or change: AMENABLE
responsive to persuasion or entreaty: EXORABLE
rest in peace: REQUIESCAT IN PACE
rest interval, postponement, delay: RESPITE
restaurant or bar that is small: BISTRO
restaurant or cafe that provides entertainment: CABARET
resting, leaning or weighing upon something: INCUMBENT
resting, nonactive: STATIC
resting place for travelers or pilgrims: HOSPICE
restless, superficial, frivolous: YEASTY
restless, unruly, fidgety: RESTIVE
restless or nervous movements: FIDGET
restlessness, anxiety: DISQUIETUDE
restlessness, uneasiness: INQUIETUDE
restoration, compensation, amends: REPARATION
restore friendship: RECONCILE
restore to perfection, renew: REDINTEGRATE
restore to rank, position, or state of health: REHABILITATE
restore youthful feeling or vigor: REJUVENATE
restrain or check, as an impulse: INHIBIT
restrained, moderate: TEMPERATE
restraint in sexual activity; moderation: CONTINENCE
restrict to a scanty amount: STINT

restriction, boundary: PALE

restriction on freight transportation: EMBARGO

result: AFTERMATH

result, effect: RAMIFICATION

result or consequence that is normal: COROLLARY

resuscitation: ANABIOSIS

retaining wall: REVETMENT

retaliation: REPRISAL

retentive, as memory: TENACIOUS

retinue, train of attendants: CORTEGE

retire, make oneself inconspicuous: EFFACE

retired from active service, but retained in honorary position: EMERITUS

retired on account of age: SUPERANNUATED

retort that is sharp and swift: RIPOSTE

retract: ABJURE

retraction: PALINODE

retreat to an earlier or worse condition: RETROGRESS

retroactive: EX POST FACTO

return by an offender to criminal acts or antisocial behavior: RECIDIVISM

return in kind or amount: RECIPROCATE

return like for like, repay evil with evil, revenge: RETALIATE

return of part of the output of a system into the input: FEEDBACK

return to a former place, position or condition: REVERT

return to normal condition or better: RALLY

reveal, bring to light, disclose: EXHUME

reveal, give vent to: UNBOSOM

reveal, tell, as a secret: DIVULGE

revelry, usually lasting for a special season or period: SATURNALIA

revenge sought by a country at the cost of war or violence: REVANCHISM

revengeful, spiteful: VINDICTIVE

reverberation, aftereffect: REPERCUSSION

revere: VENERATE

reverence, homage, respect: OBEISANCE

reverie: BROWN STUDY

reversal of opinion: ABOUT-FACE

reversal of opinion: FLIP-FLOP

reverse counting of time: COUNTDOWN

reverse of a proposition in logic: OBVERSE

reverse of truth thought of as if it were truth: DOUBLETHINK

reverse of phraseology in second of two parallel expressions: CHIASMUS

reverse reading of a word or sentence is the same as forward reading: PALINDROME

reverse side of a phonograph record: FLIP SIDE

reverse vision, as when objects are seen as in a mirror: STREPHOSYMBOLIA

reversed or opposite in order or effect: INVERSE

reversed order of things or events, used as a figure of speech: HYSTERON PROTERON

reversion, backward movement: REGRESSION

reversion to a more primitive type: ATAVISM

reversion to an earlier form or condition: THROWBACK

reviewing past occurrences, remembering: RETROSPECTION

revise, renovate: REVAMP

revise or vary, restrict or limit: MODIFY

revival, new birth: RENASCENCE

revive, bring or come back to life: RESUSCITATE

revive, refresh, renew: RENOVATE

revoke, abrogate, repeal: RESCIND

revoke a legacy: ADEEM

revoke or reverse a command: COUNTERMAND

revolve or rotate, usually around a fixed point: GYRATE

revolting, detestable, abominable: EXECRABLE

revolving, whirling or circular motion: GYRAL

rewarding partisan service with public offices: SPOILS SYSTEM

rewording of a statement with the original meaning retained: PARAPHRASE

reworked literary material, rehash: RECHAUFFÉ

rhyme composed of words similar in spelling but not in sound: EYE RHYME

rhyme in which stress falls on next to the last syllable: FEMININE RHYME

rhyme scheme in which a word within the line of verse rhymes with the final word of the line: LEONINE RHYME

rhyming game in which a rhyme must be given for word or line given by another: CRAMBO

rhythmic or measured flow: CADENCE

rhythmic placement of a tone so that its

accent does not coincide with the metric accent: SYNCOPATION

rib or ridge, as on fabric: WALE

ribbon cluster or rosette worn as a badge: COCKADE

ribbon worn as an insignia of honor or rank: CORDON

ribbons and pins in a store: NOTIONS

rice cooked in broth: RISOTTO

rich and resonant, as a tone: VIBRANT

rich man: CROESUS

rich or influential man: NABOB

rich person who has become so only recently: NOUVEAU RICHE

riches, wealth: OPULENCE

rickety: RAMSHACKLE

rid oneself of: SLOUGH

riddle, involving a pun: CONUNDRUM

riddle, puzzle, obscure or ambiguous saying: ENIGMA

ride for pleasure, reckless ride in a stolen vehicle: JOY RIDE

ridge around hatchway or skylight to keep out water: COAMING

ridge or rib, as on fabric: WALE

ridges fixed across the fingerboard of a guitar or other stringed instrument: FRETS

ridicule or scorn publicly: PILLORY

ridicule or treat with scornful mirth: DERIDE

ridicule or wit used to attack vices or follies: SATIRE

ridiculous, absurd: LUDICROUS

ridiculous or ludicrous situation: FARCE

riding the crest of a wave toward shore on a surfboard: SURFING

rifle with short barrel: CARBINE

right a wrong, make compensation: REDRESS

right- and left-handed: AMBIDEXTROUS

right angle position of a line or place to another: PERPENDICULAR

right-angled triangle's side that is opposite the right angle: HYPOTENUSE

right of feudal lords to first night with a bride: DROIT DU SEIGNEUR

right of the state to take over private property for public use: EMINENT DOMAIN

right or claim that is legal: DROIT

right or left part of something, side: FLANK

right side as opposed to the left side: DEXTER

right that is exclusive or a privilege: PREROGATIVE

right to left, a word or sentence reads the same as left to right: PALINDROME

right word or expression: MOT JUSTE

righteousness or holiness pretended: SANCTIMONIOUS

rigid, enlarged condition of the penis: ERECTION

rigid, inflexible: HARD-SHELL

rigid, severe: STRINGENT

rigidity of the muscles after death: RIGOR MORTIS

rigmarole: AMPHIGORY

ring, as for the finger, made up of two interlocked circlets: GIMMAL

ring for attaching a leash, as to a dog's collar: TERRET

ring or disk used to make a connection watertight or gastight: GASKET

ring in the ears: TINNITUS

ringing of bells: TINTINNABULATION

ringing or tinkling sound: JINGLE

ring-shaped hard breadroll: BAGEL

Rio de Janeiro resident: CARIOCA

riot, civil or political disturbance: DISTEMPER

riotous, wild: TURBULENT

rip apart forcibly: REND

ripen: MATURATE

ripple, bubble, heave: POPPLE

rise above: TRANSCEND

rise and float in the air: LEVITATE

rise or overflow of a stream occurring suddenly: FRESHET

rise somewhat from the water when moving at high speed: PLANE

rising again: RESURGENT

rising and falling gently, wavy in appearance: UNDULATING

rising and setting of a star: ACRONICAL

rising market: BULL MARKET

rising up in insurrection: INSURGENCE

risks taken to achieve some end: BRINKMANSHIP

risky: SPECULATIVE

risky, uncertain: TOUCH-AND-GO

risqué, indecent: SCABROUS

risqué, suggestive: RACY

rite considered ordained by Jesus as a means of grace: SACRAMENT

ritual of public religious worship: LITURGY

rival or vie with successfully: EMULATE

rivalry or competition: CONTENTION

river bank area: RIPARIAN

river embankment built to prevent flooding: LEVEE

river mouth where the stream's current meets the sea, an inlet of the sea: ESTUARY

river of oblivion, forgetfulness: LETHE

river of woe: ACHERON

river's head or supply of water: WATERSHED

road ascending a steep incline in a zigzag pattern: SWITCHBACK

road raised over marshy land: CAUSEWAY

road repairing utilizing forced labor: CORVEE

roam about in search of diversion, gad about: GALLIVANT

roaming, homeless: NOMADIC

rob, strip, deprive of: DESPOIL

rob a truck or seize a plane in transit: HIJACK

robber or bandit, usually one of a group: BRIGAND

robber who assaults victim from behind: MUGGER

robber who smuggles goods out of an open store: SHOPLIFTER

robe or undercoat, long sleeved and sashed: CAFTAN

robust, sound and vigorous health: HALE

robust, tough: HARDY

rock projecting and isolated: SCAR

rocket-firing schedule measured in records in reverse order: COUNTDOWN

rocket's forward separable section designed to stand intense heat: NOSE CONE

rocket's head containing explosive: WARHEAD

rocks and their characteristics, as a study: PETROLOGY

rocks' structure and composition as a scientific study: LITHOLOGY

rocky cliff that extends a distance: PALISADES

rococo: BAROQUE

rod that holds meat together for cooking: SKEWER

rod that is pointed and is used for cooking meat over a fire: SPIT

rod that is symbol of royalty: SCEPTER

rogue, rascal: RAPSCALLION

roll in shape of a crescent: CROISSANT

roll of film or magnetic tape in a case: CASSETTE

roll of hard bread that is ring-shaped: BAGEL

roll of sliced meat filled with minced meat: ROULADE

roll of minced meat or fish in a thin pastry: RISSOLE

roll or move tumultuously: WELTER

rolled up, spirally curling: VOLUTE

rollicking type of square dance: HOEDOWN

romantic in intentions but impractical: QUIXOTIC

roof that is rounded, dome: CUPOLA

roof tile with an unbalanced S shape: PANTILE

roof with single slope and its upper edge abutting a wall: LEAN-TO

roof with two slopes on each side: MANSARD

roof with two slopes on each side, the lower having a steeper pitch: GAMBREL ROOF

room or territory for expansion: LEBENSRAUM

roomy: CAPACIOUS

rooster that is castrated to make the meat better for eating: CAPON

root out, destroy wholly: EXTIRPATE

rootlike: RHIZOID

rope, cable or wire used to steady or secure something: GUY

rope or cable for mooring or towing: HAWSER

rosette or ribbon badge: COCKADE

rosy: RUBICUND

rotary combustion engine for automobiles: WANKEL ENGINE

rotate or revolve, usually around a fixed point: GYRATE

rotation force: TORQUE

rotten: CARIOUS

rotten, corrupt: PUTRID

rotten or dead flesh: CARRION

rough, crude, unrefined: UNCOUTH

rough, plain, simple: RUSTIC

rough-and-tumble clash, fracas: SCRIMMAGE

roughly handle, manhandle, abuse: MAUL

roughness: ASPERITY

round building or hall: ROTUNDA

round up: CORRAL

roundabout: AMBIGUOUS

roundabout or indirect: CIRCUITOUS

roundabout talk: CIRCUMLOCUTION

rounded, full, clear voice: OROTUND

rounded, spherical: ORBICULAR

rounded mass: GLOMERATION

rounded out, plump: ROTUND

roundness: SPHERICITY

rouse to action, stimulate, arouse: GALVANIZE

route followed in traveling: ITINERARY

routine, commonplace, ordinary: MUNDANE

routinely performed without interest: PERFUNCTORY

roving, wandering, straying, itinerant: ERRANT

royalty symbol in the form of a rod: SCEPTER

rub away: ABRADE

rub out, erase, cancel, obliterate: EFFACE

rub the body with oil: EMBROCATE

rubbing off or wearing off of particles: DETRITION

rubbish, nonsense, worthless: TRUMPERY

rubbish, refuse, leavings: OFFAL

ruddy: SANGUINE

ruddy, flushed: FLORID

rude, disorderly, boisterous: RAMBUNCTIOUS

rude, sullen: SURLY

rude or discourteous manner: INCIVILITY

rude or ill-natured person: CHURL

rudeness, insolence: IMPERTINENCE

rudeness in speech that is insulting and scornful: CONTUMELY

rudimentary: ABECEDARIAN

ruffle at the neckline or front of a bodice or shirt: JABOT

ruffle on a blouse or coat at the waist: PEPLUM

ruffle or upset the balance: DISTEMPER

ruffled or pleated strip of fabric worn about the neck or wrists of a woman's costume: RUCHE

rugged and weather-beaten: GNARLED

ruin, destruction: HAVOC

ruin, rout, sudden and ruinous breakdown or collapse: DEBACLE

ruin, wreck, pillage: RAVAGE

rule, moral guide, maxim: PRECEPT

rule by the best: ARISTOCRACY

rule of principle that is established: CANON

rule or standard by which a judgment can be made: CRITERION

rule or treat with cruel power: TYRANNIZE

ruler who governs in place of a sovereign: REGENT

ruler of a people or province: ETHNARCH

ruler or similar instrument used to punish children: FERULE

ruler who is supreme: SOVEREIGN

rulers or sovereigns reigning in succession in one line of descent: DYNASTY

rules or directions printed for use in religious services: RUBRIC

Rumanian and Israeli folk dance in which dancers lock arms in a circle: HORA

rum drink that includes lemon or lime juice and sugar: PLANTER'S PUNCH

rummage about for something: FOSSICK

rumor, gossip, the lowdown: SCUTTLEBUTT

rumor that is false: CANARD

rumpled, untidy, unkempt, tousled: DISHEVELED

rumbling noise, move with rumbling noise: LUMBER

run, go in a hurry: SCAMPER

run away to escape law: ABSCOND

run with steady swinging stride: LOPE

run-down, neglected, fallen into ruin or decay: DILAPIDATED

runners fastened to shoes for gliding over snow: SKIS

running at a slow, jolting pace: JOG

running together of final and initial sounds of two adjacent words: SANDHI

rural: AGRESTIC

rural life portrayed as peaceful and idyllic: PASTORAL

rural or farming affairs: GEORGIC

rush forward: SALLY

rush headlong: HURTLE

rush wildly: CAREEN

ruthlessly compelling conformity: PROCRUSTEAN

Russian country home: DACHA

Russian dance in which a squatting man kicks each leg out alternately: KAZATSKY

Russian for comrade: TOVARICH

Russian title equivalent to Mr.: GOSPODIN

Russian triangular shaped stringed instrument: BALALAIKA

Russian vehicle drawn by three horses abreast: TROIKA

rustic or pastoral: BUCOLIC

rustling, whispering, softly murmuring: SUSURRANT

rustling as of silk, swish, fanciness: FROUFROU

rye or bourbon cocktail made with vermouth: MANHATTAN

S

"s" shaped: SIGMATE

sable fur: ZIBELINE

sack of canvas or duck used for carrying personal possessions: DUFFLE BAG or DUFFEL BAG

sacred books of any sect or religion: CANON

sacredness maintained, unbroken: IN-VIOLATE

sacrificial offering, wholly consumed by fire: HOLOCAUST

saddened, dejected, gloomy: DIS-CONSOLATE

sad, mournful, painful: DOLOROUS

sad, pitiful, causing sorrow: PATHETIC

sad or mournful, especially in a ludicrous manner: LUGUBRIOUS

saddened or desolate through loss: BEREAVED

saddle, the hind part of which projects upward: CANTLE

sadism or masochism: ALGOLAGNIA

safe or proof against attack: UNASSAIL-ABLE

said or done for effect or as a formality: GESTURE

sail of triangular shape ahead of the fore-mast: JIB

sailboat with a single mast and fore and aft rigging: SLOOP

sailboat's mast or boom: SPAR

sailing close to the wind: LUFF

sailor ranking below an able-bodied sea-man: ORDINARY SEAMAN

sailor who is a veteran, old salt: SHELL-BACK

sailor's bag for belongings: DITTY BAG

sailors' rhythmical working song: CHAN-TEY

St. Vitus dance: CHOREA

sainted: CANONIZED

salary, pension, allowance: STIPEND

salary or fee for a service: EMOLUMENT

sale item priced near or below cost to pro-mote sale of others: LOSS LEADER

sales force manager in a store: FLOOR-WALKER

saliva, spittle: SPUTUM

salmon before it enters the ocean: PARR

salmon of a salty, smoked variety: LOX

salmon that has returned for the first time from the sea to fresh water: GRILSE

salty: SALINE

salty, briny: BRACKISH

salvage something usable from refuse: SCAVENGE

same: DITTO

same as previous reference: IBID

same kind of person or thing: CONGENER

sameness in style, tone, expression, color: MONOTONE

sample strip of fabric: SWATCH

sanctimonious: PHARISAIC

sandals with uppers made of straps: HUARACHES

sandstone used to scour the wooden decks of a ship: HOLYSTONE

sandwich with three slices of bread and two layers of filling: DOUBLE-DECKER

sandy grittiness: SABULOUS

sarcastic: ACRIMONIOUS

sarcastic, caustic, cutting: MORDANT

sarcastic or biting: CAUSTIC

sarcastic or humorous speech in which op-posite of what is said is meant: IRONY

sardinelike fish: SPRAT

sarong style loincloth worn by Samoan na-tives: LAVA-LAVA

sash, usually wide, worn as a waistband: CUMMERBUND

sassy: CHEEKY

sassy young woman: BAGGAGE

satanic: CLOVEN-HOOFED

sated, full, amply supplied: REPLETE

satire that is sarcastic or coarse and is posted publicly: PASQUINADE

satirize or abuse in humorous prose or verse: LAMPOON

satisfy or quench, as a thirst: SLAKE

saturate, permeate, fertilize: IMPREGNATE

sauce, as for fish, made of mayonnaise and chopped pickles, capers, etc.: TARTAR SAUCE

sauce made with mayonnaise and spices: RÉMOULADE

sauce of onions, butter and white sauce: SOUBISE

sauce thickened with fat and flour: ROUX

sauciness, impertinence: FLIPPANCY

saucy, brazen, shameless, bold: IMPUDENT

saucy, lively: PERT

sausage-shaped: ALLANTOID

savage, fierce, bloodthirsty, cruel: FEROCIOUS

savage, wild: FERAL

save from destruction: SALVAGE

saved material after a wreck, fire, etc.: SALVAGE

savory, pleasant tasting: SAPID

say or do over and over, repeat: REITERATE

saying long in use: ADAGE

saying something that one suggests is too obvious to say: PARALEIPSIS

sayings ascribed to Jesus but not found in Bible: AGRAPHA

scale ramparts by ladders: ESCALADE

scaly: SQUAMOUS

scanty: SKIMPY

scanty, inadequate, thin: MEAGER

scanty, small, diminutive: EXIGUOUS

scanty, stingy: NIGGARDLY

scar or scarlike marking: CICATRIX

scarcity, lack, famine: DEARTH

scarf, long and made of fur or fabric, worn over a woman's shoulders: STOLE

scarf, necktie: CRAVAT

scarf, often of lace, worn over head and shoulders by Spanish women: MANTILLA

scarf worn about the head and shoulders by Spanish and Latin American women: REBOZO

scarf worn on the head by women: BABUSHKA

scatter, drive away, dispel: DISPERSE

scatter among other things, set here and there: INTERSPERSE

scatter or diffuse, as if by sowing: DISSEMINATE

scattered, not concentrated: SPARSE

scattered, wasted: DISSIPATED

schedule or select: SLATE

scheme or plot: MACHINATE

scheming person (a derogatory term): JESUIT

schizophrenia, usually associated with puberty, characterized by unsystematic behavior, exaggerated mannerisms: HEBEPHRENIA

scholarly, learned: ERUDITE

scholarly life: ACADEME

scholarly person: SAVANT

scholarship displayed in an undiscriminating way: PEDANTRY

science of bullets, missiles, rockets, etc.: BALLISTICS

science of soil: AGROLOGY

science that treats of earth's surface and its physical, political and social characteristics: GEOGRAPHY

scientific husbandry: AGRONOMY

scoff: JEER

scold, censure, reproach: UPBRAID

scold, rake over the coals, reprove severely: KEELHAUL

scold, sharp-tongued woman: VIRAGO

scold severely, upbraid, berate: OBJURGATE

scolding: ABUSIVE

scolding, harsh reprimand: RATING

scolding and abusive woman, shrew: TERMAGANT

scope: AMBIT

scope, range, extent: PURVIEW

scorched, hot: TORRID

scorched, or colored as if by scorching: USTULATE

scorn, despise: CONTEMN

scorn, reject, refuse: SPURN

scorn or ridicule publicly: PILLORY

scornful, sneering, cynical: SARDONIC

scornful rudeness in speech: CONTUMELY

Scotch whisky and vermouth cocktail: ROB ROY

Scottish cap with a tight headband and a wide, flat top: TAM-O'SHANTER

Scottish dish containing animal's insides boiled in its stomach: HAGGIS

scoundrel: CAITIFF

scowl, look angry or sullen: LOWER
scowl sullenly: GLOWER
scrap, do away with: SCUTTLE
scrap, fragment: SNIPPET
scrape, paw or scratch: SCRABBLE
scrape away: ABRADE
scrape or grind harshly, cut, pierce: GRIDE
scratch, cut: SCOTCH
scratch, scrape or paw: SCRABBLE
scream, bawl, cry loudly: SQUALL
screen behind an altar: REREDOS
screen or shutter of overlapping horizontal slats: JALOUSIE
screw or nail inserted so that it lies flush with or below surface: COUNTERSINK
scribble: SCRABBLE
scribble or draw aimlessly: DOODLE
scribblings or drawings on wall: GRAFFITI
scruffy, uneven: SCRAGGLY
scrutinize, examine or read thoroughly: PERUSE
scrutinize, look at closely: SCAN
sculpture in which figures project slightly: BAS-RELIEF
sculptured basket of fruit: CORBEIL
scum, froth, foam: SPUME
sea arm, long and narrow path and between high banks: FIORD
sea-green or yellowish-green color: GLAUCOUS
sea spray: SPINDRIFT
sea with numerous islands: ARCHIPELAGO
seal or plug edges or crevices: CAULK
seal rings, as a subject of study: SPHRAGISTICS
seamen's short coat of heavy woolen fabric: PEA JACKET
sear: CAUTERIZE
search, pursuit, adventure: QUEST
search, scour, move rapidly: SKIRR
search for food or supplies: FORAGE
search for gold in abandoned mines: FOSSICK
search for information, investigate: DELVE
search out by careful investigation: FERRET
search thoroughly: RANSACK
search through: ROOT
search through refuse, as for food: SCAVENGE
seas, lakes, rivers, etc., studied to determine their use for navigation: HYDROGRAPHY
season of warm, hazy weather in late autumn: INDIAN SUMMER

seat behind the saddle on a horse or motorcycle: PILLION
seat for riders on an elephant or a camel: HOWDAH
seat or small stool, usually without arms or back: TABORET
seat or step in a series that rises: GRADIN
seated a great part of the time, settled, inactive: SEDENTARY
seaward current of water beneath the surface: UNDERCURRENT
seaweed or other marine vegetation cast ashore: WRACK
secluded: CLOISTRAL
secluded: SEQUESTERED
secluded, solitary person: RECLUSE
secluded garden for quiet pleasure: PLEASANCE
secluded or inactive for a period, especially winter: HIBERNATING
second experience imagined when it is actually only the first: DÉJÀ VU
second marriage: DEUTEROGAMY
second marriage: DIGAMY
second seat on a motorcycle: PILLION
second self: ALTER EGO
second sight: CLAIRVOYANCE
secondary, casual, minor: INCIDENTAL
secondary phenomenon occurring with another but having no power to produce effects: EPIPHENOMENON
secret, abstruse, unknown except by an inner few: ESOTERIC
secret, as of a meeting or plan, kept hidden for an illicit purpose: CLANDESTINE
secret, hidden, puzzling, occult, mystifying: CRYPTIC
secret, sheltered: COVERT
secret agreement, usually to defraud someone: COLLUSION
secret group joined in intrigue: CABAL
secret jargon, especially of thieves, beggars, etc.: CANT
secret meeting: CONCLAVE
secret meeting: EXECUTIVE SESSION
secret meeting, as of lovers: ASSIGNATION
secret or closed session: IN CAMERA
secret or hidden: ARCANE
secret or mystic system: CABALA
secret or private things: PENETRALIA
secret or unofficial means of relaying information, usually from person to person: GRAPEVINE
secretary: AMANUENSIS

secretly: SUB ROSA
secretly depart, to escape law: ABSCOND
secretly informed: PRIVY
section of a city in which a minority lives:
    GHETTO
secularize: LAICIZE
securities bought over a period, by the
    dollars' worth rather than by number
    of shares: DOLLAR COST AVERAGING
securities list: PORTFOLIO
securities pledged as collateral for a loan:
    HYPOTHECATION
security, pledge, challenge: GAGE
security for discharge of an obligation:
    COLLATERAL
security selling that is not done on the
    floor of a stock exchange: OVER-THE-
    COUNTER
security that is transferable by delivery:
    NEGOTIABLE
sedate, steady, sober: STAID
sedative, sleep-producing medicine:
    OPIATE
seduce, corrupt, deprave: DEBAUCH
see (reference in a book): VIDE
see before: VIDE ANTE
see below: VIDE INFRA
seed bearing: SEMINIFEROUS
seed-bearing part of flowering plants: PIS-
    TIL
seeing into the future: PRESCIENT
seeing or knowing: COGNITION
seeing things that are not visible: CLAIR-
    VOYANCE
seeming, apparent: OSTENSIBLE
seemly, proper: DECOROUS
see-through fabric: DIAPHANOUS
segment: CANTLE
seize, capture or secure: CORRAL
seize, grip tightly, struggle or contend
    with: GRAPPLE
seize and place in legal custody: IMPOUND
seize by legal means: SEQUESTER
seize by violence: WREST
seize or appropriate: CONFISCATE
seize or appropriate beforehand: PREEMPT
seize or stop on the way, prevent from
    reaching the destination: INTERCEPT
seizure of property in legal proceeding:
    ATTACHMENT
select, pick out, sort: CULL
select, schedule: SLATE
selecting from diverse sources: ECLECTIC
selections or fragments from literary
    works: ANALECTS

self, the part of the psyche that organizes
    thought and governs action: EGO
self held to be the only thing really exis-
    tent: SOLIPSISM
self-assertive, bold, indecent: IMMODEST
self-assurance: COCKINESS
self-assurance, composure, serenity: POISE
self-centered: EGOCENTRIC
self-confidence: APLOMB
self-confident, lively, brisk, dashing:
    JAUNTY
self-confident to an extreme: COCKSURE
self-contradictory, false or ridiculous
    statement: PARADOX
self-denial: ABNEGATION
self-determination: AUTONOMY
self-evident statement: AXIOM
self-examination: INTROSPECTION
self-governing: AUTONOMOUS
self-important, overdignified, pretentious:
    POMPOUS
self-important, petulant: HOITY-TOITY
self-interested person: INTROVERT
selfish person: EGOIST
selflessness: ALTRUISM
self-love: NARCISSISM
self-mortification: ASCETICISM
self-protective reaction of an organism:
    DEFENSE MECHANISM
self-reproach, guilt feeling: REMORSE
self-satisfaction: COMPLACENCY
self-satisfied, complacent: SMUG
self-service meal: BUFFET
self-supporting, as a country: SUBSTAN-
    TIVE
self-styled: SOI-DISANT
sell goods in the street, peddle: HAWK
sell property for profit: REALIZE
selling by quiet persuasion rather than
    high pressure tactics: SOFT SELL
semicircle: HEMICYCLE
semifluid, sticky, honeylike consistency:
    VISCOUS
seminar or group of people who study
    together some subject or topic:
    WORKSHOP
semiskilled worker: BLUE COLLAR
semitransparent: TRANSLUCENT
send back to one's own country: REPATRI-
    ATE
send forth or give off as light or heat:
    EMIT
send from one place to another: TRANSMIT
send or order back: REMAND
senility: CADUCITY

senility: DOTAGE
senior or eldest member of a group: DOYEN
senseless, absurd: IRRATIONAL
senseless or foolish talk: DRIVEL
senses as source of pleasure: SENSUOUS
sensibility, perception: ESTHESIA
sensible, reasoned: RATIONAL
sensitive: SUSCEPTIBLE
sensitivity in extreme to touch, heat, pain, etc.: HYPERESTHESIA
sensitivity to heat and cold: THERMESTHESIA
sensual, carnal, worldly: FLESHLY
sensual, especially concerning food: EPICUREAN
sensualist: VOLUPTUARY
sensualist, rake: ROUÉ
sentence analysis that gives the form, function and syntactical relationship of its words: PARSE
sentence in which sense and structure are not completed until the end: PERIODIC SENTENCE
sentence in which the main clause appears at the beginning and less important matter follows: LOOSE SENTENCE
sentence or word that reads the same backward as forward: PALINDROME
sentence within which one grammatical construction changes to another: ANACOLUTHON
sentimental features incorporated in a play or story to evoke emotional response: HOKUM
sentimental or emotional, tearfully so: MAUDLIN
sentimentality that is false: MAWKISHNESS
sentimentality to excess: SCHMALTZ
sentimentally pensive: LANGUISHING
sentimentality: BATHOS
separate, as the good from the bad: WINNOW
separate, disconnected: DISCRETE
separate, mark out boundaries of limits: DEMARCATE
separate, part, divide: DISSEVER
separate, set apart: SEQUESTER
separate a group into small dissenting factions: BALKANIZE
separate from, break away: DISSOCIATE
separate into opposing groups or views: POLARIZE
separate into parts: DIFFRACT
separate into two parts: DICHOTOMIZE

separate or break up into parts, analyze: RESOLVE
separated, set apart: ISOLATED
sepulchral: FERAL
sequence in logic or grammar: CONSECUTION
serene, calm, quiet: TRANQUIL
serene, calm, unmoved: IMPASSIVE
series, succession: CONSECUTION
series of reactions or events in which results become causes: CHAIN REACTION
serious, reflective, often melancholy: PENSIVE
sermon, especially one based on a biblical text: HOMILY
sermon writing and delivery, as a study: HOMILETICS
sermonize, lecture: PRELECT
serpent, reputed to be hatched from a cock's egg: COCKATRICE
serpent in the headdress of Egyptian kings: URAEUS
servant: RETAINER
servant or assistant as of a magician or scholar: FAMULUS
servant or low person: MENIAL
servile, compliant, slavish: SEQUACIOUS
servile, fawning follower: MINION
servile, fawning person: TOADY
servile, obsequious: SUBSERVIENT
servile, overly obedient, fawning: OBSEQUIOUS
servile follower, toady: LACKEY
servile or lickspittle attitude: KOWTOW
servilely flatter: ADULATE
serving or portion: DOLLOP
servitude, slavery: THRALLDOM
set, surroundings, environment, as of a play: MISE EN SCÈNE
set apart, separate: SEQUESTER
set aside, as money for a special purpose: EARMARK
set here and there, scatter among other things: INTERSPERSE
set in from the margin as the first line of a paragraph: INDENT
set of concurrent symptoms indicating a specific disease or condition: SYNDROME
set speech or recitation: DECLAMATION
set straight, undeceive: DISABUSE
set up, establish: INSTITUTE
settle one's debts: LIQUIDATE
settlement of a dispute that is advanced by

friendly intervention of a conciliator: MEDIATION

settlement of a dispute by the decision of a person or body chosen with the consent of both sides: ARBITRATION

settler on public or unoccupied land without permission: SQUATTER

seven, or seven things: HEPTAD

seven days, a week: HEBDOMAD

sevenfold: SEPTUPLE

seventh year, in ancient Jewish system: SABBATICAL YEAR

seven-year recurrences: SEPTENNIAL

several, various: DIVERS

severance of relations: RUPTURE

severe, allowing no letup: EXACTING

severe, rigid: STRINGENT

severe, stormy: INCLEMENT

severe, strict, grim: STARK

sew loosely: BASTE

sewage: SULLAGE

sewer: KENNEL

sewing together of the edges of a wound in a surgical operation: SUTURE

sex bias against females: SEXISM

sex differentiation absent, as in clothes, hair styles, etc.: UNISEX

sex glands in the male: TESTICLES

sexless: ANAPHRODISIA

sexless, asexual: NEUTER

sexless, effeminate: EPICENE

sexual, cheap: RAUNCHY

sexual abstinence: CELIBACY

sexual activity involving licking of female genitals: CUNNILINGUS

sexual activity involving licking of male genitals: FELLATIO

sexual characteristics of both sexes: ANDROGYNOUS

sexual climax in intercourse: ORGASM

sexual coupling: INTERCOURSE

sexual desire for a member of the same sex: HOMOEROTICISM

sexual desire in women that is uncontrollable: NYMPHOMANIA

sexual desire lacking: ANAPHRODISIS

sexual desire or impulse: LIBIDO

sexual desire or lust: CONCUPISCENCE

sexual desire reducer: ANTAPHRODISIAC

sexual desire that is abnormally strong: EROTOMANIA

sexual frenzy in a male elephant: MUST

sexual go-between: PANDER

sexual intercourse: COITUS

sexual intercourse: CONGRESS

sexual intercourse: COPULATION

sexual intercourse between persons so closely related that marriage is forbidden them: INCEST

sexual intercourse forced on a woman: RAPE

sexual intercourse that is illegal: FORNICATION

sexual organ of male animals: PENIS

sexual organs: GENITALS

sexual organs of female animals: VULVA, CLITORIS

sexual pervert, or to turn away from straight course: DEVIATE

sexual pleasure resulting from pain: ALGOLAGNIA

sexual potency of a man: VIRILITY

sexual practices between males, especially between men and boys: PEDERASTY

sexual restraint; moderation: CONTINENCE

sexual stimulant: APHRODISIAC

sexually abandoned, lewd: LICENTIOUS

sexually arousing: EROGENOUS

sexual arousing, pertaining to the body: SENSUAL

sexually attracted to persons of the opposite sex: HETEROSEXUAL

sexually capable at this period: PUBERTY

sexually desirous regarding those of the same sex: HOMOSEXUAL

sexually preoccupied: CARNAL

sexually stimulating: EROTIC

sexually stimulating object that in itself is not erotic, such as a shoe: FETISH

sexually unrestrained: INCONTINENT

sexually wanton man: SATYR

shabby, decayed, neglected: DILAPIDATED

shabby, decrepit: FLEA-BITTEN

shabby, dirty: DISREPUTABLE

shabby, drab: DOWDY

shackle, handcuff, fetter: MANACLE

shading, as in a picture, done with crossed lines: CROSSHATCH

shading with close parallel or crossed lines: HATCH

shadow pantomime in miniature: GALANTY SHOW

shadow that does not completely cut off light: PENUMBRA

shadows falling to north or south depending on season: AMPHISCIANS

shady: ADUMBRAL

shady or providing shade: UMBRAGEOUS

shake slightly: JOGGLE

shake suddenly or forcibly: SUCCUSS

shake up, elbow, push or crowd roughly, shove: JOSTLE

shake up and down, bounce, jolt: JOUNCE

shaking or shivering motion: TREMOR

shaky, loose: RAMSHACKLE

shallow, cursory, limited to the surface: SUPERFICIAL

sham: SIMULACRUM

sham, deceptive, pretended: FEIGNED

shameful: IGNOMINIOUS

shameful: OPPROBRIOUS

shameless: BRAZEN

shamelessness: IMPUDICITY

shank, part of leg between knee and ankle: CRUS

shape, outline, form: FIGURATION

shape distortion: ANAMORPHISM

shape or design that doesn't adhere to any rigid pattern: FREE-FORM

shapeless: AMORPHOUS

shapely buttocks: CALLIPYGIAN

share, portion, half: MOIETY

sharer of secrets: CONFIDANT

sharing the sensations of another as if one were participating in the action: VICARIOUS

sharp: ACERB

sharp: ACUATE

sharp, abrupt emphasis: STACCATO

sharp, keen, cutting, biting: INCISIVE

sharp answer or reply: RETORT

sharp but pleasant tasting, tart: PIQUANT

sharp taste, manner, speech, nature: ACRID

sharp tasting or smelling: PUNGENT

sharp-edged and pointed: CULTRATE

sharpen, as a razor, on a hone: HONE

sharpen, excite, stimulate: WHET

sharply affecting the mind: PUNGENT

sharp-tongued woman, a scold: VIRAGO

shatter, splinter into fragments: SHIVER

shattering effect of an explosion: BRISANCE

shave or pare the surface, as leather: SKIVE

shaving of the crown of the head: TONSURE

shed, get rid of: SLOUGH

shedding, or falling off, as of petals, leaves, fruit: DECIDUOUS

sheep or goat newly born: YEANLING

sheeplike: OVINE

sheepskin coat worn by Spanish shepherds: ZAMARRA

sheer or transparent: DIAPHANOUS

sheet carrying advertising or propaganda: BROADSIDE

sheet folded once and forming four pages: FOLIO

shelf above a fireplace: MANTEL

shelf above the back of an altar to hold ornaments, candles, lights: RETABLE

shelf for holding small ornamental items: WHATNOT

shell, pod or husk: SHUCK

shell containing baked minced food: COQUILLE

shell lined with mother-of-pearl: ABALONE

shell study: CONCHOLOGY

shelter or disguise: COVERTURE

sheltered, secret or concealed: COVERT

sheriff's office, term or jurisdiction: SHRIEVALTY

shield division in heraldry: CANTON

shield-shaped: SCUTIFORM

shield-shaped surface with armorial bearings: ESCUTCHEON

shift position or direction: VEER

shifting of a disease from one part of the body to another: METASTASIS

shifty, elusive: LUBRICOUS

shinbone: TIBIA

shingle knife: FROE

shining: IRRADIANT

shining, illustrious: SPLENDENT

shining back, reflecting light, bright: RELUCENT

shining with brilliance, dazzling, vividly bright: RESPLENDENT

ship opening in floor or deck giving access to area beneath: HATCH

ship portion above the main deck: TOPSIDE

ship so far away that the hull is hidden below the horizon: HULL DOWN

ship space where cargo is stored: HOLD

ship that is large: ARGOSY

ship with two or more masts, rigged fore and aft: SCHOONER

shipboard drinking fountain: SCUTTLEBUTT

ship's backbone: KEEL

ship's kitchen: GALLEY

ship's left side as one faces forward: PORT

ship's length: FORE AND AFT

ship's officer ranking next below the captain: FIRST MATE

ship's or plane's position checked by radio signals from known stations: LORAN

ship's or plane's right-hand side as one faces forward: STARBOARD

ship's permission to enter port: PRATIQUE

ship's sailing close to the wind: LUFF

ship's small boat: JOLLY BOAT
ship's upper front part: FORECASTLE
shivering or shaking motion: TREMOR
shock to the body or system, caused by an injury: TRAUMA
shocked or nauseated easily, prudish: SQUEAMISH
shocking, vivid, sensational: LURID
shoddy, poorly made, cheap: SLEAZY
shoe that is heavy and coarse: BROGAN
shoe's upper front part: VAMP
shoot (a liquid) in by mechanical or physical means: INJECT
shoot from a hiding place: SNIPE
shoot out copiously, as a liquid: SPOUT
shop that has long hours, insufficient pay, and poor conditions: SWEAT SHOP
shop that is small and fashionable: BOUTIQUE
shore or beach: STRAND
shore or coastal region: LITTORAL
shore uncovered by low tide: FORESHORE
short distance: STONE'S THROW
short fingers or toes: BRACHYDACTYLIC
short of breath: PURSY
shortage, scarcity: PAUCITY
shorten: ABBREVIATE
shorten: ABRIDGE
shortened: ELLIPTIC
shortened: TRUNCATED
shortening of a syllable that is naturally or by position long: SYSTOLE
shorthand, especially in ancient times: TACHYGRAPHY
short-lived, of short duration: TRANSIENT
short-lived, transitory, fleeting: EPHEMERAL
short takeoff and landing plane: STOL
shoulder bag, especially as used by soldiers: MUSETTE BAG
shoulder ornament, especially on the uniforms of military and naval officers: EPAULET
shout, bawl, exclaim loudly: VOCIFERATE
shout, violent denunciation: FULMINATE
shove, shake up, elbow, push or crowd roughly: JOSTLE
show clearly, manifest, demonstrate convincingly: EVINCE
show consisting of skits, songs, and dances: REVUE
showcase of glass, for displaying art objects: VITRINE
shower, scatter, sprinkle: SPARGE

showiness: OSTENTATION
showoff tendency: EXHIBITIONISM
showy, bombastic, florid: FLAMBOYANT
showy, excessively ornamented: ORNATE
showy, useless ornaments: FURBELOWS
showy and cheap: TAWDRY
showy but valueless: TRUMPERY
showy but without substance: SPECIOUS
shrew: VIXEN
shrew: XANTHIPPE
shrew, scolding and abusive woman: TERMAGANT
shrewd, practical, obstinate: HARD-HEADED
shrewd, wise: SAGACIOUS
shrewish old woman: GRIMALKIN
shrill, grating: STRIDENT
shrink or crouch in servility: CRINGE
shriveled, shrunken, withered: WIZENED
shrubs or trees cut and arranged in fantastic shapes: TOPIARY
shrunken, withered, shriveled: WIZENED
shuffle cards by bending up corners of two parts of the pack and letting cards slip together: RIFFLE
shun as unworthy: ESCHEW
shut, block or close off: OCCLUDE
shut one's eyes to wrongdoing: CONNIVE
shut out, exclude: OSTRACIZE
shut out, exclude, render impossible: PRECLUDE
shutter or screen of overlapping horizontal slats: JALOUSIE
shy, inept person (Yiddish): NEBBISH
shy, jumpy: SKITTISH
shy, meek, apologetic person: MILQUETOAST
shyly embarrassed: SHEEPISH
shyness: DIFFIDENCE
shyness, timidity, lack of confidence in self: DIFFIDENCE
sick: NAUSEATED
sick-making: NAUSEOUS
sickening to an extreme: AD NAUSEAM
sickening or insipid: MAWKISH
sickle or scythe shaped: FALCATE
sickness caused by eating or drinking too much: CRAPULENCE
sickness pretended to avoid work: MALINGER
side, right or left part of something: FLANK
side by side: ABREAST
side by side: CHEEK BY JOWL
side by side: JUXTAPOSITION

side or sides of a main thing: LATERAL
side sheltered from the wind: LEEWARD
side to side: ATHWART
side to side lurch or twist: CAREEN
side to side measurement: BREADTH
side track connecting with the main track of a railroad: SPUR TRACK
sideboard or buffet, usually without legs: CREDENZA
sideburns: BURNSIDES
sidepiece in a door or window sash: STILE
sides touching: ABUTTING
sidewise glance: ASKANCE
sievelike: CRIBRIFORM
sift, examine or analyze minutely: WINNOW
sift through a coarse sieve: RIDDLE
sighing sound, as of the wind: SOUGH
sight loss without organic defect: AMAUROSIS
sight or eye: OCULAR
sighting land: LANDFALL
sight marred by specks or threads seeming to float before the eyes: MUSCAE VOLITANTES
sign language, deaf-mute alphabet: DACTYLOLOGY
sign of a solemn pledge: SACRAMENT
sign or abbreviation representing a word, as the dollar sign: LOGOGRAM
sign or dedicate a book for presentation: INSCRIBE
sign or mark supposed to exercise occult power: SIGIL
sign or trace of something absent: VESTIGE
signal for parley, made by drum or trumpet: CHAMADE
signal for pillage and destruction: CRY HAVOC
signature, especially of a sovereign: SIGN MANUAL
signature appendage, such as a flourish or a mark: RUBRIC
signature ending made with a flourish: PARAPH
signature that authenticates another signature: COUNTERSIGNATURE
silence, subdue utterly, crush: SQUELCH
signify, hint at: IMPLY
signify, point out, indicate: DENOTE
silence, in music: TACET
silence or feigned ignorance as of a wrongdoing: CONNIVANCE
silencing or putting down, as a rumor: QUIETUS

silent, unspoken: TACIT
silk-screen process used by artist: SERIGRAPHY
silky: SERICEOUS
silky, light and fluffy: FLOSSY
silly, empty talk: TWADDLE
silly, fickle: FRIVOLOUS
silly, pointless, empty-headed: INANE
silly, vain, foppish behavior: COXCOMBRY
silver or bronze gilt: VERMEIL
silver or white in armorial bearings (heraldry): ARGENT
similar: AGNATE
similar, like, same composition throughout, uniform: HOMOGENEOUS
similar or related in structure, position, value: HOMOLOGOUS
similar thing: ANALOGUE
similarity in form: HOMOMORPHISM
similarity in sound: ASSONANCE
similarity without identity: ANALOGY
simmer: CODDLE
simple, candid, artless, unaffected: NAIVE
simple, frank, innocent, naive, straightforward: INGENUOUS
simple, rough, plain: RUSTIC
simple, sincere: UNAFFECTED
simple, unaffected, in music: SEMPLICE
simplicity, innocence and peace, portrayed as associated with rural life: PASTORAL
simultaneous: CONCURRENT
simultaneousness: SYNCHRONISM
sin, wrongful act, unjust thing or deed: INIQUITY
sincere, candid, artless: GUILELESS
sincere, real: UNAFFECTED
sinful, at fault: PECCANT
sinful, obstinate: UNREGENERATE
sing a tune heartily: TROLL
sing with trills, as a bird does: WARBLE
singing leader in church: PRECENTOR
singing that alternates falsetto and normal chest tones: YODEL
singing that is akin to ordinary speech: RECITATIVE
singing without accompaniment: A CAPPELLA
single file: INDIAN FILE
single file, one behind the other: TANDEM
single piece of stone, used in architecture or sculpture: MONOLITH
single woman: FEME SOLE
single word applied to two thoughts, each

of which gives it a different meaning: SYLLEPSIS

single word applied to two thoughts, with the linkage to one of them incorrect: ZEUGMA

single-colored: MONOCHROME

singled out for special honor because of excellence in one's achievements: LAUREATE

sink, collapse, fail: FOUNDER

sink a ship by cutting holes in the bottom of it: SCUTTLE

sink in mud, bog down: MIRE

sinuous: ANFRACTUOUS

sinuous, gliding motion: UNDULATION

sister killer: SORORICIDE

sisterhood, female student organization: SORORITY

sit and hatch eggs, develop: INCUBATE

six: HEXAD

six units: SENARY

sixfold: SEXTUPLICATE

six-ounce bottle of a beverage: SPLIT

size or extent: MAGNITUDE

skeptic: DOUBTING THOMAS

skeptical, disbelieving: INCREDULOUS

sketch of a character or a drawing of a side view: PROFILE

sketchily outline: ADUMBRATE

skewer for broiling meat: BROCHETTE

ski down a straight, steep slope: SCHUSS

skiing cross-country run: LANGLAUF

skiing jump made from a crouching position: GELÄNDESPRUNG

skiing over ice or snow in tow of a horse or motor vehicle: SKIJORING

skiing race over a winding downhill course laid out between posts: SLALOM

skiing term for a pit in the snow left by a skier who has fallen backward: SITZMARK

skill, ability: PROWESS

skill, knowledge: EXPERTISE

skill, style, technical mastery, as of an art: VIRTUOSITY

skill at a particular thing: KNACK

skill in avoiding giving offense: TACT

skill or dexterity in manipulation: SLEIGHT

skilled craftsman: ARTIFICER

skillful, adroit: DEXTEROUS

skillful, inventive, clever: INGENIOUS

skillful in use of bodily or mental powers: ADROIT

skillfully done: WORKMANLIKE

skin, remove impurities from: DESPUMATE

skim over water, glide: SKITTER

skin and its diseases, as a study: DERMATOLOGY

skin disease: ECZEMA

skin hanging loosely from neck or throat, as on turkeys: WATTLE

skin markings made by pricking with a needle and inserting indelible colors: TATTOO

skin's outer layer: EPIDERMIS

skip or rebound of a projectile after it hits a surface: RICOCHET

skirt that is full and has a gathered waist: DIRNDL

skirtlike garment worn by both sexes in the Malay Archipelago: SARONG

skip about playfully: CAPER

skip or bounce over water: DAP

skip or leap about, frolic: GAMBOL

skull: CRANIUM

skull conformations as indicating degree of development of mental facilities: PHRENOLOGY

skull study: CRANIOLOGY

skullcap worn by Orthodox and Conservative Jewish men: YARMULKE

skullcap worn by Roman Catholic clergymen: ZUCCHETTO

sky, heavens: FIRMAMENT

slake thirst: QUENCH

slander: ASPERSE

slander: CALUMNIATE

slander, calumny, curse against someone: MALEDICTION

slander, speak evil of: MALIGN

slander, mock: TRADUCE

slander, defame: VILIFY

slanted, indirect: OBLIQUE

slanting diagonal: BIAS

slanting kind of type, usually used for emphasis: ITALIC

slanting line in printing or writing: VIRGULE

slash mark in printing or writing: VIRGULE

slaughter or massacre: CARNAGE

slaughterhouse: ABATTOIR

slaughterhouse: SHAMBLES

slavery's end in U.S.: ABOLITION

Slavic alphabet: CYRILLIC

Slavic folk dance performed by a male and marked by the prisiadka step in which from a squatting position each leg is kicked out alternately: KAZATSKY

slavish, servile, compliant: SEQUACIOUS
slavish, submissive: SERVILE
sleep, desire for, which is uncontrollable: NARCOLEPSY
sleep deterrent: AGRYPNOTIC
sleep producing, narcotic: SOMNIFEROUS
sleep that is unusually deep: SOPOR
sleep-inducing medicine, relaxant: OPIATE
sleep-inducing or soothing sounds or motions: LULL
sleepiness or yawning: OSCITANCY
sleeping car on a European railroad: WAGON-LIT
sleeping sickness: ENCEPHALITIS LETHARGICA
sleepless period, as in keeping vigil: WATCH
sleeplessness or the chronic inability to sleep: INSOMNIA
sleep-producing: HYPNAGOGIC
sleep-producing medicine: SOPORIFIC
sleepwalking, somnambulism: NOCTAMBULATION
sleepy: SOMNOLENT
sleepy, drowsy: SOPORIFIC
sleeveless Arabian garment: ABA
sleight of hand: PRESTIDIGITATION
sleight of hand, trickery, hocus-pocus: LEGERDEMAIN
slender, graceful young woman: SYLPH
slender, slim, willowy: SVELTE
slender, wandlike, straight: VIRGATE
slice thinly, as leather: SKIVE
slide or glide, as a snake: SLITHER
sliding skillfully down a slope of ice or snow as in mountain-climbing: GLISSADE
slight, gracefully slender: GRACILE
slight suggestion, vague idea, notion, hint: INKLING
slighting: DISPARAGING
slightly, in music: POCO
slim, tall figure: ASTHENIC
slim, willowy, slender: SVELTE
sling for lifting or lowering a heavy object: PARBUCKLE
slink: SKULK
slip, error or fault: LAPSE
slip by, pass away (said of time): ELAPSE
slip-like undergarment: CHEMISE
slippery feeling, greasy: UNCTUOUS
slogan, rallying cry, password: WATCHWORD
slope, especially a defensive slope in front of a fortification: GLACIS

slope, incline, ramp: GRADIENT
slope, tilt: CANT
slope linking different levels: RAMP
slope or inclination of countryside: VERSANT
slope that is steep: ESCARPMENT
slope along a plateau's rim: SCARP
sloping edge: BEVEL
sloping steeply: DECLIVITOUS
slouching, awkward movement: LOP
slovenly in appearance: BLOWZY
slow, delay, hinder: RETARD
slow, dignified dance or music for such a dance: PAVANE
slow, straggler falling behind: LAGGARD
slow down: DECELERATE
slow movement, as in music: ADAGIO
slow tempo: LARGO
sluggish: INERT
sluggish, dull, inactive: TORPID
sluggish, lacking in energy: LYMPHATIC
sluggish, uninterested: STAGNANT
sluggishness, dullness, apathy: LETHARGY
slur over in pronunciation: ELIDE
sly, stealthy: FURTIVE
sly look: LEER
sly or indirect intimation, hint: INSINUATION
small: PETITE
small, cramped: INCOMMODIOUS
small, fashionable shop: BOUTIQUE
small, insignificant, trifling: MINUTE
small, scanty, diminutive: EXIGUOUS
small, stunted, as an imperfectly developed fruit or ear of corn: NUBBIN
small, trifling: NOMINAL
small, trifling work: OPUSCULE
small country that depends on a great power: SATELLITE
small decorative object: BIBELOT
small letters of the alphabet used in printing: LOWER CASE
small or insignificant amount: IOTA
small portable stove: CHAUFFER
small portion or piece: COLLOP
small quantity: MODICUM
small quantity, insufficiency: PAUCITY
small space, crack: INTERSTICE
small space between library stacks for private study: CARREL
small sum of money: PITTANCE
small to the point of being incalculable, microscopic: INFINITESIMAL
smallness of the head, to an abnormal degree: MICROCEPHALY

smallness so extreme that a thing cannot be easily seen: IMPERCEPTIBLE

smallpox: VARIOLA

smartness, style, dash: PIZZAZZ

smelling disagreeably: MALODOROUS

smelling good: ODORIFEROUS

smelling sense: OLFACTORY

smile in a silly, self-satisfied way: SMIRK

smile or smirk self-consciously: SIMPER

smoky or sooty: FULIGINOUS

smooth, flowing, graceful, expressive: FLUENT

smooth, glossy, well-groomed: SLEEK

smooth or toughen metal: PLANISH

smooth the way, as for a project or piece of work: EXPEDITE

smooth to an excess, oily-tongued: UNCTUOUS

smoothness, tact, highly refined skill: FINESSE

smug: SELF-RIGHTEOUS

smug, overexacting person: PRIG

smuggling: CONTRABAND

snake worship: OPHIOLATRY

snakelike, cunning: SERPENTINE

snake-shaped: ANGUIFORM

snap back, resume original shape after being stretched: RESILE

sneak, coward: DASTARD

sneaking, stealthy: SLINKY

sneaky, degraded, skulking: HANGDOG

sneer, laugh coarsely, jeer, deride: FLEER

sneering, ironical, taunting language: SARCASM

sneering, scornful, cynical: SARDONIC

sneeze or noise produced by it: STERNUTATION

sneeze-producing substance, snuff: ERRHINE

sniff, smell: SNUFF

snobbish person: BRAHMIN

snoring sound: STERTOROUS

snow that is coarse and granular: CORN SNOW

snowy: NIVEOUS

snub: REBUFF

snub or deliberate slight: COLD SHOULDER

snuggle for comfort, cuddle: NESTLE

so much the better: TANT MIEUX

so much the worse: TANT PIS

soak in a liquid: STEEP

soapy: SAPONACEOUS

sober, sedate, steady: STAID

soccer ball as it is moved by successive kicks: DRIBBLE

sociable: CONVIVIAL

sociable, associating habitually with others: GREGARIOUS

social only, meaningless, as applied to talk: PHATIC

social meal based on early Christian love feast: AGAPE

social status lowered: DÉCLASSÉ

society containing mixture of ethnic, racial, religious, or cultural groups: PLURALISM

Socratic method: MAIEUTIC

sodomy, sexual relations between males: PEDERASTY

sofa or bench with high back: SETTEE

sofa or couch with low cushioned seat and with arm rests or back: DIVAN

soft, rich, as certain soils: UNCTUOUS

soft spot, vulnerable point: ACHILLES' HEEL

soften, regulate, adjust or temper: MODULATE

soften by soaking in liquid: MACERATE

soften in temper, yield: RELENT

softening: MOLLESCENT

softening, soothing, relaxing especially to the skin: EMOLLIENT

softening colors or lines in a painting or drawing: SCUMBLE

softly performed in music: PIANISSIMO

soil, besmirch, defile: SULLY

soil, discolor: SMIRCH

soil deposited by water: ALLUVIUM

soil rather than climate as an affective factor: EDAPHIC

soil science: AGROLOGY

soil study: PEDOLOGY

soiled or untidy: BEDRAGGLED

soils that are soft and rich: UNCTUOUS

solar or sun: HELIACAL

soldier doing extra duty work for an officer: STRIKER

sole of the foot, palm of the hand: VOLAR

solemn declaration: ASSEVERATION

solicit for sexual purpose: ACCOST

solicit votes by going about a region: CANVASS

solid, forthright, firm: FOURSQUARE

solid, packed with meaning, terse: PITHY

solid earth: TERRA FIRMA

solidifying: CONCRETION

solitary, secluded person: RECLUSE

solo melody in opera: ARIA

solution, usually in alcohol, of a substance, used in medicine: TINCTURE solution or final unraveling in a plot: DE-NOUEMENT

solve a complicated problem: CUT THE GORDIAN KNOT

something in return for something else: QUID PRO QUO

song, often contrapuntal: MADRIGAL

song for several male voices with no accompaniment: GLEE

song of triumph or joy: PAEAN

song of unhappy love: TORCH SONG

song performed by a lover under his sweetheart's window: SERENADE

song that is short and simple: DITTY

songlike: ARIOSE

sonorous: ROTUND

soothe, pacify: SALVE

soothe, put to sleep or calm through soothing sounds or motions: LULL

soothe, quiet down, mitigate, pacify: MOLLIFY

soothing: LENITIVE

soothing, melodious, pleasant: DULCET

soothing, relieving irritation: DEMULCENT

soothing, softening or relaxing, especially to the skin: EMOLLIENT

soothing agent: ABIRRITANT

soothing pain reliever: ANODYNE

soporific, sleep producing: SOMNIFEROUS

sorceress, fortuneteller: SIBYL

sorcery: DIABLERIE

sorcery, fortune telling, black magic: NECROMANCY

sorcery or witchcraft practiced in the South, Africa and West Indies: OBEAH, OBI

sordid, low: GROVELING

sordid or worst aspect of something: SEAMY SIDE

sore, inflamed: IRRITATED

sorrow, sympathy-evoking: PATHOS

sorrow or grief, to cause: AGGRIEVE

sorrowful, mournful: PLAINTIVE

sorrowful, mournful: WOEBEGONE

sort, class, kind: ILK

sort out, pick, select: CULL

sorting of casualties to fix priorities for treatment: TRIAGE

soul: ANIMA

soul, spirit: PNEUMA

sound, pertaining to: ACOUSTIC

sound and scene reproduction: AUDIOVISUAL

sound imitated by a word: ECHOIC

sound in speech involving chiefly lips, teeth or tongue: CONSONANT

sound like cat's cries at rutting time: CATERWAUL

sound of sighing or murmuring, as made by the wind: SOUGH

sound or letter inserted into a word: EPENTHESIS

sound or vibration caused by the hitting of one body against another: PERCUSSION

sound producing or conducting: SONIFEROUS

sound reproduction: AUDIO

sound reproduction using two or more loudspeakers: STEREOPHONIC

sound with a plumb to test the depth of water: PLUMB

soundproof: ANACOUSTIC

sound-reflecting structure: SOUNDING BOARD

sound-related: SONIC

sounds in opposition in music: ANTIPHONY

sounds of speech, as a study: PHONETICS

sounds or tones in mutliplicity: POLYPHONIC

sounds repeated at the beginnings of words or in accented syllables: ALLITERATION

sound-track change from original language to another: DUBBING

sound-transmitting apparatus used under water: SONAR

sound-wave or light-wave change that seems to accompany change in distance between source and observer: DOPPLER EFFECT

soup, thick and creamy: BISQUE

soup that is clear: CONSOMMÉ

soup ingredients of dough casings filled with ground meat: KREPLACH

soup made with strained vegetables or a dish containing such vegetables or fruit: PURÉE

soup of cream and potatoes usually served cold: VICHYSSOISE

sour: ACERB

sour, fermented cabbage in shredded form: SAUERKRAUT

sour, spoiled-smelling: RANCID

sour juice of green fruit: VERJUICE

source: SPRINGHEAD

source of something: PROVENIENCE

source or forefather: PROGENITOR

source or potential for development: SEM-
INAL

souring: ACESCENT

sourness or sharpness of disposition: VER-
JUICE

South African grassland: VELDT

South African racial segregation:
APARTHEID

South African speech, based on Dutch:
AFRIKAANS

souvenir: MEMENTO

sovereign control over a locally autonomous region: SUZERAINTY

sovereigns or rulers in one line of descent reigning in succession: DYNASTY

Soviet Union collective farm: KOLKHOZ

Soviet Union's equivalent of a Cabinet:
PRESIDIUM

space for freedom of action, latitude:
LEEWAY

space from which something is missing or
has been omitted: LACUNA

space near the altar of a church: CHANCEL

spacecraft landing on water: SPLASHDOWN

spadelike tool for removing the roots of
weeds: SPUD

spangle or small metal disk: PAILLETTE

Spanish American, West Indian or Gulf
State inhabitant of European descent:
CREOLE

Spanish dialect with Hebrew elements:
LADINO

Spanish diacritical mark, as over the n in
señor: TILDE

Spanish for good day: BUENOS DIAS

Spanish for thank you: GRACIAS

sparing in eating and drinking: AB-
STEMIOUS

spark, trace: SCINTILLA

sparkle, gaiety, vivacity, lively spirits:
EFFERVESCENCE

sparkle, glitter, flash: SCINTILLATE

sparkle, glitter, shine: CORUSCATE

sparkle in intellect or action: SCINTILLATE

sparkling object: SPANGLE

spasm in a muscle: CLONUS

spasms of pain: THROES

spasm of the muscle: HYPERKINESIA

spat or trivial quarrel: TIFF

spatter, shower, pelt: PEPPER

speak at great length: PERORATE

speak dogmatically: PONTIFICATE

speak loudly or rhetorically: DECLAIM

speak or write more fully, elaborate: EX-
PATIATE

speak violently, rave: RANT

speak with clarity and exactness: ENUN-
CIATE

speaker who influences audience by his el-
oquence: SPELLBINDER

speaker's stand on which books or notes
may be placed: LECTERN

speaking fluently, glib, talkative: VOLU-
BLE

speaking impairment, or difficulty in understanding speech: DYSPHASIA

speaking in a bombastic or pompous style:
GRANDILOQUENT

speaking or writing with ease: FLUENT

speaking style, language, idiom: PAR-
LANCE

speaking trick that makes the voice seem
to come from source other than the
speaker: VENTRILOQUISM

special application, not general: AD HOC

specialty or strong point of a person:
FORTE

specific purpose and specific situation
committee: AD HOC COMMITTEE

specify: STIPULATE

specify exactly: CONCRETIZE

speck or particle: MOTE

speckled or spotted as if by drops: GUT-
TATE

specks or threads appearing to float before the eyes: MUSCAE VOLITANTES

spectacular exhibition or parade: PAGEANT

spectacular theater production: EXTRAVA-
GANZA

spectator who gives unwanted advice to
card players: KIBITZER

speculative: ACADEMIC

spectra, imiginary appearance: PHANTASM

speech constituting a bitter verbal oath:
PHILIPPIC

speech delivered simply to obstruct action:
FILIBUSTER

speech given at a formal event: ORATION

speech manner: LOCUTION

speech mechanism positions represented
by phonetic symbols: VISIBLE SPEECH

speech of fiery denunciation: TIRADE

speech or essay that is highly emotional:
DITHYRAMB

speech or sales talk: SPIEL

speech pattern: INTONATION

speech peculiar to a locality or group:
DIALECT

speech sound involving chiefly lips, teeth
or tongue: CONSONANT

speech sound that is the smallest unit of its kind and distinctive from others: PHONEME

speech sounds, as a study: PHONETICS

speech that is bombastic or flowery: RHETORIC

speech that is glib and swift: PATTER

speech that is lengthy, loud and vehement: HARANGUE

speech that is long and tiresome: SCREED

speech that is short and witty or satirical: SQUIB

speechlike sounds that are unintelligible: GLOSSOLALIA

speed: VELOCITY

speed, full speed: CAREEN

speed, promptness: DISPATCH

speed rate in music: TEMPO

speed that is dangerous: BREAKNECK

speed up, quicken, facilitate: EXPEDITE

spelling in which a letter represents different sounds in different words: HETEROGRAPHY

spelling or handwriting that is bad: CACOGRAPHY

spelling that conforms to accepted usage: ORTHOGRAPHY

spelling that varies from accepted standard usage: HETEROGRAPHY

spend wastefully, squander: DISSIPATE

spending or giving generously: LAVISH

spending to impress: CONSPICUOUS CONSUMPTION

spendthrift: WASTREL

sperm duct removal: VASECTOMY

sphere of action: AMBIT

sphere of authority: BAILIWICK

spherical, rounded: ORBICULAR

sphinxlike in having human head and animal body: ANDROCEPHALOUS

spiked wheel at the end of a spur: ROWEL

spinal column creatures: VERTEBRATES

spindle-shaped: FUSIFORM

spineless: INVERTEBRATE

spinning, whirling, dizzy: VERTIGINOUS

spinning like a top, or top-shaped: TURBINATE

spiral: HELIX

spiral coil: HELICOID

spirally curling, rolled up: VOLUTE

spire: FLÈCHE

spirit, soul: PNEUMA

spirit, wit: ESPRIT

spirit ancestors, among Pueblo Indians: KACHINA

spirit regarded as distinct from matter: ANIMISM

spirited, vital, joyful, vigorous: EXUBERANT

spiritless, not alive: INANIMATE

spiritlessness, weakness, fatigue, dreaminess, dullness, stagnation: LANGUOR

spirits or health: FETTLE

spiritual, insubstantial, nonmaterial: INCORPOREAL

spiritual, light, airy: ETHEREAL

spiritual sloth: ACEDIA

spiritual teacher or guide: GURU

spit: EXPECTORATE

spit or skewer used in broiling, usually small: BROCHETTE

spiteful, deliberately mischievous: MALICIOUS

spiteful, revengeful: VINDICTIVE

spitefulness, enmity: RANCOR

spitefulness, peevishness, ill temper: SPLEEN

splash, flounder: SLOSH

splashing or sucking noise, as when one walks in deep mud: SQUELCH

splendor, brilliance, radiance: REFULGENCE

splendor, radiance: EFFULGENCE

splinter: SLIVER

splinter into fragments, shatter: SHIVER

splinters: FLINDERS

split into factions in a church or other organization: SCHISM

split or cut into long thin pieces: SLIVER

splitting, cutting: SCISSION

splitting or breaking apart: FISSION

spoil, impair: VITIATE

spoil by indulgence: COCKER

spoil someone, pamper or pet: COSSET

spoiled-smelling: RANCID

spoiling for a fight: PUGNACIOUS

spoils, booty: PILLAGE

spoken, oral: VIVA VOCE

spoken error thought to disclose a person's true thinking: FREUDIAN SLIP

spoken in an undertone, privately: SOTTO VOCE

spoken statement of a false or defamatory nature: SLANDER

spokesman: PROLOCUTOR

sponsor: AEGIS

sponsorship, support: PATRONAGE

spontaneous, unprepared: IMPROMPTU

spontaneous talk by a patient in psychoanalysis: FREE ASSOCIATION sports, a player in the front line of attack or defense: FORWARD

sports feat that is highly unusual: HAT TRICK

sports term for an extra period in a tied game during which the first side to score wins: SUDDEN DEATH

spot, streak, blotch: MOTTLE

spot or blemish, blurred impression in printing: MACKLE

spotted, especially in white and black: PIEBALD

spotted horse or pony: PINTO

spotted or speckled as if by drops: GUTTATE

spotted or variegated: DAPPLED

spotting on animals or plants: MACULATION

spouse: CONSORT

spouse murder: MARITICIDE

spread, as information: DISSEMINATE

spread, pour or send out in all directions: DIFFUSE

spread, publicize, disseminate: PROPAGATE

spread about loosely for drying, as mown hay: TED

spread apart or branch out at a wide angle, diverge: DIVARICATE

spread false charges: ASPERSE

spread in all directions, circulate: DIFFUSE

spread or branch out, diverge: DIVARICATE

spread out, extend: SPLAY

spread out into divisions, divide: RAMIFY

spread the word far and wide: DISSEMINATE

spread thinly: SPARSE

spread through: PERVADE

spread through completely, penetrate: PERMEATE

spreading of a disease from one part of the body to another: METASTASIS

spree, fling, prank, reckless behavior: ESCAPADE

spring back, snap back, recoil, resume original shape after being stretched: RESILE

springlike, youthful, fresh: VERNAL

sprinkle: ASPERSE

sprinkle, shower, scatter: SPARGE

sprinkle, suffuse or cover with a liquid or color: PERFUSE

sprout, breed rapidly, swarm: PULLULATE

sprout, proliferate: BURGEON

spur into action, urge on, stir up: INCITE

spur of the moment, offhand: IMPROMPTU

spur on, goad, incite, foment, provoke to some drastic action: INSTIGATE

spurious: APOCRYPHAL

spurt or gush of liquid from a narrow orifice: JET

spy who infiltrates opposing espionage system to betray it: DOUBLE AGENT

squabble, heated argument: HASSLE

squall, brief windstorm: FLAW

squander, spend wastefully: DISSIPATE

squander or deal recklessly with: PLAY DUCKS AND DRAKES WITH

square dance of a rollicking kind: HOEDOWN

square dancing term for a change of step or figure: CALL

square surrounded by buildings: PIAZZA

squatting Slavic dance step in which a man kicks out each leg alternately: PRISIADKA

squeamish: QUEASY

squint: SKEW

squirm in agony: WRITHE

squirt, gush forth: SPURT

stab, pierce or tear painfully: LANCINATE

stable adjunct, enclosure for exercising horses: PADDOCK

stage curtain that can be raised and lowered: DROP CURTAIN

stage fabric, light and sheer, used as a backdrop: SCRIM

stage front: DOWNSTAGE

stage of a theater including its arch: PROSCENIUM

stage performer without speaking part, as in a mob scene: SUPERNUMERARY

stage scenery, flat, on side of stage: COULISSE

stage surrounded by seats: ARENA THEATER

stagnation, weakness, fatigue, dreaminess, dullness, spiritlessness: LANGUOR

stain or drench especially with blood: IMBRUE

stale joke: CHESTNUT

stall for time: TEMPORIZE

stamp collecting: PHILATELY

stamp out, stifle: SCOTCH

stamped or hammered, as the figure or design on a coin: INCUSE

stand on the hind legs and stretch out the forelegs: RAMP

stand on which a speaker may place notes or books: LECTERN

stand with shelves, usually ornamental: ÉTAGÈRE

standard of quality: BENCH MARK

standard or criterion for testing the qualities of something: TOUCHSTONE

standard or rule by which a judgment can be made: CRITERION

standards of polite society: THE PROPRIETIES

standing out, striking, conspicuous: SALIENT

standstill because of disagreement by two forces: DEADLOCK

star grouping: GALAXY

star mapping: URANOGRAPHY

star that suddenly becomes brilliant then fades: NOVA

star with six points and composed of two equilateral triangles: STAR OF DAVID

star used as guide in navigation; guiding principle or example: LODESTAR

stare at, make eyes at suggestively: OGLE

stare stupidly, gape: GAWK

stare with an angry frown: GLOWER

staring eyes, as in a fish: WALLEYED

starlike symbol in printing (*): ASTERISK

starlike very distant object that emits strong radio waves: QUASAR

stars, of and pertaining to: SIDEREAL

star's rising and setting, said of: ACRONICAL

star-shaped: ASTEROID

star-shaped, radiating: STELLATE

start, beginning: INCEPTION

start a discussion: BROACH

start of something: CONCEPTION

starting existence, newly conceived: NASCENT

starting point: JUMPING-OFF PLACE

startle, thrill, arouse: ELECTRIFY

state, declare, detail: EXPOUND

state or affirm something on basis of known facts or conditions: PREDICATE

state positively: ASSEVERATE

stately, impressive, grand: IMPOSING

stately beauty: JUNOESQUE

stately passage or movement of music: MAESTOSO

statement that decides the matter: CLINCHER

state's right to take over private property for public use: EMINENT DOMAIN

stationary, resting: STATIC

statistician dealing with vital statistics, as of births, deaths, disease: DEMOGRAPHER

status of holding one's position on an enduring basis: TENURE

statute, especially of a municipal body: ORDINANCE

staunch, brave: YEOMANLY

staves ready for assembling into barrels or boxes: SHOOK

stay or dwell temporarily: SOJOURN

steadfast, brave: UNFLINCHING

steadfast, firmly directed, unwavering: INTENT

steadily at work, diligent: SEDULOUS

steady, sober, sedate: STAID

steady stream, as of people or things: INFLUX

steal: PURLOIN

steal, take by fraud: EMBEZZLE

steal funds, especially public funds, embezzle: PECULATE

steal in a petty way: PILFER

steal slyly in small amounts: FILCH

stealthily approach game: STALK

stealthily move about: SKULK

stealthy, sly: FURTIVE

stealthy, sneaking: SLINKY

steam-bath room: SAUNA

steam-whistle organ: CALLIOPE

steep: PRECIPITOUS

steep downward slope: DECLIVITY

steep slope: ESCARPMENT

steep slope: SCARP

steering instrument: RUDDER

stench: MEPHITIS

stencil process that forces ink through open meshes of a silk screen: SILK-SCREEN PROCESS

steps at the entrance to a house: STOOP

step recorder to measure walking distance: PEDOMETER

sterile, barren, fruitless: INFECUND

stern, gloomy, morose, ill-tempered: DOUR

stern, rear, toward the stern on a boat: ABAFT

stern, toward the stern on a boat: AFT

stew of meat and vegetables well seasoned: RAGOUT

stick for stirring drinks: MUDDLER

sticking together: COHERENT

sticky, adhesive: VISCID

sticky, honeylike, semifluid: VISCOUS

stifle, stamp out, suppress: SCOTCH

stigmatize: BRAND
still, placid: QUIESCENT
stimulate, enliven, arouse: QUICKEN
stimulate, excite, raise the spirits of: ELATE
stimulate, excite, rouse to action: GALVANIZE
stimulate, push or touch with a slight jar, shake lightly: JOG
stimulate, sharpen, excite: WHET
stimulating, arousing: PROVOCATIVE
stimulating, racy: PIQUANT
stimulus, incentive: FILLIP
stimulus that hastens a result: CATALYST
stimulus to action: INCENTIVE
stinginess: PARSIMONY
stingy, also poor: PENURIOUS
stingy, scanty: NIGGARDLY
stingy or mean practice: CHEESE-PARING
stinking: MALODOROUS
stinking, offensive, disgusting, noxious: NOISOME
stinking or foul odor: FETID
stipulation or condition: PROVISO
stir or cut up the surface, as of topsoil: SCARIFY
stir up, instigate, incite: FOMENT
stir up, spur into action, urge on: INCITE
stirring stick used for mixed drinks: MUDDLER
stitch used in surgery: SUTURE
stitching that is loose and temporary: BASTING
stock bought in order to repay stock previously borrowed, a short sale operation: SHORT COVERING
stock bought in such quantity as to give the buyer control over the price: CORNER
Stock Exchange, New York: BIG BOARD
stock in a corporation that entitles the owner of the shares to dividends after other obligations have been met: COMMON STOCK
stock issued but reacquired by a company: TREASURY STOCK
stock market on the decline: BEAR MARKET
stock market on the rise: BULL MARKET
stock of a company known for its quality and, therefore, for its ability to make money for investors: BLUE CHIP
stock of a company with good prospects for future earnings: GROWTH STOCK
stock of goods of a business listed: INVENTORY

stock on which dividends must be paid ahead of those on common stock: PREFERRED STOCK
stock on which omitted dividends must be paid before dividends are paid on common stock: CUMULATIVE PREFERRED
stock options to sell a fixed number of shares at a specified price within a certain period or to buy a fixed number of shares at a specified price within a certain period of time: PUTS or CALLS
stock or bond sales that are not made on the floor of a stock exchange: OVER-THE-COUNTER
stock phrases: CANT
stock purchaser does not receive recent dividend: EX-DIVIDEND
stock purchase at one broker and equivalent sale at another to make trading seem active: WASH SALE
stock that is high-priced and good: BLUE CHIP
stock that is traded on a securities exchange: LISTED STOCK
stock trading of fewer than the established 100-share unit: ODD-LOT
stock's market price divided by earnings per share for a 12-month period: PRICE-EARNINGS RATIO
stocks selling at less that $1 a share: PENNY STOCKS
stocky, fleshy: PYKNIC
stomach ache resulting from muscular spasms: COLIC
stomach inflammation: GASTRITIS
stomach pit: SOLAR PLEXUS
stone for sharpening knives: WHETSTONE
stone or block on which a column or statue stands: PLINTH
stone shaft that tapers to a pyramidal top: OBELISK
stone slab carrying an inscription or design: STELE
stone to death: LAPIDATE
stone used to scour the wooden deck of a ship: HOLYSTONE
stones set up as marker or memorial: CAIRN
stony, hard: PETROUS
stony, stonelike: LITHOID
stool or small seat, usually without arms or back: TABORET

stoop to an action or person, condescend: DEIGN

stop, impede, block, hinder: OBSTRUCT

stop, keep back, suppress: STIFLE

stop or check the flow of: STANCH

stop or pause at intervals or temporarily: INTERMIT

stop or seize on the way, prevent from reaching the destination: INTERCEPT

stop someone or something from all activity: IMMOBILIZE

stoppage in the flow of any bodily fluid: STASIS

stoppage of growth: ATROPHY

storage place for goods: REPOSITORY

store carrying general merchandise: EMPORIUM

store as in a granary, gather, accumulate: GARNER

storm characterized by sudden burst of wind, usually with rain or snow: SQUALL

storm consisting of a whirling column of air: TORNADO

stormy, severe: INCLEMENT

stormy, violent: TEMPESTUOUS

story, always long, sometimes poetic, chronicling adventure or heroic acts: SAGA

story between two main floors, a partial balcony: MEZZANINE

story or statement issued to news media: HANDOUT

story that is highly improbable: COCK-AND-BULL STORY

story with a moral: PARABLE

story with hidden or symbolic meanings: ALLEGORY

storyteller of great skill: RACONTEUR

stout: PORTLY

stove of cast-iron, open-faced and resembling a fireplace: FRANKLIN STOVE

stove that is small and portable: CHAUFFER

straggler, slow, falling behind: LAGGARD

straight, slender, wandlike: VIRGATE

straight line over a vowel indicating long sound: MACRON

straightforward, frank, innocent, simple, naive: INGENUOUS

strain, stretch, irritate: RACK

strained, done with great effort: LABORED

strained, forced: FAR-FETCHED

strained as in aiming at effect: AGONISTIC

strange, extraordinary, remarkable: UNACCOUNTABLE

strange, freakish: OUTLANDISH

strange, weird, unnatural, eerie: UNCANNY

strangle: GARROTE

strap encircling the body of a horse: SURCINGLE

strap passing across the forehead that helps to support a load carried on the back: TUMPLINE

stratagem or tactic to outwit someone: PLOY

strategies in games, economics, warfare: GAME THEORY

stratagem that is a sudden, telling blow: COUP

stratagem to avoid unpleasantness, dodge: SUBTERFUGE

straw bed that lies on the floor: PALLET

straw mattress: PALLIASSE

stray: WAIF

stray animal enclosure: PINFOLD

stray from script: AD LIB

stray or wander aimlessly: DIVAGATE

straying from the right course: ERRANT

streak, blotch, spot: MOTTLE

stream or bay leading into the land from a larger body of water: INLET

stream or creek: KILL

street, usually narrow, lined with dwellings that were formerly stables: MEWS

street for pedestrians, with stores on each side: MALL

street show, peep show: RAREE SHOW

strength, vigor: STAMINA

strength or degree of some quality, feeling, action: INTENSITY

stretch out, swell, expand: DISTEND

stretchable, capable of being drawn out: TENSILE

strict: EXACTING

strict, grim, severe: STARK

strict, tightly enforced: STRINGENT

strict disciplinarian: MARTINET

strict in religious or moral matters: PURITANICAL

strictness, exactness: RIGOR

stride that is steady and swinging: LOPE

strike against, bump: JAR

strike against, fall upon: IMPINGE

strike hard: SLOG

strike in which workers stay in plant but refuse to work: SIT-DOWN

string looped over the fingers into intricate arrangements: CAT'S CRADLE

stringed instrument used in Hindu music: SITAR

strip, deprive, as of possessions: DIVEST
strip, deprive of, rob: DESPOIL
strip, edging or selvage, as of cloth: LIST
strip as of clothes, deprive as of rights or possessions: DIVEST
strip blubber or skin from a whale or seal: FLENSE
strip of leaves: DEFOLIATE
strip of material sewn to a seam: WELT
strip of ornamentation as along the top of a wall: FRIEZE
strip or row of cut grass or grain: SWATH
striped, grooved: STRIATED
strips of meat or vegetables cut very thin: JULIENNE
stripteaser: ECDYSIAST
striving: CONATION
stroll, walk leisurely: SAUNTER
strong: PUISSANT
strong, determined, brave: STALWART
strong, sturdy, masculine: VIRILE
strong and dark in color, said of cigars: MADURO
strong physically: POTENT
strong point of a person: FORTE
stronghold: REDOUBT
structural unit used in planning or building: MODULE
structure, framework: FABRIC
structure or outline of something: CONFORMATION
structure that projects and is supported at only one end: CANTILEVER
struggle clumsily, move awkwardly, stumble: FLOUNDER
struggle of people that is confused and noisy: MELEE
struggle or contend with: GRAPPLE
strut, bluster: SWAGGER
strut or promenade: CAKEWALK
stubborn, cantankerous: CROTCHETY
stubborn, cranky: PERVERSE
stubborn, determined: HEADSTRONG
stubborn, obstinate: PERTINACIOUS
stubborn, unmanageable: REFRACTORY
stubborn, persevering: INDOMITABLE
stubborn, persistent, tough: TENACIOUS
stubborn, pitiless, hardhearted: OBDURATE
stubborn, rebellious, disobedient: RECALCITRANT
stubborn, unruly, difficult: INTRACTABLE
stubborn, unyielding: INFLEXIBLE
stubborn, unyielding, pig-headed: OBSTINATE
studio: ATELIER

study intensively for an examination: CRAM
study of insects: ENTOMOLOGY
study or read intently: PORE
study or write laboriously: LUCUBRATE
study space between library stacks: CARREL
stumble or move clumsily: FLOUNDER
stun, amaze, bewilder: STUPEFY
stunted, small, as an imperfectly developed fruit or ear of corn: NUBBIN
stupid: ADDLED, ADDLEBRAINED, ADDLEHEADED, ADDLEPATED
stupid, foolish, unmoved, brutish: INSENSATE
stupid, foolish person: SCHMO
stupid, graceless fellow: LOUT
stupid, idiotic, inane: FATUOUS
stupid, senseless: VACUOUS
stupid, ungainly individual: GAWK
stupid in a gross way: CRASS
stupid person: CLODPATE, CLODPOLL
stupid person: IGNORAMUS
stupid person, blockhead, dunce: DOLT
stupor, apathy: TORPOR
stupor, muscular rigidity and occasional mental agitation: CATATONIA
sturdy, athletic physical structure: MESOMORPHIC
sturdy, strong, masculine: VIRILE
style, skill, technical mastery, as of an art: VIRTUOSITY
style, smartness, dash: PIZZAZZ
style of great brilliance: BRAVURA
style of speech or writing that is artificially elegant: DUPHUISM
style that is spirited, dash: PANACHE
suave, refined, polite: URBANE
subconscious mind exhibited in art and literature: SURREALISM
subdue or suppress by force, allay: QUELL
subdue utterly, silence, crush: SQUELCH
subject to the law or rule of another: HETERONOMOUS
subjective aspect of an emotion: AFFECT
sublime, celestial, superior, fiery: EMPYREAL
submerge, engulf, overpower: WHELM
submissive: AMENABLE
submissive, slavish: SERVILE
submission to or respectful regard for the wishes or opinions of another: DEFERENCE
subsidiary business on certain premises: CONCESSION

subsidy to support a study or institution: SUBVENTION

substance produced chemically: SYNTHETIC

substitute: SURROGATE

substitute: VICAR

substitute, deputy: ALTER EGO

substitute, especially for an actor or actress: UNDERSTUDY

substitute, usually inferior: ERSATZ

substitute for or authority to act for another: PROXY

substitute goals or abilities to make up for personal lack: COMPENSATION

substitutes on an athletic team: BENCH

substituting a roundabout word for another to avoid giving pain or offense: EUPHEMISM

substitution of title or epithet for proper name: ANTONOMASIA

subtle: FINE-DRAWN

subtle, as a distinction made: NICE

subtle, vague: INDEFINABLE

subtle and gradual introduction: INSINUATION

subtle or fine variation or gradation: NUANCE

subtraction term for the number from which the subtrahend is to be deducted: MINUEND

subverting person or group that undermines from within: TROJAN HORSE

success that comes unexpectedly to this venture or person: SLEEPER

success that is sudden and removes an obstacle to progress: BREAKTHROUGH

successful or prosperous period: FLORESCENCE

succor, aid: SUBVENTION

sudden, abrupt: PRECIPITATE

sudden and overwhelming: FOUDROYANT

sudden and turbulent outburst: PAROXYSM

sudden burst of activity or energy: SPURT

sudden change of mind without adequate motive: CAPRICE

sudden impulse: IMPETUOSITY

sudden inspiration: BRAINSTORM

sudden sharp twist: QUIRK

sudden start: SALLY

sudden success that removes an obstacle to progress: BREAKTHROUGH

suffering, capable of feeling: PASSIBLE

suffering, distress, pain, anguish: TRAVAIL

suffering that affords pleasure: MASOCHISM

sufficient grounds for, justify: WARRANT

suffocating someone to death: BURKE

suffocation: ASPHYXIATION

suffuse or cover with a liquid or color: PERFUSE

sugar raw in the cane: MUSCOVADO

sugared or candied, iced, frozen: GLACÉ

suggest, imply: CONNOTE

suggest, propose: PROPOUND

suggest or mention for the first time: BROACH

suggestive, off-color: RISQUÉ

suggestive, risqué: RACY

suggestive in a delicate way: SUBTLE

suggestive of something, fragrant: REDOLENT

suicidal Japanese air attack: KAMIKAZE

suicide: FELO-DE-SE

suicide by disembowelment as a Japanese ritual: HARA-KIRI

suitable: APROPOS

suitable, advisable, proper: EXPEDIENT

suitable, practicable: FEASIBLE

sulkily pugnacious: TRUCULENT

sullen, stern, gloomy, morose: DOUR

sullen or angry look, scowl: LOWER

sum of the squares of the two legs of a right-angle triangle equals the square of the hypotenuse: PYTHAGOREAN THEOREM

summarize: RECAPITULATE

summary: PROSPECTUS

summary: RÉSUMÉ

summary, diagram, or synopsis as of a process: SCHEMA

summary, digest: CONSPECTUS

summary, general view of a subject: SYNOPSIS

summary in concise form, abstract: PRECIS

summary of a document: ABSTRACT

summary of the main points of a course of study: SYLLABUS

summary or synopsis of the plot of a dramatic work: SCENARIO

summary that is brief but comprehensive: COMPENDIUM

summation of an oration: PERORATION

summer, to pass the: ESTIVATE

summer and that which pertains to it: ESTIVAL

summer home, Russian: DACHA

summerhouse or similar structure: GAZEBO

summerhouse, tent or canopy: PAVILION

summer's beginning when the sun is farthest north of the Equator, about June 22: SUMMER SOLSTICE

summon, draw or call forth: EVOKE

summons or formal demand: REQUISITION
sun, solar: HELIACAL
sun as the center: HELIOCENTRIC
sun at its greatest distance north or south of the equator: SOLSTICE
sunroom: SOLARIUM
sun-dried brick: ADOBE
sunken design, incised carving: INTAGLIO
sunset occurrence: ACRONICAL
superficial: FACILE
superficial follower of an art or science: DILETTANTE
superficial or little knowledge: SMATTERING
superfluous: DE TROP
superfluous: EXCRESCENT
superfluous, extraneous: SUPEREROGATORY
superfluous, redundant word or phrase: PLEONASM
superintendence or management: INTENDANCE
superior to all others: SUPERLATIVE
superiority in weight, influence: PREPONDERANT
superiority worshiper who shows contempt for supposed inferiors: SNOB
superstition or story passed on from generation to generation: OLD WIVES' TALE
superstitious regard for an object thought to have magical powers: FETISHISM
supplant, replace: SUPERSEDE
supple, agile, lithe, pliant: LISSOME
supplement, piece out: EKE
supply or feed to excess: SURFEIT
support: ABET
support: ADMINICLE
support, approval, encouraging look: COUNTENANCE
support, sponsorship: PATRONAGE
support for wood in a fireplace: ANDIRON
support of wood or metal to keep a broken bone in place: SPLINT
support or advocacy, as of a cause: ESPOUSAL
support or aid as an auxiliary: ANCILLARY
supporter or originator of a cause: PROPONENT
supporters or voters: CONSTITUENCY
suppose or conclude from incomplete evidence: CONJECTURE
suppress, keep back: STIFLE
suppress, keep secret: HUGGER-MUGGER
suppress, stamp out, stifle: SCOTCH
suppress or put down forcibly: QUASH

suppression of truth to procure some favor or reward: SUBREPTION
suppressing or silencing, as a rumor: QUIETUS
supreme and independent authority: SOVEREIGN
supreme command, absolute power: IMPERIUM
supreme or highest good: SUMMUM BONUM
sureness: CERTITUDE
surface elegance: VENEER
surfeit, glut: SATIATE
surgery on living animals for medical research purposes: VIVISECTION
surmountable, conquerable: SUPERABLE
surname: COGNOMEN
surname: PATRONYMIC
surpass, excel, beat: TRUMP
surpassing others: PREEMINENT
surprise attack: AMBUSH
surrender of a prerogative: ABDICATE
surround, beset: BELEAGUER
surrounded by land: LANDLOCKED
surroundings: AMBIENCE
surroundings, environment, set, as of a play: MISE EN SCÈNE
surroundings, setting, environment: MILIEU
survey of a subject: CONSPECTUS
survey or map used for taxation basis: CADASTER
survey to gain information: RECONNAISSANCE
survive, pass through, as a crisis: WEATHER
surviving, existing: EXTANT
susceptibility or tendency to: PREDISPOSITION
suspend, supplant, annul: SUPERSEDE
suspend temporarily punishment or pain: REPRIEVE
suspense or state of anxiety: ON TENTERHOOKS
suspenseful story: CLIFF-HANGER
suspension of action: ABEYANCE
suspicious, cautious, wary: LEERY
suspicious, questionable: EQUIVOCAL
sustained or held, in music: TENUTO
sustenance: ALIMENT
swagger, bluster: FANFARONADE
swaggering self-assurance: COCKINESS
swallow food: INGEST
swallow up, overwhelm: ENGULF
swallowing difficulty: DYSPHAGIA
swampy body of water: BAYOU
swarm, teem, breed rapidly: PULLULATE

sway, totter, waver: VACILLATE
swayback: LORDOSIS
swear falsely, perjure oneself, renounce: FORSWEAR
sweat: SUDOR
sweater, knitted, collarless and long-sleeved that opens down front: CARDIGAN
sweating in excessive or abnormal manner: SUDATION
sweating that is excessive: HIDROSIS
sweet or rich in excess, cloying: LUSCIOUS
sweet sounding: MELLIFLUOUS
sweet-sounding, melodious, pleasant: DULCET
sweet to excess: SACCHARINE
swell, expand, widen: DILATE
swell, stretch out, expand: DISTEND
swelling: INTUMESCENCE
swelling, knot or knob: NODE
swelling, protuberance: TUBEROSITY
swelling, puffiness: TUMEFACTION
swelling in the body: EDEMA
swelling or tumor formed by an effusion of blood: HEMATOMA
swerve: SKEW
swift, dashing, large, vigorous: SPANKING
swift, dazzling, brilliant: METEORIC
swift, rapid, galloping: TANTIVY
swimmer's breathing tube that projects above water's surface: SNORKEL
swimming kick in which both legs are parted and bent at the knees, then thrust backward together: SCISSORS KICK
swimming pool: NATATORIUM
swimming under water with equipment such as flippers, scuba apparatus, etc.: SKIN DIVING
swindle: BUNCO
swindle: SKIN GAME
swindle, cheat: ROOK
swindle after the victim's confidence has been won: CONFIDENCE GAME
swine castrated after maturity: STAG
swing around: SLUE
swing to and fro, fluctuate: OSCILLATE
swirling motion of air, water, or gas, etc.: TURBULENCE
swish, fanciness, rustling as of silk: FROUFROU
switch from the lofty to the commonplace: BATHOS
switching of letters or sounds that changes a word: METATHESIS

swollen: BULBOUS
swollen: TUMESCENT
swollen: TUMID
swollen, distended: TURGID
swollen, bulging: VENTRICULAR
sword, short and curved: SCIMITAR
sword without cutting edge used in dueling: EPEE
swordlike in shape: XIPHOID
swordlike knife: SNICKERSNEE
sword-shaped: GLADIATE
sworn, written statement: AFFIDAVIT
syllable or letter appended to a word: PARAGOGE
syllable or syllabes placed at the beginning of a word: PREFIX
syllable or syllables placed at the end of a word: SUFFIX
syllable shortened although it is naturally or by position long: SYSTOLE
syllable third from last in a word: ANTEPENULT
syllables, used in music, as do, re, mi, etc.: SOLMIZATION
symbol for "and" (&): AMPERSAND
symbol of fruitfulness: CALATHUS
symbol or emblem by a publisher, used on title page of a book: COLOPHON
symbol or picture representing a word, sound or object: HIEROGLYPHIC
symbol or representative of something, as of a doctrine or a cause: EXPONENT
symbols devised to represent phonetically the positions of the speech mechanism: VISIBLE SPEECH
sympathize or grieve with someone: CONDOLE
sympathy-evoking, sorrow: PATHOS
symptom of an approaching disease: PRODROME
symptoms indicating a disease or condition: SYNDROME
synonyms and antonyms arranged in categories, in a book: THESAURUS
synopsis, summary or diagram as of a process: SCHEMA
synopsis or summary of the plot of a dramatic work: SCENARIO
syntax: COLLOCATION
synthesis of separate elements of emotion or experience that constitutes more than the mechanical sum of the parts: GESTALT
syphilis: LUES
systematized course of living: REGIMEN

T

table companion: COMMENSAL
table for holding a tea service: TEAPOY
table or its uses: MENSAL
table supported wholly or in part by brackets: CONSOLE TABLE
table wine: VIN ORDINAIRE
table with swinging legs that support drop leaves: GATE-LEG TABLE
tablet on a wall for decoration or to mark an event: PLAQUE
tableware: FLATWARE
tact, knowledge of the right thing to say or do: SAVOIR-FAIRE
tact, smoothness, highly refined skill: FINESSE
tactic or stratagem to outwit someone: PLOY
tactlessness: GAUCHERIE
tadpole: POLLIWOG
tail part that is fleshy, in animals: DOCK
tailless: ACAUDAL
take apart: DISMANTLE
take attention away from: PRESCIND
take away a legacy: ADEEM
take away from, detract: DEROGATE
take back, recant: RETRACT
take exception to, hesitate, object: DEMUR
take note: COGNIZANCE
take off, remove: DOFF
take over property from the owner, usually for public use: EXPROPRIATE
take place, happen: SUPERVENE
take the place of: SUPERSEDE
take parts from one piece of equipment to use in another: CANNIBALIZE
taking risks to achieve some end: BRINKMANSHIP
talisman or charm: GRIGRI
talk, conference of opposing sides: PARLEY

talk about publicly: BRUIT
talk boastfully: COCKALORUM
talk down or against something: DEPRECATE
talk foolishly: TWADDLE
talk in a wandering, incoherent manner: MAUNDER
talk quickly or incoherently: GABBLE
talk or chatter that is rapid, nonsensical or unintelligible: JABBER
talk rapidly and incoherently: GIBBER
talk senselessly, chatter: PRATE
talk that is foolish or senseless: DRIVEL
talk that is idle, also a discussion: PALAVER
talk that sounds important but isn't: BOMBAST
talk to oneself: SOLILOQUIZE
talkative: LOQUACIOUS
talkative, foolish person: BLATHERSKITE
talkative, glib, speaking fluently: VOLUBLE
talkativeness: GARRULITY
talkativeness to an abnormal degree: LOGORRHEA
talked-about object: CONVERSATION PIECE
talking about a traumatic situation for release from it: ABREACTION
talking foolishly: BLITHERING
talks learnedly in table conversation: DEIPNOSOPHIST
tall, lean, often awkward: LANKY
tall, slender figure: ASTHENIC
tall building: HIGH-RISE
tall story: COCK-AND-BULL STORY
Talmudic literature devoted to legal elements: HALAKHA
Talmudic stories and account of the Exodus read at Seder service: HAGGADAH

tangible, touchable: TACTILE
tangle or make intricate: INVOLVE
tangle: RETICULAR
tantrum: CONNIPTION
tap dancing without metal taps: SOFT SHOE
tap firmly: PERCUSS
tap or drum monotonously: THRUM
tart or pleasantly sharp taste: PIQUANT
taste, flavor: SAPOR
taste or flavor that is sickeningly sentimental: MAWKISH
taste that is saline and distasteful: BRACKISH
tasteless, flat, bland, dull: INSIPID
tasting, taste: GUSTATION
tasty, appetizing: SAVORY
tasty, savory: SAPID
taunt, gibe: GIRD
taunt, jeer: GIBE
taunt or annoy by reminding of a fault: TWIT
taunting, sneering, ironical language: SARCASM
tautological, wordy: REDUNDANT
tax: IMPOST
tax of one tenth: TITHE
teacher: PRECEPTOR
teacher, lecturer, tutor without faculty rank: DOCENT
teacher or guide, in the East, especially in spiritual matters: GURU
teaching or learning through discovery and investigation: HEURISTICS
teacher who is narrow-minded, pedantic: PEDAGOGUE
tear, chafe, or burn away strips of: EXCORIATE
tear apart, as in searching for plunder: RANSACK
tear apart forcibly: REND
tear raggedly, mangle: LACERATE
tear to pieces: DILACERATE
tearful: LACHRYMOSE
tearfully emotional or sentimental: MAUDLIN
tearing away: AVULSION
tease or disappoint by repeated frustration of expectations: TANTALIZE
teasing talk, jesting: RAILLERY
teasing that is playful: BADINAGE
technical mastery, skill, style, as of an art: VIRTUOSITY
technicians as rulers: TECHNOCRACY
tedious, boring: WEARISOME
tedious, troublesome, tiresome: IRKSOME

teething, cutting teeth: DENTITION
telepathy, clairvoyance: CRYPTESTHESIA
telephone transactions in unlisted stocks: OVER-THE-COUNTER
television: VIDEO
television magnetic tape on which the video and audio parts of a program can be recorded: VIDEO TAPE
television or radio melodramatic series: SOAP OPERA
television's picture as distinguished from its sound, or audio: VIDEO
television's sound as distinguished from its picture, or video: AUDIO
tell, disclose, reveal: DIVULGE
temperate in eating and drinking: ABSTEMIOUS
temperature sense lacking, unable to recognize heat or cold: THERMANESTHESIA
temperature standard used to estimate fuel requirements for heating of buildings: DEGREE DAY
tempo and expression of music at performer's pleasure: A CAPRICCIO
temporary: INTERIM
temporary, brief: TRANSIENT
temporary buildings for housing troops: CANTONMENT
temporary camp, usually without shelter: BIVOUAC
temporary inaction: ABEYANCE
temporary or makeshift, as applied to a ship's rigging: JURY-RIGGED
temporary residence or stay: SOJOURN
temporary stitching: BASTING
tendency, bent: PROPENSITY
tendency, trend, liking, leaning or bent: INCLINATION
tendency or drift that is hidden: UNDERCURRENT
tendency or inclination: BENT
tendency or way of reacting: DISPOSITION
tendency or inclination, usually toward something objectionable: PROCLIVITY
tendency or susceptibility to: PREDISPOSITION
tendency that is inborn: INSTINCT
tender, emotional, sometimes mawkish: SENTIMENTAL
tender part of a loin of meat: TENDERLOIN
tending to a particular point of view: TENDENTIOUS
tendon at the back of the human knee: HAMSTRING

Ten Commandments: DECALOGUE
ten-year anniversary: DECENNIAL
ten-year period, decade: DECENNARY
tennis: SPHAIRISTIKE
tennis ball returned before it hits the ground: VOLLEY
tennis court's screened gallery for spectators, especially in court tennis: DEDANS
tennis return in which softly stroked ball barely clears the net: DROP SHOT
tennis rule violation of failing to keep both feet behind the base line when serving: FOOT FAULT
tennis set in which the winner wins every game: LOVE SET
tennis stroke in which the ball is arched high into the air: LOB
tennis stroke in which the hand holding the racket hits the ball from the opposite side of the body: BACKHAND
tennis stroke made on the same side of the body as that of the hand wielding the racket: FOREHAND
tense, bewildered, agitated, worried: DISTRAUGHT
tenth part of anything: TITHE
terminology, names: NOMENCLATURE
territory surrounded by that of another country or class: ENCLAVE
terse, concise, brief and meaningful: SUCCINCT
terse, pithy, axiomatic: SENTENTIOUS
terse, solid, packed with meaning: PITHY
test for diphtheria: SCHICK TEST
test for uterine cancer: PAP TEST
test or gauge the weight of by lifting: HEFT
test the depth of water: SOUND
test word, password: SHIBBOLETH
textiles, also perishable goods: SOFT GOODS
ticket selling above regular rates: SCALPING
tickle or excite pleasurably: TITILLATE
tidal wave: TSUNAMI
tide occurring at or shortly after the new or full moon: SPRING TIDE
tide when rise and fall show least change: NEAP TIDE
tides in conflict producing turbulent water: RIP TIDE
tidy: KEMPT
tie, a race in which two competitors finish together: DEAD HEAT

tie or draw, as in a game: STANDOFF
tie or fasten together: COLLIGATE
tie that connects, bond: LIGAMENT
tie together the four feet, or the feet and hands: HOG-TIE
tight spot, predicament: QUANDARY
tighten up or make concise: CONDENSE
tight-rope walker: FUNAMBULIST
tilelike, either in shape or arrangement: TEGULAR
tilt or slope: CANT
timber driven into the earth to support a building or pier: PILE
timber in a stand: STUMPAGE
time between periods or events, meantime: INTERIM
time counted in reverse, as in rocket launching: COUNTDOWN
time flies: TEMPUS FUGIT
time, in addition to length, width and thickness: FOURTH DIMENSION
time erroneously associated with an event or a thing: ANACHRONISM
time nature of a verb form: TENSE
time or rate agreement arranged: SYNCHRONIZED
time out from work, for a short period: COFFEE BREAK
time period memorable for important events or influence: EPOCH
time to be off the streets: CURFEW
time-consuming tactics to obstruct action: FILIBUSTER
time-honored, venerable, classic: VINTAGE
time-measuring science: CHRONOLOGY
timepiece: HOROLOGE
time-to-get-up signal on bugle or drum: REVEILLE
timid: PIGEON-HEARTED
timid, fearful: TIMOROUS
timid or cowardly: CHICKEN-HEARTED or CHICKEN-LIVERED
timid or fearful, trembling: TREMULOUS
timidity, shyness, lack of confidence: DIFFIDENCE
tin mine region: STANNARY
tinder of decayed wood: PUNK
tint, light color: TINCTURE
tiny: IOTA
tiny, very small: MINUSCULE
tiny person: HOP-O'-MY-THUMB
tiny quantity: SOUPÇON
tip: POURBOIRE
tip, gift of money: GRATUITY
tirade: HARANGUE

tireless, unflagging: INDEFATIGABLE

tiresome, tedious, troublesome: IRKSOME

tissue and tissue structure, as a biological study: HISTOLOGY

tissue growing abnormally, as a tumor: NEOPLASM

tissue removed from living organism for examination: BIOPSY

title or epithet substituted for proper name: ANTONOMASIA

title or heading of a section in a law: RUBRIC

that's life: C'EST LA VIE

theater bulletin board: CALLBOARD

theater fabric, light and sheer, used as a backdrop: SCRIM

theater space above the stage containing drop curtain and lighting: FLY

theater waiting room for performers when they are off-stage: GREEN ROOM

theater with stage surrounded by seats: ARENA THEATER

theaters, tents, modified barns, usually in resort areas, for plays, concerts: STRAW-HAT CIRCUIT

theatrical, overly emotional: HISTRIONIC

theatrical collection of works prepared for production: REPERTORY

theatrical stage objects: PROPS

theft: LARCENY

theme used throughout a work of art to indicate a certain person, event or idea: LEITMOTIF

theoretical, as opposed to practical: ACADEMIC

theoretical, not concrete: ABSTRACT

theological branch dealing with facts and proofs concerning Christianity: APOLOGETICS

theoretical or conjectural: SPECULATIVE

theory or supposition used as basis for further investigation: HYPOTHESIS

therapy using doses of medicines that produce symptoms of the disease treated: HOMEOPATHY

thesis established by showing its opposite to be absurd: APAGOGE

thick and dense, as heavy smoke: TURBID

thicken: INCRASSATE

thicken as by evaporation: INSPISSATE

thickening of artery walls: ATHEROSCLEROSIS

thief: GONIF or GANEF

thin, flimsy, delicate: TENUOUS

thin, lean: SPARE

thin, scanty, inadequate: MEAGER

thin and pale: PEAKED

thin biscuit or cooky: WAFER

thin down, emaciate: MACERATE

thin sheets of fabric, wood, etc., bonded together: LAMINATED

thing that goes into a mixture: INGREDIENT

think, reason: INTELLECTUALIZE

think about, reflect, consider carefully: PONDER

think of separately: PRESCIND

think out carefully, devise: EXCOGITATE

thinker, clever man: SOPHIST

thinking, using the intellect: INTELLECTION

thinly diffused: SPARSE

third anniversary: TRIENNIAL

third syllable from end in a word: ANTEPENULT

thirst-causing, dry up: PARCH

thirteen: BAKER'S DOZEN

this side of the Atlantic: CISATLANTIC

thorough, thorough-going: INGRAINED

thoroughfare or open space for crowds: CONCOURSE

thought, idea: INTELLECTION

thought apart from matter: ABSTRACT

thoughtful, serious, often melancholy: PENSIVE

thoughtless, unthinking: INCOGITANT

thousand, as by the thousand: PER MILL

thousand, or thousand years: CHILIAD

thousand tons: KILOTON

thousand-year period: MILLENARY

thrash severely, punish or beat: TROUNCE

threat or denunciation, especially from a divine source: COMMINATION

threaten: IMPEND

threatening, menacing: MINACIOUS, MINATORY

threatening and dark, as the weather: LOWERING

. . . (three dots) indicating the omission of words in a sentence: ELISION

three in a governing group: TROIKA

three miles: LEAGUE

three persons or things: TRIAD

three rhyming lines: TERCET

three separate but related literary or dramatic works: TRILOGY

three spots, as on a card or domino: TREY

three-figure design, with branches, arms, or legs coming from a common center: TRISKELION

threes, grouped in threes: TERNARY

thrift or economy in managing: HUS-BANDRY
thriftless, rash, incautious: IMPROVIDENT
thrifty: FRUGAL
thrifty, careful: CANNY
thrill, arouse, startle: ELECTRIFY
throat irritation often causing loss of voice: LARYNGITIS
throb regularly, vibrate: PULSATE
throbbing, pulsing: VIBRANT
throw forth or forward: PROJECT
throw goods or cargo overboard: JETTISON
throw in or introduce abruptly: INJECT
throw things at: PELT
throwing out of a window: DEFENESTRA-TION
thrust away from, push down: DETRUDE
thumb: POLLEX
thumb one's nose: SNOOK
thumb rapidly through a book's pages: RIFFLE
thus passes away worldly glory: SIC TRANSIT GLORIA MUNDI
to the point: APROPOS
toady, cringe fondly: FAWN
toady, servile follower: LACKEY
toast or bread, in small pieces, dipped in gravy or sauce: SIPPET
toasted slices of bread that has been baked yellow: ZWIEBACK
tobacco ash left in pipe after smoking: DOTTLE
tobacco grown in Louisiana, dark and strong: PERIQUE
toe with joint bent downward: HAMMER-TOE
toeless: ADACTYLOUS
toes linked by membrane: WEB-FOOTED
together: IN CONCERT
together, cooperative: SYNERGETIC
toilet bowl for bathing genitals: BIDET
toilet for numbers of people, as in a camp: LATRINE
toilet in nautical language: HEAD
token of a solemn pledge: SACRAMENT
token or counter: JETON
tolerate by use or exercise, accustom: INURE
tomato juice mixed with vodka as a cock-tail: BLOODY MARY
tomato juice served as if it were a cock-tail: VIRGIN MARY
tomboy: HOYDEN
tombstone inscription: EPITAPH

tomcat: GIB
tomorrow (Spanish): MAÑANA
tone color, as of a voice or an instrument: TIMBRE
tongue lashing: EXCORIATION
tonguelike: LANGUET
tonguelike or pertaining to language: LINGUAL
too glib, facile: PAT
too great or too numerous to be deter-mined: INCALCULABLE
too much, in music: TANTO
too much sweetness: CLOYING
tooth cleanser: DENTIFRICE
tooth extraction: EXODONTIA
tooth that is broken or projects: SNAGGLE-TOOTH
tooth with two points: BICUSPID
toothache: ODONTALGIA
toothless: EDENTATE
tooth-gnashing: BRUXISM
top, apex: VERTEX
top course of a wall or roof: COPING
top grade or quality: FIRST WATER
top having four, lettered sides, used in a gambling game: TEETOTUM
topmost point, acme: PINNACLE
top-shaped, or spinning like a top: TUR-BINATE
top rank: PREEMINENT
torch, candlestick that is large and deco-rated: FLAMBEAU
torment, tease, rant, browbeat, bluster: HECTOR
tornado: TWISTER
torpor: ACEDIA
Torrid Zone inhabitants whose shadows fall according to season: AMPHISCIAN
tortoiselike: TESTUDINAL
tortuous: ANFRACTUOUS
tossing or twitching to an abnormal de-gree: JACTITATION
total, end-to-end: OVERALL
touch at sides or ends: ABUT
touch or meet lightly: KISS
touch or push with a slight jar, shake lightly, stimulate: JOG
touchable: TANGIBLE
touchable, perceptible: PALPABLE
touchable, tangible: TACTILE
touching: TANGENT
touching, emotionally moving: POIGNANT
tough, robust: HARDY
tough, unyielding: HARD-BITTEN

toughen or smooth metal: PLANISH
tour rural districts: BARNSTORM
tournament: JOUSTS
tournament in which each player engages every other player: ROUND ROBIN
tousled, untidy, unkempt: DISHEVELED
toward the center: CENTRIPETAL
toward the stern on a boat: ABAFT
tower or keep of a castle: DONJON
tower that tapers to a point: SPIRE
trace, sign of something absent: VESTIGE
trace, slight hint: SOUPÇON
trace, spark: SCINTILLA
trace out, portray verbally, describe: DELINEATE
track, trail, footprint or other trace of a wild animal: SPOOR
track and field event in which an athlete uses a long pole to leap over a high horizontal bar: POLE VAULT
track or trail behind any moving thing, such as a ship: WAKE
tractable, yielding: PLAINT
trademark of a publishing house: COLOPHON
trader: CHANDLER
trader or dealer: MONGER
trading of votes and influence between politicians: LOGROLLING
trading unit on a stock exchange, usually 100 shares: ROUND LOT
tragic muse: MELPOMENE
trail, track, footprint or other trace of a wild animal: SPOOR
train of persons or animals fastened together as for marching: COFFLE
train to a behavior pattern: CONDITION
training of employes to develop skills, etc.: IN-SERVICE COURSES
traitor: RECREANT
traitor, deserter: RENEGADE
traitor, renegade: TURNCOAT
tramp, wanderer: VAGABOND
tranquil, calm, untroubled: SERENE
tranquil, serene, uniform: EQUABLE
tranquillity: ATARAXIA
transaction conditionally authorized when, as, and if a security is issued: WHEN ISSUED
transference of an emotion to something other than the original object: DISPLACEMENT
transform: TRANSMOGRIFY
transform, convert: RESOLVE

transformation: PERMUTATION
transformation of form, character, or appearance: METAMORPHOSIS
transient, fickle, unstable, fleeting: VOLATILE
transitional form: INTERGRADE
transitory, fleeting: FUGACIOUS
transitory, lasting a short time, fleeting, of short life or duration: EPHEMERAL
transitory or passing: CADUCITY
translation literally of a word or construction from one language to another: LOAN TRANSLATION
translation word for word: METAPHRASE
translucent, limpid: PELLUCID
transmit to another: BEQUEATH
transmutation process: ALCHEMY
transparent, lucid, pure, clear: LIMPID
transparent, radiant: LUCENT
transparent or translucent, as a cloth: DIAPHANOUS
transposing letters of a word to form another: ANAGRAM
transposition of letters or sounds that changes a word: METATHESIS
transposition of sounds or of parts of words unintentionally: SPOONERISM
trap, situation with no escape: CUL DE SAC
trapeze acrobat: AERIALIST
trashy art or literature: KITSCH
travel a route: PEREGRINATE
travel urge: WANDERLUST
traveler, wayfarer: VIATOR
travelers moving in a group: CARAVAN
traveling or going from place to place: ITINERANT
traveling salesman who sells or gives away religious books: COLPORTEUR
tray: SALVER
treacherous: PERFIDIOUS
treacherous woman: DELILAH
treacherous, wily, cunning: INSIDIOUS
treason, offense against sovereign authority: LESE MAJESTY
treasurer: BURSAR
treatise: DISSERTATION
treatise, formal discourse: DISQUISITION
treatise or pamphlet usually on a political or religious subject: TRACT
treatment of disease by manipulation of joints: CHIROPRACTIC
treatment of disease by producing incompatible conditions: ALLOPATHY
treaty, contract, agreement: PACT

tree grown from seed: STAND
tree rings used to estimate dates of past events: DENDROCHRONOLOGY
tree with its top cut to cause growth of shoots: POLLARD
trees, like or living in: ARBOREAL
trees as studied in botany and forestry: DENDROLOGY
trees or shrubs cut and arranged in fantastic shapes: TOPIARY
trembling paralysis: PALSY
trench mouth: VINCENT'S ANGINA
trespass, intrude, advance beyond proper limit: ENCROACH
trespass for hunting or fishing: POACH
triangle with two equal sides: ISOSCELES
triangles and the relationship of their sides and angles, as a study: TRIGONOMETRY
triangular jet aircraft: DELTA WING
triangular or wedge-shaped piece of fabric set into a garment to provide greater fullness: GORE
triangular roof feature: GABLE
triangular stringed instrument (Russian): BALALAIKA
tribute, elaborate praise: PANEGYRIC
trick, cajole, entice by flattery or guile: INVEIGLE
trick, cheat, deceive: FINAGLE
trick, maneuver, device for obtaining advantage: STRATAGEM
trick or cheat: HOODWINK
trick or deceive someone: BAMBOOZLE
trickery: CHICANERY
trickery, deceitfulness, double-dealing: DUPLICITY
trickery, deception: HOCUS-POCUS
trickery, hocus-pocus, sleight of hand: LEGERDEMAIN
trickery, rascality, deceitfulness: KNAVERY
trickery, underhandedness: SKULDUGGERY
tricky or fraudulent action: JOCKEYING
tricky or lewd: LUBRICOUS
trifle: BAGATELLE
trifle, little something: QUELQUE CHOSE
trifle with or flirt: COQUET
trifles, unimportant details: MINUTIAE
trifling, small work: OPUSCULE
trifling or insignificant size or amount: NEGLIGIBLE
trifling, small: NOMINAL
trifling, unimportant, frivolous: FRIBBLE
trifling, unimportant, insignificant: PETTY

trilling sound, as that of grasshoppers or birds: CHIRR
trim or cut the branches as from a tree: LOP
trimming for women's gowns, as beaded lace or braid: PASSEMENTERIE
trimming on edges or seams of material: PIPING
trinket: BIBELOT
trinket: GEWGAW
trinket or ornament either gaudy or trifling: FALLAL
triplicate: TERNATE
trite, commonplace, banal remark: PLATITUDE
trite, commonplace, worn out by overuse (as a phrase): HACKNEYED
trite expression: BROMIDE
trite or hackneyed: HACK
trite, worn-out, overused expression: CLICHÉ
trite story, song, saying: CHESTNUT
triumphant, joyful: JUBILANT
trivial, of small importance: FEATHERWEIGHT
trivial, petty: INSIGNIFICANT
trivial, petty: PICAYUNE
trivial, petty, contemptible: PALTRY
trivial, silly, unimportant: FRIVOLOUS
trivial, unimportant: INCONSEQUENTIAL
trivial or worthless matter: CHAFF
trolley in parallelogram shape that draws current for an electric locomotive: PANTOGRAPH
troop call for service, review, etc.: MUSTER
trouble: TSOORIS
trouble, bother, inconvenience: DISCOMMODE
trouble, torment relentlessly: HARASS
trouble with persistent demands: IMPORTUNE
trouble-free state: ATARAXIA
troublemaker: ENFANT TERRIBLE
trouble-making: PESTILENT
troublesome, tiresome, tedious: IRKSOME
trousers of women resembling a skirt: CULOTTE
trudge laboriously: PLOD
true apparently but open to doubt: PLAUSIBLE
truism: PLATITUDE
truly so: VERITABLE
trumpet mute: SOURDINE

trumpet or drum signal for a parley: CHA-MADE

trustee, guardian: FIDUCIARY

truthful, accurate: VERACIOUS

truthful appearing: VERISIMILITUDE

tub for boiling and bleaching fabrics: KIER

tube between mouth and stomach: GULLET

tube of small size, often graduated: PI-PETTE

tuck made in a garment to achieve good fit: DART

tuft of ribbons, yarn, feathers: POMPON

tuft or clump, as of grass or hair: TUSSOCK

tumbler, vaulter: VOLTIGEUR

tumor that is malignant: SARCOMA

tumult, confusion: TURMOIL

tune an instrument: TEMPER

turbulent, dangerous condition or place: MAELSTROM

Turkish confection: HALVAH

Turkish title of respect (formerly): EF-FENDI

turmoil, confusion: HURLY-BURLY

turmoil, haste, excitement: HECTIC

turn, as the hand, so that the palm is upward or forward: SUPINATE

turn, rotate or swing, as on a pivot: PIVOT

turn aside: SHUNT

turn aside, deflect, distract, amuse, entertain: DIVERT

turn aside, swerve: SKEW

turn aside, wander from the main subject: DIGRESS

turn aside, ward off, avoid: PARRY

turn away from straight course, or sexual pervert: DEVIATE

turn or go back to a former place, position or condition: REVERT

turn out finally, result ultimately: EVEN-TUATE

turn outward or inside out: EVERT

turned up at the tip: RETROUSSÉ

turncoat, traitor: RENEGADE

turning of one's interest inward upon oneself: INTROVERSION

turning point in action, belief, etc.: WA-TERSHED

turreted like a castle: CASTELLATED

tutor, teacher, lecturer, without faculty rank: DOCENT

tuxedo, semiformal attire: BLACK TIE

twelve or twelfths: DUODECIMAL

twentieth: VIGESIMAL

twenty-one, a card game: VINGT-ET-UN

twenty-year period: VICENNIAL

twice a week: SEMIWEEKLY

twice a year: BIANNUAL

twilight, dusk: GLOAMING

twilight dimness, obscure: CREPUSCULAR

twin-bearing: BIPAROUS

twinge of fear: QUALM

twist, bend, contort: WRITHE

twist, bend, misrepresent: DISTORT

twist or bend out of shape: DISTORT

twist or lurch from side to side: CAREEN

twist or pull away: WREST

twisted cord used for ornamentation: TORSADE

twisting or being twisted: TORSION

twitching or tossing to an abnormal degree: JACTITATION

two, double or paired: BINARY

two bids made simultaneously are decided by a flip of a coin: MATCHED AND LOST

two dancers in a ballet figure: PAS DE DEUX

two dots over a Germanic vowel to indicate sound change (ü): UMLAUT

two dots over second of two consecutive vowels to indicate different pronunciation: DIERISIS

two equally accented syllables making up a poetic metrical foot: SPONDEE

two meanings in a phrase, one of them risqué: DOUBLE ENTENDRE

two months apart: BIMONTHLY

two months duration: BIMESTRIAL

two names or two terms: BINOMIAL

two negatives in a single sentence ("I don't have no pencil"): DOUBLE NEGATIVE

two or more husbands at once: POL-YANDRY

two or more wives at once: POLYGYNY

two persons sharing ruling power: DIARCHY

two prosecutions for the same offense: DOUBLE JEOPARDY

two sections or two opposed parts: DI-CHOTOMY

two-sided: BILATERAL

two loudspeakers for stereophonic effect: BINAURAL

two tickets for the price of one: TWOFER

two tones rapidly alternated, in music: TRILL

two vowel sounds that blend into one syllable: DIPHTHONG

two years apart: BIENNIAL

two-colored: DICHROMATIC

two-edged battle ax: TWIBIL

two-footed animal: BIPED

two-god theology: DITHEISM

two-handed: BIMANOUS

two-part division of groups or classes that are often opposed: DICHOTOMY

tying up or binding together; also two or more letters united in print: LIGATURE

type assortment of all the characters in one size and style: FONT

type in which the letters slant, usually to denote emphasis: ITALIC

type or kind, as in art or literature: GENRE

type measure equal to square of the type body: EM

type measure half the width of an em: EN

type plate containing company's distinctive form of name, trademark, newspaper nameplate, etc.: LOGOTYPE

type set by printers that exceeds the space available: OVERSET

type that is heavy and black: BOLDFACE

type that looks like handwriting: CURSIVE

type 12 points high used as a unit of measurement in printing: PICA

typesetter: COMPOSITOR

typewriter operated by telephone: TELEX

typify: PERSONIFY

typical example, model, pattern: EXEMPLAR

typical or specific language, style, etc, as in art, literature: IDIOM

typographical error: TYPO

typographical ornament or symbol: DINGBAT

typographical term for part of a letter that extends below the line: DESCENDER

typographical term for part of a letter that extends upward: ASCENDER

typographical unit of measurement, 12 points: PICA

tyrant: DESPOT ·

tyrannical subordinate official: SATRAP

U

U-shaped piece of metal with pointed ends used as a fastener: STAPLE

ugly, unpleasant in appearance, disagreeable: ILL-FAVORED

ugly and malicious old woman: BELDAM

umpire: ARBITER

unable to produce the desired effect: INEFFECTUAL

unable to survive: INVIABLE

unable to swallow: APHAGIA

unabridged: IN EXTENSO

unacceptable, unwelcome person: PERSONA NON GRATA

unaccompanied singing: A CAPPELLA

unadorned, as speech or writing: LITERAL

unaffected, simple, candid, artless: NAIVE

unaffected by pain or pleasure: STOICAL

unalike, varied: DIVERSE

unalive, spiritless: INANIMATE

unambiguous: UNEQUIVOCAL

unattractive, dingy: SNUFFY

unavoidable, authoritative, urgently necessary: IMPERATIVE

unavoidable, certain: INEVITABLE

unavoidable, inevitable: INELUCTABLE

unaware, unmindful: OBLIVIOUS

unbearable: INSUFFERABLE

unbeliever: INFIDEL

unbelieving, irreligious: HEATHEN

unbending: INTRANSIGENT

unbiased: INDIFFERENT

unbiased, impartial: DISPASSIONATE

unbiased, objective, impartial: DISPASSIONATE

unbreakable: INFRANGIBLE

unbreakable: IRREFRANGIBLE

unbiased, detached: OBJECTIVE

uncalled for: GRATUITOUS

unceasing: INCESSANT

uncertain: AMBIVALENT

uncertain: VACILLATING

uncertain, risky: TOUCH-AND-GO

uncertain or unforeseen but possible event: CONTINGENCY

unchangeable: IMMUTABLE

unchangeable: INVARIABLE

unchangeable, fixed: INFLEXIBLE

unchanged, undamaged, whole: INTACT

unchaste, morally unrestrained: LIBERTINE

unchecked, wild: RAMPANT

unclean: UNSAVORY

unclear: AMBIGUOUS

unclear, hazy, misty, vague: NEBULOUS

uncle-like: AVUNCULAR

uncomfortably small, cramped: INCOMMODIOUS

uncommunicative: TACITURN

uncommunicative, quiet, reserved: RETICENT

unconcealed: ABOVEBOARD

unconcealed, open, evident: OVERT

unconcerned, apathetic: INDIFFERENT

unconcerned, lighthearted, carefree: INSOUCIANT

unconquerable: INEXPUGNABLE

unconquerable, not capable of being injured: INVULNERABLE

unconscious, lethargic, torpid: COMATOSE

unconscious part of the psyche regarded as source of instinctual drives: ID

unconscious perception: SUBLIMINAL

unconsciousness caused by injury or disease: COMA

unconsciousness caused by too little oxygen: ASPHYXIA

uncontrolled response by a patient in psychoanalysis to a given stimulus: FREE ASSOCIATION

unconventional, odd: OUTRÉ

unconvincing, inadequate, fragile: FLIMSY

uncultivated, unseeded: FALLOW
undamaged, whole, unchanged: INTACT
undeceive, free from false or mistaken ideas: DISABUSE
undecided, wavering: IRRESOLUTE
undeniable: INCONTROVERTIBLE
undependable person in a group: WEAK SISTER
underdeveloped countries, especially in Asia and Africa: THIRD WORLD
underdone, poorly made: SLACK-BAKED
underground structure or vault: HYPOGEUM
underhanded and secret activity, plot: INTRIGUE
underhanded or shady dealing: CHICANERY
underhandedness, trickery: SKULDUGGERY
undermine the morale, corrupt: SUBVERT
understand, interpret, puzzle out: FATHOM
understandable, clear: PELLUCID
understandable with ease, rational, clear, bright, shining: LUCID
understanding, compatible: SIMPATICO
understanding, knowledge, or grasp of ideas or things: PERCEPTION
understanding or agreement: ENTENTE
understatement for effect, a form of litotes: MEIOSIS
understood, implied: IMPLICIT
understood only by an inner group: ESOTERIC
undertone: SOTTO VOCE
underwater breathing apparatus: SCUBA
underwater work chamber: CAISSON
underworld vocabulary: ARGOT
undeveloped: LATENT
undisclosed, beyond what is spoken of: ULTERIOR
undiscovered, unused, untrod hitherto: VIRGIN
undo, void: NULLIFY
uneasiness, anxieties, restlessness: INQUIETUDE
uneasiness, misgiving: QUALM
uneasy: QUEASY
uneatable: INEDIBLE
uneducated, illiterate: UNLETTERED
unemployed people or vagrants: FLOTSAM
unending: AD INFINITUM
unequal: DISPARATE
unequaled: PEERLESS
unequaled, matchless: NONPAREIL
unequaled: SANS PAREIL

unerring: IMPECCABLE
unerring: INFALLIBLE
unessential: UNIMPORTANT
unethical clash of public duty and self-interest: CONFLICT OF INTEREST
unexplored land or area: TERRA INCOGNITA
unexpected, without warning: UNAWARES
unexpressed, unspoken: INARTICULATE
unfair: INEQUITABLE
unfaithful, cowardly: RECREANT
unfavorable, inauspicious: UNTOWARD
unfeeling, hardened: INDURATE
unfeeling, impassive: STOLID
unfeeling, invulnerable: IMPASSIBLE
unfeeling, stupid, foolish: INSENSATE
unfilled orders: BACKLOG
unflagging, tireless: INDEFATIGABLE
unflinching, resolved, determined: RESOLUTE
unfortunate: STAR-CROSSED
unfortunate, unlucky: HAPLESS
unfriendly: DISAFFECTED
unfriendly: ILL-DISPOSED
unfriendly: INIMICAL
unfruitful, barren: STERILE
ungodliness, lack of reverence: IMPIETY
ungrateful person: INGRATE
unified: INDISCRETE
uniform, similar, like, same composition throughout: HOMOGENEOUS
uniform worn by male household servants or employes: LIVERY
unify, bring together into a whole, fit together: INTEGRATE
unimaginative: LITERAL
unimportant, frivolous, trifling,: FRIBBLE
unimportant, trivial: INCONSEQUENTIAL
unimportant, trivial, petty: FRIVOLOUS
unimportant or small details, trifles: MINUTIAE
unimportant person or thing: CIPHER
unimportant person or thing: NONENTITY
uninjured, whole, untaxed: SCOT-FREE
unintelligible: INCOMPREHENSIBLE
unintelligible speech or sounds: GLOSSOLALIA
unintentional: INADVERTENT
uninterested: APATHETIC
uninterrupted or extended: CONTINUOUS
union man who represents fellow workers: SHOP STEWARD
union members alone allowed to be employed: CLOSED SHOP

union membership not required for employment: OPEN SHOP

union membership required after employment: UNION SHOP

unique, one of a kind: SUI GENERIS

unit of trading on a stock exchange, usually 100 shares: ROUND LOT

unit that is indivisible: MONAD

united: IN CONCERT

united in opinion, all assenting: UNANIMOUS

United States and Soviet Union: SUPERPOWERS

uniting of atomic nuclei into one of heavier mass: NUCLEAR FUSION

unity of purpose relations or interests: SOLIDARITY

universal, all-embracing knowledge: PANSOPHY

universal, widespread, also general epidemic: PANDEMIC

universal, world-wide, general, especially concerning the church: ECUMENICAL

universe, especially when viewed as a unity: MACROCOSM

universe, theories of its creation, structure, etc.: COSMOLOGY, COSMOGONY

universe in miniature: MICROCOSM

unjust: INIQUITOUS

unjustifiable: INSUPPORTABLE

unjustifiable, unprincipled: UNCONSCIONABLE

unjustly: UNDULY

unkempt, tousled, rumpled, untidy: DISHEVELED

unknowable through physical perception: NOUMENON

unknown except by a few specially instructed individuals; secret, abstruse: ESOTERIC

unknown or hidden difficulty: JOKER

unlawful, unauthorized: ILLICIT

unlawful dispossession: DISSEIZIN

unlawful manner of performing a lawful act: MISFEASANCE

unlike, dissimilar, unequal: DISPARATE

unlike, dissimilar, unrelated: HETEROGENEOUS

unlikeness: DISSIMILITUDE

unlikeness, inequality: DISPARITY

unlimited as to subject, duration, etc., or, in an investment company, as to number of shares: OPEN-ENDED

unlimited authority in a government: ABSOLUTISM

unlimited money or authority made available: BLANK CHECK

unlucky: ILL-STARRED

unlucky, unfortunate: HAPLESS

unmanly, womanlike, weak, soft: EFFEMINATE

unmarried, abstaining from sexual congress: CELIBATE

unmindful, unaware: OBLIVIOUS

unmoved, calm, serene: IMPASSIVE

unnatural or disfiguring outgrowth, such as a wart: EXCRESCENCE

unoccupied, idle: VACUOUS

unorganized: AMORPHOUS

unorthodox: HETERODOX

unorthodox in his attitudes: MAVERICK

unorthodox or liberal in attitudes or beliefs: LATITUDINARIAN

unpardonable: IRREMISSIBLE

unperceivable by the sense of touch: IMPALPABLE

unperceptive: PURBLIND

unpleasant appearance: EYESORE

unpleasant in appearance, ugly, disagreeable: ILL-FAVORED

unplowed land near fence or at end of furrows: HEADLAND

unpolished, crude: INURBANE

unpolished, uncouth: AGRESTIC

unpractical, though romantic in intentions: QUIXOTIC

unpredictable, uncertain: INCALCULABLE

unpremeditated: EXTEMPORANEOUS

unpremeditated: SPONTANEOUS

unpremeditated homicide in a sudden fight: CHANCE-MEDLEY

unprepared, spontaneous: IMPROMPTU

unprincipled, unjustifiable: UNCONSCIONABLE

unprovoked, unjust, malicious: WANTON

unquestionable: VERITABLE

unquestionable, certain: INDUBITABLE

unquestionable, unassailable: INCONTESTABLE

unreadable: INDECIPHERABLE

unreal, false, artificially invented: FICTITIOUS

unreasonable: ABSONANT

unreasoning: IRRATIONAL

unreasoning devotion to one's race country, etc.: CHAUVINISM

unreasoning passion, foolish love: INFATUATION

unreceptive, not open: IMPERVIOUS

unrefined, coarse, natural: EARTHY

unrefined, rough, crude: UNCOUTH
unrelated, unlike, dissimilar: HETEROGE-
NEOUS
unrelated to the matter at hand, coming
from without: EXTRANEOUS
unrelenting, merciless: IMPLACABLE
unreliable: IRRESPONSIBLE
unreliable: SKITTISH
unreserved, absolute: IMPLICIT
unresolved: PENDENT
unrestrained: IMMODERATE
unrestrained, excessive: WANTON
unrestrained, unchecked: INCONTINENT
unrestrained as in speech or action: IN-
TEMPERATE
unrestricted authority: CARTE BLANCHE
unrivaled: INAPPROACHABLE
unruffled, calm: IMPERTURBABLE
unruly, boisterous: OBSTREPEROUS
unruly, difficult, stubborn,: INTRACTABLE
unruly, fidgety, restless: RESTIVE
unruly, loud: RAUCOUS
unruly, malicious, fierce: VICIOUS
unruly, rebellious, irritable, cranky:
FRACTIOUS
usage-based law, rather than legislation:
UNWRITTEN LAW
unscrupulous: UNCONSCIONABLE
unseeable because of smallness: IMPER-
CEPTIBLE
unseeded, uncultivated: FALLOW
unseemly: INDECOROUS
unselfish devotion to others: ALTRUISM
unserviceable: IMPRACTICABLE
unsettled, difficult to solve: PROBLEMATIC
unsettled, vague: INDETERMINATE
unskilled or inexperienced: FRESH-WATER
unskilled worker: BLUE COLLAR
unsociable, fierce, wild: FAROUCHE
unsophisticated, artless, unaffected, unin-
structed, simple: NAIVE
unsophisticated, narrow: PROVINCIAL
unspoken, unexpressed: INARTICULATE
unspoken, silent: TACIT
unstable, changeable: LABILE
unstable, fleeting, transient, fickle: VOLA-
TILE
unsteady, wavering: FLUCTUATING
unsteady or irregular movement at sea:
YAW
unsubstantial, flimsy, weak: TENUOUS
unsuccessful, fruitless: INEFFECTUAL
unsuccessful, futile: UNAVAILING
unsuccessful, short of goal: MANQUÉ
unsuccessfully conclude a project: ABORT

unsuitability: INAPTITUDE
unsuitable, inappropriate, at odds with:
INCONGRUOUS
unsuitable, untimely: INOPPORTUNE
unsure, risky,: PRECARIOUS
unsurmountable: INSUPERABLE
untanned skin of a calf or lamb: KIP
untaxed, uninjured, whole: SCOT-FREE
unthinking, thoughtless: INCOGITANT
untidy, slovenly: UNKEMPT
untidy, unkempt, tousled, rumpled: DI-
SHEVELED
untidy in appearance: BLOWZY
untidy or careless person: SLOVEN
untidy or soiled: BEDRAGGLED
untidy or slovenly woman: SLATTERN
untimely, unsuitable: INOPPORTUNE
untruthful: MENDACIOUS
unusable: IMPRACTICABLE
unused, brand new, original condition:
MINT CONDITION
unused condition, neglected: DESUETUDE
unusual happening: PHENOMENON
unutterable: INEFFABLE
unwavering, firmly faithful: STEADFAST
unwavering, steadfast, firmly directed:
INTENT
unwelcome or unacceptable person: PER-
SONA NON GRATA
unwholesome, noxious atmosphere, influence, effect, etc.: MIASMA
unwieldly, ponderous, enormous: ELE-
PHANTINE
unwilling, reluctant: LOATH
unwise: INADVISABLE
unwise, imprudent: INDISCREET
unyielding: ADAMANT
unyielding: INDUCTILE
unyielding, aggressive: TRUCULENT
unyielding, resistant: IMPREGNABLE
unyielding, refusing to compromise or
come to terms: INTRANSIGENT
unyielding, stubborn: INFLEXIBLE
up for consideration: ON THE TAPIS
up to date: AU COURANT
upbraid or denounce scathingly: EX-
CORIATE
upheaval that is violent: CATACLYSM
upholstery or drapery fabric with varicolored stripes of satin or moiré: TAB-
ARET
uplift, enlighten, benefit: EDIFY
upper class, aristocrat: PATRICIAN
upper class rule: ARISTOCRACY
upright, honest: INCORRUPT

uprightness, correctness of judgment: RECTITUDE

uproar: BALLYHOO

uproar: BROUHAHA

uproar, brawl, conflict, fight: FRAY

uproar, confused sound: HUBBUB

uproar of a crowd: TUMULT

uproot, eradicate, dislocate, extirpate: DERACINATE

uproot, pull up by the roots, destroy utterly, erase: ERADICATE

uprooting, extracting forcibly: EVULSION

upset, confuse, frustrate: DISCONCERT

upset, disturb, alarm: PERTURB

upset or irritate: RUFFLE

upstart: JACKANAPES

upstart, newly rich or influential: PARVENU

upward leap, made by a trained horse: CAPRIOLE

upward stroke of a small letter (typography): ASCENDER

urban complex: CONURBATION

urbane, cheerful, lively: DEBONAIR

urbane, gracious: SUAVE

urge on, drive or force to action: IMPEL

urge on, stir up, spur into action: INCITE

urge by earnest appeal, recommend strongly, advise: EXHORT

urgent: IMPERIOUS

urgent, demanding immediate action: EXIGENT

urgently necessary, unavoidable, authoritative: IMPERATIVE

urinary system, as a branch of medicine: UROLOGY

urinate: MICTURATE

urination that is excessive: DIURESIS

urination that is involuntary: ENURESIS

urine-increasing substance: DIURETIC

urine of cattle or horses: STALE

urn of metal for heating water for tea: SAMOVAR

used to or accustomed to, habituated: WONT

useless: INUTILE

useless, ineffectual: OTIOSE

useless person or thing: DEADWOOD

useless work: BOONDOGGLE

usurp: ARROGATE

utensils and serving dishes that are concave: HOLLOWWARE

uterine cancer test: PAP TEST

uterus surgery: HYSTERECTOMY

V

"v" shaped insignia: CHEVRON

vacation for one year, or less, originally granted every seven years: SABBATICAL YEAR

vacillate, veer, shift about: WHIFFLE

vagrant on beach living off what he can find: BEACHCOMBER

vagrants or unattached persons: FLOTSAM

vague: AMBIGUOUS

vague, confused: HAZY

vague, subtle: INDEFINABLE

vague, unclear, hazy, misty: NEBULOUS

vague, unsettled: INDETERMINATE

vague concept, general idea: NOTION

vague idea, notion, slight suggestion, hint: INKLING

vague or indefinite: INTANGIBLE

vague state between two others: LIMBO

vain, silly, foppish behavior: COXCOMBRY

valiant, courageous: METTLESOME

valley or mountain pass that is narrow: DEFILE

value, in proportion to: AD VALOREM

value of a business in excess of liabilities: EQUITY

value of a bond, as it appears on the security: FACE VALUE

value of a nation's annual output of goods and services before any deductions: GROSS NATIONAL PRODUCT

value per share, calculated by totaling market price and deducting all liabilities: NET ASSET VALUE

valueless: TINKER'S DAMN

valueless though showy: TRUMPERY

valve or faucet used to drain off water or air: PETCOCK

vanish gradually, disappear by degrees: EVANESCE

vanquish, as in battle, or defeat the purposes of: DISCOMFIT

variation or inflection of words: ACCIDENCE

variations or changes occurring irregularly, as of fortune: VICISSITUDES

varied, diverse to a great degree: MULTIFARIOUS

varied, unalike: DIVERSE

varied with many forms: MANIFOLD

varied without limit: OMNIFARIOUS

variegated in color or other elements: MOTLEY

variegated or spotted: DAPPLED

various, several, many: DIVERS

vary or change often and in irregular manner: FLUCTUATE

vary or diversify by interjecting something different: INTERLARD

vary or revise, restrict or limit: MODIFY

vary the products of a business so as to expand it: DIVERSIFY

vary the tone or pitch of the voice, modulate: INFLECT

vast indefinite number, innumerable: MYRIAD

vast or limitless: INFINITE

vat used by brewers for fermenting: TUN

veal cutlet breaded and garnished: WIENER SCHNITZEL

veal thin-sliced and sautéed: SCALOPPINE

veer, vacillate, shift about: WHIFFLE

vegetate, become dull or inert: STAGNATE

vehemently censure: INVEIGH

vehicle that carries passengers for a small fee: JITNEY

vehicle with three wheels moved by pedaling: PEDICAB

vehicles traveling together: CARAVAN

velvety, covered with soft hairs: VELU-
TINOUS

venerable, classic, time-honored: VINTAGE

vengeance or just retribution as identified
with an antagonist or thing: NEMESIS

verb form that relates to time of action:
TENSE

verb mood used to express hypothesis,
possibility, or nonfactual condition:
SUBJUNCTIVE

verb of weak form that links subject and
predicate: COPULA

verb that forms its past tense by internal
vowel change, as "swim": STRONG
VERB

verb that is a copula, serving mainly as a
connection between subject and predicate: LINKING VERB

verbal contention, or argument about
words: LOGOMACHY

verbal noun: GERUND

verbose: PROLIX

verbose: REDUNDANT

verbose, wordy: DIFFUSE

verse containing eight lines and two
rhymes (a-b-a-a-a-b-a-b) with the
first line repeated as the fourth and
seventh, and the second as the eighth:
TRIOLET

verse, humorous and often bawdy, containing five lines with the rhyme
scheme a-a-b-b-a: LIMERICK

verse free of conventional meter and
rhyme: FREE VERSE

verse in praise of wine and sensual pleasures: ANACREONTIC

verse of three stanzas and an envoy, with
last line of each the same: BALLADE

verse rhythm analysis: SCANSION

verse that is trivial and awkwardly written:
DOGGEREL

verse that is humorous, metrical and
usually rhymed: LIGHT VERSE

verse that ends with a lack of a syllable in
its final foot: CATALECTIC

verse with two feet to the line: DIMETER

verse's feet analyzed: SCANNED

vertical: PERPENDICULAR

vertical sidepiece in a door or a window
sash: STILE

vertical takeoff and landing plane: VTOL

very much: BEAUCOUP

vessel that services another at sea: TEN-
DER

veto performed by the U.S. President by
not signing a bill by the time
Congress adjourns: POCKET VETO

vex, annoy, weary: IRK

vibrate, throb regularly: PULSATE

vibrating effect produced on a stringed instrument or with the voice: TREMOLO

vibration or sound caused by the hitting of
one body against another: PERCUS-
SION

vicarious sharing of another's emotions or
feelings: EMPATHY

vice-ridden and corruption-ridden area of
a city: TENDERLOIN

vicious, inhuman, cruel: FELL

victimized or injured by one's plans to injure another: HOIST BY ONE'S OWN
PETARD

victims of poverty or discrimination: UN-
DERPRIVILEGED

victory at great cost, Pyrrhic victory:
CADMEAN VICTORY

vie with or rival successfully: EMULATE

view in all directions: PANORAMA

view of the proportional relation of parts
to the whole: PERSPECTIVE

vigilant, watchful: JEALOUS

vigor, dash: VERVE

vigor, strength, endurance: STAMINA

vigor or youthful feeling restored: REJU-
VENATION

vigorous, interesting: SUCCULENT

vigorous, large, shift, dashing: SPANKING

vigorous, lively: VIBRANT

vile, base, degraded: SORDID

vile, contemptible: DESPICABLE

vile, evil: NEFARIOUS

vileness, depravity, baseness: TURPI-
TUDE

vilify, abuse: REVILE

village: HAMLET

vinegary: ACETOUS

violation of a law or a pledge: INFRAC-
TION

violation of conventional language usage:
SOLECISM

violation or profaning of anything sacred:
SACRILEGE

violent, impetuous, ardent: VEHEMENT

violent, intermittent: SPASMODIC

violent, stormy: TEMPESTUOUS

violent, sudden outburst: PAROXYSM

violent and loud denunciation: FULMINA-
TION

violent disturbance: CATACLYSM

violent outbreak: RAMPAGE

violent reaction: BACKLASH

violently destructive: BERSERK

violinist who leads his section of an orchestra: CONCERT MASTER

violin-like instrument, but slightly larger and tuned lower: VIOLA

virgin, woman of pure character: VESTAL

visible or observable occurrence or experience: PHENOMENON

visible to the naked eye: MACROSCOPIC

vision blurring or temporary loss caused by oxygen deficiency, experienced especially by pilots: GRAYOUT

vision defect in which specks or threads appear to float before the eyes: MUSCAE VOLITANTES

vision, dimmed: PURBLIND

vision less distinct by day than by night, day blindness: HEMERALOPIA

vision of something not actually present: HALLUCINATION

vision or discernment faulty: MYOPIA

vision that is distorted: ASTIGMATISM

vision that is normal at 20 feet: 20-20 VISION

visionary or dreamer: FANTAST

visionary or imaginary semblance: SIMULACRUM

visit frequently or habitually: RESORT

visitor who frequents a place: HABITUÉ

visual arts involving the use of lines or strokes on a flat surface, as painting or drawing: GRAPHIC ARTS

visual defects treated by exercises: ORTHOPTICS

visualizing objects previously seen: EIDETIC IMAGERY

vital principle: ANIMA

vital statistics as of births, deaths, disease: DEMOGRAPHY

vivacity, enthusiasm, dash: ÉLAN

vivacity, lively spirits, gaiety, sparkle: EFFERVESCENCE

vivid: GRAPHIC

vivid, sensational, shocking, violent: LURID

vividly bright, shining with brilliance, dazzling: RESPLENDENT

vocabulary of a class or group: ARGOT

vocabulary or jargon of a profession or class: LINGO

vocabularly that is specialized or technical and used by members of a particular group: JARGON

vocal quality that is dry and rough or coarse: HUSKY

vocalist's runs and trills: COLORATURA

vodka and tomato juice cocktail: BLOODY MARY

vodka and orange juice cocktail: SCREWDRIVER

voice of a male higher than a tenor: COUNTERTENOR

voice of the people: VOX POPULI

voice on television commenting on the picture or narrating: VOICE-OVER

voice tone or pitch variations or modulations: INFLECTION

voice-affecting throat irritation: LARYNGITIS

void, undo: NULLIFY

voiding, nullifying: DEFEASANCE

voiding, nullifying: DIRIMENT

volatile, lively, changeable: MERCURIAL

volume of bids and offers on stocks is relatively low: THIN MARKET

vomit: REGURGITATE

vomit-causing medicine: EMETIC

vomiting: EMESIS

vomiting action causing strain: RETCH

vote against: BLACKBALL

vote to obtain the people's will on an issue: PLEBISCITE

vote that is unofficial and used to determine group opinion: STRAW VOTE

voters or supporters: CONSTITUENCY

votes and influence traded between politicians: LOGROLLING

votes for a candidate in excess of the number cast for his nearest opponent: PLURALITY

vowel for changed tense, etc.: ABLAUT

vowel inserted into word: ANAPTYXIS

vowel lost at beginning of a word (alone, lone): APHESIS

vowel marking (straight line) over vowel to indicate long sound: MACRON

vowel that is neutral, occurring in unstressed syllables in English: SCHWA

vulgar, common: PLEBEIAN

vulgar, disreputable, tawdry: RAFFISH

vulgar, obscene: FESCENNINE

vulgar language or behavior: BAWDRY

vulgar or coarse joking: RIBALD

vulgar, sexual, cheap: RAUNCHY

vulgar talk: BILLINGSGATE

vulnerable: PREGNABLE

vulnerable point: ACHILLES' HEEL

W

wad of compressed cotton or lint used for a wound: PLEDGET

wages remaining after payroll deductions: TAKE-HOME PAY

wagon maker: WAINWRIGHT

wagon without sides: LORRY

wail, howl, hoot: ULULATE

wail, whimper, cry: PULE

wailing lament for the deceased: KEEN

waist measure: GIRTH

waistband that is broad and worn with men's formal clothes: CUMMERBUND

wait for and accost: WAYLAY

waiter or waitress at a drive-in restaurant: CARHOP

waiting room in theater used by performers when they are off-stage: GREEN ROOM

walk, able to: AMBULATORY

walk about idly or aimlessly, gad about: TRAIPSE

walk around something: CIRCUMAMBULATE

walk clumsily with short steps, swaying from side to side: WADDLE

walk heavily: CLUMP

walk laboriously, trudge: PLOD

walk leisurely: AMBLE

walk leisurely, stroll: SAUNTER

walk with a latticework roof, arbor: PERGOLA

walker: PEDESTRIAN

walking or moving about, itinerant: PERIPATETIC

walking space that is narrow and elevated: CATWALK

walking with short, dainty steps: MINCING

wall bracket that holds candles or lights: SCONCE

wall hanging attached to a roller devised by Japanese: KAKEMONO

wall of stone, cement, etc., for protective purposes: REVETMENT

wall painting by an artist: MURAL

wall paneling or wood or marble: WAINSCOT

wall scribblings or drawings: GRAFFITI

wan, colorless: PALLID

wand or staff of Mercury, symbol of medical profession: CADUCEUS

wander from main subject: DIGRESS

wander idly or without plan: MEANDER

wander or stray aimlessly, digress: DIVAGATE

wander or turn aside from main subject: DIGRESS

wanderer, tramp: VAGABOND

wanderer without a permanent home: NOMAD

wandering, roving, straying, itinerant: ERRANT

wandering away from the right way: ABERRANCE

wandering from the point, passing quickly from one subject to another: DISCURSIVE

wanting one's own way: WAYWARD

wanton or lewd: CYPRIAN

ward off: STAVE OFF

ward off, avoid, turn aside: PARRY

ward off, drive back: REPEL

warding off, preventing: PREVENTIVE

wardrobe with drawers on one side: CHIFFOROBE

warhead of a missile: PAYLOAD

warlike, brave, disciplined: SPARTAN

warm, glowing, earnest: FERVENT

warmth, or increasing warmth: CALESCENCE

warn, presage, foreshadow: PORTEND
warning: CAVEAT
warning, danger sign, especially in zoology: SEMATIC
warning notice: MONITION
warning, omen, portent: PRESAGE
warning system by radar in North America: DEW LINE
war-provoking event: CASUS BELLI
wart or other skin growth: KERATOSIS
washing the body: ABLUTION
wasps or a wasp colony: VESPIARY
waste matter, refuse: DROSS
waste matter from the bowels, feces: EXCREMENT
waste matter removal, as by kidneys or intestines: EMUNCTORY
waste or entrails of a butchered animal: OFFAL
waste time, dawdle, loiter: DILLY-DALLY
waste time, dwadle: PIDDLE
waste time, loiter: DAWDLE
wasted, scattered: DISSIPATED
wasteful, extravagant, lavish: PRODIGAL
wasting away: TABESCENT
wasting or withering away: ATROPHY
watch kept over one: SURVEILLANCE
watch kept, usually at night: VIGIL
watchful, alert: VIGILANT
watchful, suspicious: JEALOUS
watching and guarding carefully: WARY
watchman, keeper, guard: WARDER
water channel made with a gate to regulate the flow: SLUICE
water craft with winglike structures that lift the hull above water at certain speeds: HYDROFOIL
water cure: HYDROPATHY
water nymph: NAIAD
water nymph of folklore, who could obtain a soul by marrying a human and bearing his child: UNDINE
water of the soil not available to plants: ECHARD
water or land vehicle or creature: AMPHIBIAN
water search with a divining rod: DOWSE
water signs as a means of divination: HYDROMANCY
water tower: STANDPIPE
waterfront or river vessels laborer: ROUSTABOUT
waterproof hat: SOUTHWESTER
waters of the earth, as a study: HYDROLOGY

waters under the jurisdiction of a state: TERRITORIAL WATERS
watertight chamber for construction in a body of water: COFFERDAM
watery: AQUEOUS
wave or flood: SPRING TIDE
wave that breaks on reef, rock or shore: BREAKER
wavelike or watered appearance, as in fabrics: MOIRÉ
waver, sway, totter: VACILLATE
wavering, undecided: IRRESOLUTE
wavering, unsteady: FLUCTUATING
waving motion: WAFTURE
wavy, winding: SINUOUS
wavy in appearance or motion: UNDULATING
way of entry: ACCESS
wayfarer, traveler: VIATOR
waylay: AMBUSH
weak: ANILE
weak, barren: EFFETE
weak, careless, reckless: FECKLESS
weak, cowardly: PUSILLANIMOUS
weak, emaciated condition: CACHEXIA
weak, flimsy, unsubstantial: TENUOUS
weak, ineffective: IMPOTENT
weak, listless, lacking animation: LANGUID
weak, loose: SLACK
weak, self-indulgent: EFFEMINATE
weak, unconvincing, fragile: FLIMSY
weaken, destroy the affection of: DISAFFECT
weaken, hang down: FLAG
weaken, make feeble or languid: DEBILITATE
weaken, pine, droop gradually: LANGUISH
weaken, sap the strength of, devitalize: ENERVATE
weaken by degrees, impair secretly: UNDERMINE
weakness, fatigue, spiritlessness, dreaminess, dullness, stagnation: LANGUOR
weakness or failing in one's character: FOIBLE
wealth, riches: OPULENCE
wealthy, fashionable people: JET SET
wealthy, powerful industrialist: TYCOON
wealthy man: CROESUS
wealthy person who has become so only recently: NOUVEAU RICHE
wear away by friction: ABRADE
wearied, exhausted, sated, worn-out, dulled from overindulgence: JADED

wearing away or eating away of a substance: CORROSION

wearing off or rubbing off of particles: DETRITION

wearisome, boring: TEDIOUS

weary, vex, annoy: IRK

weather that is dark and threatening: LOWERING

weather and atmospheric conditions, as a science: METEOROLOGY

weather-beaten and rugged: GNARLED

weave together, combine, blend: INTERLACE

webfooted: SYNDACTYL

wedding song or poem: HYMENEAL

wedged or packed firmly: IMPACTED

wedge-shaped especially as used in ancient writing: CUNEAL, CUNEIFORM

weed killer: HERBICIDE

weeping or grief that is false: CROCODILE TEARS

weigh down, burden, hamper: CUMBER

weighing, resting, leaning upon something: INCUMBENT

weight: HEFT

weight a missile can lift and carry to a target: THROW-WEIGHT

weight lost, abnormally lean: EMACIATED

weight of container deducted to find weight of contents: TARE

weight unit for gems: CARAT

weightlessness, in space: ZERO GRAVITY

weird, ghostly: EERIE

weird, unnatural, eerie, strange: UNCANNY

welcome or acceptable person: PERSONA GRATA

welcome with an outburst of applause: OVATION

well-being, relaxation, happiness: EUPHORIA

well-being or happiness as found in a life of moderation: EUDEMONIA

well-bred, distinguished, dignified: DISTINGUÉ

well-bred in one's ways, refinement: GENTILITY

well-chosen, apt, agreeable in manner or style: FELICITOUS

well-groomed: SOIGNÉ

well-groomed, smooth, glossy: SLEEK

werewolf: LYCANTHROPE

West Indian, Spanish American or Gulf State inhabitant of European descent: CREOLE

western hemisphere: OCCIDENT

whale oil: TRAIN OIL

wharf for loading and unloading vessels: QUAY

wharf or pier to protect a harbor or beach: JETTY

wheedle: CAJOLE

wheedle or flatter: BLANDISH

wheel, spiked or toothed, at the end of a spur: ROWEL

wheel about: CARACOLE

wheel heavy enough to resist sudden changes of speed: FLYWHEEL

wheel on a fixed axis and containing seats hanging from frame: FERRIS WHEEL

wheel-shaped: ROTIFORM

wheels with the rims slanted in or out from the hub: DISHED

while away the time: BEGUILE

whim: CAPRICE

whimper, wail, cry: PULE

whining, complaining, fretful: QUERULOUS

whip or scourge: FLAGELLATE

whiplash-like, long, slender and flexible: FLAGELLIFORM

whirling, revolving or circular motion: GYRAL

whirling, rotating rapidly: VORTICOSE

whirling, spinning, dizzy: VERTIGINOUS

whirling on the toes in ballet dancing: PIROUETTE

whirlwind or whirlpool: VORTEX

whirlpool: MAELSTROM

whisky and vermouth cocktail: MANHATTAN

whisper intended to be overheard: STAGE WHISPER

whispering, rustling, softly murmuring: SUSURRANT

whistle or call derisively: CATCALL

white linen worn around the neck by a priest: AMICE

white- or gray-haired, ancient, venerable: HOARY

whiten or turn yellowish, as a plant does when kept from sunlight: ETIOLATE

whitening: ALBESCENT

white-skinned and pink-eyed person: ALBINO

who goes there?: QUI VIVE?

whole, unchanged, undamaged: INTACT

whole composed of originally separate parts: SYNTHESIS

whole number: INTEGER

whole, untaxed, uninjured: SCOT-FREE

whole that is uninterrupted: CONTINUUM
wholesaler: JOBBER
wholesome: SALUTARY
whore: HARLOT
whorehouse: BORDELLO
wicked: INIQUITOUS
wicked, atrocious: FLAGITIOUS
wicked, atrocious, odious: HEINOUS
wicked, erring: PERVERSE
wicked, ominous: SINISTER
wicked, vicious woman: JEZEBEL
wicked, vile: NEFARIOUS
wickedness, monstrous act: ENORMITY
wicker receptacle for documents or valuables: HANAPER
wide-awake, on the alert: ON THE QUI VIVE
widely practiced, common: PREVALENT
widen, swell, expand: DILATE
widespread: RAMPANT
widespread, prevalent: RIFE
widespread, universal, also general epidemic: PANDEMIC
wife: HELPMEET
wife or husband: CONSORT
wifely: UXORIAL
wig for a man: TOUPEE
wild: BERSERK
wild, irresponsible, reckless: HARUM-SCARUM
wild, riotous: TURBULENT
wild, savage: FERAL
wild, unchecked: RAMPANT
wild, unexpected action: VAGARY
wild or wanton revelry, drunken carousal, debauchment: ORGY
wild party: BACCHANAL
wild prank or escapade: CAPER
wild uproar: PANDEMONIUM
wildly excited: DELIRIOUS
will exercised: VOLITION
will maker, one who has left a will: TESTATOR
will rather than reason stressed as the active factor in man's role in a hostile world: EXISTENTIALISM
willful, capricious: WAYWARD
willing, desirous: SOLICITOUS
willingly, readily: LIEF
willingly or unwillingly: WILLY-NILLY
willingness that is cheerful: ALACRITY
will-o'-the-wisp, delusion: IGNIS FATUUS
willowy, slender, slim: SVELTE
willy-nilly: NOLENS VOLENS
wily, treacherous, cunning: INSIDIOUS

win by cleverness: OUTWIT
win over, appease: PROPITIATE
win the favor or confidence of others by deliberate effort: INGRATIATE
wind, cold and dry, that blows from the north through southern France: MISTRAL
wind, hot, dry, and full of sand, especially in deserts: SIMOOM
wind, hot and dusty, that blows from the African coast to Europe: SIROCCO
wind, soft and gentle: ZEPHYR
wind direction indicator consisting of a cone-spaced cloth bag, as at an airfield: WINDSOCK
wind from ahead blowing directly opposite to the course of a ship: HEAD WIND
wind from the east in Mediterranean regions: LEVANTER
wind from the Sahara that blows in the Middle East before the vernal equinox: KHAMSIN
wind in a sudden, violent burst, usually accompanied by rain or snow: SQUALL
wind in and out: SINUATE
wind is blowing toward this direction: LEEWARD
wind moving in a cold, sudden, violent blast down a mountain to the sea: WILLIWAW
wind of the Argentine pampas: PAMPERO
wind science: ANEMOLOGY
wind-driven rain or snow: SCUD
winding: TORTUOUS
winding and turning: ANFRACTUOUS
winding or bending, wavering, unsteady: FLEXUOUS
winding path: AMBAGE
window, a throw out of: DEFENESTRATION
window, balcony or porch with an excellent view, in Spanish architecture: MIRADOR
window division, a vertical dividing piece in the opening: MULLION
window frame: SASH
window in a spire: LUCARNE
window opening vertically in the middle as a double door does: FRENCH WINDOW
window or any small opening suggestive of a window: FENESTELLA
window or doorway covering that covers

only top half of opening: LAM-BREQUIN

window side post: JAMB

window slats, horizontal and overlapping: LOUVER BOARD

window that opens on hinges at the side: CASEMENT

window that projects from a sloping roof: DORMER

windstorm that is brief, gust of wind: FLAW

windy pomposity, pretentiousness: FLATULENCE

wine aroma: BOUQUET

wine bottle holding almost four quarts: JEROBOAM

wine bottle or large vessel with handle and spout used for serving liquids: FLAGON

wine bottle twice the ordinary size: MAGNUM

wine measure of about 18 wine gallons: RUNDLET

wine merchant: VINTNER

wine named for the principal grape from which it is made: VARIETAL

wine named for the region where its type originated: GENERIC WINE

wine of no distinction, cheap red wine: VIN ORDINAIRE

wine steward: SOMMELIER

wines and winemaking as a study: OENOLOGY

wing: PINION

wink: NICTITATE

winning of every event, as in a series: SWEEP

winter's beginning when the sun is farthest south of the Equator, about Dec. 21: WINTER SOLSTICE

wintry,: HIBERNAL

wintry: HIEMAL

wipe off or cleanse: DETERGE

wipe out: EXPUNGE

wipe out, destroy completely: OBLITERATE

wire, rope or cable used to steady or secure something: GUY

wisdom, discernment: SAGACITY

wise: SAPIENT

wise, prudent: JUDICIOUS

wise, prudent, diplomatic: POLITIC

wise, shrewd: SAGACIOUS

wise person, infallible authority: ORACLE

wise saying, maxim: GNOME

wise statement: APHORISM

wishful thinking modifying reality: AUTISM

witches' sabbath on April 30, the eve of May Day: WALPURGIS NIGHT

with reference to: APROPOS

withdraw, move backward: RECEDE

withdraw a contestant from a race, etc.: SCRATCH

withdraw formally from an organization: SECEDE

withdraw in fear, lose heart: QUAIL

withdraw or end by plan: PHASE OUT

withdraw or remove from former habits: WEAN

withered, shriveled, shrunken: WIZENED

withering or wasting away: ATROPHY

withering, mercilessly severe, harsh: SCATHING

within the same school, college, etc.: INTRAMURAL

without a center: ACENTRIC

without a date being set (for the next meeting): SINE DIE

without dividend: EX-DIVIDEND

without warning: UNAWARES

witness's sworn statements in court: TESTIMONY

witticism: SALLY

witty, characterized by higher and finer qualities of the mind: SPIRITUEL

witty, quick replies: REPARTEE

witty, short saying: MOT

witty, terse statement: EPIGRAM

witty remark: BON MOT

witty remark or gibe: QUIP

wizard, sorcerer: WARLOCK

woeful tale, complaint, lament: JEREMIAD

woman, elderly, dignified, wealthy: DOWAGER

woman, old and ugly: CRONE

woman adviser: EGERIA

woman beside herself with frenzy or excitement: MAENAD

woman hater: MISOGYNIST

woman hired to suckle a child of another: WET NURSE

woman living under canon law in a community, but not under vows: CANONESS

woman-man relationship without sexual activity: PLATONIC

woman or women forming the government: GYNARCHY

woman servant in Orient: AMAH

woman to whom a man is engaged: FIAN-CÉE

women who have lost social position and reputation because of promiscuity: DEMIMONDE

woman who is abusive and scolding, shrew: TERMAGANT

woman who is aggressive, domineering: BATTLE-AX

woman who is disreputable, ill-tempered, perverse: JADE

woman who is divorced, separated or lives apart from her husband: GRASS WIDOW

woman who is dowdy and sometimes also ill-tempered: FRUMP

woman who is homosexual: LESBIAN

woman who is sharp-tongued or a scold: VIRAGO

woman who is untidy or slovenly: SLATTERN

woman who is vicious or hateful: HARRIDAN

woman who is voluptuous but treacherous: DELILAH

woman who is wicked and vicious: JEZEBEL

woman who lives with a man though not married to him: CONCUBINE

woman whose allure leads to downfall of men: FEMME FATALE

womanhood, femininity: MULIEBRITY

womanlike, unmanly, weak, soft: EFFEMINATE

woman's dressing room: BOUDOIR

woman's legal status in marriage: COVERTURE

woman's paid escort: GIGOLO

woman's trousers that resemble a skirt: CULOTTE

woman's work and domain traditionally: DISTAFF

women in general: DISTAFF

wonderful or marvelous to tell: MIRABILE DICTU

wood from broad-leaved deciduous trees, as oak or maple: HARDWOOD

wood in a thin, broad piece, as that forming the back of a chair: SPLAT

wood in thin flexible strips, as used for basketmaking: SPLINT

wood layers glued together: PLYWOOD

wooded: ARBORACEOUS

wooden vessel for butter or lard: FIRKIN

woodworking knife with a handle at each end: DRAWKNIFE

woodworking training system: SLOYD

woolly or crispy hair: ULOTRICHOUS

word, phrase, or clause inserted into a sentence to add explanation or comment: PARENTHESIS

word adopted from another language and partly or completely naturalized: LOANWORD

word blindness: ALEXIA

word categories, of which there are eight in English: PARTS OF SPEECH

word choice and arrangement in speaking or writing: DICTION

word coined for a single or special occasion: NONCE WORD

word derived from the same root as another: PARONYM

word-for-word: TEXTUAL

word formed by combining parts of two words: PORTMANTEAU WORD, CENTAUR WORD, BLEND WORD

word formed by transposing letters of another: ANAGRAM

word formed from initial letters of lines: ACROSTIC

word formed from initial letters or syllables of series of words: ACRONYM

word game in which a rhyme must be given for word or line given by another: CRAMBO

word group between punctuation stops: SENTENCE

word hard to pronounce: JAWBREAKER

word having the same, similar, or equivalent meaning as another word: SYNONYM

word identical with another in spelling, but having different origin and meaning: HOMOGRAPH

word inflection: ACCIDENCE

word interpretation largely spiritual and mystical: ANAGOGE

word list, with definitions, of technical, obscure or foreign words of a work or field: GLOSSARY

word of more than three syllables: POLYSYLLABLE

word opposite in meaning to another word: ANTONYM

word or expression that is not standard: BARBARISM

word or phrase often repeated, as a slogan: CATCHWORD

word or phrase serving only to complete a rhythm or a pattern: EXPLETIVE

word or prhase that is an exclamation or obscene oath: EXPLETIVE

word or phrase that is substituted for another to avoid giving offense or pain: EUPHEMISM

word or saying that is familiar to most people: HOUSEHOLD WORD

word or sentence that reads the same backward as forward: PALINDROME

word order inverted: ANASTROPHE

word origin popularly conceived but erroneous: FOLK ETYMOLOGY

word origins and development, as a study: ETYMOLOGY

word puzzle, as an anagram: LOGOGRIPH

word selection and arrangement: PHRASEOLOGY

word spelled like another but having a different sound and meaning: HETERONYM

word spoken, considered only as sound: VOCABLE

word structure, as a study: MORPHOLOGY

word that has been coined or existing word that has been given a new meaning: NEOLOGISM

word that is a compound and is divided by an intervening word: TMESIS

word that makes a statement misleading or ambiguous: WEASEL WORD

word use that is effective: RHETORIC

word used humorously in two different meanings: PUN

word used in cabalistic charms: ABRACADABRA

word used in sense opposite to its meaning, ironically,: ANTIPHRASIS

word widely used without regard to its exact meaning: COUNTER WORD

word with no accent but pronounced as part of preceding word: ENCLITIC

word with several different meanings: POLYSEMY

word with the same sound as another but different meaning: HOMONYM

wordiness: VERBIAGE

wordiness, circumlocution: PERIPHRASIS

wordless drama played with gestures: PANTOMIME

word's alteration by shifting to its beginning the final consonant of a preceding word: PROVECTION

words altered by transposing sounds or parts unintentionally: SPOONERISM

words and word groups, their development and changes of meaning, as a subject of study: SEMANTICS

words in phrases, clauses and sentences in terms of their arrangement and interrelationship: SYNTAX

words in a series each having same initial sound: ALLITERATION

word's last syllable: ULTIMA

words of one language altered to resemble words in another, usually for humorous effect: MACARONIC

words of wisdom: APOTHEGM

words or book of an opera: LIBRETTO

words or expressions placed next to each other, the second explaining the first: APPOSITION

words that reflect natural sounds, or the use of such words: ONOMATOPOEIA

wordy, long-winded: DIFFUSE

wordy, superfluous: REDUNDANT

wordy, tedious: PROLIX

wordy, wearisome in conversation: VERBOSE

work at: PLY

work avoided by pretending of sickness: MALINGER

work clumsily: BUNGLE

work crew selection, especially among longshoremen: SHAPEUP

work expands to fill the time allotted to it: PARKINSON'S LAW

work for which one is particularly suited; forte: MÉTIER

work shift beginning at midnight: GRAVEYARD SHIFT

work shift usually from 4 p.m. until midnight: SWING SHIFT

work slowdown caused by employes' ostensibly following the rules closely: JOB ACTION

work tediously: PLOD

work that is dull and wearisome: DRUDGERY

workable, practicable: VIABLE

worker, clerical or professional: WHITE COLLAR

worker who is ultraconservative: HARD HAT

worker, unskilled or semiskilled: BLUE COLLAR

workers employed in excess of actual needs: FEATHERBEDDING

workers' organization in a single company and unaffiliated with other unions: COMPANY UNION

working class: PROLETARIAT

working independently, as a writer or artist, for instance, rather than for one employer: FREE LANCE

working on a job in addition to one's regular occupation: MOONLIGHTING

working or moving, effective: OPERATIVE

working with the hands, work done by hand: HANDICRAFT

workshop: ATELIER

world and life as viewed comprehensively: WELTANSCHAUUNG

world betterment: MELIORISM

worldly, as opposed to narrow or parochial: COSMOPOLITAN

worldly, sensual, carnal: FLESHLY

worldly as distinguished from spiritual or religious: SECULAR

worldly-wise: SOPHISTICATED

world-weariness: WELTSCHMERZ

world-wide, general, universal, especially concerning the church: ECUMENICAL

worn, gaunt, or wild look, as from fatigue, hunger or anxiety: HAGGARD

worn out, exhausted, sated, dulled from overindulgence: JADED

worn out or enfeebled by age or use: DE-CREPIT

worried, tense, bewildered, agitated, crazed: DISTRAUGHT

worry, harass: CHEVY

worry, harass: HARRY

worry, torment relentlessly: HARASS

worry-free, carefree: SANS SOUCI

worse, inferior, morally degraded: DEGENERATE

worsen as in quality or power: IMPAIR

worsening, declining, going backward: RETROGRADE

worship given properly only to God, in the Roman Catholic Church: LATRIA

worship of idols: IDOLATRY

worthless: CHEESE-PARING

worthless, meaningless: NUGATORY

worthless, rubbish, nonsense: TRUMPERY

worthlessness or futility imposed on something or someone: STULTIFIED

wounds that Christ received during the Passion and Crucifixion: STIGMATA

wrangle, bandy words: SPAR

wrangling, quarrel: JANGLE

wreck, pillage, ruin: RAVAGE

wreckage that is afloat or washed up on shore: FLOTSAM

wrestler or boxer over 175 pounds: HEAVYWEIGHT

wrestler or boxer weighing between 127 and 135 pounds: LIGHTWEIGHT

wrestler or boxer weighing between 136 and 147 pounds: WELTERWEIGHT

wrestler or boxer weighing between 147 and 160 pounds: MIDDLEWEIGHT

wrestler or boxer weighing between 161 and 175 pounds: LIGHT HEAVY-WEIGHT

wrestler weighing up to 134 pounds or a boxer up to 126 pounds: FEATHER-WEIGHT

wrestling hold in which an arm is passed under the opponent's armpit and the hand pressed against the back of his head: HALF NELSON

wrestling hold in which arms are under the opponent's armpits from the back and hands against his neck: FULL NELSON

wrestling hold in which opponent's arm is twisted behind his back and upward: HAMMERLOCK

wrestling hold in which the wrestler's head is gripped between his opponent's arm and body: HEADLOCK

wrestling term for head caught and held under opponent's arm: CHANCERY

wrestling throw: FLYING MARE

wretched, cheerless, abandoned, deserted: FORLORN

wrinkle or pucker: COCKLE

writ authorizing seizure of property: AT-TACHMENT

writ ordering that a person be brought before a court: HABEAS CORPUS

write: INDITE

write, mark or engrave, especially for some solemn or public purpose: IN-SCRIBE

write or speak more fully, elaborate: EX-PATIATE

write or study laboriously: LUCUBRATE

write out, compose or edit: REDACT

writer of articles, books, speeches for someone else to whom the authorship will be attributed: GHOSTWRITER

writer of polemical pamphlets: PAM-PHLETEER

writers, scholars, men of letters: LITERATI

writer's assumed name: PEN NAME

writer's name at head of article: BYLINE

writing describing a pleasant, peaceful scene: IDYLL

writing desk: ESCRITOIRE

writing difficult to decipher: HIERO-GLYPHICS

writing in which lines alternately read left to right and right to left: BOU-STROPHEDON

writing of an ancient mode: PALEOGRAPHY

writing of words or phrases erroneously because of cerebral injury: PARA-GRAPHIA

writing or printing with flowing lines: CURSIVE

writing paper measuring about 13 by 16 inches: FOOLSCAP

writing prose in line lengths corresponding to the sense: STICHOMETRY

writing technique that records inner thoughts and feelings of characters: STREAM-OF-CONSCIOUSNESS

writing that is backward and readable in a mirror: MIRROR WRITING

writing that is long and tiresome: SCREED

written statement or graphic representation that is false or malicious and damaging to person's reputation: LIBEL

wrong; if anything can go wrong, it will: MURPHY'S LAW

wrong name: MISNOMER

wrongdoing, especially by a public official: MALFEASANCE

wrongdoing or guilt implied: INCRIMINA-TION

wrongful act, unjust thing or deed, sin: INIQUITY

wrongful act not involving breach of contract but a possible basis for a suit: TORT

wrongful use: ABUSE

Y

yarn length: SPINDLE
yarn length equaling 80 yards for wool, 120 for cotton, 300 for linen: LEA
yarn or thread wound in a coil: SKEIN
yawning or sleepiness: OSCITANCY
yearn, desire, crave: HANKER
year or period that is critical: CLIMACTERIC
year-old animal: YEARLING
yellow fever: VOMITO
yellowish complexion: SALLOW
yellowish-green color, sea-green: GLAUCOUS
yelp or bark: YAWP
yes, just so; used after a quoted word or phrase to indicate that it is accurate: SIC
yield to or gratify, as one's desires: INDULGE

yield weakly or with bad grace, cringe: TRUCKLE
yielding, persuadable: PLIANT
yielding courteously or respectfully to the wishes or opinions of another: DEFERENCE
yielding readily in an emotional way: SUSCEPTIBLE
young and innocent woman: INGÉNUE
young man, youth: SPRIG
young or becoming young: JUVENESCENCE
youthful, fresh, springlike: VERNAL
youthful days of freshness and inexperience: SALAD DAYS
youthful feeling or vigor restored: REJUVENATION
you've scored a point, you've got me: TOUCHÉ

zeal that is extravagant or frenzied: FA-
    NATICISM
zenith, highest point of anything: MERID-
    IAN

zest, enthusiasm: GUSTO
zestless, dull: PERFUNCTORY
zigzag course in sailing: TACK

Index of Key Words

aba 9, 72, 161
abacus 5, 24
abaft 167, 179
abalone 111, 157
abase 83, 103, 143
abashed 48, 56
abate 47, 99, 143
abattoir 160
abbreviate 33, 158
abbreviated 35
abdicate 73, 145, 172
abduct 25, 95
abecedarian 7, 15, 16, 55, 99, 117, 150
aberrance 46, 191
aberration 45, 46, 108
abet 10, 56, 80, 172
abeyance 45, 172, 175
abhor 46
abhorrence 46, 102
abigail 97, 104
abiosis 3, 100
abirritant 108, 163
abjure 143, 145, 146, 147
ablaut 27, 190
ablegate 125
abluent 29, 46
ablution 15, 26, 144, 192
abnegation 45, 145, 154
abnegate 73
abnormality 92, 105
abode 53, 82, 146
abolition 160
a bon marché 14
A-bomb 11, 117
aboriginal 88, 115, 135
abort 56, 62, 110, 134, 186
about-face 27, 147
aboveboard 117, 121, 183
abracadabra 104, 107, 117, 197
abrade 150, 153, 192
abreaction 144, 174
abreast 158
abridge 33, 99, 158
abridgment 64

abrogate 8, 50, 145
abscission 41, 145
abscond 45, 58, 150, 154
absolution 69, 135, 145
absolutism 46, 75, 185
absonant 48, 185
abstain 45, 82, 144
abstemious 52, 54, 164, 175
abstract 117, 171, 177
abstruse 33, 47, 79, 81
abuse 199
abusive 90, 152
abut 20, 178
abutting 56, 159
academe 152
academic 131, 164, 177
a cappella 159, 183
a capriccio 112, 175
acatalectic 131
acaudal 174
accede 6, 31, 34, 57
access 5, 9, 57, 122, 126, 192
accidence 89, 188, 196
accidental 17, 117
accommodation ladder 97
accordion pleats 130
accost 162
accreditation 9
accrescence 60, 76
acculturation 5, 40
acedia 108, 165, 178
acentric 26, 195
acephalous 80, 99
acerb 10, 18, 79, 157, 163
acerbate 56, 92
acescent 164
acetous 189
acheron 78, 149
Achilles' heel 162, 190
achromatopsia 31
acolyte 7, 10
acoustic 163
acquest 4
acquiesce 34

acquiescence 10, 126, 139
acrid 18, 137, 157
acrimonious 18, 26, 151
acronical 148, 167, 172
acronym 89, 196
acrophobia 128
acrostic 89, 131, 196
actuary 24, 90
acuate 157
acumen 90, 95, 108, 139
acupuncture 28, 108, 116
adactylous 65, 178
adage 137, 152
adagio 161
adamant 79, 86, 186
addled 34, 110, 170
addle-brained 34, 110, 170
addleheaded 34, 110, 170
addlepated 34, 110, 170
adduce 29
adeem 147, 174
a deux 91
ad hoc 125, 164
ad hoc committee 32, 164
ad hominem 8, 134
adiaphorous 52, 111
adieu 63, 74
ad infinitum 69, 101, 184
adipose 63
adjudicate 4, 94
adjure 8, 54
ad lib 60, 87, 169
adminicle 11, 80, 172
admonish 5, 145
admonition 73, 109
ad nauseaum 158
adobe 21, 172
Adonis 78, 105
adoptive parents 125
adroit 46, 60, 160
adulate 61, 64, 66, 133, 155
adulterate 36, 43, 87
adumbral 123, 156
adumbrate 69, 123, 160
ad valorem 188
advent 133
adventitious 4, 61, 117
adversative 121
aegis 11, 137, 165
aerialist 81, 179
aerate 138
aerie 81, 116
aeroneurosis 6, 67
aerophobia 128
aesopian language 33, 98

afebrile 64, 70
affable 54, 70
affect 56, 170
affectation 10, 134
affective 8, 56
affidavit 119, 173
affinity 115, 144
afflatus 87
affray 21, 50, 65, 137
affront 88, 90
aficionado 46, 57, 63
Afrikaans 164
Afro-American 18
aft 142, 167
aftermath 34, 147
agape 103, 162
agate line 5, 107
agent provocateur 6, 137
age of consent 5
agglomerate 72, 94, 107
aggrandize 57, 85, 90
aggrieve 73, 76, 163
aghast 49, 82
agiotage 110
agnate 144, 159
agnation 104
agnosticism 74, 139
agog 54
agonistic 9, 169
agora 10, 106, 137
agoraphobia 128
agrapha 93, 152
agrarian 6, 97
agrestic 115, 150, 185
agrology 152, 162
agronomy 97, 152
agrypnotic 134
ahimsa 6, 50
aichinophobia 128
ailuromania 105
ailurophobia 128
akimbo 78
a la carte 47, 108
alacrity 28, 102, 194
albescent 76, 193
albinism 129
albino 129, 193
albumen 55
Albuquerquean 6
alchemy 108, 179
al dente 28, 66
aleatory, 45, 72
alexia 142, 196
algolagnia 106, 151, 156
algophobia 128

algorism 9, 43
alienation 89, 108
aliment 67, 117, 172
allantoid 152
allegory 169
allegro 63, 113
alliteration 89, 145, 163, 196
allonym 115
allopathy 48, 179
allusion 88
alluvium 119, 162
aloha 79
alopecia 13
altercation 7, 49, 139
alter ego 70, 91, 153, 171
altimeter 7, 80
altruism 103, 154, 186
amah 195
amalgam 18, 31
amanuensis 106, 153
amaurosis 102, 159
amazon 106
ambage 88, 126, 194
ambagious 46
ambidexter 51, 84
ambidextrous 20, 99, 148
ambience 11, 57, 64, 109, 172
ambiguous 51, 119, 149, 183, 188
ambit 101, 152, 165
ambitendency 34
ambivalent 27, 183
ambivalence 35
amble 99, 191
ambsace 13, 99, 110, 116
ambulatory 16, 191
ambush 172, 192
ameliorate 15, 87, 104
amenable 6, 146, 170
amenity 130
amenities 29, 74, 131
ament 64, 85, 108
amentia 85, 108
amerce 45, 137
American plan 83, 107
amicable 70, 126
amice 193
amnesia 102, 108
amnesty 73, 125
amorphous 69, 111, 157, 185
amortization 75, 144
amortized 43, 100
ampere 55
ampersand 7, 173
amphibian 97, 192
amphibology 7, 51

amphigory 23, 117, 148
amphiscians 156, 178
amplification 57, 60
ampliation 57, 60
amulet 27, 58, 74
anabiosis 147
anabiotic 43
anachronism 58, 176
anacoluthon 75, 155
anacoustic 163
anacreontic 189
anadiplosis 145
anagoge 90, 120, 196
anagogic 114
anagram 179, 196
analects 31, 59, 69, 154
analeptic 52, 144
analgesia 124
analgesic 124
analogue 159
analogy 146, 159
analysand 137
anamnesis 143
anamorphism 49, 157
ananthous 67
anapest 131
anaphora 16, 145
anaphrodisis 156
anaphrodisia 156
anaptyxis 60, 190
anarchic 8
anarchism 75
anarchy 3, 49, 98, 132
anastrophe 91, 197
anathema 14, 40
anchorite 81, 143
anchor man 22, 35, 65
ancillary 6, 11, 172
andante 110, 113
andiron 66, 172
androcephalous 80, 165
androgynous 20, 81, 156
android 83, 105
androphobia 128
androsterone 82, 104
anemology 194
anencephalous 21
anergy 97
anfractuous 160, 178, 194
angary 16
Angelino 102
angelus 16
anglophobia 128
anguiform 162
anguilliform 55

angustate 33, 115
anile 64, 120, 192
anima 58, 163, 190
animadversion 39, 48
animism 87, 165
animus 79, 83
anodyne 124, 163
anomalous 3, 46, 92
antaphrodisiac 156
antediluvian 7, 8, 16, 120, 123
antemeridiem 16
antepenult 173, 177
anthology 31
anthomania 105
anthropocentric 105
anthropomorphism 83
anthroponomy 105
anthropopathy 83
anthropophagi 24
antiphony 163
antiphrasis 91, 197
antipodal 47, 121
antithesis 35, 47
antonomasia 57, 115, 171, 177
antonym 121, 196
apagoge 131, 177
apartheid 141, 164
apathetic 36, 56, 88, 184
apeirophobia 128
aperitif 6, 8
aphagia 183
aphanisis 64
aphasia 102
apheresis 52, 89
aphesis 102, 190
aphorism 4, 137, 195
aphotic 42
aphrodisiac 156
apiary 16
apimania 105
aplisade 64
aplomb 154
apocope 52
apocryphal 11, 166
apodictic 27, 45, 88
apodosis 33
apogee 30, 81, 122
apologetics 177
apologia 44
apologue 62
apophasis 108, 117
aposiopesis 21
apostasy 3, 46, 69, 99
apostrophe 5, 10, 47
apothegm 107, 129, 133, 197

apotheosis 44, 59, 74
appanage 45, 56, 115
appellation 115
apperception 34, 127
appetence 37, 46, 136
apposition 94, 197
apprise 89, 117
approbation 9
appurtenance 4, 5, 10
apraxia 87, 108
a priori 26, 73, 134
apropos 171, 178, 195
aqueous 192
aquiline 82
arable 40, 97
arbiter 43, 94, 183
arbitrage 23
arbitration 156
arboraceous 196
arboreal 180
arcane 81, 114, 153
archeology 47, 59, 82
archetype 122, 127, 137
archipelago 92, 153
arena theater 166, 177
areola 117
argent 80, 159
argonaut 24
Argonauts 74
argosy 66, 157
argot 93, 184, 190
aria 162
ariose 108, 163
aristocracy 17, 150, 186
Armageddon 15, 56
arithmetic progression 136
arpeggio 29, 117
arrant 117, 122
arrogate 11, 29, 187
arroyo 22, 77
ars gratia artis 10
articulated 94
artifact 83, 119
artificer 37, 160
art nouveau 10
ascender 135, 182, 187
ascetic 11
asceticism 154
ashcan school 10
askance 50, 159
asperity 18, 79, 149
asperse 160, 166
aspersions 62
asphyxia 183
asphyxiation 171

assassins 111
asseverate 44, 167
asseveration 132, 162
assiduous 11, 46, 127
assignation 103, 153
assonance 100, 159
asterisk 167
asteroid 167
asthenic 112, 161, 174
astigmatism 49, 190
astraphobia 129
astride 99, 121
astringent 11, 18, 79
astrophobia 129
asyndeton 34, 120, 121
ataraxia 126, 179, 180
atavism 135, 147
ataxia 102, 112
atelier 170, 198
athanasia 86
atheism 74, 144
atheneum 101
atherosclerosis 10, 177
athwart 4, 35, 87, 159
atonality 113
atrabilious 13, 108
atrophy 76, 169, 192, 195
attachment 136, 154, 198
attrition 128, 144
au courant 89, 186
audio 163, 175
audiovisual 163
audit 101
au fait 89
auf wiedersehen 73
au gratin 28
augury 69, 120, 132
august 12, 81, 86, 104
au jus 76
au lait 109
aural 54
aureole 78, 141
autarchy 3, 75
autarky 55
auteur 65
autism 43, 195
autocracy 3, 121
automania 105
automaton 8, 127
autonomous 88, 154
autonomy 154
autophobia 128
autumnal equinox 43
avant garde 99, 116
avarice 82

avaricious 110
avatar 87
aviary 17, 24
avulsion 69, 175
avuncular 183
axiom 107, 154

babushka 95, 152
baccalaureate 5, 75
bacchanal 52, 122, 194
backbencher 22
backdrop 40
backfield 68
backhand 176
backlash 142, 143, 189
backlog 146, 184
backstretch 141
badger 115
badinage 130, 175
baedeker 77
bagatelle 180
bagel 148, 149
baggage 87, 152
bagman 141
baguette 72, 119
bailiwick 9, 50, 165
baker's dozen 177
balalaika 150, 180
baldachin 25
balderdash 107, 117
balk 15
balkanize 21, 155
ballade 131, 189
ballerina 13
balletomania 105
ballistics 23, 152
ballistophobia 128
ballyhoo 5, 187
balneology 109
baluster 132
balustrade 78
bamboozle 28, 110, 180
banal 53, 122
bandolier 7
bandy 73, 75
bane 50
banquette 16
banter 130
barbarism 196
bard 131
bar-mitzvah 93
barnstorm 179
barnstorming 132
baroque 61, 122, 149

barrelhouse 93
bashaw 132
bas mitzvah (or bat or bath mitzvah) 93
bas-relief 142, 153
bassoon 90
baste 156
basting 168, 175
bastinado 15
bastion 69
bathophobia 128
bathos 63, 90, 155, 173
bathysphere 44
batten 63, 101
battle-ax 196
Bauhaus 9
bawdry 119, 190
bayou 106, 172
bay stater 107
beachcomber 188
be-all and end-all 6
bear market 44, 106, 168
bearer bond 19
bearish 128
beaucoup 189
beau geste 75
bedlam 34, 117
bedraggled 162, 186
beer and skittles 25, 52
beetle-browed 61
begrudge 146
beguile 28, 43, 193
behoove 116
belabor 15, 123
beldam 78, 183
beleaguer 17, 172
belie 63, 110, 137
belles-lettres 101
bellicose 139
bellicosity 7, 83
bellweather 98
belvedere 83
bemused 17, 50, 134
bench 171
benched 130
bench mark 167
benday 51
benedict 106, 116
benediction 18
benefactor 73
beneficiary 143
Benelux 55
benighted 85
benign 63, 73, 95, 109
benignant 75
bent 87, 175

bequeath 73, 78, 179
bereaved 46, 151
beret 25
Bernstein's first law 62
berserk 189, 194
besotted 52
bespoke 41, 104
bête noire 52, 79
bevel 55, 161
bevy 73, 76
bewitch 27
bewitching 92
biannual 181
bias 46, 119, 160
bibelot 161, 180
bibliography 20
biblomania 105
bibliophile 20
bibliopole 142
bibulous 6, 52
bicuspid 178
bid 134
bidet 178
biennial 182
bifocals 61, 73
bigamy 106
big board 116, 168
bikini 15
bilateral 114, 181
bilious 85, 126
billet 102
billet-doux 103
billingsgate 190
bimanous 182
bimonthly 181
binary 51, 124, 181
binaural 181
binestrial 181
binomial 181
biogenesis 100
biopsy 59, 177
biparous 181
biped 182
birdie 74
biretta 25, 29
bisque 163
bisextile 60, 99
bistro 146
bivouac 24, 175
biweekly 58, 69
blackball 122, 190
blackmail 126
black tie 181
blandish 24, 66, 193
blank check 185

blank check 185
blasphemy 40, 92
blatherskite 68, 174
blazon 89, 137
bleachers 16
blend word 196
blithe 28
blithering 93, 174
blitzkrieg 11
blockbusting 109
bloody Mary 178, 190
blooper 15
blowzy 63, 161, 186
blue chip 168
blue collar 88, 106, 154, 186, 197
blue sky laws 98
blurb 20
bogey 74
boiler room 81
boldface 182
bombast 174
bonhomie 74
boniface 89
bon jour 70
bon mot 30, 195
bon soir 70
bon vivant 128
boondoggle 187
bordello 22, 194
borscht circuit 26
botch 13
botched 30
boudoir 52, 196
boulevardier 105
bounteous 73, 130
bouquet 67, 195
bourgeois 109
boustrophedon 199
boutique 158, 161
bowdlerization 137
bowdlerize 26, 55, 60
boycott 144
brachycephalic 22, 80
brachydactylic 158
brackish 151, 175
brad 115
braggadocio 19, 134
brahmin 79, 128, 162
Braille 78
brainstorm 22, 171
brainstorming 85
brainwash 27, 35
brainwashing 88
brand 97, 106, 168
brash 4, 86, 142

brasserie 14
brassy 28, 90
brattle 29, 117, 142
bravado 19, 21
bravura 22, 76, 170
brawn 112
bray 79
brazen 157
bread-and-butter 32, 128
breadth 107, 159
break bread 54
breaker 192
breakneck 42, 165
breakthrough 171
breech delivery 17
breezeway 125
brevet 136
breviary 20, 42
bric-a-brac 95
brickbat 39
bricole 17, 88
bridgehead 109
bridle 7
briefing 99
brigand 149
brinkmanship 60, 148, 174
brio 102
brisance 60, 157
broach 66, 108, 167, 171
broad jump 102
broadside 132, 157
brochette 107, 160, 165
brogan 80, 158
brogue 91
broker 6, 128
bromide 30, 130, 180
Bronx cheer 35, 45
brouhaha 187
brownout 47
brown study 3, 147
bruit 75, 174
brume 67, 110
brut 52
bruxellois 22
bruxism 76, 178
bucket shop 22
bucolic 126, 150
buenos dias 164
buffet 95, 107, 154
bulbous 173
bulimia 8, 83
bull market 106, 148, 168
bulldog edition 54, 116
bullish 121
bullpen 15, 129

bumper 40, 73
bumpkin 12, 30, 36
bumptious 6, 33
bunco 28, 173
bungle 20, 30, 197
bunt 15
buoyant 28, 100
bureaucracy 75, 143
burgeon 136, 166
burke 171
burnoose 9, 82
burnsides 159
bursar 179
bursitis 124
busby 71
bush league 15, 109
busman's holiday 82
butterfingers 30, 70, 128
buttocks 16
by-election 55
byline 115, 198
byword 63, 128

cabal 91, 153
cabala 114, 120, 153
cabalistic 114
cabana 15
cabaret 24, 146
cacoethes 105
caboose 70, 142
cabriolet 25
cache 49, 81
cachet 106
cachexia 105, 192
cachinnate 98
cacography 13, 78, 165
cacophany 48, 79
cadaster 106, 172
cadaverous 43, 72, 124
cadence 58, 147
cadenza 87, 113
cadge 16, 73
Cadmean victory 44, 138, 189
cadre 36, 56, 117
caduceus 108, 191
caducity 120, 154, 179
caesarean section 13, 17
caesura 21
caftan 102, 149
cafe au lait 31
cafe noir 31
cahier 135, 145
cairene 24

cairn 106, 168
caisson 7, 184
caitiff 14, 152
cajole 30, 193
Cajun 102
cakes and ale 74
cakewalk 136, 170
calathus 173
calculation 69, 137
caldron 19
calefacient 80
calender 74, 104
calescence 191
caliber 44, 128
calipers 47, 90
calisthenics 59, 77
calk 131
call 131, 166
callboard 22, 177
call girl 137
callable 19
calligraphy 127
calliope 122, 167
callipygian 15, 157
call letters 141
call loan 102
callosity 79
callow 86, 88
calorific 80
calorimetry 80
calumet 126
calumniate 4, 160
calvities 13
calypso 113
camaraderie 64
camarilla 5, 24, 30
Camelot 95
camera 94
camouflage 48, 81
campanile 16
campanology 16
camp follower 78
canalize 47
canapé 8
canard 63, 150
cancroid 37
candelabrum 24
canister 34
canker 36
cannibalize 22, 174
cannikin 24
canny 26, 137, 178
canon 58, 150, 151
canoness 195
canonized 151

canorous 108, 113
go to Canossa 50
cant 84, 90, 153, 161, 168, 176
Cantabrigian 24
cantankerous 13, 139
cantata 113
cantatrice 64
canticle 27
cantilever 136, 170
cantle 22, 129, 151, 154
canton 81, 157
cantonment 175
canvass 46, 59, 162
capacious 149
cap-a-pie 80
caparison 30
caper 130, 160, 194
capital expenditure 87, 136
capital gain 136
capital goods 136
capital loss 102
capitalization 36
capitation 132
capitulate 73
capon 26, 149
caprice 171, 193
capriole 187
capstone 81
captious 39, 63, 139
captive audience 127
caracole 78, 193
caraqueno 25
carat 72, 193
caravan 179, 188
caravansary 89
carbine 148
carcinogen 24
carcinoma 24
cardigan 173
cardinal virtues 94, 115
careen 103, 150, 159, 165, 181
caret 90, 91
carhop 191
carillon 16
carioca 148
carious 43, 149
carminative 66
carmine 44
carnage 18, 107, 160
carnal 19, 66, 156
carnivores 66
carom 17, 82
carp 32
carpetbagger 132
carrel 161, 170

carrion 43, 149
carte blanche 18, 186
cartography 106
cartulary 144
caryatid 31, 64
casbah 117
casement 195
cashier 49
cassandra 128, 136
cassette 149
castanets 30
caste 29
castellated 26, 181
castigate 28, 143
casting vote 43
castrate 56
casual 120
casuistry 142
casus belli 192
catachresis 110
cataclysm 48, 186, 189
catafalque 31
catalectic 189
catalepsy 112
catalyst 6, 168
catamite 21
catapult 83, 98
catastrophe 24
catatonia 112, 170
catcall 24, 193
catchall 35
catchpenny 28
catchword 197
catechesis 121
catechism 139
catechize 139
categorical 3, 117, 132
catena 27
catenate 34
cater-cornered 46
caterwaul 163
catharsis 48, 138
Catherine wheel 129
cathexis 33
catholic 22
catholicon 124, 145
cat's cradle 169
cat's-paw 53, 100
catwalk 115, 191
caucus 132
cauliflower ear 20, 54
caulk 131, 153
cause celèbre 87
causerie 28, 35
causeway 149

caustic 18, 151
cauterize 23, 153
cavalcade 125
cavalier 36, 70, 72, 79, 120
caveat 192
caveat emptor 23
caviar to the general 3
cavil 25, 139, 142
cavort 70, 133
cede 73
cedilla 4, 106
celibacy 156
celibate 3, 185
Celtic cross 40
cenotaph 56, 111
censorious 63
censure 18, 33
centaur 76, 78
centaur word 196
centenary 121
centennial 121
centrifugal 11
centripetal 179
centuple 83
ceramics 29
ceremonious 123
certitude 32, 172
c'est la vie 100, 177
chaff 14, 180
chagrin 47, 56
chain reaction 155
chaise longue 36
chalk talk 99
chalumeau 29
chamade 52, 159, 181
chamber music 113
chameleon 27
chamfer 17
champ 28, 112
champaign 66
champerty 31, 85
chancel 164
chancemedley 87, 185
chancery 82, 198
chandler 24, 179
change ringing 16
chantey 151
chaps 37
chapfallen 44, 51
charade 107
charades 77
charisma 99
charley horse 9, 99
charnel 73
chary 25, 26, 70

chaser 52
chatelaine 27, 110
chatoyant 26, 27
chattel 128
chauffer 161, 169
chauvinism 126, 185
checkmate 44
cheek by jowl 91, 158
cheeky 151
cheese-paring 107, 168, 198
chemise 52, 161
cheromania 105
cheroot 29
cherrystone 29
chestnut 166, 180
cheval glass 109
chevron 90, 188
chevy 79, 198
chez 10
chiaroscuro 18, 100
chiasmus 35, 91, 147
chicanery 156, 180, 184
chicken cacciatore 28
chicken-hearted 37, 176
chicken-livered 37, 176
chiffonier 23, 28
chifforobe 191
chignon 23, 95
chiliad 177
chimera 65, 82, 86
chimerical 63
chintzy 28, 128
chionophobia 128
chipper 22, 28
chip shot 74
chirography 78, 127
chiromancy 124
chirr 180
chivalrous 36, 72
chlorophyll 76
chock-a-block 93
choker 116
cholesterol 63, 80
chorea 151
choreography 42
choreomania 105
chorography 106
chortle 28, 74
chrematomania 105
chrestomathy 31
chrism 82, 120
chromatics 31
chronic 35, 98, 143
chronology 9, 43, 176
chukker 132

churl 85, 150
chutzpah 11, 21, 87
cicatrix 152
cicerone 77
cicisbeo 103, 106
cimmerian 42, 74
cincture 16, 36
cinematography 65, 111, 112
cinéma vérité 65
cinereous 10
cinquain 66
cipher 184
circa 3, 9
Circe 56
circuitous 88, 149
circumambulate 191
circumference 29, 49
circumflex accent 4
circumlocution 102, 149
circumscribe 51, 106
circumspect 11, 25, 26
circumvent 11, 123
cirrocumulus 30
cirrostratus 30
cirrus 30
cisatlantic 177
citizens' arrest 9
claiming race 83
clairvoyance 153, 154
clambake 89
clamorous 117
clandestine 71, 153
claptrap 28, 134
claque 9, 81
clarion 29
classicism 5
clavichord 129
cleavage 21
cliché 22, 32, 180
cliff-hanger 172
climacteric 39, 200
clincher 43, 167
clipping 68
clique 29, 59, 90
clitoris 156
cloche 16
clock 56
clodhopper 30
clodpate 18, 170
clodpoll 18, 170
cloisonné 56, 109
cloistral 153
clone 122
clonus 112, 164
closed shop 184

closet drama 130
closure 56
cloture 56
clout 15
cloven-hoofed 46, 152
cloverleaf 81
cloying 178
clump 191
clutch 55, 72
coadjutor 10, 37
coagulation 18
coalesce 18, 71
coalition 6
coaming 40, 148
coaxial 12
coccyx 19
cockade 148, 149
cock-a-hoop 55, 81
cock-a-leekie 28
cockalorum 174
cockamamie 37
cock-and-bull story 169, 174
cockatrice 155
cockcrow 43, 54
cocker 31, 165
cockerel 31
cockiness 154, 172
cockle 198
cockney 102
cock of the walk 28, 98
cocksure 27, 154
cocotte 137
coda 113
coddle 35, 124, 159
codicil 5, 8
coeval 35
coffee break 143, 176
cofferdam 192
coffin corner 68
coffle 125, 179
cogent 35, 128
cognition 95, 154
cognizance 127, 174
cognomen 63, 172
cognoscente 90, 128
cohabit 101
coherent 82, 104, 167
cohort 14, 67
coiffeur 78
coign of vantage 5, 119
coincide 6
coitus 156
cold shoulder 162
cold turkey 52
colic 3, 168

colitis 91
collage 10
collate 32, 72
collated 106
collateral 20, 130, 154
collation 100, 107, 144
collect 133
collective 63
collective bargaining 116
collectivism 75
collegiality 11
colligate 63, 176
collocate 9, 130
collocation 173
collop 107, 161
colloquial 35
colloquialism 89
colloquy 33, 35
collude 34, 35
collusion 153
colonnade 31
colophon 137, 173, 179
coloratura 190
colporteur 20, 126, 179
columbarium 116
coma 183
comate 71, 78
comatose 183
comforter 15
comity 29, 36
commando 141
commensal 54, 174
commensurate 57, 66, 136
commination 45, 177
comminute 137
commission plan 112
committee of the whole 32
commode 27
common denominator 6
common law, 98
Common Market 55, 58
common multiple 118
common stock 168
commune 76
companionate marriage 106
company union 197
compendium 3, 171
compensation 171
complacency 35, 154
complaisance 6, 119
complex 142
compositor 182
compote 70
comprise 34, 87
compunction 77, 145

comstockery 26
conation 11, 170
concatenation 27, 101
concave 40
concavity 90
conceit 63
concentric 26
conception 16, 167
concert, in 178, 185
concertina 4
concerto 113
concert master 190
concession 170
conchology 157
concierge 51
concinnity 9, 79
conclave 153
concoct 46, 104, 110
concomitant 4, 120
concordance 88
concourse 31, 40, 177
concretion 76, 162
concretize 104, 164
concubine 196
concupiscence 103, 156
concurrence 6
concurrent 108, 159
condense 3, 176
condescend 103
condescending 126
condign 46, 109
condition 4, 179
conditioned reflex 99, 142, 146
condole 76, 173
condom 35
condominium 8
condone 30, 123
conducive 80, 99
confabulate 28, 75, 91
confidant 128, 157
confidence game 173
configuration 9
confiscate 154
conflagrant 23
conflation 18
conflict of interest 184
confluence 40, 67
conformation 123, 170
confound 34
confrere 31, 64
confrontation 39, 62
confute 137, 145
congé 49, 99
congener 34
congenital defect 44

conglomerate 31, 36
congress 156
congruent 6, 33
congruity 66
conjecture 33, 77, 88, 172
conjugal 106
conjunction 31
conjunctive 94
conjuncture 31, 39
conjuration 104
conjurer 104
conniption 84, 175
connivance 159
connive 30, 134, 158
connoisseur 60
connotation 86
connote 171
connubial 106
consanguinity 18
conscription 33, 51
consecution 155
consensus 6, 121
consequential 67, 86
conservative 26, 110, 146
consign 73, 78
on consignment 74
console table 174
consommé 163
consonance 6
consonant 163, 164
consort 84, 166, 194
consortium 6, 76
conspectus 47, 171, 172
conspicuous consumption 61, 165
consternation 7, 64, 124
constituency 172, 190
contemn 46, 152
contend 9, 43
contention 32, 148
contentious 139
contiguity 116
contiguous 30
continence 146, 156
contingency 183
contingent 100, 132
continual 144, 145
continuous 117, 184
continuum 194
contraband 75, 85, 162
contumacious 49, 90, 143
contretemps 56
controvert 9, 121
contumely 90, 150, 152
contuse 22
conundrum 148

conurbation 187
convenance 137
conversant 4, 96
conversation piece 9, 32, 174
conversion 68
convex 40
conveyance 136
convivial 162
convoke 24
convolute 31
cooper 14
cooperative 8
co-opt 9, 133
copesetic 59, 65
coping 178
coprology 65, 88, 132
copula 189
copulation 156
copy editor 55
coq au vin 28
coquet 67, 180
coquille 157
corbeil 15, 153
cordiform 80
cordon 77, 101, 148
cordon sanitaire 14
coriaceous 99
corinthian 9, 76
corneous 82
corner 110
corn snow 162
cornucopia 82
corollary 34, 117, 147
coronary thrombosis 80
corporal 19
corporeal 19
corpulent 63, 66
corpus delicti 39, 136
corral 25, 149, 154
corrida 23
corrigible 36
corrosion 54, 193
cortege 26, 147
coruscate 164
corvee 69, 149
coryphee 14
coryza 31, 79
cosher 31, 124
cosmetic 8
cosmology 185
cosmogony 185
cosmopolitan 198
cosset 124, 165
costive 34
coterie 29, 76

couch 129, 138
couchant 103
coulisse 76, 166
countdown 36, 147, 149, 176
countenance 9, 172
counterbalance 120
counterfoil 28
countermand 147
countermine 131
counterpane 16
counterpart 32, 107, 146
counterpoint 108
counterpoise 69
counterpose 55
countersignature 159
countersink 153
countertenor 190
countervail 32, 104, 120
counter word 197
coup 107, 169
coup de grace 43, 111
coup d'état 75, 123
courier 11, 109
courtesan 137
court-martial 109
cousinry 63
couturier 52
couvade 28, 63
covenant 6, 32
send to Coventry 122
coverall 72
cover charge 27
cover-up 33, 81
covert 33, 153, 157
coverture 48, 106, 157, 196
covet 46, 103
covetous 76
cowboy 26
cowhand 26
cowpuncher 26
cowled 82
cowlick 78
coxcombry 159, 188
cozen 28, 43
crab 32
crackbrained 37
crackdown 48
cracker-barrel 48
crack of doom 56
cram 170
crambo 147, 196
craniology 160
cranium 160
cranky 54, 139
crapulence 74, 158

crapulent 52
crash program 56, 130
crass 170
cravat 116, 152
craven 37
crawl 39, 101
craze 37
crazy quilt 139
creature terms 37
crèche 29
credenza 22, 159
credits 101
credibility 16
credulity 16, 77
creel 66
crenelated 117
Creole 77, 164, 193
crêpes 124
crêpes suzette 124
crepitate 37, 142
crepuscular 47, 119, 181
crescendo 113
crest 80
crestfallen 45
crevasse 28, 66
crevice 37
cribriform 159
criminal conversation 5
criminology 39
crimp 81, 119
cringe 40, 64, 158
criterion 150, 167
crocodile tears 76, 193
Croesus 148, 192
croissant 149
crone 78, 195
cropper 62
come a cropper 62
crossbeam 15
crosscheck 82
crosshatch 156
crotchety 25, 170
cruciate 40
crucifer 40
cruciform 40
cruet 20
cruller 51
crumpet 24
crus 157
cryptanalysis 31, 44
cryptesthesia 29, 108, 175
cryptic 114, 138, 153
cryptography 31
cuckold 84
cuisine 35

cul de sac 18, 179
culinary 35
cull 129, 154, 163
cullet 73
culotte 180, 196
culpable 18
cultrate 131, 157
culvert 27
cumber 193
cum laude 82
cummerbund 151, 191
cumulative preferred 168
cumulus 30
cuneal 193
cuneiform 193
cunnilingus 156
cupidity 11, 76
cupola 50, 149
curator 40, 112
curfew 176
curiosa 20
curling 85
curmudgeon 76, 92
cursive 135, 182, 199
cuspid 24
cutlery 54
cyanosis 18
cybernetics 33, 35
cyclone cellar 26
cyclorama 40
cyclothymia 105
cynomania 105
cynophobia 128
cynosure 26, 119
cyprian 100, 191
cyrillic 160
cystitis 18
cystoscopy 18
cytology 26

dacha 36, 150, 171
dactyl 131
dactylogram 65
dactylology 43, 159
Dada 10
dado 126
daedal 40, 89, 91
daily double 17
dais 130, 142
daltonism 31
damascene 122
sword of Damocles 42, 127, 133
danseur 13, 104
danseur noble 14, 104
dap 47, 160

dappled 166, 188
dark horse 24, 131
dart 181
dastard 37, 162
Davy Jones's locker 120
dawdle 78, 102, 192
day order 23, 122
dead heat 176
deadlock 167
deadwood 187
dearth 97, 152
debacle 21, 150
debauch 36, 45, 154
debauchee 100
debenture 19, 27, 43
debilitate 192
debonair 28, 101, 187
debouch 31, 56
decadence 43, 44, 111
decalomania 135
decalogue 176
decant 133
decanter 20
decapitate 16
decathlon 11
decedent 43
decelerate 161
decennary 176
decennial 176
decibel 102, 117
deciduous 62, 157
decimate 46, 95
decision 21
deckle edge 55, 141
declaim 164
declamation 121, 155
déclassé 162
declivity 167
declivitous 161
decoct 19, 33
decolletage 103, 116
decor 44
decorous 16, 136, 154
decrepit 57, 198
decretory 44, 94
decry 33, 45
decubitus 16
decumbent 76, 103
decussate 40, 91
dedans 176
deduction 51, 73, 102, 143
de facto 62
defalcate 56, 109
default 62, 116
defeasance 190

default 62, 116
defeasance 190
defecate 59, 144
defenestration 178, 194
defense mechanism 58, 154
deference 170, 200
deficit financing 55, 75
defile 188
definitive 60
deflagrate 23
deflation 111, 134
defoliate 170
defunct 43, 60, 122
degenerate 111, 198
degree day 175
deign 33, 169
deipnosophist 174
déjà vu 85, 153
dejeuner 21
de jure 99
delectation 57
deleterious 83, 89
Delft 54, 133
Delilah 179, 196
delineate 123, 132, 179
deliquescent 110
delirious 194
delphic 7, 121
delta wing 180
delude 98, 110
delve 91, 153
demagogue 99, 132
demarcate 106, 155
démarche 105, 112
demean 16, 33, 44, 103
demeanor 16, 45, 105
dementia 108
demesne 50
demijohn 94
demimonde 137, 196
demise 43
demission 73, 146
demitasse 31
démodé 120
demographer 167
demography 132, 190
demoniac 45, 65, 103, 105
demophobia 128
de mortuis nil nisi bonum 43
demos 107
demotic 32, 107, 132
demulcent 144, 163
demur 81, 119, 174
demure 37, 110, 146
dendrochronology 29, 76, 180

dendrology 180
denigrate 18, 44, 49
denizen 78, 89
denominator 107
denote 88, 131, 159
denouement 65, 122, 163
dentifrice 178
dentil 9, 18
dentition 41, 175
deontology 58
depilatory 78
depletion 102, 115
deploy 129
deployment 15
deprave 36
deprecate 48, 130, 144, 174
deprecatory 8
depreciate 16
depredate 129, 131, 134
depurative 138
deracinate 57, 60, 187
dereliction 62, 116
deride 98, 148
de rigueur 63
dermatology 160
dernier cri 98
derogate 16, 46, 174
derriere 16, 23
descant 48, 82
descender 135, 182
descry 48, 119
desecrate 136
desegregation 141
desiderate 46, 116
despicable 35, 189
despoil 45, 149, 170
despondency 45, 82
despot 182
despotism 133
despumate 160
desuetude 116, 183
detail 109
detail man 52
detente 54
deterge 29, 195
determinism 26, 70
detonate 60
detrition 150, 194
detritus 69
de trop 172
detrude 138, 178
deus ex machina 87, 122
deuterogamy 106, 153
deviate 156, 181
devil-may-care 25, 143

devil's advocate 9, 121
devoirs 146
DEW line 141, 192
dexter 148
dexterous 5, 160
diablerie 163
diadem 40, 80
dialect 164
dialectic 102
dianoetic 102
diaphanous 154, 157, 179
diaphoresis 128
diaphragm 35
diarchy 181
diaspora 94
diastrophism 44
diathermy 80
diathesis 133
diatribe 4, 39, 79
dichotomize 41, 50, 155
dichotomized 124
dichotomy, 181, 182
dichromatic 31, 182
dicrotic 51, 80
diction 196
didactic 90, 111, 126
diddle 28, 43
dido, 8, 25
die-hard 119
dieresis 4, 51, 181
diesis 42, 51
diffidence 33, 158, 176
diffract 155
diffuse 29, 102, 127, 133, 166, 189, 197
dig 9, 59
digamy 106, 145, 153
digit 65
digital computer 118
digits 118
digress 142, 181, 191
dilacerate 175
dilapidated 22, 43, 116, 150, 156
dilate 60, 173, 194
dilatory 45
dilemma 17, 29, 133, 135
dilettante 42, 172
dillydally 43, 192
diluvial 67
dimeter 189
diminishing returns 99
dimidiate 50, 78
dingbat 122, 135, 182
dingus 72
diocese 18, 28
diorama 60, 129

diphthong 182
diplomatic immunity 59, 98, 99
diplopia 51, 61
dipsomania 6, 105
diptych 51
direct primary 135
dirge 71
diriment 117, 190
dirndl 160
disabuse 155, 184
disaffect 46, 192
disaffected 6, 58, 184
disaffection 70, 103
disaffiliate 21
disaffirm 35, 45, 146
disbarred 98
disburse 126
discalced 14
disc brake 21
discern 127, 143
discipline 99
disc jockey 141
discography 129
discomfit 34, 44, 70, 188
discommode 20, 50, 87, 180
disconcert 34, 187
disconsolate 45, 74, 151
discontinuous 90
discophile 60, 129
discord 49
discothèque 116
discovery 48, 58
discredit 79
discrepancy 35, 50, 87
discreet 25, 137
discrete 48, 49, 155
discursive 125, 143, 191
disdain 144
disfranchise 45
dishabille 30, 48, 52
dishearten 48
dished 193
disheveled 150, 179, 185, 186
disingenuous 37, 90
disinflation 134
disinterest 119
disinterested 86, 119
disjointed 31, 48
dismantle 174
disorient 34, 110
disorientation 47
disparage 16, 138
disparagement 46, 103
disparaging 161
disparate 47, 49, 184, 185

disparity 88, 185
dispassionate 24, 86, 119, 183
dispatch 49, 55, 136, 139, 165
dispatch, with 49, 139
dispel 52, 145
dispensation 59
dispense 59, 73
disperse 52, 152
dispirited 44, 45, 51
displaced person 82
displacement 179
disport 7, 70, 120
disposition 70, 78, 175
disputable 9, 121
disputation 43
disputatious 9, 35
disquietude 8, 146
disquisition 179
disreputable 156
disseizin 49, 185
dissemblance 84
dissemble 33, 48, 64
disseminate 47, 152, 166
dissension 47, 48, 139
dissent 47, 117
dissentious 139
dissertation 179
disservice 89
dissever 50, 125, 155
dissidence 47
dissident 47
dissimilitude 46, 185
dissimulate 33, 134
dissipate 49, 52, 165, 166
dissipated 152, 192
dissipation 88, 90
dissociable 85, 87
dissociate 21, 155
dissolute 43, 86
dissonance 48, 87, 89
dissonant 83, 89
dissuade 7, 27, 46
distaff 196
distaff side 64, 107
distemper 50, 85, 148, 150
distend 60, 169, 173
distillation 3, 58
distingué 47, 49, 193
distort 16, 110, 181
distract 34, 50
distrait 3
distraught 6, 17, 37, 176, 198
ditheism 53, 182
dither 8, 116
dithyramb 164

ditto 53, 151
dittography 145
ditty 163
ditty bag 13, 151
diuresis 187
diuretic 108, 187
diurnal 42, 43
divan 36, 162
diva 64, 121, 135
divagate 47, 169, 191
divaricate 21, 50, 166
diverge 47
divergence 47
divergent 112
divers 188
diverse 47, 156, 183, 188
diversify 60, 188
diversion 7, 125
divert 7, 44, 49, 57, 181
divertissement 7
divest 45, 170
dividend 126
divination 69, 136
divine 77
divining rod 69
divulge 48, 147, 175
docent 99, 175, 181
dock 174
doff 145, 174
dog days 83, 94
doggerel 189
doggery 105, 107
dogma 16, 50
dogmatic 10, 132
dolabriform 12, 79
doldrums 20, 45, 51, 53
dollar cost averaging 154
dollop 132, 155
dolly 130
dolichocephalic 102
dolorous 112, 124, 151
dolt 18, 170
domicile 53, 82
domino 82, 106
donjon 179
donnybrook 21, 70
doodle 51, 153
dope sheet 83
doppelganger 73
Doppler effect 100, 163
Doric 9, 76
dormer 195
dot 51
dotage 5, 68, 120, 155
dottle 178

double agent 166
double-dealing 43
double-decker 151
double entendre 181
double indemnity 100
double jeopardy 181
double negative 181
double play 15
double take 45
doublethink 147
double truck 124
doublure 19
doubting Thomas 160
dour 74, 167, 171
dowager 55, 195
dowdy 51, 156
downbeat 45
Down's syndrome 111
downstage 166
down tick, minus-tick 103
double talk 7
dowse 192
doxology 74, 84
doyen 55, 155
drabble 51, 97
draff 52
dragnet 116
dragoman 77, 90
dragonnade 109, 127
draw 17, 39, 40
drawback 47
drawknife 95, 196
dress rehearsal 130
dribble 15, 82, 162
drip-dry 72
drivel 68, 155, 174
droit 148
droit du seigneur 148
dromedary 24
dromomania 105
drone 102
drop curtain 166
drop kick 68
drop letter 100
drop shot 176
dross 144, 192
drub 15, 44, 123
drudgery 197
drumhead court-martial 36
dryad 118
dry nurse 118
dry point 129
dry rot 111
dry run 144
duad 124

dubbing 112, 163
dubiety 51
dubious 51, 139
ducks and drakes, play with 143, 166
dude 42, 105
dudgeon 146
due bill 43
duff 67
duffel bag 151
duffle bag 151
dulcet 108, 163, 173
dulcimer 113
dumb waiter 56
dun 128, 134
duodecimal 181
duphuism 170
duple 51
duplicity 43, 51, 180
durance 34, 86
duress 31, 68
dust jacket 125
Dutch courage 36
Dutch door 51
dutchman 89
Dutch treat 126
Dutch uncle 5, 39
duteous 119
duumvirate 75, 94
dwindle 47, 99
dybbuk 45
dynamics 69
dynamism 57
dynasty 150, 164
dysgenic 17, 46
dyslexia 42
dyspeptic 74, 126
dysphagia 172
dysphasia 164
dysphenism 49
dysphoria 48, 85
dyspnea 21
dystrophy 118

eagle 74
eagre 67
earmark 106, 155
earthly 86, 132
earthy 30, 115, 185
ebullient 22, 57
ecchymosis 18, 22
ecclesiology 28
ecdysiast 170
ecesis 55
echard 55, 192

echelon 32, 69, 100, 142
echinate 22
echoic 86, 163
echoism 121
echolalia 145
eclampsia 35
eclat 22, 145
eclectic 50, 154
eclipse 119, 123
eclogue 131
ecology 57, 122
ecosystem 15, 55
ecotone 55
ecstasy 142
ectomorphic 99
ectype 86, 145
ecumenical 185, 198
eczema 160
edaphic 55, 162
eddy 46
edema 173
edentate 178
edict 44
edify 57, 186
eerie 73, 193
efface 58, 147, 150
effect 4, 22
effeminate 185, 192, 196
effendi 181
effervescence 102, 164, 190
effete 14, 192
efficacious 136
efficiency apartment 8
effigy 86, 100
effloresce 18, 67
effluence 67
effluent 123
effluvium 56, 120
efflux 56
effrontery 11, 19, 87
effulgence 141, 165
effuse 56, 61
effusive 77, 123
e.g. 68
egalitarian 57
egeria 195
eggshell china 28, 132
ego 33, 154
egocentric 154
egoist 154
egregious 13, 66
egress 60, 74
eidetic imagery 108, 190
eidolon 85, 128
ejaculate 48, 59

ejaculation 133
ejecta 25
eke 129, 172
élan 42, 57, 190
elapse 125, 161
elate 59, 168
Electra complex 43
electrify 9, 167, 178
electrocardiogram (EKG) 80
electroencephalogram (EEG) 21
electron 125
eleemosynary 6, 27
elegy 97, 112
elenchus 144
elephantine 57, 186
elicit 51, 58
elide 121, 136, 161
elision 120, 177
elite 17
ellipsis 120
elliptic 158
eloign 145
elude 11, 58
elusive 79
elutriate 138
Elysian Fields 125
em 182
emaciated 193
emancipate 70
emasculate 26, 72
emasculated 55
embargo 147
embarrass 33, 48, 86
embellish 44, 122
embezzle 167
emblazon 5
embody 31, 87
emboss 122
embossed 142
embracery 85
embrangle 33, 57
embrocate 110, 150
embroider 59
embroil 34, 91, 112
emend 36
emeritus 147
emesis 190
emetic 108, 190
emigrant 99
emigrate 99
eminence grise 6
eminent domain 148, 167
emir 111
emit 73, 154
emollient 162, 163

emolument 126, 151
empathy 64, 189
emphysema 21
empiricism 60
emporium 73, 169
empyreal 26, 170
emulate 86, 148, 189
emulous 32
emulsion 109
emunctory 192
en 182
enamor 27
enate 64, 111
encaenia 27
enceinte 134
encephalitis 21
encephalitis lethargica 161
enchase 44
enchiridion 78, 106
enchorial 88, 115
enclave 176
enclitic 136, 197
encomium 58, 133
encore 127
encroach 91, 180
enculturation 5
encumber 81, 86
encyclical 125
endemic 115, 126
endocrine 73
endogamy 106
end paper 125
end zone 68
enema 108
energumen 63
enervate 46, 192
enfant terrible 180
enfilade 77, 142
enfranchise 70
enfranchisement 29
English 14
English horn 113
engorge 54
engrail 122
engrailed 55
engross 3, 35, 120
engulf 123, 172
enigma 119, 148
enjoin 32, 122
ennui 20, 101
enormity 111, 194
en rapport 79
entente 6, 184
enteric 91
enthymeme 9

entity 16, 142
entomology 89, 170
entomomania 105
entourage 11, 67
entr'acte 17
entrechat 14
entree 104
entrepreneur 23
entropy 49, 88
enunciate 10, 164
enuresis 16, 187
envenom 56, 131
envoy 44, 65, 131
eon 58, 127
eonism 104
epaulet 158
epée 53, 173
epenthesis 89, 100, 163
epexegesis 70
ephemeral 98, 158, 179
epicedium 47, 71
epicene 55, 156
epicure 67, 75
epicurean 155
epidemic 34, 48
epidermis 160
epigram 145, 195
epigraph 89, 111, 140
epilogue 56
epiphany 8, 105
epiphenomenon 153
episcopate 18
episodic 22, 49
epistaxis 117
epistemology 83, 96
epistle 100
epitaph 178
epithalamium 118
epithet 27
epizootic 57
epoch 176
eponym 115, 127
equable 179
equanimity 24, 33
equestrian 83
equilibrium 13
equinox 43, 116
equiponderate 13, 36
equitable 62, 86
equity 62, 86, 188
equivocal 7, 51, 139, 172
equivocate 43, 110
eradicate 46, 57, 187
erection 127, 148
eremiomania 105

erethism 92
ergo 80
eristic 9
erogenous 156
erotic 156
erotomania 156
errant 150, 169, 191
errata 58
erratic 54, 92
errhine 162
ersatz 89, 171
eruct 16
erudite 99, 152
erythrophobia 128
escalade 152
escalate 60, 76, 88
escapade 133, 166
escarpment 161, 167
escharotic 36
eschatology 43
escheat 136
eschew 158
escritoire 199
esculent 55
escutcheon 157
esoteric 3, 153, 184, 185
ESP 33
Esperanto 97
espousal 5, 172
esprit 165
esprit de corps 76
esthesia 155
esthetics 15
estival 171
estivate 171
estuary 89, 149
esurient 83
étagère 122, 167
etesian 8
ethereal 6, 100, 165
ethnarch 150
ethnology 141
ethos 11, 27
etiolate 193
etiology 26
et seq. 7
etude 113
etymology 45, 197
euchre 28, 123
eudemon 74
eudemonia 79, 193
eugenics 81, 83, 141
euhemerism 114
eulogy 133
eunuch 26

eupepsia 47
eupeptic 79, 80
euphemism 109, 171, 197
euphonious 79, 130
euphoria 59, 79, 193
euphuism 10, 67
European plan 83
eurythmic 75, 112
euthanasia 43, 109
euthenics 83
evacuee 127
evanesce 47, 188
evanescent 66
evangelism 75
eventuality 122, 132
eventuate 79, 181
evert 181
evince 45, 105, 158
eviscerate 48
evitable 11
evoke 24, 51, 171
evolve 46, 121
evulsion 131, 187
ewer 94, 129
exact 45, 60, 69, 146
exacting 45, 156, 169
ex cathedra 11
excelsior 124
excogitate 46, 177
excommunicate 41
excommunication 54
excoriate 175, 186
excoriation 178
excrement 64, 192
excrescence 123, 185
excrescent 172
excruciating 6, 124
exculpate 70
exculpatory 89
excursive 47, 142
ex-dividend 168, 195
execrable 3, 46, 89, 147
execrate 40, 45
executive session 30, 153
exegesis 7, 60, 90
exemplar 110, 126, 182
exemplary 42, 85
exergue 31
exhibitionism 14, 158
exhilarate 91, 127
exhort 5, 187
exhume 47, 48, 147
exigent 39, 187
exiguous 152, 161
existentialism 106, 194

ex libris 20
exodontia 178
exonerate 4, 29
exorable 146
exorbitant 59
exoteric 32, 122
ex parte 121
expatiate 55, 164, 198
expatriate 60
expectorate 165
expediency 5, 9
expedient 136, 171
expedite 62, 162, 165
expertise 96, 160
expiate 11, 104
expiry 56
expletive 59, 65, 197
explicate 60, 90
explication 60
explicit 29, 44, 123
exponent 60, 145, 173
ex post facto 5, 147
expostulate 9, 143
expound 46, 167
expressionism 10
expropriate 174
expunction 45
expunge 57, 195
expurgate 26, 45, 145
exquisite 4, 5, 95
exscind 41
exsert 138
exsertile 137
exsiccate 52
extant 60, 172
extemporaneous 4, 87, 185
extenuate 59, 99
externalize 104
externalized 123
extirpate 46, 149
extol 133
extort 73
extradite 45
extradition 135
extraneous 31, 186
extrapolate 58, 136
extrapolation 10
extrasensory perception 127
extrasystole 80
extraterritorial 123
extravaganza 164
extricate 48
extrinsic 123
extrovert 123
exuberant 94, 98, 123, 165

exude 121, 141
exult 144
exultant 94
eye rhyme 147
eyesore 146, 185

fabric 70, 170
fabricate 91, 104
fabrication 63, 100
facade 62
face off 82
facet 10, 128
facetious 66, 93
face value 19, 188
facile 54, 139, 142, 172
facility 142
facsimile 35, 59
faction 30, 76
factitious 5, 10
factor 6, 26, 55
fag end 98
fail-safe 137
faineant 85, 88, 98
fait accompli 4, 51
falcate 158
faldstool 133
fallacious 58
fallal 122, 180
fallible 100
fallout 52
fallow 85, 184, 186
falsetto 81
famulus 10, 155
fan 14
fanaticism 201
fanfaronade 19, 172
fantast 52, 190
farce 31, 103, 148
farceur 94
far-fetched 169
farouche 65, 186
farrago 34, 108
farrow 14, 36
fasciate 14, 20
fascicle 20
fastidious 42, 79, 123, 144
fatalism 88, 133
fata morgana 109
fathom 138, 184
fatuous 68, 85, 170
fauna 8
faux pas 63, 75, 110
fawn 39, 178
fealty 62, 103, 119
feasible 133, 143, 171

featherbedding 56, 197
featherweight 20, 180, 198
febrile 64
feces 59
feckless 25, 143, 192
feculence 65, 69
fecund 64, 70, 136
feedback 110, 147
feigned 43, 134, 157
feint 43, 134
feisty 6, 101
felicitate 34
felicitous 6, 9, 193
feline 26
fell 40, 65, 79, 89, 189
fellatio 104, 156
felo-de-se 171
felony 39
feme covert 106
feme sole 159
feminine rhyme 147
femme fatale 196
fenestella 194
feracious 64, 70
feral 152, 155, 194
feretory 144
ferocious 152
ferret 52, 153
Ferris wheel 193
ferule 137, 150
fervent 54, 191
fervid 86
fervor 9, 56
fescennine 119, 190
fester 34, 142
festoon 27
fet 137
fetch 10, 142
fete 82, 123
fête champêtre 123
feticide 64
fetid 168
fetish 119, 156
fetishism 172
fettle 80, 165
fettuccine 117
feuilleton 116
fey 72
fiancé 196
fiancée 196
fiasco 62
fiat 11, 122
fibrillation 80
fickle 27, 87
fictitious 62, 91, 185

fiddlehead 20
fidelity 4, 62
fidget 116, 146
fiduciary 77, 181
fielder's choice 14
fifth 65, 101
figment 62, 65
figurant 13
figuration 69, 123, 157
figurative 67, 109
figurehead 20, 99
filch 129, 167
filet mignon 16
filial 28
filiation 125
filibuster 119, 164, 176
filicide 28
fillip 65, 87, 168
finagle 28, 43, 105, 180
fin de siècle 26
fine-drawn 60, 171
finesse 10, 40, 162, 174
finicky 63, 71, 133
finite 101
fiord 89, 153
firebreak 97
firkin 196
firm 125
firmament 80, 160
first cause 74
first mate 157
first water 81, 178
fiscal 65
fish-eye lens 24
fission 165
fist 135
fistic 20
fixation 11, 137
flabbergast 7, 10
flabellum 63
flag 44, 52, 192
flagellate 193
flagelliform 193
flagitious 11, 194
flagon 195
flagrant 48, 123
flagrante delicto 26, 143
flake 141
flam 52, 63, 100
flambé 66
flambeau 178
flamboyant 19, 67, 122, 158
flank 148, 158
flashback 21, 35
flat-footed 47, 130

flattop 6
flatulence 134, 195
flatus 72
flatware 174
flaunt 21, 49, 87, 125
flaw 166, 195
flay 11, 60
flea-bitten 22, 156
flea market 106
flèche 165
flection 16, 40
fledgling 16
fleer 45, 93, 162
Fleet Street 102
flense 170
fleshly 155, 198
fleshpot 19
fletcherism 28
flexuous 17, 194
flick 112
flighty 64, 70
flimsy 183, 192
flinders 165
flinty 66, 79
flip-flop 147
flippancy 152
flip side 147
flocculent 36
floorwalker 151
flora 130
florescence 18, 137, 171
floriculture 67
florid 67, 122, 150
flossy 159
flotsam 67, 184, 188, 198
flounce 112
flounder 170
flourish 49, 56, 63
flout 44, 93, 110
flow chart 46
fluctuate 27, 188
fluctuating 186, 192
fluent 75, 162, 164
fluff 58
fluke 103
flume 72
flummery 40, 56, 66
flump 52, 112
fluoroscope 90
flush 6, 58, 131, 135, 137
fluted 76
flux 27, 34, 67, 112
fly 177
flying buttress 23
flying mare 198

flyleaf 18
flyweight 20
flywheel 193
fob 8, 49, 124
fog 75
fogdog 29
fogy 34, 120
foible 63, 192
foist 86, 91
foliate 99, 118
folio 124, 157
folk etymology 88, 132, 196
foment 87, 90, 168
font 135, 182
foofaraw 71
foolscap 125, 199
foot-candle 100
foot fault 176
footloose 25
foozle 70, 110
fop 42
forage 67, 153
foray 131, 141
force majeure 69
force-out 14
forceps 129
fore 74
fore and aft 157
forecastle 158
forehand 176
forensic medicine 107
forensics 9, 43
forereach 26
foreshore 158
foreshorten 51
forestall 23, 77, 81, 134
forfeit 73, 126
forge 112
forlorn 3, 46, 198
forlorn hope 51, 82
formality 136
format 9, 104
formidable 12, 64, 79
fornication 156
forswear 127, 145, 173
forte 164, 170
fortissimo 113
fortuitous 4
forward 166
forward pass 68
fosse 50
fossette 47
fossick 150, 153
foudroyant 171
foul shot 15

forswear 127, 145, 173
forte 164, 170
fortuitous 4
forward 166
forward pass 68
fosse 50
fossette 47
fossick 150, 153
foudroyant 171
foul shot 15
foul tip 14
fortissimo 113
founder 26, 31, 62, 160
fourchette 74
four-flush 131
foursquare 66, 69, 162
fourth dimension 176
fracas 65, 117
foyer 57, 102
fractious 92, 143, 186
fragmentation bomb 19
fragmentary 22, 87
frangible 21
frank 135
franked mail 104
Franklin stove 169
frappé 85
fraternize 10, 109
Frankenstein's monster 37
fratricide 95
fraught 27, 65
free association 165, 183
fray 21, 65, 187
free-form 46, 157
free lance 10, 198
free verse 131, 189
French window 194
frenetic 59, 64
fresco 124
freshet 123, 148
French horn 113
fresh-water 186
frets 148
fretwork 122
friable 40
fribble 180, 184
Freudian slip, 58, 165
frieze 44, 170
frigorific 28
frippery 28, 66
frivolous 159, 180, 184
fringe benefit 126
frontispiece 124
froe 95, 157
froufrou 122, 150, 173

frugal 178
frugivorous 70
fruition 4, 57, 70, 142
frump 51, 196
frump 40
frustum 33, 38
fugacious 66, 179
fugleman 98, 124
fulgurate 66
fuddy-duddy 71, 120
fuliginous 162
fugue 113
fullback 68
full-fashioned 95
full-fledged 32, 107
full house, 131
full nelson 198
fulminate 158
fulmination 45, 189
fulsome 59, 90, 120
funambulist 81, 176
functional illiterate 85, 142
fundament 23
fundamentalism 144
fungo 14
furbish 22, 131
funk 45, 70
furcate 69
furfur 42
furbelows 158
furlong 49
furtive 161, 167
fusain 27
fusiform 165
fustian 19, 132
fustigate 15
futurity 83
fusty 113, 120

gable 180
gadfly 8, 137
gabble 87, 174
gaff 82
gage 130, 154
galaxy 167
gainsay 35, 45, 121
galanty show 125, 156
galimatias 34, 73
galley 135, 136, 157
gallimaufry 82
gallivant 74, 149
galore 4
galumph 30
galvanize 59, 150, 168
gambado 8, 25

garner 31, 72, 169
garnishee 11
garniture 56
garrote 31, 36, 59, 169
garrulity 142, 174
gascon 19
gasconade 19, 21
gasket 148
gastritis 168
gastronomy 10, 54
gatefold 124
gate-leg table 174
gauche 12, 30
gaucherie 174
gaunt 56, 74, 78
gauntlet, throw down the 27
gavage 64, 69
gawk 72, 167, 170
gazebo 171
geländesprung 160
gelding 26, 83
gelid 70, 85
geminate 57
gemination 53
gemology 73
genealogy 45, 63
generative grammar 75
generic wine 195
genitals 156
genitive 75, 132
genocide 8, 46, 60
genre 95, 182
gentility 144, 193
gentleman's agreement 6
genuflect 16, 95
geognosy 54
geography 152
geology 54
geomancy 50
geometric progression 107, 118
georgic 63, 150
geriatrics 120
german 20, 125
germane 128, 144
germicide 73
gerontocracy 75, 120
gerontology 6
gerrymander 50, 132, 143
gerund 189
gesso 130
gestalt 173
gestation 134
gesticulate 60
gesture 51, 151
gewgaw 180

ghetto 50, 154
ghostwriter 198
ghoul 76
gib 178
gibber 174
gibberish 87
gibbet 72
gibe 93, 175
Gibson 106
gigolo 95, 105, 196
gilt-edged 17, 19
gimlet 73
gimmal 148
gingerly 25, 26
gingivitis 77
girandole 24, 66
gird 175
girth 29, 191
gist 104
glabella 69
glacé 24, 171
glaciology 73
glacis 161
glade 29
gladiate 173
glair 55, 73
glassy 18, 66
glaswegian 73
glaucoma 61
glaucous 153, 200
glee 113, 163
glissade 161
glissando 113
gloaming 181
gloat 61
glockenspiel 113
glomerate 69
glomeration 150
gloriole 78
gloss 32, 43, 60
glossary 101, 196
glossolalia 165, 184
glower 7, 153, 167
gloze 60
gluttonous 54
glyptics 25
glyptograph 46
gnarled 150, 193
gnathic 93
gnocchi 126
gnome 107, 195
gnostic 96
goad 136
goatee 15
goffer 67

glossolalia 165, 184
glower 7, 153, 167
gloze 60
gluttonous 54
glyptics 25
glyptograph 46
gnarled 150, 193
gnathic 93
gnocchi 126
goad 136
gnostic 96
gnome 107, 195
goffer 67
goatee 15
gonfalon 14, 66
gore 180
Gordian knot 135,163
gossamer 45, 66
gouache 124
gouge 28
gourmand 54
gourmandise 54
gourmet 48, 54
grabble 64
gospodin 150
governance 5
gracile 161
gradate 125
grace note 113
gradation 9, 136
gradient 142, 161
gradin 153
gracias 164
graffiti 89, 153, 191
graminivorous 75
grandiloquent 19, 132, 164
grandiose 75, 86, 134
grand slam 14, 21
grandstand play 127
grangerize 85, 113
grapevine 32, 153
graphic 190
graphic arts 190
graphite 126
graph 28
grapple 154, 170
graphics 46
grass widow 196
gravamen 58, 76
grave accent 4
gratis 70
gratuitous 73, 183
gratuity 73, 176
acute accent 4
graveyard shift 197

gravid 134
grayout 190
gray matter 21, 90
greaves 37
green room 120, 177, 191
gregarious 67, 162
Gregorian calendar 24
gremial 30
gride 76, 153
Gresham's law 13
grig 102
grigri 28, 174
grilse 151
grimace 62, 104
grimalkin 26, 158
gringo 98
grisaille 124
griseous 76
grisette 70
grist 75
grizzled 76
grolier 20
grommet 61
gross national product 115, 136, 188
grotesque 18
grounder 15
grouse 76
grout 111
grovel 37, 43
growth stock 168
groveling 163
grubstake 10, 111
Grubstreet 78
guaranteed bond 19
gudgeon 13
guesstimate 58
guerrilla 65
guffaw 98
guinea pig 60
guile 40, 43
guileless 10, 24, 159
guipure 97
guise 8, 62, 134
gules 143
gullet 181
gullible 28, 67
gull 54
gumption 36
gunwale, gunnel 19
gusher 120
guru 165, 175
gusset 7, 62
gustation 175
gusto 57, 201
gutta 52

habeas corpus 198
haberdashery 108
habitué 70, 190
hack 52, 141, 180
hackles 64
hackney 83
hackneyed 180
hafiz 111
haft 78
Haggadah 126, 174
haggard 72, 198
haggis 152
haggle 14, 78, 105
hagiarchy 75, 82
hagiocracy 75, 82
hagioscope 121
ha-ha 64, 80
haiku 93
hairbreadth 115
hair space 135
halakha 174
halcyon 24, 85
hale 32, 69, 80, 149
halfback 68
half binding 20
half-breed 120
half-cocked 79, 87
half gainer 50
half-life 141
half nelson 198
halfway house 130
haligonian 78
halitosis 13
hallah or challah 21
hallmark 106
hallow 34
hallucination 127, 190
hallux 17
halvah 181
hamadryad 118
hamlet 189
hammer and sickle 32
hammerlock 198
hammertoe 178
hamper 15, 81, 86
hamstring 95, 175
hanaper 194
handball 13
handbill 5
handbook 77, 106
handicap 47
handicraft 198
handily 54
handiness 60, 106

handoff 68
handout 73, 169
handpick 29
handsel 73
hand-to-hand 30
hangar 6
hangdog 10, 44, 162
hanging indentation 88
hanker 37, 46, 200
Hansard 22
hapahazard 4, 142
hapless 184, 185
happenstance 4, 27
haptephobia 128
hara-kiri 93, 171
harangue 165, 176
harass 180, 198
harbinger 5, 80
hard-bitten 178
hard-cover book 19
hard goods 53
hard hat 197
hard hats 34
hard-headed 119, 133, 158
hardihood 19, 42
hardpan 66, 76
hardset 17
hard-shell 89, 148
hardtack 17
hardtop 11
hardware 33, 109
hardwood 196
hardy 149, 178
harebrained 66, 68, 73
harelip 101
haricot 95
hark 101
harlequinade 31, 124
harlot 137, 194
harness hitch 95
harpsichord 113
harpy 76
harridan 78, 196
harrier 40
harrow 50
harry 141, 198
harum-scarum 92, 194
hasenpfeffer 141
hashish 115
hassle 166
hassock 68
hasta la vista 74
hasta luego 74
hasta manana 74

hatch 156, 157
hatchment 80
hat trick 166
haughty 81
haut couture 81
haut cuisine 67
haut monde 81
havelock 25
haversack 13
havoc 46, 150, cry havoc 159
haw 81, 83
hawk 19, 29, 36, 126, 154
hawkshaw 46
hawser 24, 111, 149
haywire 37
hazard 74
haze 89
hazy 34, 188
head 178
head gate 72
headland 30, 185
headlock 198
headlong 142, 143
headstrong 170
head wind 194
hearsay 80
hearten 56
hearth 65, 71
heathen 92, 183
heat lightning 100
heaviside layer 141
heavy-handed 23, 30
heavyweight 20, 198
hebdomad 156
hebephrenia 152
hebetate 53
hebetude 100
heckle 8, 79
hectic 59, 79, 181
hector 22, 23, 178
hedonics 130
hedonism 130
hedonomania 105
heft 100, 176, 193
hegemony 50, 99
hegira 94
heifer 37
heighten 90
heinous 11, 58, 194
heliacal 162, 172
helicline 142
helicoid 31, 165
heliocentric 172
heliograph 109
heliport 80

helix 165
hellbox 135
hellion 110
hellkite 40
helpmeet 194
helter-skelter 34, 83
hem and haw 81
hematoma 173
hemeralopia 43, 190
hemicrania 80
hemicycle 154
hemiplegia 125
hemophilia 18
hemophobia 128
hemorrhage 18
hemorrhoids 129
hendecagon 56
hendiadys 65, 117
henotheism 16
hepatitis 102
heptad 156
heraldry 30, 73
herbicide 193
herbivorous 64, 130
herculean 47, 73, 133
hereat 10, 15
heresy 16, 44, 121
heretofore 16, 134
hereupon 86
hermaphrodite 64, 104
hermeneutics 17, 90
hermetic 6, 104
heroic couplet 131
herpes labialis 31
herpetology 145
herringbone 125
hesperus 58
heterodox 121, 185
heterogeneous 47, 49, 185, 186
heterography 165
heteronomous 170
heteronym 197
heteronymous 47
heterosexual 156
heterotaxis 3, 9
heuristics 48, 91, 99, 175
hexad 160
heyday 80
hiatus 72, 121, 126
hibernal 195
hibernating 87, 153
hidebound 17, 115, 119
hidrosis 173
hie 79, 83
hiemal 195

hierarch 81, 134
hierarchy 76, 120
hierocracy 75, 135
hieroglyphic 129, 173
hieroglyphics 199
hierology 144
higgle 9
higgledy-piggledy 49, 94
highball 101, 141
highboy 28
highfalutin 61
highflier 134
highhanded 9, 123
highlight 86, 123
high muck-a-muck 86
high rise 22, 174
high-test 72
hijack 32, 149
hilarity 72, 117
hindsight 5, 127
hinny 84, 120
hinterland 13, 89
Hippocratic oath 108
hippodrome 9
hippomania 105
hircine 74
hirsute 78
histology 177
historical present 134
histrionic 56, 177
hit-and-run play 14
hoary 7, 76, 193
hobnob 10
Hobson's choice 29
hocus-pocus 43, 180
hodomania 105
hoedown 149, 166
hogshead 101
hog-tie 176
hoi polloi 32, 107
hoity-toity 66, 73, 128, 154
hokku 93
hokum 155
hold 157
holding company 36
hole-high 74
hole in one 74
holism 122
hollowware 187
holocaust 46, 151
holograph 50, 78
holotype 7, 130
holus-bolus 6
holystone 151, 168
homeopathy 177

homeostasis 57, 122
homer 14
homeric laughter 98
home run 14
homestretch 98, 141
homicidal 112
homicide 95
homiletics 155
homily 155
hominoids 105
homochromatic 111
homoeroticism 156
homogeneous 159, 184
homograph 196
homologous 144, 159
homomorphism 159
homonym 197
homosexual 156
homunculus 53, 109
hone 157
hoodwink 28, 180
hookah 129
hooker 137
hoosier 88
hootenanny 67
hop-o'-my-thumb 176
hopper 99
hora 29, 42, 92, 150
horal 83
horn-mad 71, 104
horologe 176
horoscope 10
horrendous 70
horripilation 75
hors de combat 122
hors d'oeuvres 9
horseplay 71
hortatory 56, 60
horticulture 72
hospice 129, 146
hospitable 70, 143
hostage 135
hot line 32
hot rod 11
household word 197
housemaid's knee 95
house organ 127
hovel 53
Hovercraft 6
howdah 153
howitzer 24
hoyden 178
hubris 10
hue and cry 122
huaraches 151

hubbub 187
hugger-mugger 49, 172
hull down 157
humbug 110
humdrum 53
humid 42, 110
humidor 93
humoresque 113
hunter's moon 70
hurly-burly 83, 181
hurry-scurry 23
hurtle 112, 150
husbandry 55, 63, 178
hush money 111
hush puppy 36
husky 190
hustings 132
hutch 35
hybrid 78, 110
hydrocephalus 80
hydrofoil 192
hydrography 153
hydrology 192
hydromancy 192
hydropathy 192
hydrophobia 141
hydroponics 76, 130
hyetography 141
hygrometry 110
hylozoism 100
hymeneal 193
hyperbole 59, 123
hyperborean 9, 70
hypercritical 39, 79
hyperesthesia 155
hyperkinesia 164
hypermetropia 63
hypethral 121
hyphen 106
hypnagogic 52, 161
hypnophopia 128
hypochondria 8, 86
hypocorism 128
hypocrisy 134
hypodermic 89
hypogeum 184
hypostasis 15, 71
hypostatize 34
hypotenuse 148
hypothecation 130, 154
hypothesis 10, 177
hypothetical 86
hypsography 54
hysterectomy 187
hysteron proteron 13, 65, 147

iamb 131
iambus 131
ibid 151
ichnography 76
ichthylogy 66
ichthyomania 105
icon 86, 129
iconoclast 46
iconography 86
icterus 93
id 183
ID card 85
idée fixe 66, 119
ideograph 75
ideomania 105
ideophobia 128
idiom 129, 182
idiosyncrasy 106, 140
idolatrous 18, 46
idolatry 198
idyll 198
idyllic 129
igneous 65
ignescent 66
ignis fatuus 194
ignoble 14, 44, 49
ignominious 49, 157
ignoramus 170
ilk 29, 95, 163
illation 44, 88
ill-disposed 105, 184
ill-favored 47, 183, 185
illicit 136, 185
illiquid 25
ill-starred 185
illuminate 44
illusion 62
illustrious 49, 63, 145
imago 88
imbecile 108
imbibe 52
imbricate 123
imbroglio 33, 34
imbrue 52, 166
imbue 90, 128
immaculate 29
immanence 88
immediacy 47, 91
immerse 57
immersion 44
imminent 3, 86
immobile 111, 117
immobilize 66, 169
immoderate 186
immodest 19, 88, 154

immunity 60, 146
immunology 86
immure 33, 56, 86
immutable 183
impacted 40, 124, 132, 193
impair 99, 198
impale 52, 66, 81, 129
impalpable 90, 185
impart 17, 48, 104
impartial 49, 62
impassible 91, 184
impassive 24, 155, 185
impasto 124
impeach 27
impeachment 4
impeccable 58, 63, 66, 184
impecunious 127, 132
impede 45, 81
impediment 119
impedimenta 13, 22, 51
impel 52, 69, 187
impend 3, 177
impenetrable 45, 87
imperative 11, 183, 187
imperceptible 162, 186
imperial 125
imperious 10, 50, 187
imperium 3, 11, 172
impersonate 109
impertinence 90, 92, 150
imperturbable 24, 186
impervious 30, 87, 185
impetrate 119
impetration 146
impetuous 79, 87, 142
impetuousity 171
impetus 52, 69, 87, 111
impiety 184
impinge 56, 62, 169
impious 18, 92
implacable 108, 186
implant 89
implement 25
implementation 138
implicate 34, 57, 91
implicit 3, 184, 186
implode 31
implore 16
implosion 91
imply 81, 91, 159
impolitic 87
importunate 45
importune 79, 127, 180
impose 89, 119
imposing 75, 86, 167

imposition 119, 126
impost 83, 175
imposter, impostor 43
imposture 132, 134
impotence 80
impotent 80, 133, 192
impound 154
impoverish 104
impracticable 186
imprecate 40, 133
impregnable 66, 146, 186
impregnate 127, 152
impresario 105, 122
impress 27, 106
impressionism 10
imprest 102
imprimatur 120
improbity 49, 90
impromptu 120, 165, 166, 185
impropriated 55
improvident 87, 142, 178
improvise 91, 127, 136
impudent 19, 21, 152
impudicity 157
impugn 11, 27, 49
impuissance 97
impuissant 133
impunity 60, 70
imputation 4, 27
inadvertence 123
inadvertent 184
inadvisable 186
inalienable 87
inane 131, 159
inanimate 165, 183
inapposite 92
inapproachable 186
inapt 30
inaptitude 186
inarticulate 184, 186
inaugurate 16, 32, 90
inauspicious 184
inborn 115
incalculable 178, 185
in camera 30, 153
incandescent 22, 74, 103
incantation 27, 104
incapacitate 47
incarcerate 33, 86, 138
incarnate 128
incarnation 83
incense 7, 57
incentive 168
inception 16, 167
inceptive 89

incertitude 51
incessant 35, 183
incest 156
inchoate 14, 69
incidence 44
incident 57, 79
incidental 26, 109, 153
incinerate 23, 39
incipient 16, 31
incise 25, 41, 57
incision 72
incisive 4, 18, 95, 157
incite 166, 168, 187
incivility 48, 150
inclement 79, 156, 169
inclination 99, 101, 175
incogitant 177, 186
incognito 10, 48
incoherent 34, 49, 142
incombustible 66
incommensurable 49
incommensurate 87, 97, 122
incommode 20, 50
incommodious 37, 161, 183
incommunicado 34
incompatible 34, 48, 110
incomprehensible 119, 184
incongruous 87, 186
inconsequential 180, 184
inconsistent 27
inconsolable 22, 44
inconstant 64
incontestable 88, 185
incontinent 156, 186
incontrovertible 184
incorporate 5, 87, 89, 174
Interpol 90
incorporeal 90, 117, 165
incorrigible 82
incorrupt 82, 186
incrassate 177
incredible 7, 79
incredulous 48, 51, 160
increment 5, 88
increscent 57, 76, 88
incriminate 4
incrimination 77, 199
incrust 44, encrust 44
incubate 46, 160
incubus 23, 117, 121
inculcate 86, 90
inculpate 18, 88
incumbency 82
incumbent 99, 119, 146, 193
incunabula 16, 20, 54

incur 22
incursion 91, 141
incurvate 40
incuse 78, 166
indeciduous 58
indecipherable 185
indecorous 186
indefatigable 177, 184
indefinable 171, 188
indelible 127
indelicate 40
indemnify 137
indemnity 32, 60
indent 41, 135, 155
indention 88, 117
indenture 35
indeterminate 186, 188
index 135
Index Expurgatorious 26
index finger 69
Indian file 159
Indianian 88
Indian summer 153
indicia 57, 106
indict 4, 27
indifferent 8, 108, 183
indigence 133
indigene 115
indigenous 115
indignation 7
indignity 5, 90
indirect discourse 140
indirection 43
indiscreet 87, 186
indiscrete 184
indiscriminate 34, 142
indisposition 85
indissoluble 53, 66
indite 198
individuate 125
indoctrinate 90
indolent 98
indomitable 127, 170
indubitable 27, 185
induce 26, 128
inducement 111
inductile 186
indulge 76, 200
indulgent 99
indurate 79, 184
inebriate 59, 60
inebriated 52
inedible 184
ineffable 17, 186
ineffectual 70, 133, 183, 186

ineluctable 88, 183
inept 12, 30, 87
inequitable 184
inert 161
inestimable 134
inevitable 27, 183
inexorable 144
inexpugnable 183
in extenso 70, 183
inextricable 86
infallible 184
infamous 117, 120
infamy 58, 117
infanticide 28
infatuated 25
infatuation 68, 125, 185
infectious 26, 59
infecund 14, 167
infer 4, 33
inference 44
inferiority complex 116
inferno 80
infest 123
infidel 183
infield 14
infinite 101, 188
infinitesimal 109, 161
in flagrante delicto 26, 143
inflate 57, 88
inflated 19
inflation 134
inflect 188
inflection 190
inflexible 66, 170, 183, 186
inflorescence 67
influent 67
influx 31, 167
inform 8, 128
infraction 21, 30, 189
infra dig 17
infrangible 183
infrastructure 69
infuscate 42
ingenious 91, 160
ingénue 89, 200
ingenuity 86
ingenuous 30, 70, 115, 159, 169
ingest 172
inglorious 48
ingrained 44, 58, 177
ingrate 184
ingratiate 40, 194
ingredient 177
ingress 57, 74
ingurgitate 52, 54

inhabit 101
inherent 20, 58, 87
inhibit 28, 146
inhibition 56, 108
in high dudgeon 7, 146
inhume 23, 90
inimical 8, 83, 184
inimitable 107
iniquitous 185, 194
iniquity 159, 199
initiate 16, 32, 116, 122
inject 91, 158, 178
injudicious 94, 132
injunction 94, 122, 136
inkling 81, 161, 188
inlaid 44
inlay 56
inlet 15, 169
in medias res 109
innate 87, 89
inning 15
innocuous 79
innominate 115
innovate 91
innovation 116
innoxious 79
innuendo 81, 90
inoculate 86, 91
inopportune 186
inordinate 59
input 33
inquest 43
inquietude 146, 184
inquisition 91, 139
inquisitorial 40, 137
in re 33, 87
insatiable 76
inscribe 44, 159, 198
inscrutable 57, 114
inseminate 86
insensate 22, 68, 170, 184
in-service courses 179
insidious 40, 112, 179, 194
insignificant 128, 180
insinuate 91
insinuation 81, 161, 171
insipid 18, 53, 66, 175
insolate 18, 60
insolent 49, 90
insolvent 14
insomnia 161
insouciant 25, 100, 183
inspissate 177
installment 125
instance 25, 59

instantaneous 86
instanter 10, 86
instep 68
instigate 74, 87, 166
instill 86, 138
instinct 95, 115, 175
institute 155
instrument landing 97
insubordinate 49, 143
insubstantial 86
insufferable 183
insufficiency 44
insufflate 21
insular 46, 92, 115, 137
insulate 92
insuperable 186
insupportable 185
insurgence 90, 148
insurgent 143
insurrection 146
insusceptible 86, 146
intact 183, 184, 193
intaglio 25, 87, 172
intangible 88, 188
intarsia 111
integer 193
integral 32, 58, 88
integrate 66, 184
integration 57, 141
integrity 32, 82
integument 36, 123
intellection 177
intellectualize 143, 177
intelligence quotient 108
intelligentsia 55
intelligible 29
intemperate 59, 61, 186
intendance 105, 172
intensity 44, 133, 169
intent 6, 47, 138, 167, 186
inter alia 7
interbreed 40
intercalary 43
intercalate 89
intercede 91
intercept 154, 169
intercession 57, 133
interchange 7, 27, 59
intercourse 32, 156
interdict 59, 68, 136
interference 68
intergrade 109, 179
interim 107, 175, 176
interject 89, 91
interjection 59

interlace 18, 193
interlard 50, 188
interline 8
interlinear 17
interlocution 47
interlope 91, 107
interlude 113, 127
intermediary 74
intermezzo 113
interminable 56
intermission 91, 143
intermit 126, 169
intern 34, 46, 50, 107
internecine 43
internuncio 74
interpellation 99
interpolate 89, 91
interpolations 5, 91
interpose 31, 138
interpret 29, 60
interregnum 21, 90
interrogate 10, 139
intersect 41, 50
intersperse 152, 155
interstice 37, 161
intervale 97
intervening 17
intestate 47
intimacy 30, 33
intimate 81, 86
intimidate 22, 23, 70
intolerance 17
intolerant 30
intonation 4, 164
intone 27
in toto 7, 57
intoxicant 52
intoxicate 55, 59, 88
intractable 47, 170, 186
intramural 195
intransigent 183, 186
intrepid 19, 43, 64
intricate 33, 91, 138
intrigue 9, 34, 63, 102, 131, 184
intrinsic 58, 89
introjection 85
intromission 90
introspection 119, 154
introversion 181
introvert 154
intrude 57, 69
intuition 96
intumescence 173
inundant 123
inundate 67

inurbane 40, 185
inure 4, 178
inutile 187
invalid 117
invalidate 8, 145
invaluable 134
invariable 34, 183
invective 4, 45
inveigh 26, 188
inveigle 57, 180
inventory 101, 168
inverse 121, 147
invertebrate 27, 66, 165
invest 90, 129
investiture 90
investment banker 109
investment trust 32
inveterate 58, 66, 78
inviable 183
invidious 37, 137
in vino veritas 87
inviolate 90, 151
invite 11, 26
invocation 57, 87, 133
invoice 17, 101
invoke 24, 44
involution 33, 57, 91
involve 86, 175
involved 91
invulnerable 86, 183
Ionic 9, 76
iota 90, 161, 176
ipse dixit 50
ipso facto 23
IQ 108
irascible 92, 139
irate 7, 57
irenic 126
iridescence 31, 141
irk 8, 189, 193
irksome 175, 177, 180
irony 121, 151
irradiant 157
irradiate 29, 57, 100
irrational 3, 155, 185
irrefrangible 183
irremissible 119, 185
irreproachable 18
irresistible 32, 63
irresolute 81, 184, 192
irresponsible 186
irritated 89, 163
irruption 21, 23, 91
isagoge 91
isochronal 57

isochroous 31
isocracy 57
isolated 7, 155
isomerous 57
isometric 57
isosceles 180
isthmus 97
italic 160, 182
iterate 145
ithyphallic 100
itinerant 74, 179
itinerary 77, 150

jabber 174
jabot 150
jackanapes 187
jackass 18
jackpot 135
jactitation 19, 178, 181
jade 49, 84, 196
jaded 53, 192, 198
jai alai 72
jalousie 153, 158
jamb 51, 195
jangle 48, 79, 139, 198
jape 94, 110
jar 23, 169
jargon 25, 73, 101, 190
jaunt 94
jaunty 22, 43, 101, 154
jawbreaker 196
jaywalker 126
jealous 189, 192
jeer 45, 152
jejune 14, 52, 90, 115
je ne sais quoi 79, 88
jeopardy 42, 100
jeremiad 97, 195
jeroboam 195
jerrybuilt 66
jess 62
jest 70, 130, 139
Jesuit 152
jet 18, 77, 166
jeton 178
jetsam 25
jet set 63, 192
jettison 48, 178
jetty 129, 193
jezebel 194, 196
jib 13, 144, 151
jibe 6
jigger 40, 73
jiggle 93
jihad 40

jilt 25, 48
jimmy 23, 40, 137
jingle 148
jingo 28, 126
jitney 188
job action 197
jobber 194
job lot 74
jockey 105
jockeying 70, 180
jocose 93, 130
jocund 28, 72
jodhpurs 21
jog 117, 150, 168, 178
joggle 156
joie de vivre 94
joists 15
joker 81, 185
jollity 72
jolly boat 158
jorum 52
jostle 40, 138, 157, 158
jounce 20, 94, 157
jousts 179
jowl 66
joy ride 143, 148
jubilant 94, 180
judicious 25, 195
judo 44
juggernaut 46, 68
jujitsu 93
julienne 170
jump bid 21
jumping-off place 123, 167
jump shot 15
jumpsuit 36
junk 19
junket 64, 129, 130
junoesque 167
junta 24, 91
jurant 119
jurisprudence 98
jury-rigged 56, 175
juvenescence 200
juxtaposition 158

kabuki 93
kachina 50, 165
kaddish 93
kaffiyeh 9, 95
kakemono 191
kaleidoscopic 27
kamikaze 93, 171
kana 93
kangaroo court 36

karma 58, 146
katzenjammer 34, 82
kayak 25
kazatsky 42, 99, 150, 160
kebab 107
keel 157
keelhaul 143, 152
keen 97, 191
kef 52
kempt 176
kennel 77, 156
kepi 109
keratosis 192
kerf 41, 117
kettledrum 52
key 92
khaki 30
khamsin 194
kibbutz 31, 92
kibitzer 107, 164
kickback 111
kickoff 68
kier 181
kilderkin 25
kill 39, 169
killick 7
kiln 71, 123
kilometer 49
kiloton 60, 177
kilowatt 133
kinematics 111
kinesophobia 128
kinesthesia 112
kingpin 86
kiosk 20, 116
kip 24, 97, 186
kismet 63
kiss 25, 178
kite 13
kitsch 10, 101, 179
kitty 111
klaxon 82
kleptomania 105
klieg light 67
knack 3, 160
knapsack 13
knavery 43, 49, 180
knell 16, 43, 120
knesset 92
knight-errantry 28
knoll 81, 111
knurl 23, 103
koine 47
kolkhoz 31, 164
Koran 111

kosher 93
koto 93
kowtow 155
kraft 22
kreplach 163
kris 42
kudos 39, 133
kumiss 109
kyphosis 83

labiate 101
labile 27, 186
labored 51, 169
labyrinth 107
lace 6
lacerate 105, 175
lachrymose 175
laciniate 70
lackadaisical 101
lackey 155, 178
lackluster 53
laconic 22, 33, 64
lacteal 109
lactescent 109
lacuna 18, 72, 164
Ladino 164
lag 14
laggard 62, 161, 169
lagniappe 60, 76
laicize 154
laid paper 125
laissez faire 100, 117
laity 127
lallation 97, 136, 141
lalomania 105
lalophobia 128
lambent 22, 66
lambrequin 51, 195
lame duck 44, 120
laminated 177
lampoon 4, 152
lancet arch 9
lancinate 166
landfall 159
landlocked 172
landlubber 12
landmark 108, 119, 136
langlauf 40, 160
languet 178
languid 97, 101, 192
languish 52, 101, 129, 192
languishing 155
languor 53, 63, 88, 165, 166, 192
lanky 174
lanuginous 51

lapidary 57, 72
lapidate 168
lapin 141
lapse 161
larboard 132
larceny 177
lard 56, 63
lardon 13
lares and penates 83
largess 73
largo 113, 161
laryngitis 178, 190
lascivious 103
laser 15
latent 51, 184
lateral 159
lateral pass 68
latitude 70, 142
latitudinarian 100, 185
latria 198
latrine 178
laud 133
laudatory 31
laureate 82, 160
lava-lava 102, 151
lavish 73, 165
lax 102
layup 15
lazaretto 83
lea 200
leach 65
leader 51
league 177
lean-to 149
lebensraum 149
lecherous 100, 103
lectern 164, 167
lectionary 20
leer 99, 102, 105, 161
leery 172
lees 52
leeward 159, 194
leeway 98, 164
left 141
left-handed 7, 90
leftist 100, 141
legal cap 125
legatee 17
legato 113
legend 25, 60
legerdemain 82, 161, 180
leitmotif 177
lenitive 163
lentigo 70
lento 113

leonine 101
leonine rhyme 90, 147
leotard 72
lepidopteran 23, 111
lesbian 82, 196
lese majesty 49, 120, 179
lesion 89
lethal 43, 63
lethargy 8, 53, 161
lethe 69, 119, 149
letter of credence 50
letter press 135
leukemia 24
levanter 54, 194
levee 149
leverage 32, 54
leviathan 73, 83
levigate 137
levitate 148
levity 65, 70, 72, 100
levy en masse 29
lexicography 47
libation 101
libel 42, 63, 199
libertarian 29
libertine 111, 142, 183
libidinous 103
libido 156
libretto 121, 197
licentious 100, 156
licit 98
lied 73
lief 142, 194
lien 29
lieu 87
ligament 19, 176
ligature 135, 182
lightface 135
light heavyweight 20, 198
light verse 189
lightweight 20, 198
light year 49
limbo 188
limbus 20
limelight 34, 137
limerick 189
limn 45
limpid 29, 103, 179
linage 101
lineage 7
lineament 49, 62
lineate 101, 106
linebacker 68
line drive 14
line of scrimmage 68

linesman 68
lingo 93, 190
lingua franca 97
lingual 178
linguistics 97
linking verb 189
lintel 51
lion's share 17
lipoid 63
liquescent 108
liquidate 155
liquidity 27, 134, 146
lissome 101, 131, 172
list 55, 170
listed stock 168
listless 8, 88, 97
litany 101, 133
literal 59, 107, 183, 184
literati 198
lithe 16, 75, 101
lithography 135
lithoid 168
lithology 149
litigation 98
litigious 139
litotes 5, 10, 65, 116
little finger 129
little neck 29
littoral 158
liturgy 144, 148
liverpudlian 102
livery 184
livid 18, 71, 98
load 32, 36
loan shark 99
loan translation 101, 179
loanword 196
loath 144, 186
loathing 3, 48, 49
loathsome 146
lob 176
lobbyist 145
lobster shift 76, 116
lockout 56
locution 106, 129, 164
lodestar 77, 167
logaoedic 109, 110
loggerheads, at 47, 139
loggia 72
logistics 109
logogram 3, 159
logogriph 7, 197
logomachy 65, 189
logorrhea 174
logotype 115, 182

loan translation 101, 179
loanword 196
loath 144, 186
loathing 3, 48, 49
loathsome 146
lob 176
lobbyist 145
lobster shift 76, 116
lockout 56
locution 106, 129, 164
lodestar 77, 167
logaoedic 109, 110
loggerheads, at 47, 139
loggia 72
logistics 109
logogram 3, 159
logogriph 7, 197
logomachy 65, 189
logorrhea 174
logrolling 132, 179, 190
logy 53
logotype 115, 182
loll 52, 78, 100
loiter 101
long 123
longe 144
longevity 5, 102
long jump 22
long shot 17
long-winded 51
loom 8, 31
loop 35
loose sentence 104, 155
lop 12, 41, 52, 78, 161, 180
lope 150, 169
lopsided 121
loquacious 174
lordosis 173
lorgnette 61
lorry 191
loran 157
Los Angelean 102
Los Angeleno 102
loss leader 151
lotus-eater 88
loupe 93, 104
lout 12, 20, 170
louver board 195
love set 176
low 111
lowboy 28
lower 7, 153, 171
lowering 42, 177, 193
lower case 7, 161
lowery 30

lox 123, 151
luau 79
lubricate 76, 120
lubricous 100, 157, 180
lucarne 194
lucent 141, 179
lucid 22, 29, 142, 184
luciferin 65
lucrative 111, 136
lucubrate 23, 170, 198
lucubration 101, 126
lucullan 60
ludicrous 3, 148
lues 173
luff 151, 157
lugs 54
lugubrious 112, 151
lull 161, 163
lumber 112, 150
lumbering 30, 80
luminiferous 100
luminous 22, 74
lurch 25
lurid 158, 190
luscious 30, 45, 173
lustrate 138
lustrum 66
luteous 76
luxate 49
lycanthrope 193
lymphatic 161
lyonnaise 133

machismo 106
macabre 76
macaronic 101, 110, 197
macedoine 110
macerate 56, 162, 177
machinate 34, 152
mackle 19, 51, 135, 166
macrocosm 98, 185
macrograph 100
macron 101, 169, 190
macroscopic 98, 190
maculation 18, 166
mad money 110
Madrilenian 104
madrileño 104
maculation 106
madding 70, 141
maduro 29, 170
madrigal 163

maelstrom 181, 193
maenad 195
maestoso 113, 167
magnanimous 73, 76, 81
magnitude 160
maestro 113
magnum 195
magnum opus 76, 107
mahdi 92, 109, 136
mahout 56
maiden over 39
maieutic 162
mainer 104
maisonette 36
majuscule 98
make short shrift of 49
maladroit 18, 30
malapropos 87, 122
malediction 40, 160
malfeasance 199
malefactor 39, 58
maleficent 79, 110
malevolent 85, 105
malign 44, 160
malicious 79, 165
malinger 158, 197
malleable 66, 131
mall 169
malodorous 162, 168
Manxman 92
manacle 78, 156
mammals 8
Mancunian 105
mandamus 32, 112
mandatory 119, 146
mañana 178
maneuvers 10, 112
Manhattan 150, 193
manifest 8, 58, 130
mannerism 5, 126
manifold 106, 188
mannequin 110
manipulate 35, 78, 105
manqué 97, 186
mania 37, 119
mantel 157
mantic 136
mansard 149
manumit 56, 70, 100
marasmus 56
maraca 142
marathon 56, 68
mantilla 152
maraud 131, 141
marc 75

mare's tail 30
mare's nest 34, 109
margin 7, 25, 127
margin call 45
marinate 129
marina 19
market order 122
market price 134
marsupium 133
martinet 48, 169
martingale 51, 72
martini 73
marimba 90
masochism 130, 171
Massachusettsan 107
massé 17
massif 111
mastectomy 21
master-at-arms 131
masthead 116
materiel 109
matador 23
matched and lost 17, 181
matin 111
matriarchy 111
mariticide 112, 166
matriculate 57, 144
matriculation 31
matrix 110
maverick 117, 185
maturate 148
maturity 43
matutinal 54, 87
maudlin 56, 155, 175
maul 4, 105, 149
maunder 52, 112, 174
maven or mavin 34, 60
mawkishness 63, 155
mawkish 158, 175
mazer 52, 74
meager 152, 177
mea culpa 18, 85
meander 191
meandering 6, 142
mean 90
mechanical 11, 100
medical jurisprudence 99
medley 110, 113
median 109
mediation 156
megaton 109
megillah 102
meiosis 184
mélange 82
melburnian 108

merry Andrew 22, 30
mesalliance 106
mesomorphic 11, 170
mesostich 4, 131
metabolism 19, 137
metallurgy 109
metamorphosis 27, 179
metaphor 32, 65
metaphrase 179
metaphysical 33
metaphysics 3
metastasis 48, 157, 166
metathesis 173, 179
meteoric 22, 43, 173
meteorology 11, 193
meticulous 124, 134
métier 69, 120, 197
metonymy 65, 115
mettle 36, 131
mettlesome 36, 188
mews 6, 169
mezuzah 93
mezzanine 169
mezzo 108, 113
miasma 11, 117, 186
michigander 109
michiganite 109
Mickey Finn 52
microcephaly 161
microcosm 101, 185
microfiche 65
microfilm 65
micturate 187
middleweight 20, 198
mien 8, 105
migrant 31
miliaria 135
milieu 57, 172
militate 5
millenary 177
millennium 127
millstone 23
milquetoast 8, 108, 158
mimesis 86
minacious 108, 177
minatory 108, 177
mincing 5, 42, 191
minify 143
minimize 143
minion 67, 155
mint 31, 91
mint condition 21, 122, 186
minuend 117, 171
minuscule 176
minute 90, 161

minutiae 180, 184
mirabile dictu 106, 196
mirador 13, 194
mire 9, 160
mirror writing 13, 199
mirth 109
MIRV 110
misandry 79, 105
misanthrope 105
misanthropy 50
misbegotten 20
miscarriage 62
miscegenation 90
miscreant 58
misdemeanor 98, 120
mise en scène 155, 172
misfeasance 98, 185
misgiving 9, 51, 139
misnomer 58, 199
misogynist 195
misology 49
misprison 33, 39, 110
mistral 194
miter 94
mitigated 99, 109
mitzvah 74
mnemonic 108
mocha 31
mockup 110
moderate 134
modicum 161
modify 147, 188
modulate 5, 144, 162
module 170
modus operandi 106
modus vivendi 6
Mohole 82
moiety 78, 132, 157
moiré 192
mollescent 162
mollify 124, 139, 163
Molotov cocktail 19
molto 112
momentum 86
momism 111
momus 63
monad 185
monandrous 121
monger 43, 179
monition 192
monochrome 121, 160
monody 131
monograph 20
monolith 159
monomania 37, 105

monopoly 59
monorail 141
monosodium glutamate 66
monotone 151
monotype 135
monsoon 142
monstrous 57, 81
montage 129
monthly investment plan 23, 144
moonlighting 198
moot 43, 84
morass 19, 47, 106
moratorium 45
mordant 26, 151
mores 40, 67
morganatic 106
morose 74, 85
morpheme 98
morphology 7, 101, 130, 197
mortarboard 31
mortification 63
mortise 135
Moscovite 111
mossback 34
mot 195
mote 125, 164
motel 83
mother wit 32
mot juste 148
motley 188
mottle 18, 166, 169
moue 133
moulage 26, 110
mountebank 27, 139
muchacha 73
muckrake 60
muckraker 137
mudder 83
muddler 167, 168
muff 23
mufti 29
mug 10
mugger 149
mugwump 88
mukluk 20
mulct 28, 44
muliebrity 64, 196
mullion 194
multifarious 50, 188
multitudinous 118
mummery 27, 84, 134
mundane 122, 150
munificent 20, 73, 98, 121
mural 10, 191
murky 42, 110, 119

Murphy's law 85, 199
murrey 138
murrhine glass 73
muscae volitantes 61, 159, 164, 190
muscovado 142, 171
musette bag 158
musophobia 128
must 56, 94, 156
muster 24, 180
mutable 27, 64
muumuu 75
myalgia 37, 112
myology 112
myopia 190
myopic 116, 120
myriad 89, 118, 188
myrmidon 62, 103
mysophobia 128
mystique 114
mythical 65
mythomania 103

nabob 133, 148
nacelle 6
nachus 135
nacreous 91, 126
nadir 103
naiad 192
naive 10, 39, 159, 183, 186
nape 13
napery 101
napped 62
narcissism 154
narcolepsy 161
nascent 116, 167
natant 67
natatorium 173
nates 23
nauseated 158
nauseous 158
navel 16
neap tide 176
nebbish 158
nebulous 79, 183, 188
necromancy 18, 69, 163
necrophobia 128
née 104
nefarious 58, 189, 194
negativism 51, 146
negligible 90, 180
negotiable 154
nemesis 8, 121, 189
neologism 116, 197
neophobia 128
neophyte 16, 116, 117

neoplasm 177
nepenthe 119
nephology 30
nephrectomy 95
nephritis 95
ne plus ultra 127
nepotism 64
nescience 85
n'est-ce pas 92
nestle 40, 62
net 145
net asset value 188
nether 17, 103
nether world 80
neuritis 116
neurology 116
neuter 156
neutron 11
nevus 17
newel 132
newspeak 98
New York Stock Exchange 17
nexus 19, 34, 101
nice 4, 58, 133, 171
nicety 65
niche 82, 132
nicht wahr? 92
nictitate 195
niello 18
niggardly 152, 168
niggling 65, 71, 115, 123, 128
nigrescence 18
nihilism 48, 144
nimbus 11, 78
nirvana 18, 144
niveous 162
no 93
noblesse oblige 117
noctambulation 161
nocuous 79, 89
node 95, 173
noetic 90
noisome 48, 120, 168
nolens volens 194
nolo contendere 117
nomad 191
nomadic 82, 149
nom de plume 11, 126
nomenclature 115, 176
nominal 87, 99, 161, 180
nonagenarian 117
nonce 134
nonce word 196
nonchalant 35, 88
non compos mentis 108

noncumulative 134
nondescript 27, 97
nonentity 184
nonpareil 107, 125, 184
nonplus 17, 53, 127
non sequitur 92
nonuple 117
nose cone 110, 149
no-show 6
nosography 48
nostalgia 82, 102
nostrum 108, 139, 145
notion 73, 188
notions 129, 148
notwithstanding 116
noumenon 90, 185
nouveau riche 148, 192
nova 167
novella 117
novena 117, 133
novice 9, 16
noxious 79, 89
noyade 52
nuance 65, 75, 171
nubbin 161, 170
nubile 106, 129
nubilous 30, 67, 88
nucha 115
nucleus 26, 36
nuclear fission 11
nuclear fusion 185
nugatory 107, 133, 198
nullify 184, 190
numen 69, 77, 89
numerus clausus 140
numismatics 31
nuncio 132
nuncupative 121
nurture 22, 64, 117, 142
nutation 117
nutriment 67
nyctalopia 116
nycotophobia 128
nymphomania 156

obdurate 79, 129, 170
obeah 163
obeisance 82, 146, 147
obelisk 168
obese 36, 63
obfuscate 17, 34, 112, 119
obi 93, 163
obiter dictum 32, 145
objective 46, 183
objectivism 50

objet d'art 10
objet trouve 10
objurgate 17, 143, 152
oblation 144
obligato 113
oblique 88, 160
obliterate 46, 55, 195
oblivion 49, 69
oblivious 183, 185
obloquy 4, 44, 48, 88
obnoxious 119, 120
oboe 113
obscurantism 121
obscure 62, 81
obsequies 71
obsequious 64, 119, 155
obsession 33, 134
obsolescent 125
obsolete 122
obstinate 129, 170
obstreperous 19, 186
obstruct 18, 86, 169
obtrude 69, 91
obtuse 19, 53, 89
obverse 36, 62, 70, 147
obviate 11, 49, 134
Occident 193
occlude 18, 30, 158
occult 50, 104
ochlocracy 110
ochlomania 105
ochlophobia 128
octave 55
octennial 55
ocular 61, 159
odd-lot 168
odious 48, 79, 102, 146
odontalgia 178
odoriferous 162
odorous 70
oenology 195
offal 150, 192
offer 134
offertory 31
officiate 4, 127
officinal 108
officious 120, 138
offset 13, 32, 135
offside 68, 82
ogle 61, 104, 167
ogre 40, 81
Old English 18, 135
old wives' tale 172
oleaginous 120
olfactory 162

oligarchy 75
olla 93, 132
ombudsman 32
omnifarious 188
omnipotent 6
omnipresence 58
omniscient 95
omnivorous 6, 54
omphalos 26
omphaloskepsis 35, 116
onanism 107
oneirocritic 52
onerous 23
onomastics 115
onomatopoeia 197
onomatopoeic or onomatopoetic 55
onslaught 11
ontology 142
opalescence 91
opaque 53, 100
open-ended 185
open shop 185
operational 142
operative 55, 198
operetta 113
ophidiomania 105
ophidiophobia 128
ophiolatry 162
ophthalmology 61
opiate 144, 154, 161
oppidan 29
opprobrious 4, 48, 157
opt 29, 55
optician 61
optimize 46
option 28
optometrist 61
opugn 24, 49
opulence 148, 192
opuscule 161, 180
oracle 88, 195
oracular 57, 136
oration 164
oratorio 113
oratory 27
orbicular 149, 165
ordain 44, 56, 122
ordeal 56, 124
ordinance 98, 167
ordinary seaman 151
ordnance 10, 24, 109
oread 111
organic 15, 71
orgasm 30, 156
orgy 194

oriel 15
Orient 54
orientation 5
orifice 112, 121
oriflamme 80
origami 93
ormolu 74
ornate 67, 122, 158
ornithology 17
ornitomania 105
orography 112, 165
orotund 29, 70, 132, 149
orphrey 56
orthodontics 45
orthodox 35, 136
orthoepy 136
orthography 165
orthopedics 19, 112
orthoptics 190
oscillate 67, 173
oscitancy 53, 161, 200
osculant 30
osculation 95
osmosis 10, 47, 127
ossification 19
ossify 79
ostensible 8, 154
ostentation 158
osteopathy 48, 105
ostracize 59, 158
otalgia 54
o tempora! o mores! 122
otiose 85, 88, 98, 187
otology 54
ottoman 36
outage 21, 41, 90
outboard motor 57, 111
outlandish 70, 169
outpatient 126
outrageous 11
outré 120, 183
outrigger 19
outstrip 59
outwit 44, 194
ovation 9, 193
overall 58, 178
overbearing 50, 123
overblown 89, 134
overcompensation 142
overhead 36, 60
override 44
overset 135, 182
overt 58, 121, 183
over-the-counter 154, 168, 175
overweening 10, 33

overwrought 116, 123
ovine 157
oxonian 123
oxymoron 35, 65, 121
oyez 36

pachyderms 17
pacific 126
pacify 139
pact 6, 179
paddock 65, 166
paean 163
pageant 60, 125, 164
paginate 118
paillette 109, 164
painstaking 25, 47
paisley 30
palaver 85, 174
pale 20, 80, 147
paleography 7, 199
paleontology 69
palimpsest 125
palindrome 13, 104, 142, 147, 148, 155, 197
palinode 131, 147
palisade 14
palisades 30, 133, 149
pall 20, 49
pallet 16, 169
palliasse 107, 169
palliate 6, 60
pallid 31, 124, 191
palmistry 69
palomino 83
palpable 178
palpate 59, 64
palpitate 15, 67, 140
palsy 180
palter 100, 139
paltry 35, 128, 180
paly 81
palynology 132
pampero 194
pamphleteer 198
pan 112
panacea 40, 145
panache 43, 131, 170
panatela 29
pandemic 73, 185, 194
pandemonium 194
pander 129, 156
panegyric 133, 180
panjandrum 120, 134
panorama 189
pansophy 185

pantheism 74
pantile 149
pantograph 35, 180
pantomime 73, 197
paperback 19
paper profit 136
paper tiger 133
Pap test 176, 187
parable 169
paradigm 59, 126
paradox 35, 62, 154
paragoge 173
paragon 59
paragraphia 110, 199
paraleipsis 152
paralogism 63, 85, 143
paramedic 50, 107
paramount 3, 81
paramour 103
paranoia 45, 127
paraph 67, 159
paraphernalia 57, 72
paraphrase 147
paraplegia 125
parapraxis 29, 108, 110
parasite 127
parataxis 29
parboil 19
parbuckle 161
parch 52, 177
parenthesis 129, 196
par excellence 3
parget 130
pariah 122
parimutuel 17, 141
parity 57
Parkinson's law 197
parlance 85, 97, 164
parlay 17, 141
parley 33, 174
parmesan 28
parochial 101, 115, 137
parody 23, 86
paronomasia 137, 138
paronym 196
parotitis 112
paroxysm 122, 171, 189
parquet 122
parquetry 67
parr 151
parricide 125
parry 11, 44, 181, 191
parse 75, 155
parsimony 110, 168
partial 17, 63, 134

particeps criminis 4
participating preferred 134
particolored 31
parti pris 133
parts of speech 196
parturition 13, 28
parvenu 116, 187
pas de deux 181
pasquinade 152
passant 80
passé 120
passed ball 15
passed dividend 50
passementerie 180
passible 171
passim 8, 81
passive resistance 117, 121
pastiche 110
pastoral 89, 150, 159
pat 9, 62, 94, 178
patent 58, 105, 120
paternal 63
pathetic 129, 151
pathetic fallacy 83
pathology 48
pathos 163, 173
patina 76
patio 121
patisserie 126
patois 47
patriarchy 75, 104
patrician 9, 186
patrimony 56
patronage 120, 132, 165, 172
patronymic 63, 172
patter 74, 165
paucity 64, 158, 161
paunch 16, 17
pauper 27, 132
pavane 161
pavé 93
pavilion 25, 171
pavonine 91
pax vobiscum 126
pay dirt 136
payload 191
pea jacket 153
peaked 124, 177
peccadillo 63
peccant 36, 159
pecking order 142
pecksniffian 84, 90
pectin 93
pectoral 21
peculate 56, 167

pecuniary 110
pedagogue 126, 175
pedantry 152
pederasty 156, 162
pedestrian 53, 108, 137, 191
pediatrics 28
pedicab 188
pediculophobia 128
pediculosis 102
pedicure 68
pedigree 7
pedology 162
pedomania 105
pedometer 167
pedophobia 128
peer 57
peerless 184
pejorative 45
pelagic 120
pelf 20, 110
pellage 71
pellet 13
pell-mell 49
pellucid 29, 179, 184
pelt 82, 178
penalty box 82
penance 11
penchant 101
pendant 122
pendent 186
pending 12, 35
pendulous 78
penetralia 89, 153
peninsula 97
penis 156
penitence 35
pen name 198
penny stocks 103, 168
penology 39
pensile 78
pensive 144, 155, 177
pentateuch 111
pentathlon 11
penultimate 116
penumbra 156
penurious 132, 168
peplum 150
pepper 126, 164
percept 96
perception 184
Percherons 83
percuss 175
percussion 163, 189
per diem 42, 60
perdition 42

perdurable 53, 127
peregrinate 179
peremptory 3, 44, 47, 86, 132
perennial 35, 98
perfecting press 135
perfecto 29
perfervid 9, 64
perfidious 179
perforate 137
perforce 116
perfunctory 53, 150, 201
perfuse 36, 166, 171
pergola 9, 191
pericope 60, 125
perigee 103, 122
perihelion 122
perimeter 20
periodic 143, 144
periodic sentence 104, 155
periodontics 45
peripatetic 191
peripheral 106, 123
periphery 55
periphrasis 197
periphrastic 29, 88
perique 178
peristalsis 91
perjury 103
permeate 127, 166
per mill 177
permissive 6, 99
permutation 179
pernicious 43, 89, 105
perorate 164
peroration 143, 171
perpendicular 148, 189
perpetrate 32, 50
perpetuity 98
perplexed 17, 138
perquisite 17, 126, 135
perseverance 127
perseveration 143
persiflage 14, 66
persona grata 193
personal equation 47
persona non grata 183, 186
personification 56, 65, 83, 128
personify 182
perspective 131, 189
perspicacious 48, 95, 127
perspicuous 29, 103
pert 101, 152
pertinacious 127, 170
pertinacity 119
pertinent 144

perturb 6, 50, 187
peruse 59, 142, 153
pervade 166
perverse 35, 37, 46, 58, 117, 170, 194
perversion 46
pervert 36, 49, 109
pervious 121, 126
pestilent 42, 180
petard, hoist by one's own 89, 189
petcock 63, 188
Peter principle 56, 87
petite 161
petite bourgeoisie 103
petrify 43, 79, 125
petrology 149
petrous 79, 168
pettifogger 28, 98, 139
pettish 126
petty 90, 107, 115, 180
petulance 92, 126
phagophobia 128
phantasm 86, 164
phantasmagoria 8
phallic 127
phallus 127
pharisaic 151
pharisaism 84
pharmacology 52
pharmacopoeia 108
pharos 100
phase out 56, 195
phatic 107, 162
phenology 130
phenomenon 60, 186, 190
philander 103, 104
philanthropy 27
philately 166
philippic 164
philistine 35
philogyny 103
philology 101
philoprogenitive 136
philter 103
phlegmatic 8, 88
phobia 52, 64
phoneme 165
phonetics 163, 165
phonophobia 128
phosphorescence 100
photoengraving 135
photo finish 141
photogenic 11, 129
phraseology 197
phrenology 160
phylacteries 93

phylogeny 58
physics 57, 107
physiognomy 8, 62
physiology 7
phytography 20
pi 29, 135
piacular 11
piaffer 83
pianissimo 113, 162
piazza 166
pica 182
picador 23
picaresque 81
picaroon 129
picayune 124, 128, 180
piccolo 113
picot 55
piddle 43, 192
pidgin English 47
piebald 111, 166
pièce de résistance 104
pie chart 29, 75
pied-à-terre 102, 125
piedmont 111
pier glass 109
piety 144
pigeon-hearted 176
pigment 31
pile 62, 176
pilfer 167
pill 35
pillage 20, 131, 165
pillion 153
pillory 148, 152
pilot film 65
pimp 137
pince-nez 61
pinfeather 64
pinfold 169
pinguid 120
pinion 17, 82, 195
pinked 117
pinnacle 4, 81, 178
pinto 166
pipette 181
piping 36, 180
pipkin 132
piquant 101, 141, 157, 168, 175
pique 146
pirouette 14, 193
pistil 154
pith 58, 73
pithy 162, 176
pittance 161
piu 113

pivot 131, 181
pivotal 40, 86
pixie 56
pizzazz 162, 170
pizzicato 131
placable 8, 69
placard 132
placate 8
placebo 79, 108
placenta 64
placid 24, 126
placket 121
plafond 26
plagiarize 9, 129
plain-dealing 82
plaint 32, 76, 179
plaintive 112, 163
plait 21
plane 148
planetarium 130
plangent 37, 117
planish 162, 179
plankton 106
planned parenthood 17
planter's punch 150
plaque 174
plastic 110, 131
plateau 81
platitude 14, 32, 180
platonic 106, 195
plaudit 9, 31
plausible 16, 143, 180
play upon words 137
pleach 91, 130
pleasance 72, 153
pleasantry 74, 131
pleasure principle 130
pleat 67
plebeian 32, 190
plebiscite 190
pledget 191
plenary 3, 32, 70
plenipotentiary 70
plenum 70
pleonasm 59, 144, 172
plethora 123
plethoric 89, 123
plexus 116
pliable 16, 66
pliant 128, 200
plicated 67, 130
plight 12, 33, 133
plinth 18, 126, 168
plod 180, 191, 197
ploy 105, 169, 174

plumb 47, 99, 107, 163
plummet 52, 62
plunder 20, 131
pluralism 110, 162
plurality 190
plutocracy 75
plutomania 105
pluvious 141
ply 134, 139, 197
plywood 196
pneuma 163, 165
poach 66, 83, 180
pocket veto 189
poco 113, 161
pococurante 88
podagra 75
podiatry 68
podium 130
poetaster 131
poetic justice 94
poetic license 49
pogonip 67
pogrom 107
poignant 83, 112, 178
point 50, 121
point-blank 6, 18, 47
pointe 14
pointillism 51, 124
poise 33, 154
poitrine 21
polar 121
polarize 50, 155
polemic 9
pole vault 11, 179
policlinic 83, 123
politic 47, 60, 137, 195
polity 75, 132
pollard 7, 82, 180
pollenosis 79
pollex 178
polliwog 174
pollute 44, 47
poltergeist 73, 117
poltroon 37
polyandry 181
polygamy 111
polyglot 98, 112
polygyny 181
polyphagia 54
polyphemus 121
polyphonic 163
polysemy 197
polysyllable 196
polyunsaturated 63
pomander 9

pompon 181
pompous 134, 154
ponder 34, 144, 177
ponderous 22, 30, 97, 103
pontifical 50, 79, 132
pontificate 164
pontoon 67
ponytail 78
pooh-pooh 16
popple 22, 148
porcine 82, 129
pore 142, 170
pork barrel 64
porous 127, 132
port 99, 157
portal 51, 57
porte-cochère 72
portend 69, 192
porteño 22
portentous 12, 120
portfolio 92, 101, 154
portico 132
portieore 51
portière 40
portly 169
portmanteau word 196
posse 19
poseur 5
posit 10
posterior 16
posterity 71
posthaste 83
posthumous 5
postiche 10, 36
post-mortem 7, 59
postprandial 5
postulant 128
postulate 4, 10, 29, 134, 146
posture 70, 108
potable 52
pot-au-feu 107
potent 35, 55, 129, 170
potential 132
pother 20, 23, 32, 67
pothole 82
potion 101
potpourri 108, 110
potsherd 22, 54
pot shot 142
potter's field 26
poulard 80
poultice 113
pourboire 176
pousette 42
pousse-café 101

pou sto 129
powwow 33
pragmatic 51, 133
prandial 107
prank 44
prate 28, 85, 174
pratique 157
prattle 28
praxis 4, 133
preamble 91
prebend 29, 126
precarious 186
precentor 98, 159
precept 107, 111, 150
preceptor 175
precious 5, 123
precipice 30
precipitate 3, 22, 26, 83, 171
precipitous 167
precis 3, 33, 171
precise 58
preclude 59, 134, 158
precocious 5, 46, 134
preconceive 16, 69
preconception 17, 121, 134
precursor 69, 133
predatory 64
predicate 14, 167
predilection 17, 125, 134
predisposition 172, 175
preeminent 123, 172, 178
preempt 9, 154
preen 52, 135
preface 91
preferred stock 168
prefix 16, 173
pregnable 91, 190
pregnant 70, 91, 136
prehension 75
prelacy 28
prelate 28
prelect 99, 155
premier 66
premier danseur 14, 104
premiere 121
premise 15
premium 7, 143
premonition 69
preoccupy 50, 57
preponderant 172
preponderate 87
prepossessing 11, 130
prepuce 69
prerequisite 146
prerogative 148

presage 120, 132, 192
presbycusis 80
prebyopia 63
prescience 69, 96
prescient 63, 154
prescind 92, 145, 174, 177
prescriptive 146
presentative 95
presentiment 64, 69, 75
presidium 164
pressure cooker 35, 133
prestidigitation 104, 161
prestigious 49, 86, 145
prestissimo 113
presto 113
presumptuous 10, 69
pretentious 5, 122
preterition 121
pretermit 116, 123
preternatural 3
prevalent 32, 70, 194
prevaricate 57, 100
prevenient 8, 74, 133
preventive 191
priapism 58, 127
price-earnings ratio 168
prie-dieu 133
prig 126, 162
prima ballerina 14
prima donna 64
prima facie evidence 58
primal 66, 122, 135
primate 134
primipara 134
primogenitor 7, 69
primordial 55, 122
prim'oro 105
primp 52
primrose path 130
prince consort 84
printout 33
prisiadka 166
pristine 135, 138
privy 87, 154
prix fixe 66
probate 136
probity 90
problematic 139, 186
pro bono publico 137
proboscis 117
proclivity 49, 99, 175
procrastinate 132, 138
procreant 70
procreate 16, 136
procrustean 34, 150

proctology 143
procurator 105
prodigal 61, 98, 192
prodigious 7, 57, 106
prodigy 28
prodrome 173
proem 91, 133
profane 46, 132
proffer 120
profile 160
pro forma 69
profound 44
profuse 4, 98
progenitor 69, 163
progeny 120
prognosis 133
prognosticate 69
project 130, 178
prolate 99
prolegomenon 91, 133
prolepsis 65, 71
proletariat 198
prolific 64, 136
prolix 102, 189, 197
prolocutor 165
prolusion 136
promethean 37, 122
promiscuous 26, 88
promontory 80, 97
promulgate 8, 137
prone 62, 103
pronunciamento 136
propaedeutic 55, 91
propagate 21, 112, 166
propensity 87, 175
prophylaxis 48, 134, 137
propinquity 30, 95, 116
propitiate 8, 33, 194
propitious 11, 63, 95
proponent 5, 13, 172
propound 136, 171
proprietary 123, 137
proprieties, the 167
propriety 136
props 177
prorate 50
prorogue 56
prosaic 32, 52, 122
proscenium 166
prosciutto 78
proscribe 33, 123, 136
prosecute 90, 138
proselyte 35
prosody 131
prosopopeia 128

prospectus 123, 136, 171
prosthesis 10
prostrate 60, 103
protagonist 99
protasis 33
protean 27
prothesis 5
prothonotary 36
protocol 47, 58
proton 11
prototype 110
protuberant 22
provection 197
provenance 122
provender 26
provenience 163
providence 69, 130
provincial 115, 186
proviso 33, 168
provocative 168
prowess 3, 160
proximate 116
proximity 116
proxy 171
prudery 5
pseudonym 65
psychedelic 78
psychoanalysis 108
psychokinesis 109
psychological moment 17
psychosomatic 19
psychrophobia 128
puberty 156
public domain 36
pudency 110
pudendum 64
puerile 28, 94
pugilism 20
pugnacious 31, 139, 165
puissant 109, 133, 170
pulchritude 15
pule 40, 191, 193
pullulate 21, 166, 172
pulsate 178, 189
pulverized 133
pulverulent 53, 133
pummel 15, 82
pun 197
punch-drunk 76
punctilio 65
punctilious 25, 58
pundit 99
pungent 4, 18, 26, 157
punk 176
punt 68

purblind 97, 185, 190
purée 163
puritanical 169
purgative 20
purl 95
purlieu 79, 123
purloin 167
purple prose 122, 125
purport 86, 107
pursuant 34
pursuit 120
pursy 158
purvey 71
purview 60, 142, 152
pusillanimous 37, 192
putative 146
putrefy 43
putrid 36, 149
puts or calls 168
putt 74
pyknic 168
pyre 71, 129
pyrexia 64
pyriform 126
pyrogenic 80
pyromania 105
pyrophobia 128
pyrosis 80
pyrotechnics 22, 66
pyrrhic victory 44
pythagorean theorem 171
pythonic 136

quadrennium 69
quaff 52
quagmire 47, 106
quahog 29
quail 102, 195
qualm 110, 181, 184
quandary 127, 133, 176
quantum 7, 139
quarry 83, 134
quarterback 68
quasar 167
quash 138, 172
quatrain 131
quay 193
queasy 115, 166, 184
quell 138, 170
quelque chose 180
quench 60, 160
querulous 32, 63, 193
quest 138, 153
quibble 39, 58
quiche lorraine 129

quicken 59, 168
quiddity 58, 119
quidnunc 23
quid pro quo 59, 163
quiescent 87, 168
quietus 95, 159, 172
quintessence 58, 138
quip 73, 195
quirk 106, 171
qui vive? 193
qui vive, on the 121, 194
quixotic 149, 185
quondam 69
quorum 118
quotation 81, 134
quotidian 42

rabbit punch 18
rabid 63, 141
rack 169
raconteur 169
racy 148, 171
raffish 49, 142, 190
ragamuffin 141
raglan 30
ragout 167
raillery 14, 93, 175
raison d'être 59, 143
rake 86
rakish 43, 72, 93
rallentando 113
rally 11, 22, 147
rambunctious 49, 150
ramification 21, 55, 120, 147
ramify 50, 166
ramose 21
ramp 87, 161, 166
rampage 122, 189
rampant 80, 122, 183, 194
rampart 23, 69
ramshackle 46, 148, 157
rancid 142, 163, 165
rancor 57, 79, 85, 105, 165
random 79, 138
random sample 88, 108
randy 100, 103
rankle 7, 9, 56, 92
ransack 129, 131, 153, 175
ransom 126
rant 142, 164
rapacious 75, 76
rape 131, 156
rappel 112
rapport 4, 79
rapporteur 145

rapprochement 51
rapscallion 142, 149
rara avis 142
raree show 126, 169
rarefy 138, 144
rapt 3, 57
rapture 94
rating 145, 152
ratiocinate 44, 143
rational 143, 155
rationale 143
rationalize 60
raucous 30, 49, 102, 186
raunchy 156, 190
ravage 129, 150, 198
ravenous 83
ravishing 45
raze 45, 100
reactionary 5, 121
real income 87, 138
reality principle 5
realize 154
realpolitik 132
ream 57, 125
rebate 44
reboant 55, 146
rebound 26
rebozo 152
rebuff 44, 144, 145, 162
rebus 138
recalcitrant 49, 170
recant 48, 146
recapitulate 171
recede 112, 195
recension 55
receptacle 34
recessive 13
rechauffé 67, 147
recherché 144
recidivism 147
reciprocal 114
reciprocate 147
reciprocity 59
recitative 159
recluse 153, 162
recoil 13
recompense 145
reconcile 146
reconciled 5, 34, 79
recondite 3, 81, 136
reconnaissance 60, 172
recorder 67
recoup 144
recreant 37, 179, 184
recriminate 4

recrimination 36
recrudesce 21
recrudescence 142
rectitude 36, 187
recumbent 99, 103, 143
recuperate 143
recurrent 145
recusant 49, 117
redact 33, 55, 198
red-dog 68
redeem 25, 143
redemption price 134
red-handed 26, 88
redintegrate 145, 146
redolent 70, 171
redoubt 170
redoubtable 64, 69
redound 142
redress 32, 143, 148
reductio ad absurdum 4
redundant 175, 189, 197
reduplication 51
refection 107
refectory 47
reflation 89
reflet 91
refluent 54, 67
reflux 54, 67
refraction 17, 80, 100
refractory 119, 146, 170
refulgence 22, 141, 165
refute 49
regale 7, 45, 57
regalia 63, 65
regatta 19
regeneration 116, 143
regent 150
regicide 95
regimen 35, 173
reginal 139
regnant 50, 134
regrate 23
regression 13, 147
regulation T 39
regulation U 64
regurgitate 22, 190
rehabilitate 146
reify 33, 107
reimburse 32, 126
reiterate 145, 152
rejuvenate 146
rejuvenation 189, 200
relegate 14, 34
relent 162
relentless 35, 79, 129

relevant 9, 128
relict 7, 130
reliefer, reliever 14
relinquish 3, 73, 100, 145
relucent 144, 157
remand 122, 154
reminiscence 143
remiss 25, 116
remissible 69, 125
remnant 99
remonstrate 121, 130, 137
remorse 77, 154
rémoulade 152
remunerate 32, 126
remunerative 136
renascence 116, 147
rend 21, 148, 175
rendezvous 9, 108
rendition 90, 127
renegade 46, 179, 181
renege 13, 62
renovate 145, 147
renown 26, 63
renowned 63
reparation 7, 146
repartee 35, 145, 195
repast 107
repatriate 154
repel 52, 144, 191
repent 144
repercussion 5, 147
repertory 31, 177
repine 32, 70
replete 70, 152
replevin 143
replica 35, 53
replicate 67
replication 55, 146
répondez s'il vous plait 130, 145
repository 129, 169
repoussé 46, 144
reprehend 18, 39, 143
repression 138
reprieve 132, 172
reprimand 26, 143
reprisal 73, 147
reprise 145
reproach 18, 26, 143
reprobation 45
reproof 18, 143
repudiate 49, 144
repugnant 8, 83, 87, 121
repulse 143, 144, 145
reputable 82
repute 58, 81

requiem 84
requiescat in pace 146
requisite 88, 146
requisition 45, 172
requite 32, 145
reredos 153
rescind 3, 145, 147
rescript 44
residency 129
residue 99, 145
resile 143, 162, 166
resilience 23, 55
res judicata 43
resolute 46, 146, 184
resolve 7, 21, 35, 60, 155, 179
resonant 146
resort 190
respectable 11, 110
respire 21
respite 45, 132, 146
resplendent 43, 157, 190
restive 13, 65, 70, 94, 146, 186
résumé 171
resurgent 148
resurrectionist 19, 76
resuscitate 147
retable 157
retainer 64, 155
retaliate 145, 147
retaliation 61
retard 45, 81, 161
retardation 100
retch 190
retention 108
reticent 139, 146, 183
reticular 175
reticulation 116
reticule 78
retinue 11, 58
retort 8, 145, 157
retouching 129
retract 51, 174
retrench 41, 143
retribution 137
retrieve 143, 144, 145
retroactive 55
retrocede 73
retrochoir 28
retroflex 17
retrograde 13, 44, 198
retrogress 147
retrospection 143, 145, 147
retroussé 181
retroversion 13
revamp 104, 145, 147

revanchism 147
reveille 111, 176
revel 26, 45, 104
revenant 73
reverie 43, 113
revers 30, 98
revert 147, 181
revetment 147, 191
revile 4, 189
revivalist 58
revoke 24, 143
revue 158
rhabdomancy 50
rhapsody 113
rhetoric 97, 165, 197
rhetorical question 139
rhinology 117
rhizoid 149
rhomboid 125
riant 98
riata 98
ribald 30, 190
ricer 95
Richter scale 54
rick 79
ricochet 143, 160
rictus 72, 112
riddle 39, 42, 159
rife 4, 131, 194
riffle 158, 178
rifle 142
rift 21, 48
rightist 34
rights 135
rigmarole 68, 91
rigor 169
rigor mortis 148
rimose 37, 66
ring finger 65
riparian 148
riposte 147
riprap 69
rip tide 176
risible 98
risotto 148
risqué 18, 120, 171
rissole 149
risus 76
ritardando 113
rivet 63, 66
roan 83
robot 11, 107
Rob Roy 152
rococo 67, 123
rodomontade 10, 19, 21

rollicking 25, 72, 100
roman à clef 117
rondeau 131
rook 28, 173
roorback 63
root 153
Rorschach test 89, 128
roseate 28
Rosetta stone 81, 95
Rosh Hashana 93
roster 101
rotary press 135
rote 107, 108
rotiform 193
rotund 131, 150, 163
rotunda 149
roué 142, 155
roughage 30, 67
roulade 149
roundhouse 141
round lot 179, 185
round robin 35, 100, 179
roustabout 97, 192
roux 152
rowel 165, 193
rowen 5, 75
rubato 117
rubber 25
rubescent 143
rubicund 149
rubric 67, 150, 159, 177
ruche 150
ruck 32, 40, 122
rucksack 95
rudder 167
rudiment 66
rudimentary 55
rue 144, 145
ruffle 50, 92, 187
rule of thumb 107, 133
ruminate 108, 132
rump 98
runcible spoon 69
rundlet 195
rundown 15
rune 114, 119
run-off 55, 65
rupture 21, 156
rustic 130, 149, 159
ruthless 108

sabbatical year 156, 188
sabotage 42
sabra 92
sabulous 76, 151

saccharine 173
sacerdotal 135
sachem 28, 132
sachet 13, 127
sacrament 148, 159, 178
sacred cow 146
sacrifice 15
sacrilege 136, 189
sadiron 91
sadism 124
safari 60, 94
safe-conduct 125
safety 68
saga 169
sagacious 158, 195
sagacity 48, 195
salaam 76
salacious 99, 100, 119
salad days 200
salient 34, 136, 167
saline 151
sallow 200
sally 139, 150, 171, 195
salmagundi 48, 108
salubrious 80
salutary 17
salutation 76
salutatory 121, 194
salvage 152
salve 124, 163
salver 179
salvo 59, 146
samaritan 80
samovar 187
sampan 19
samsara 22
sanative 80
sanctimonious 82, 148
sanctimony 84
sanction 9, 127, 142
sanctions 31
sanctum 92, 135
sandhi 150
sang-froid 33, 35
sanguinary 18
sanguine 23, 28, 121, 150
sanitarium 80
sannup 7, 106
sans doute 27
sansei 93
sans pareil 184
sans souci 25, 198
sapid 90, 130, 152, 175
sapient 195
saponaceous 162

sapor 66, 175
sarcasm 162, 175
sarcoma 181
sarcophagus 31
sardonic 41, 152, 162
sari 81
sarong 72, 160
sartorial 108
sash 194
satellite 122, 161
satiate 74, 172
satire 67, 148
satrap 46, 120, 182
saturnalia 147
saturnine 74, 76, 111
satyr 99, 104, 156
sauerbraten 16
sauerkraut 163
sauna 167
saunter 170, 191
sauté 70
savanna 100
savant 99, 152
savoir-faire 96, 174
savoir-vivre 74
savory 9, 146, 175
scabrous 47, 88, 148
scagliola 86
scaloppine 188
scalping 176
scamper 83, 150
scan 73, 100, 102, 142, 153
scanned 189
scansion 189
scant 87
scapegoat 18
scapular 13
scar 30, 149
scarify 40, 41, 168
scarp 30, 161, 167
scathing 26, 79, 195
scatological 119
scavenge 151, 153
scenario 171, 173
scepter 149, 150
schatchen 93, 106
schema 46, 171, 173
scherzo 102, 130
Schick test 47, 176
schism 50, 165
schizophrenia 108, 137
schlemiel 23
schlep 25, 51, 79
schlock 28
schmaltz 155

schmo 170
schmooze 28
schnapps 6
schnitzel 41
schnorrer 16
scholium 106
schooner 157
schottische 42
schuss 160
schwa 190
sciamachy 65
scilicet 115
scimitar 173
scintilla 164, 179
scintillate 74, 164
sciolism 27, 96
scion 45, 120
scission 41, 50, 165
scissors kick 173
scofflaw 98
sconce 191
scone 17
scotch 41, 153, 166, 167, 172
Scotch woodcock 55
scot-free 184, 186, 193
scotoma 18
scrabble 153
scraggly 153
scratch 195
screed 79, 137, 165, 199
screwball 14
screwdriver 190
scrim 166, 177
scrimmage 68, 69, 149
scrimmage line
scrimshaw 25, 92
scrip 27, 125
script 78, 106
scrod 31
scrofulous 36, 44, 111
scrooge 110
scrub 130
scruff 115, 116
scruple 81
scrupulous 58, 82
scrutinize 59
Scuba 184
scud 194
scull 19
scumble 19, 162
scurf 42
scurrilous 4, 30
scutiform 157
scuttle 3, 153, 160
scuttlebutt 103, 150, 157

Scylla and Charybis, between 42
seadog 29
seamy side 153
seat 108
secant 41, 91
secede 195
secern 48, 49
second nature 44, 78
secular 198
sedentary 87, 153
Seder 93
sedulous 47, 167
seismology 54
sejant 81
selenography 111
self-conscious 34
self-liquidating 126
self-righteous 162
self-sufficient 88
sellout 17
selvage 55, 62
semantic 107
semantics 107, 197
sematic 42, 192
semblance 8, 102
semé 80
seminal 133, 136
seminar 36, 164
seminiferous 154
semipostal 132
semiweekly 181
semper fidelis 62
semper paratus 7
semplice 159
senary 160
senescent 6, 76
senile 5, 120
sensual 156
sensuous 155
sentence 196
sententious 12, 111, 176
sentience 34
sentimental 175
Sephardim 94
sepia 22
septennial 156
septicemia 18
septuple 156
sepulcher 23
sepulchral 74, 108
sequacious 155, 161
sequela 34
sequester 154, 155
sequestered 153
seraph 7

sere 27, 130
serenade 163, 179
serendipity 103
serene 24
seriatim 121
sericeous 159
serif 135
serigraphy 159
serotinous 18, 98
serpentine 162
serrated 117
servile 161, 170
sesquicentennial 26
sesquipedalian 102, 132
setaceous 22
settee 162
seventh heaven 79
severance pay 126
sexism 156
sextuplicate 160
sforzando 4
shagging 15
shaitan 46, 58, 111
shalom 93
shambles 49, 160
shandygaff 6, 16
shapeup 197
shard 22, 69
sharkskin 51, 62
sharp-set 95
shashlik 97
sheepish 158
shellback 40, 120, 151
shepherd's pie 107
shibboleth 126, 129, 176
shiftless 98
shirred eggs 55
shirring 62
shish kebab 97
shiva 93
shiva, to sit 93
shiver 157, 165
shoddy 88
shoestring 25
shofar 142
shoji 93
shook 19, 167
shoplifter 149
shop steward 184
short covering 168
short position 7
short sale 20
shortstop 14
shotgun wedding 106
shovel hat 79

shrievalty 157
shrink 137
shtick 127
shuck 84, 131, 157
shunt 181
shutout 72
shyster 98
sibilant 82
siblings 22
sibyl 69, 163
sic 4, 200
siccative 52
sickened 115
sic transit gloria mundi 74, 178
sidereal 167
sidestep 50
sideswipe 82
sidle 112
siècle 26, 57, 127
sierra 112
signalize 104
sigil 159
sigmate 150
signalment 46
sign manual 159
silhouette 42, 136
silk-screen process 167
silva 69
s'il vous plait 85, 130
simian 8, 111
simile 65, 101
simmer 19
simony 23
simoom 194
simpatico 32, 34, 184
simper 162
simple interest 90
simplistic 85, 123
simulacrum 86, 157, 190
simulate 86, 102, 134
simultaneous 33, 120
sinecure 120, 132
sine die 195
sine qua non 58, 88
singspiel 121
sinister 81, 99, 194
sinistral 99
sinker 14
sinking fund 71
sinuate 16, 40, 194
sinuses 26
sinuous 192
sippet 178
sirloin 16
sirocco 194

sisyphean 47, 56, 90
sitar 169
sit-down 169
sitomania 105
sitzmark 160
size 65
skein 200
skep 16
skeptic 51
skew 119, 166, 173, 181
skewed 102
skewer 149
skiascopy 61
skid row 82
skijoring 160
skim 73, 142
skimble-scamble 117
skimpy 152
skin diving 173
skinflint 110
skin game 173
skirl 13
skirr 112, 153
skis 150
skitter 74, 160
skittish 64, 70, 94, 158, 186
skittles, beer and 25, 52
skive 157, 161
skiver 20, 99
skulduggery 180, 184
skulk 71, 161, 167
skylark 70
slab 66
slack 102, 192
slack-baked 132, 184
slake 139, 152
slalom 160
slander 44, 121, 165
slang 98
slapstick 31
slate 24, 101, 152, 154
slattern 136, 186, 196
slave driver 56
slaver 52
sleazy 28, 132, 158
sleek 162, 193
sleeper 68, 171
sleight 37, 40, 46, 160
sleight of hand 104
slider 14
slight 49, 116
slink 110, 134
slinky 162, 167
slipshod 25
slither 74, 161

sliver 41, 165
sloe-eyed 61
slog 131, 169
sloop 151
slosh 67, 165
slothful 98
slough 19, 25, 73, 148, 157
slough of despond 45, 46
sloven 25, 186
sloyd 106, 196
slue 129, 173
sluggard 98
sluice 192
slumlord 97
slur 10
slush fund 111
smack 19
small talk 35
smalto 73
smart money 110
smattering 172
smearcase 36
smirch 44, 49, 162
smirk 162
smithy 18
smoke-jumper 65
smorgasbord 22
smug 32, 154
smut 132
snafu 34
snaggletooth 178
snap 68
snare drum 52
sneak preview 112
snickersnee 95, 173
snide 105
sniggling 55
snipe 158
snippet 18, 153
snit 7, 92
snob 79, 172
snook 178
snorkel 173
snow job 66, 128
snuff 162
snuffle 21, 115
snuffy 183
snuggle 40
soap opera 175
sobriquet 116
sociometry 144
Socratic irony 85
Socratic method 139
sodality 10, 32, 64
soft goods 176

soft sell 154
soft-shoe 175
soi-disant 154
soigné 193
soilage 76
soiree 125
sojourn 53, 167, 175
solace 31, 34
solarium 72
solar plexus 129, 168
solatium 32
solecism 75, 189
solemnize 127
solicitous 33, 194
solicitude 8
solidarity 185
solid geometry 73
solid state 55
soliloquize 174
soliloquy 111
solipsism 154
solmization 113, 173
solon 98
solstice 40, 81, 172
somatic 19, 36
somber 45, 53, 74
sommelier 195
somniferous 161, 163
somnolent 52, 161
Sonar 163
sonic 163
soniferous 163
sonnet 131
sonorous 70, 102, 117, 146
soothsayer 69, 133
sop 8, 21
sophist 30, 177
sophisticated 33, 198
sophistry 143
sophomoric 24, 86, 121
sopor 161
soporific 161
sordid 14, 47, 189
sororicide 160
sorority 160
sorry 88, 124, 129
sortie 6, 109
sostenuto 80, 136
sotto voce 135, 165, 184
soubise 152
souffle 48, 100
sough 112, 159, 163
soul food 67
sound 50, 176
sounding board 163

sojourn 53, 167, 175
solace 31, 34
solar plexus 129, 168
solarium 172
solatium 32
solecism 75, 189
solemnize 127
solicitous 33, 194
solicitude 8
solid geometry 73
solidarity 185
soliloquize 174
soliloquy 111
solipsism 154
solid state 55
solmization 113, 173
solon 98
solstice 40, 81, 172
sonnet 131
sonic 163
somnolent 52
somatic 19, 36
somber 45, 53, 74
sommelier 195
somniferous 161, 163
somnolent 161
sonar 163
soniferous 163
sonorous 70, 102, 117, 146
soothsayer 69, 133
sop 8, 21
sophistry 143
sophist 30, 177
sophisticated 33, 198
sophomoric 24, 86, 121
sopor 161
sotto voce 135, 165, 184
soporific 161
sordid 14, 47, 189
sorority 160
sororicide 160
sorry 88, 124, 129
sortie 6, 109
sostenuto 80, 136
soubise 152
souffle 48, 100
sough 112, 159, 163
soul food 67
sound 50, 176
sounding board 163
soupçon 176, 179
sourdine 180
souse 22, 47
soutache 21

soutane 25
southpaw 15
southwester 192
sovereign 88, 150, 172
soviet 75
space-time 35, 69
spadework 134
spall 21
span 78, 83, 107, 117, 124
spangle 74, 164
spanker 128
spanking 43, 112, 173, 189
spar 20, 107, 151, 198
spare 28, 55, 70, 99, 177
sparge 158, 166
spartan 21
sparkplug 4, 90, 98
sparse 152, 166, 177
spasmodic 35, 189
spartan 191
spate 123
spatula 66
spawn 22, 45, 66, 122
spay 7, 123
specialist 22
specie 31
species 17
spellbinder 164
spelunker 26
specious 8, 43, 130, 158
specter 8, 73
spectrum 100
speculative 148, 177
speleology 26
sphacelate 72
sphairistike 176
sphericity 150
sphincter 112
sphragistics 153
sphygmic 137
spiccato 20
spider 70
spiel 164
spinet 79
spindle 107, 200
spindrift 153
spin-off 23, 87
spire 179
spinster 120
spinous 134
spiracle 6
spiral 40
spirituel 195
spit 97, 149

squelch 40, 159, 165, 170
squib 65, 165
squinting modifier 5
stabile 66
staccato 3, 113, 117, 157
staff 34
stag 173
stage whisper 193
stagnate 188
stagnant 161
staid 154, 162, 167
stakeout 131
stalactite 26
stalag 73
stalagmite 26
stale 187
stalemate 28, 43
stalk 9, 167
stalking horse 24
stallion 83
stalwart 21, 46, 170
stamina 56, 169, 189
stammel 143
stance 132
stanch 28, 169
stanchion 14
stand 76, 180
standardbred 83
standoff 51, 176
standpipe 192
stannary 176
staple 28, 125, 135, 142, 183
starboard 157
star chamber 36
star-crossed 85, 184
stark 14, 18, 76, 156, 169
star of David 167
stasis 169
static 146, 167
status quo 33
statute 44
statute of limitations 98
staunch 45, 66, 103
stave off 191
steadfast 66, 186
steatopygia 23, 63
steelhead 141
steep 162
steeplechase 40, 141
steer 16, 104
stele 168
stellate 141, 167
stellular 17
stentor 102
stentorian 102

steppe 130
stereochromy 112
stereophonic 163
sterile 14, 184
stern 142
sternutation 162
stertorous 162
stet 100
sthenic 11
stichometry 199
stickle 9, 35
stickler 47
stifle 95, 169, 172
stigma 48, 106
stigmata 198
stile 159, 189
stillborn 43
stilted 69, 132
stint 66, 73, 146
stipend 6, 127, 151
stipendiary 127
stipple 51, 124
stipulate 76, 136, 164
stirpiculture 21
stirps 63, 127
stirrup cup 63
stoat 58
stock car 11
stock dividend 50
stockfish 66
stockpile 74, 146
stock-still 111
stodgy 32, 53
stogie 29
stoical 86, 88, 183
stol 130, 158
stole 152
stolid 86, 184
stomatology 112
stone's throw 158
stoneware 133
stool pigeon 89
stoop 130, 132, 167
stopgap 87
stoup 82
stover 36, 64, 67
strabismus 40, 61
strafe 6
straight man 4
straitjacket 93
strand 158
strand line 20
strangle 29, 95
stratagem 105, 180
stratocracy 75, 109

stratocumulus 30
stratosphere 11
stratum 15, 75, 98
straw-hat circuit 177
straw vote 190
stream-of-consciousness 199
street name 22, 115
strephosymbolia 147
striated 76, 170
striation 101
stricture 39
strident 76, 79, 81, 158
stridor 117
strikeout 15
striker 162
stringendo 79
stringent 148, 156, 169
stringer 116
strip mining 30
strong verb 189
struck jury 94
structural linguistics 98
stucco 26
stud book 126
studied 130, 134
stud poker 131
stultified 3, 68, 198
stump 55
stumpage 176
stupefy 17, 170
stygian 42, 74, 89, 91
style book 19
stymie 18, 74, 119
suave 187
subaltern 88
subito 139
subjective 128
subjoin 4, 8
sub judice 36
subjunctive 189
sublimate 35
subliminal 127, 183
subordinate 88
suborn 21, 88, 90
subpoena 36
subpoena duces tecum 36
subreption 88, 172
sub rosa 154
subsequent 67
subservient 119, 155
subside 3, 24, 139
subsist 3, 35, 105
substantive 4, 88, 142, 154
subterfuge 50, 169
subtitle 112

subtle 88, 89, 95, 171
subtrahend 118
subvention 6, 171
subvert 36, 123, 184
succinct 22, 33, 176
succubus 64
succulent 94, 189
succuss 156
sudation 173
sudden death 166
sudor 173
sufferance 34, 126, 127
suffix 5, 56, 173
suffragan 17
suffuse 123
sui generis 121, 185
sui juris 32
sukiyaki 93
sulky 83, 85
sullage 112, 156
sullen 74, 146
sully 44, 162
summa cum laude 81
summer 15
summer solstice 171
summum bonum 172
sumpter 124
sumptuary 60
sundries 92
sunna 111
superable 172
superannuated 119, 123, 147
supercilious 10, 48
supererogatory 60, 172
superficial 157
superfluity 59
superlative 81, 172
supernal 26, 80
supernumerary 111, 166
superpowers 185
supersede 8, 145, 172, 174
supersonic 63
supervene 67, 79, 174
supinate 181
supine 62, 87, 88, 101, 103
supple 66
suppliant 17, 57, 83
supplicate 10, 16, 133
suppurate 64
surcease 56
surcingle 169
surd 107
surfeit 59, 64, 172
surfing 148
surly 150

surplice 29
surrealism 10, 170
surrogate 171
sursum corda 100
surveillance 192
susceptible 155, 200
suspension points 51
sustenance 67, 102, 107
susurrant 112, 150, 193
sutler 126
suture 156, 168
suzerainty 164
svelte 161, 194
swagger 170
swale 106
swan song 53
sward 75
swarm 30
swarthy 42, 53
swashbuckler 19
swatch 62, 151
swath 170
sweatshop 158
sweep 195
sweepstakes 102
sweltering 80
swindle sheet 60
swing shift 197
switchback 149
switch-blade knife 95
switch hitter 15
sybarite 130
sycophant 66
syllabus 123, 171
syllepsis 65, 160, 197
syllogism 44, 102
sylph 75, 161
symbiosis 102, 125
symposium 108
synchronism 159
synchronized 176
synchronous 79
syncopation 148
syncope 52
syncretize 18, 31, 143
syndactyl 193
syndic 29, 145
syndicate 6, 10
syndrome 155, 173
synecology 55
synedoche 125
syneresis 18, 109
synergetic 35, 178
synod 54
synonym 196

synonymous 144
synopsis 22, 171
syntax 97
synthesis 10, 44, 193
synthetic 171
syssarcosis 19
systole 80, 158, 173

tabaret 186
tabescent 192
tabetic 56
tableau vivant 129
table d'hôte 47, 107
tabloid 116
taboo 14, 68, 136
taboret 153, 168
tabula rasa 29
tabulature 113
tacamahac 87
tacet 159
tachygraphy 158
tacit 86, 159, 186
taciturn 30, 146, 183
tack 201
tackle 68
tact 43, 160
tactics 105
tactile 175, 178
tagmemics 98
tailgating 52
take 15, 111
take-home pay 191
tales 94
talion 137
talisman 7, 27
tallith 133
tallow 63
Talmud 93
talon 25
tamales 109
tambour 52
tambourine 52
tam-o'-shanter 152
tamp 69, 124
tandem 121, 159
tang 16
tangent 34, 178
tangential 144
tangible 107, 142, 178
tankard 40
tantalize 175
tantamount 57
tantivy 142, 173
tant mieux 162
tanto 178

tant pis 162
tantrum 13, 66
tap dance 42
taphephobia 128
tapis, on the 21, 186
taps 22
tarantism 42
tarboosh 25
tare 35, 193
tarlatan 113
tarsus 8
tartar sauce 152
tartuffe 84
tatterdemalion 141
tattersall 28, 130
tattoo 52, 160
taunt 93, 145
taurine 23
tautology 144, 145
taw 99, 106
tawdry 28, 122, 158
taxidermy 7
taxonomy 29
teapoy 174
technical knockout 21
technocracy 175
tectonics 22, 54
ted 166
tedious 20, 193
teeming 70, 123
teetotaler 3
teetotum 178
tegmen 30
tegular 176
teknonymy 115, 145
telamon 104, 129
telekinesis 112
telemetry 49, 107
teleology 46, 65
telepathy 32
telesis 136
telesthesia 60, 127
telestich 4, 131
Telex 182
telic 138
tellurian 54
temblor 54
temerarious 142, 143
temerity 67, 80
temper 109, 110, 181
tempera 124
temperate 110, 146
tempestuous 169, 189
template 72, 126
tempo 165

temporization 58
temporize 33, 125, 166
tempus fugit 176
tenable 44, 104
tenacious 30, 79, 127, 147, 170
tendentious 17, 175
tender 19, 120, 189
tenderloin 29, 175, 189
tenebrous 42, 74
tenet 16, 50, 135
tenor 107
tense 176, 189
tensile 169
tenterhooks, on 8, 172
tenuous 66, 177, 186, 192
tenure 82, 167
tenuto 80, 172
tepid 103
tequila 109
teratism 64, 111
teratoid 3
tercet 177
tergiversate 27, 46, 57
termagant 139, 152, 158, 196
ternary 177
ternate 180
terpsichore 42
terpsichorean 42
terra firma 162
terrain 76
terra incognita 184
terrestrial 54
terret 148
territorial waters 192
terse 33
tertium quid 107
tessellated 111
tessera 111
testaceous 79
testator 194
tester 25
testicles 156
testimony 195
testudinal 178
tête-à-tête 33, 135
tether 34, 101, 142
tetrad 69
tetragonal 139
Texas leaguer 15
textual 196
T formation 68
thalassophobia 128
thallasic 120
thanatophobia 128
thaumatology 109

thaumatrope 121
thaumaturge 104
theanthropism 74
theism 16
thenar 124
theopathy 55, 144
theorem 137
therapeutic 40, 80
theriomorphic 15
thermanesthesia 175
thermesthesia 80, 155
thermonuclear 80
thersitical 4, 102
thesaurus 173
thespian 4
theurgy 50, 104
thin market 23, 190
third world 36, 184
thralldom 155
thrasonical 21
three-point landing 6
threnody 47, 71
throes 124, 164
thrombosis 18
throwaway 22
throwback 147
throw-weight 102, 193
thrum 52, 175
thunderhead 30
thurifer 7
thwart 67, 70, 119
tiara 40, 80
tibia 157
tickler 108
tiff 164
tilde 4, 164
timbale 126
timbre 178
timocracy 82, 136
timorous 64, 176
timpani 95
tincture 66, 162, 176
tinder 31
tinge 31
tinker's damn 188
tinnitus 54, 148
tintinnabulation 16, 148
tirade 45, 164
titanic 83
tithe 175, 176
titillate 176
titillated 130
titivate 44, 52
tittle 91, 94
tittup 25, 101, 133

titular 115, 117
tmesis 89, 197
TNT 60
toady 64, 155
toby 94, 112
tocsin 6, 16
tole 56, 109
tolerable 6, 15, 32
tolling 16
tomalley 102
tomentose 36, 78
tonsure 111, 157
tooling 122
top banana 31
topee 80
toper 52
topiary 158, 180
topography 106
toponym 115, 129
topside 157
toque 79
Torah 93, 111, 127
torchier 97
torch song 163
toreutics 122
tornado 169
torose 95
torpid 53, 87, 117, 161
torpor 8, 170
torque 149
torrefy 52
torrid 9, 83, 125, 152
torsade 122, 181
torsion 181
tort 199
torte 24
torticollis 112, 116
tortile 31
tortilla 109
tortuous 46, 194
tory 34
total recall 145
touch-and-go 148, 183
touchback 68
touchdown 68
touché 34, 200
touchstone 39, 167
toupee 194
tour de force 5
tourniquet 14
tout à fait 57
tout de suite 86
tovarich 150
toxemia 18
toxic 131

toxicophobia 128
tract 179
tractable 33, 105
traduce 44, 160
trailer park 110
train oil 193
traipse 72, 191
trajectory 126
trammel 81, 86, 101
trampoline 4, 25
tranquil 24, 139, 155
transact 25
transcend 59, 148
transferred epithet 5
transfigure 27, 74, 85
transfix 129
transfixed 111
transformational grammar 75
transhumance 26
transient 158, 175
transilient 3, 112, 125
transistor 55
transliteration 7
translucent 100, 154
transmit 154
transmogrify 27, 35, 179
transmute 27
transpire 15, 99, 125
transubstantiate 27
transverse 40
transvestitism 52
trattoria 92
trauma 56, 89, 158
travail 7, 28, 50, 97, 124, 171
traverse 59, 112, 121
travesty 23, 86
trawler 19
treacle 145
treasury stock 168
treatise 10
trek 94
tremolo 189
tremor 157, 158
tremulous 64, 176
trenchant 95
trepidation 64
trey 177
triad 177
triage 26, 163
tribune 137
trice 142
trencherman 54
tresses 78
tribulation 110
tribute 127

trice, in a 90
trichinosis 48, 91
tricorn 79
tricot 95
triennial 177
trifle 57
trifocal 61
trifocals 73
trigonometry 180
trill 181
trilogy 177
trimurti 81
triolet 131, 189
triple 14
triple play 14
triskaidekaphobia 128
triskelion 177
trismus 102
tritanopia 18
triturate 137
troche 36, 103
trochee 131
trochoid 129
troglodyte 26, 143
troika 150, 177
Trojan horse 171
troll 159
trolling 66
trollop 137
trombone 113
trompe l'oeil 85, 142
trope 65
trophic 118
tropism 11, 146
tropophyte 130
trounce 15, 137, 177
trousseau 21
troy 93
truant 138
truce 26
truck farm 63
truckle 200
truculent 40, 44, 64, 137, 171, 186
trump 25, 59, 172
trumped-up 62, 70
trumpery 117, 150, 158, 188, 198
truncate 41
truncated 158
tryst 9, 108
tsimmes 71
tsooris 180
tsunami 120, 176
tuba 113
tuberosity 137, 173
tumefaction 173

trek 94
trepidation 64
treatise 10
trenchant 95
trey 177
triad 177
triage 26, 163
tribune 137
trencherman 54
trice 142
tresses 78
tribulation 110
tribute 127
trice, in a 90
tricorn 79
tricot 95
triennial 177
trichinosis 48, 91
trifle 57
trifocal 61
trifocals 73
trigonometry 180
trilogy 177
triolet 131, 189
triple 14
triple play 14
triskaidekaphobia 128
troika 150, 177
trochee 131
Trojan horse 171
trill 181
trimurti 81
triskelion 177
trismus 102
tritanopia 18
triturate 137
troche 36, 103
trochoid 129
troglodyte 26, 143
troll 159
trolling 66
trollop 137
trombone 113
trompe l'oeil 85, 142
trope 65
trophic 118
tropism 11, 146
tropophyte 130
trounce 15, 137, 177
troy 93
trousseau 21
truck farm 63
truckle 200
truce 26
truculent 40, 44, 64, 137, 171, 186

truant 138
trump 25, 59, 172
trumpery 117, 150, 158, 188, 198
trumped-up 62, 70
truncate 41
truncated 158
tryst 9, 108
tsunami 120, 176
tuberosity 137, 173
tumefaction 173
tsooris 180
tumid 89
tsimmes 71
tumid 19, 132, 173
tuba 113
tumescent 173
tumpline 169
tumulose 81, 111
tumulus 23, 111
tun 188
tumult 117, 187
tundra 130
tunic 18
tup
turban 80
turbid 30, 112, 177
turbidity 34
turbinate 165, 178
turbulent 6, 148, 194
turbulence 32, 173
tureen 48
turncoat 179
turmoil 181
turgid 19, 49, 75, 89, 173
turnstile 72
turnverein 10, 77
turpitude 15, 45, 189
tussock 30, 181
tutti 6
twaddle 159, 174
TV dinner 47
tweedle 158
twenty-twenty vision 190
twibil 15, 182
twister 178
twit 8, 145, 175
two-dollar broker 22
twofer 181
tycoon 192
tympanic 52
typhoon 41
tyrannize 150
tyranny 40
tyro 16, 117
tzigane 77

upper case 25
upright 82
uproarious 71, 102, 117
upset price 134
up tick, plus-tick 81, 134
Uraeus 155
uranism 82
uranist 82, 104
uranography 167
urbane 131, 144, 170
Uriah Heep 84
urning 82, 104
urology 187
uropygium 17
urticaria 82
usage 98
ustulate 152
usufruct 99
utility player 15
uxorial 194
uxoricide 84
uxorious 67, 84

vacillate 173, 192
vacillating 88, 183
vacuity 56, 87
vacuous 85, 170, 185
vade in pace 74
vagabond 179, 191
vagary 120, 194
vagrant 82, 85
vainglorious 19, 33, 132
valance 51
vale 63
valedictory 63, 75
valetudinarian 80, 91
valgus 95
vamp 158
van 80
vandalism 42
vandyke 15
vanity press 137
vapid 53, 66, 90
varicella 28
varietal 195
variola 162
variorum 19
vasectomy 105, 165
vatic 136
vaticinate 69
vaunt 21
vector 25
veer 157
vegetate 101
vehement 9, 86, 189

veldt 75, 164
veloce 139, 142
velocity 165
velour 62
velutinous 78, 189
venal 21, 36, 108
venality 137
vendetta 64
vendible 106
vendue 11, 137
veneer 172
venerate 146, 147
venial 59, 125
venire 124
venison 44
veni, vidi, vici 85
venom 105
ventricular 173
ventriloquism 164
venue 129
veracious 181
veracity 82
verbiage 197
verbigerate 145
verbose 197
verboten 68
verdant 76, 88
verisimilitude 8, 181
veritable 180, 185
verjuice 163, 164
vermeil 22, 73, 159
vernacular 32, 98, 115
vernal 70, 166, 200
vernal equinox 43
versant 87, 161
versatile 5, 106
versicolor 31, 91
verso 99, 124
vertebrates 13, 165
vertex 8, 178
vertiginous 50, 165, 193
vertigo 50
verve 43, 57, 189
vesicant 18
vespers 58, 133
vespiary 192
vestal 190
vestige 159, 179
vestment 72
veterinarian 7, 50
veto 95
vexatious 8, 92
viable 25, 133, 197
via media 109
viand 67

viaticum 58, 137
viator 179, 192
vibrant 101, 137, 148, 178, 189
vibrato 113
vibrissa 78
vicar 6, 45, 171
vicarious 157
vicennial 181
viceroy 95
vichyssoise 163
vicinal 116
vicinal road 102
vicious 65, 105, 186
vicious circle 29, 135
vicissitudes 27, 188
vide 154
vide ante 154
vide infra 154
video 175
video tape 175
vie 32
vigesimal 181
vigil 192
vigilant 6, 192
vignette 101
vigorish 20
vigoroso 56
vile 13, 58, 146
vilify 44, 160
vilipend 44, 46, 49
Vincent's angina 180
vinculum 19
vindicate 3, 4, 29, 94
vindicatory 11, 138
vindictive 147, 165
vingt-et-un 25, 181
viniculture 75
vin ordinaire 28, 174, 195
vintage 29, 59, 176, 189
vintner 195
viola 190
virago 152, 157, 196
virescent 76
virga 30
virgate 161, 169
virgin 184
Virgin Mary 178
virgule 101, 160
virile 106, 170
virility 105, 106, 156
virtue 55, 74, 133, 139
virtuosity 160, 170, 175
virtuoso 31, 34, 107
virulent 18, 79, 105, 117, 142
visa 126

visage 62, 102
vis-à-vis 62
viscera 89, 90
visceral 77, 91
viscid, 5, 167
viscous 81, 154, 167
visible speech 164, 173
visionary 86
visor 22
vital 100
vitellus 55
vitiate 36, 43, 86, 91, 165
viticulture 75
vitreous 73
vitrine 73, 158
vitriolic 23, 26, 39
vituperate 141
vituperation 4, 63
vivace 22, 101, 139
vivacious 4, 101
viva voce 121, 165
vive 102
vivid 22, 28
viviparous 105
vivisection 172
vixen 158
viz. 115
vocable 197
vocation 120
vociferate 15, 59, 158
vociferous 117
voice-over 190
voila 16
voir dire 119
volant 67
volar 124, 162
volatile 64, 66, 179, 186
vol-au-vent 126
volition 45, 194
volley 176
volt 83
voltage 55
volte-face 3
voltigeur 181
voluble 74, 164, 174
voluminous 22
voluptuary 103, 155
voluptuous 103
volute 149, 165
vomito 200
voracious 54, 76, 89
vortex 193
vorticose 193
votary 20, 34, 46
vouch 10, 76

vouchsafe 33, 44, 75, 127
voyeur 126
vox populi 190
vtol 130, 189
vulgar 32
vulgate 4, 58, 132
vulnerable 100, 121
vulpine 37, 69
vulva 156

waddle 191
wafer 177
waffle 15
waft 25, 67
wafture 192
wag 94
waggery 94, 110
waggish 83
wagon-lit 161
waif 82, 169
wainscot 124, 191
wainwright 191
waive 44, 69, 73, 132, 144
wake 5, 116, 179
wale 36, 148
walkaway 35
walk-on 127
walkover 83
walleye 61
walleyed 167
Walpurgis night 195
wanderlust 179
Wankel engine 11, 149
wanton 49, 59, 102, 103, 105, 185, 186
wapiti 56
warble 159
warder 76, 95, 192
warhead 110, 149
warlock 195
warrant 11, 56, 94, 171
warranty 76
warren 40, 141
wary 26, 77, 192
wash-and-wear 72
wash sale 168
wastrel 102, 165
watch 74, 95, 161
watchword 126, 161
watermark 125
watershed 149, 161
wattle 160
waul 26, 40
waybill 101
waylay 7, 191
wayward 25, 58, 191, 194

weak sister 88, 184
wean 145, 195
wearisome 20, 175
weasel word 197
weather 125, 172
weathercock 64
web-footed 178
web press 135
weft 40
weir 42
Wellington boot 20
well-nigh 6, 116
Welsh rabbit 28
welt 170
weltanschauüng 198
welter 112, 149
welterweight 20, 198
weltschmerz 108, 128, 198
western omelet 120
wetback 109
wether 142
wet nurse 195
whatnot 157
wheedle 30, 66, 128
whelm 57, 170
when issued 33, 179
wherewithal 116
whet 59, 157, 168
whetstone 95, 168
whey 109
wheyface 62, 124
whiffle 18, 137, 188
whim 63, 117
whimper 40
whimsical 120
whimsy 25, 63, 139
whiplash 94, 116
whirligig 109
whirlwind 6
white collar 30, 136, 197
whited sepulcher 84
white elephant 132
white heat 59
white lie 100
white paper 75
whitlow 65
whodunit 114
whorl 65
widow's mite 73
widow's peak 78
widow's walk 119
wiener schnitzel 188
wild-goose chase 71
wild oats 88
wild pitch 14

wile 37, 40
williwaw 194
willy-nilly 100, 194
wilton 25
wimple 118
windrow 79
windsock 194
windsor chair 27
windsor tie 116
wing chair 27
winnow 59, 155, 159
wino 6
winsome 11, 130
winter solstice 195
wire-wove 125
withers 13
wittingly 34, 45
wizened 158, 195
woebegone 112, 163
wold 130
womb 129
wont 4, 40, 78, 187
workmanlike 160
workshop 154
worm fence 64
wove paper 125
wrack 153
wraith 8
wrangle 7, 9, 139
wrest 49, 137, 154, 181
wretch 110
writhe 16, 166, 181
wrought 25, 45, 69
wunderkind 28

xanthippe 158
xenogamy 40
xenophobia 128
xeric 52
xerography 36

xiphoid 173
xylophone 113

yahrzeit 43
yarborough 21
yarmulke 160
yaw 112, 186
yawp 14, 200
yeanling 74, 116, 157
yearling 200
yeasty 70, 146
yeomanly 21, 167
yeshiva 93
Yeti 3
yodel 63, 159
yoga 81
yogurt 109
Yorkshire pudding 137

zabaglione 92
zamarra 157
zapateado 80
zarf 40
zarzuela 121
zealot 63, 125
zealous 57
zenith 40, 81
zephyr 194
zero gravity 193
zeugma 65, 160
zibeline 150
zoolatry 8
zoomania 105
zoom lens 99
zoophobia 128
zucchetto 160
zwieback 21, 178
zymolysis 64
zymurgy 21